MW01223081

Advanced
Structured BASIC

James F. Clark
Fulton County Schools
Atlanta, Georgia

James E. LaBarre
University of Wisconsin-Eau Claire
Eau Claire, Wisconsin

Published by

J87 **SOUTH-WESTERN PUBLISHING CO.**

CINCINNATI   WEST CHICAGO, IL   DALLAS   PELHAM MANOR, NY   PALO ALTO, CA

Reviewer Acknowledgment

The authors would like to acknowledge the contributions of the following people in reviewing the manuscript and recommending excellent changes for revisions.

Judy M. Senden
West High School
Anchorage, Alaska

Verle Smith
Jefferson High School
Portland, Oregon

Preface

As microcomputers have come into widespread use in businesses and homes, more and more people have discovered the need to develop some degree of programming skill. Frequently the skill developed, while useful, has stopped short of being sufficient for real-world programming.

Advanced Structured BASIC teaches the BASIC language in a structured fashion, with an emphasis on developing a level of skill with which production programs for business use may be planned and coded. The great majority of career opportunities in programming are in business, and this text presents programming concepts in the context of such practical applications. The use of this text is recommended after the student has developed at least a minimal level of skill in BASIC programming. Several features of the text make the learning of advanced programming easier.

The first four chapters review the process of planning and coding structured programs, as well as reviewing all commonly used BASIC keywords. The emphasis is on doing things the correct way so that results are obtained with the least effort and smallest number of errors. Chapters are presented in two topics. Topic 1 presents general principles that apply regardless of the computer language being used. Topic 2 explains how to apply those principles using the BASIC language. As each BASIC keyword is presented, its general form and an example are given. Each chapter contains an example program using newly presented keywords. This helps integrate the new keywords with previously learned material. Each topic includes review questions. At the end of each chapter are lists of vocabulary words and BASIC keywords that were presented.

Each chapter includes six programming assignments. Assignments 1 and 2 are easiest and can generally be completed by reference to similar examples in the chapter. Assignments 3 and 4 require a bit more effort, while assignments 5 and 6 are generally most difficult, requiring the progressive application of higher levels of understanding. Two continuing projects are started in Chapter 5 and continue through Chapter 13. These projects require the progressive development of complex business systems as new concepts are learned.

Proper documentation is emphasized throughout the text. The use of structured programming techniques is developed without the use of burdensome jargon. Hierarchy charts, program documentation sheets, and module documentation sheets are used instead of flowcharts. These forms of documentation are much easier to understand and use, and lead more quickly to error-free programs. Their use makes documentation much less a chore and, therefore, much more likely to be done.

Three end-of-book items are handy references once particular programming ideas have been learned. A glossary contains all new vocabulary words presented in the text, making review much easier. A quick guide to all BASIC keywords is included. This guide is a handy reference for referesher purposes once the keyword has been learned. Each entry in the reference guide refers to the page in the text that will give full information. An ASCII code table is convenient for use when writing programs that do character manipulation.

The versions of BASIC used by several popular microcomputers are emphasized throughout the text. Differences between computers are pointed out in each chapter and alternate methods of programming are presented where necessary. There is never any doubt as to which keywords apply to the particular computer and version of BASIC being used. The computers covered are the Apple® II and IIe[1], the Commodore 64[2], the IBM PC and the IBM PCjr[3], and the Radio Shack TRS-80 Models III and 4[4]. All items that apply to the IBM Personal Computer are valid with other computers that are fully IBM compatible.

---

[1]Apple® II Plus, Apple® IIe, and Applesoft® are trademarks of Apple Computer, Inc. Any reference to Apple II Plus, Apple IIe, or Applesoft refers to this footnote.

[2]Commodore® is a trademark of Commodore Business Machines, Inc. Any reference to the Commodore 64 refers to this footnote.

[3]IBM PC and IBM PCjr are trademarks of International Business Machines. Any reference to IBM, the IBM PC, or IBM PCjr refers to this footnote.

[4]TRS-80® is a trademark of the Radio Shack Division of Tandy Corporation. Any reference to the TRS-80 or the Radio Shack microcomputer refers to this footnote.

Contents

Unit 4   Advanced Data Files

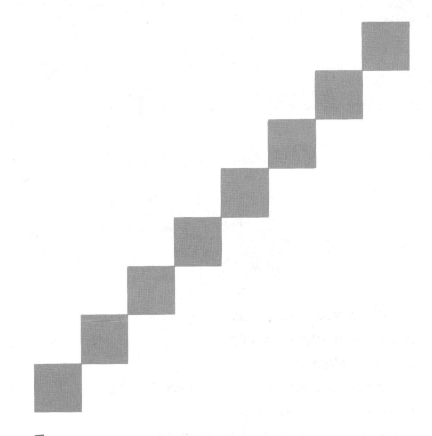

Unit 1 • Review of Basic Concepts

Chapter 1

Program Development

Objectives: 1. List the steps in program development.

2. Define structured programming.

3. Plan a hierarchy chart.

4. List the rules for planning a hierarchy chart.

5. Plan a structured program.

6. Identify the purpose of subroutines.

7. List the principles of structured programming.

8. Explain the usage of BASIC keywords.

The computer is one of the most fascinating machines ever built. Recently, the developments in technology have caused the internal parts of the computer to be built smaller and smaller. This enabled computers to sell for hundreds of thousands of dollars less than the larger computers previously used in business. Today many people have computers in their homes. These same computers are being used in business and industry.

The computer must be programmed to make it usable. A program is a series of steps telling the computer what to do. Usually the program will provide the computer with input data (raw data to be processed). The input data is processed into a usable form known as output. Since the computer operates only with machine language (a language using a code understood by the computer) it is very difficult for the programmer to write the steps in this form. To eliminate this problem, high-level languages were developed. High-level languages use English-like instructions that are translated into machine language by the computer. This translation process is accomplished by an interpreter or compiler program. The interpreter or compiler is provided with the computer.

BASIC (Beginner's All-Purpose Symbolic Instruction Code) is one of many high-level languages. BASIC is used on small computers as well as large computers. BASIC is easy to learn and uses many keywords (English words that have a special meaning to the translator program of the computer). A list of keywords will be given at the end of each chapter as well as in Appendix A.

Topic 1.1— CONCEPTS OF STRUCTURED DESIGN

Several years ago there was much discussion about the manner in which computer programs were being written. Some thought that the development of a computer program was an art and the programmer should have the right to develop the logic in any manner. Others felt that better programs could be written if programmers would work within a set of rules. Perhaps the first step in this direction was during the early 1960s when the American National Standards Institute (ANSI) standardized the symbols used in flowchart templates (structures for program logic). These flowchart templates identified the symbols to be used in designing the basic processing of data whether it be manual, mechanical, or electronic. The basic operation of all computers can be identified by the flow process diagram illustrated in Figure 1.1.

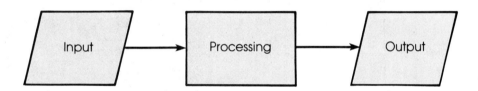

Figure 1.1   Flow Process Diagram for Computer Processing

The use of flowchart templates helped make it easier for others to understand the logic of a program. But the use of the flowchart templates did not help the programmer design better program logic nor did it identify a set of rules for programmers to follow when developing program logic. For the most part, program logic continued to be developed in the same manner as an artist painting a creative picture.

Several programmers all over the world were concerned about the problem of understanding the logic developed by other programmers. One of the first computer scientists to write about the problem was Edsger W. Dijkstra of the Technological University of the Netherlands. He identified that there should be a set of rules for all programmers to follow in program design. Even though he did not specifically identify a set of rules, he helped others become more aware of program planning. He caused the implementation of the concept of "GOTO-less" logic.

DEFINING THE PROBLEM

The problem must be defined and programmed before the computer will know what to process. As a programmer, you need to know who is going to use the results. In the classroom this is easy to determine because the instructor will usually assign the problem to be solved. Therefore, the instructor is the user. However, you must still identify the input and the output. The input is generally obtained from a source document (document containing information to be processed). For example, consider a program used by the utility company to produce the monthly utility bill. This bill is produced once a month and the input is frequently the result of reading a meter and recording the numbers on a source document. The input will include information such as that recorded on the document in Figure 1.2. The output must be planned by the final user of the information with the help of the programmer.

```
              North-South Utility Company
                      Utility Bill

          Floyd Stromme
          126 Clairemont
          Devils Lake, ND   58201-8671


          Residential Gas Used              764
          Residential Electricity Used      428


              1/2/--
```

Figure 1.2   Utility Bill Source Document

Generally, you will be asked to plan the output on a Report Spacing Chart (see Figure 1.3). In the utility bill case, the user will be responsible for approving the output shown on the Report Spacing Chart. The program will provide logic for generating the output.

Every report planned by the programmer should contain a title. In the report shown in Figure 1.3, the title is "NORTH-SOUTH UTILITY COMPANY." The subtitle is "UTILITY BILL" and explains the purpose of the report. The remainder of the Report Spacing Chart is used to detail the report. In Figure 1.3 the actual data has been written in to illustrate where each of the items is to be printed. Notice that the name and address begin in column 1 on rows 4, 5, and 6. This represents variable data and will change from customer to customer. Sometimes the programmer will use a row of letters or symbols such as a pound sign (#) to illustrate the name. The following example will illustrate how they may be used.

```
# # # # # # # # # #  # # # # # # # # # # # # #
# # # # # # # # # # # # # # # # # # # # # # # # # # # # # #
# # # # # # # # # # # # # # # # # # # # # # # # # # # # # # # # #,
# #  # # # # #-# # # #
```

When you wish to have a blank line in the report, the line is left blank on the Report Spacing Chart. "RESIDENTIAL GAS CHARGE", "RESIDENTIAL ELECTRICITY CHARGE", and "STATE TAX" are headings which will appear on each report. The data following each of these words must be represented by a number since each of these will be calculated. The last line of the report contains the date, the words "AMOUNT DUE", and the calculated total.

Now that you have had a chance to see the Report Spacing Chart on paper, you will recognize that the purpose of the chart is to help you determine where each of the items of the report is to be printed. Notice how the dollar signs ($) are all aligned. The gas charges, electricity charges, taxes, and total charges are to begin printing in Column 32. By maintaining a consistent column, the output will be neatly arranged and pleasing to the eye.

PROBLEM ANALYSIS

Once the input and output of the program have been determined, the next step is the analysis of the necessary processing steps. This is usually done by preparing a hierarchy chart.

Description of the Hierarchy Chart

The hierarchy chart is a diagram of the program logic. The logic of the program is the steps the computer will complete to perform the process designated. The preparation of a hierarchy chart requires the programmer to identify each of the modules within the program. A module performs a series of logic steps. The individual subroutines (programs under the control of the main module) to be performed within the program are known as submodules. You do not have to be concerned about the specific programming language while planning the hierarchy chart. The hierarchy chart should stand alone

```
                1         2         3
      123456789012345678901234567890
 1         NORTH-SOUTH UTILITY COMPANY
 2              UTILITY BILL
 3
 4    FLOYD STROMME
 5    126 CLAIREMONT
 6    DEVILS LAKE, ND 58201-8671
 7
 8    RESIDENTIAL GAS CHARGE        $ 22.44
 9    RESIDENTIAL ELECTRICITY CHARGE $ 43.28
10    STATE TAX                     $  2.63
11
12    2/16/-- AMOUNT DUE            $ 68.35
```

Figure 1.3   Report Spacing Chart

and should define the logic of the problem. Most high-level programming languages such as BASIC have specific keywords which are used to perform the logic desired.

Developing the Hierarchy Chart

The easiest way to design a hierarchy chart is by listing each of the submodule activities. You need not worry about the order of the submodules. After all of the submodules are identified, you should list them in order of hierarchy. The process of identifying the submodules for the utility bill may be identified as follows:

1. *Initialize the variables.* The bill sent to the customer must contain the correct data. In the utility bill example, it is necessary to initialize the rate to be charged for each cubic foot of gas and each kilowatt of electricity. Since the rates are numbers and will not change during the processing of the data, they are known as constants. Constants are not enclosed within quotation marks. Unchanging alphanumeric data is known as a literal. A literal is always enclosed in quotation marks.

2. *Input the data.* The data needed to process the utility bill includes the name, street address, city, state, ZIP Code, amount of gas used, and amount of electricity used.

3. *Calculate the charges.* To calculate the amount of the charges for gas and electricity for the utility bill, it is necessary to multiply the cubic feet of gas used by the constant which represents the rate for each cubic foot of gas. The program must also multiply the constant representing the rate for electricity by the number of kilowatts used. The taxes must be calculated next. The total cost of gas and electricity must also be calculated.

4. *Print the bill.* The utility bill is created by having the computer print the title, name and address, the line for the cost of gas, the line for the cost of electricity and the amount for taxes, and the last line for the billing date and the amount due.

5. *Terminate processing.* This will end the processing of the program and will not represent a separate submodule.

The relationship between the main module and the submodules is shown in Figure 1.4. The hierarchy chart illustrates top-down design. In this design the main module controls each of the submodules.

The main module is the highest in the hierarchy order. The submodules are arranged under the main module in the order that they are presented. The hierarchy chart should show the main module and the submodules in the order they appear in the program. A number and a name must be given to each module.

With many programs, the modules are performed in order. Control is passed from the main module to the first submodule. When the logic in the first submodule has been performed, control is returned to the main module.

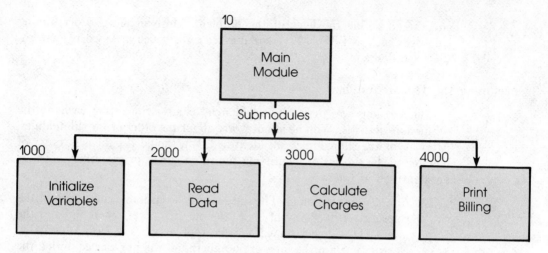

Figure 1.4   Hierarchy Chart for the Utility Bill

Control then passes to the second module. Upon completion, the control is returned to the main module. Control passes to the third submodule and returns to the main module. Processing continues until all submodules have been executed and control is returned to the main module. Processing of the program is terminated in the main module. When necessary, modules may be performed repeatedly in whatever order required.

Designing the Logic Functions

After the hierarchy chart has been prepared, the input, processing, and output will be listed for each program. The program documentation sheet shown in Figure 1.5 will illustrate what has to be completed in order to produce the desired report. The next step in problem solving is to design the logic in each of the modules. The logic to be performed by each module is described in English-like statements. These statements are known as pseudocode. To help the design of each of the modules, you should use a module documentation sheet shown in Figure 1.6 to record the logic to be performed.

A module documentation sheet is prepared for each of the modules. You should begin with the main module and continue until each of the submodules illustrated on the hierarchy chart is completed. The module documentation sheet is used to define the name of the program and module, line numbers for the module, description of the function the module will perform, and identification of the pseudocode. The module documentation sheet for the utility program's main module is shown in Figure 1.7. The program is identified as EXC1E1, which represents Example Chapter 1, Example 1.

PROGRAM DOCUMENTATION		
Program: Utility Bill	Programmer: Clark and LaBarre	Date: 2/1/--

Purpose:

To produce the utility bill for gas and electricity usage for the month of 1/--.

Input: DATA Statement	Output: Utility Bill Report to be sent to the customer

Data Terminator:

Variables Used:

NAM$	=	Name
STREETADDRESS$	=	Street Address
CITY$	=	City
STATE$	=	State
ZIPCODE$	=	ZIP Code
GAS	=	Cubic Feet of Gas
ELECTRICITY	=	Kilowatts of Electricity
CURRENTDATE$	=	Date of Bill
GASRATE	=	Gas Rate
ELECTRICITYRATE	=	Electricity Rate
STATETAX	=	State Tax Rate
GASTOTAL	=	Gas Amount
ELECTRICITYTOTAL	=	Electricity Total
CURRENTBILL	=	Total Billing
TAX	=	Total Tax
ENERGYCHARGE	=	Total Gas and Electricity

Figure 1.5   Program Documentation Sheet

MODULE DOCUMENTATION	Program: _____	Module: _____
		Lines: _____ _____
Module Description:		
Module Function (Program Design):		

Figure 1.6   Module Documentation Sheet

MODULE DOCUMENTATION	Program: EXC1E1	Module: MAIN
		Lines: 10-999

Module Description:

This is the main module which controls all other modules.

Module Function (Program Design):

1. Identify the program.
2. Clear memory space for string data (TRS-80).
3. Perform the initialization module.
4. Perform the read input data module.
5. Perform the calculate charges module.
6. Perform the print utility bill module.
7. End processing.

Figure 1.7   Main Module Documentation Sheet

The module name is MAIN and the lines of the module will be 10-999. The module description identifies that the main module controls all the submodules. The module function portion of the module documentation sheet describes the logic steps to be performed in the module. The processing begins and ends within the main module.

Designing Submodules

You will follow the same procedure identified for the main module as the module documentation sheets are prepared for each of the submodules. Because each submodule is to be controlled by the main module, you must follow a set of rules. These rules will make the program easier to understand.

RULES GOVERNING SUBMODULE CONSTRUCTION

1. Each module shall perform one logic function. A logic function may consist of one or more program statements.
2. Each submodule shall be called by the main module or by the higher module on the hierarchy chart.
3. When the logic within a module has been performed, the control should be returned to the module from which it was called. The main module in this case would continue with the next statement.
4. Each module shall be entered at the top and processing should end at the bottom. This top-down design will ensure that there is only one entry point and only one exit point.
5. No submodule shall make a decision that would result in it controlling any module above it on the hierarchy chart. However, a submodule may call another submodule controlled by another module within the hierarchy chart.
6. Each submodule shall be documented within the program to identify its function.

Using these rules will result in better programs containing top-down logic. Study the following module documentation sheets in Figures 1.8, 1.9, 1.10, and 1.11. These submodules are used in the utility bill example.

MODULE DOCUMENTATION	Program: __EXC1E1__	Module: __INITIALIZATION__ Lines: __1000-1999__

Module Description:

The purpose of this module is to set up variables with constant amounts. These rates will be used in the computation of billing amounts.

Module Function (Program Design):

1. Set the date equal to the current date.
2. Set the gas rate equal to the current rate per cubic foot of gas.
3. Set the electricity rate equal to the current rate.
4. Set the tax rate equal to the state tax rate.

Figure 1.8   Initialization Module Documentation Sheet

MODULE DOCUMENTATION	Program: __EXC1E1__	Module: <u>READ INPUT DATA</u> Lines: <u>2000-2999</u>

Module Description:

The purpose of this module is to read the data to be used as input into the processing of the utility bill.

Module Function (Program Design):

1. Read the name.
2. Read the street address.
3. Read the city.
4. Read the state.
5. Read the ZIP code.
6. Read the number representing the amount of gas used.
7. Read the number of kilowatts used.

Figure 1.9   Read Input Data Module Documentation Sheet

MODULE DOCUMENTATION	Program: __EXC1E1__	Module: <u>CALCULATE CHARGES</u> Lines: <u>3000-3999</u>

Module Description:

Calculate the charges for gas and electricity as well as the total bill.

Module Function (Program Design):

1. Multiply the rate for gas by the number of cubic feet of usage.
2. Multiply the rate for electricity by the number of kilowatts used.
3. Add the amount for gas to the amount for electricity.
4. Calculate the state taxes by multiplying the total of gas and electricity by the percentage rate initialized.
5. Add the tax to the total of the gas and electricity.

Figure 1.10   Calculate Charges Module Documentation Sheet

MODULE DOCUMENTATION	Program: EXC1E1	Module: PRINT UTILITY BILL Lines: 4000-4999

Module Description:

The purpose of this module is to print the utility bill.

Module Function (Program Design):

1. Print the name and address.
2. Print the detail line for gas.
3. Print the detail line for electricity.
4. Print the detail line for taxes.
5. Print the summary line for billing date and billing amount.

Figure 1.11   Print Utility Bill Module Documentation Sheet

REVIEW QUESTIONS

1. What is a hierarchy chart? (Obj. 2)
2. Define the function of the main module. (Obj. 3)
3. Identify the steps involved in solving a problem. (Obj. 1)
4. List the rules for developing each submodule. (Obj. 4)

Topic 1.2— IMPLEMENTING STRUCTURED DESIGN WITH BASIC

After the program has been planned, the next step is to code it. Coding is writing the program in a high-level programming language. The coding of the examples and problems in BASIC has been completed using the rules set by the BASIC language for the IBM Personal Computer. Where the text refers to the IBM Personal Computer, the BASIC structure should work for IBM Computers, IBM compatible computers, and other computers using Microsoft BASIC. Microsoft BASIC is generally referred to by other manufacturers as MBASIC or GW-BASIC. Where the text makes no distinction in the requirements for a statement, the code should work on any computer. Where differences exist in the BASIC language used by Apple computers, Commodore computers, and Radio Shack computers, they will be pointed out. Where differences are pointed out for the Apple, they should also be the same for the Apple compatible computers. The writing of the program may be divided into a number of steps.

WRITING A BASIC PROGRAM

A BASIC program contains a number of sequential instructions telling the computer what to do. Each instruction will be executed in the order that it appears unless the computer is told to branch to a different instruction in the program. The instructions begin with numbers. The most common procedure is to begin with the number 10 and increment by 10. The purpose for this is to provide space for future changes to the program if they are needed.

STEPS FOR DEVELOPING PROGRAMS

1. Determine which line numbers will be assigned to each module.
2. Code the main module.
3. Code the stub for each of the submodules (beginning and ending lines).
4. Test the logic of the main module. Debug if necessary.
5. Code each of the submodules. Begin at the top and work down. Test the module and debug if necessary.

These steps will ensure that the program written will perform as planned. Also, you will be assured that all modules are contained within the program and the output generated is correct.

Assigning Line Numbers

The line numbers are assigned based upon the logic of the hierarchy chart. The main module should always begin with the lowest number. The numbers should always be in increments of 10. For the problem defined earlier in the chapter, the modules were assigned line numbers as follows:

Line Numbers	Module
10-999	Main
1000-1999	Initialization
2000-2999	Read Input Data
3000-3999	Calculate Charges
4000-4999	Print Utility Bill

Although these line numbers were assigned for each of the modules, their usage is recommended but not required. Generally, you should begin numbering with the main module and move to the next lower level numbering from left to right. If additional submodules exist below the submodules, you would return to the left side of the hierarchy chart, add one zero to the number of the previous submodule, and begin to number from left to right. For example, submodule 1000 would have submodules numbered by 10000. Once the hierarchy chart has been developed, you need only look at it for the ranges to be used as the modules are being programmed.

Writing the Main Module

You should review the module documentation sheet for the main module shown in Figure 1.7. Since the main module serves as the supervisor of all other modules, it must contain the code to identify the program. This code is not executed when the program is processed. Rather, it serves as internal documentation. Documentation enables another person to understand the purpose of the source code without looking at the program documentation sheets.

Keywords for Writing Simple Programs

Each of the statements in BASIC contains a line number, one or more BASIC keywords, variable names if needed, arithmetic operators if needed, string literals if needed, and constants if needed. The design of a particular BASIC statement is known as the syntax of the language. Just as the English language must be written without errors, so must the programming language used by the computer. In this text, the syntax for each keyword will be presented in the following form. Each general form will be followed by an example.

General Form: *line number BASIC keyword statement*

Example: 10 REM THIS IS STANDARD STATEMENT FORMAT

DOCUMENTATION OF THE PROGRAM

The keyword **REM** is used to internally document the program. REM is an abbreviation of the word remark. Any statement following the REM statement will not be executed. This means that the information is shown in the program but is not manipulated by the computer. On some computers (for example, the IBM Personal Computer and the TRS-80), the apostrophe (') is used in place of the REM. You may use REM; however, the (') may not be as distracting when reading the program. Most examples in this text will use the apostrophe. The general form of the REM statement is as follows.

General Form: *line number* REM *statement*

Example: 10 REM   THIS IS A PROGRAM REMARK

or

General Form: *line number ' statement*

Example: 10 '   THIS IS ALSO A PROGRAM REMARK

Each of the statements in the example will be ignored by the computer when the program is executed. However, each of the above statements is very important to the program. Any character on the keyboard may be used following REM. REM statements may occur anywhere within the program and are helpful in identifying the submodules.

CLEARING MEMORY SPACE

The keyword CLEAR is used on the TRS-80 Model III to clear string space within the memory of the computer. Even though the computer does set aside some space for the storage of string characters, TRS-80 Model III may require additional space. Therefore, it is a good idea to include the CLEAR statement in your program. Note that with most other computers the CLEAR statement performs other functions used only for very advanced programs.

General Form: *line number* CLEAR *number*

Example: 50 CLEAR 1000

CLEARING THE SCREEN

The BASIC keyword CLS is used to clear the screen on the IBM and TRS-80. This statement is very helpful if you are writing a program to produce output on the screen. Any command previously displayed on the screen will be erased before the output for the report is displayed.

General Form: *line number* CLS

Example: 40 CLS

To clear the screen on the Commodore, you must add a line to the beginning of the program. The general form is as follows:

General Form: *line number* PRINT *"shift and clr/home"*

Example: 40 PRINT "◨"

To clear the screen on the Apple, you must also add a line to the beginning of the program. The general form is as follows:

General Form: *line number* HOME

Example: 40 HOME

PRINTING ON THE SCREEN

The keyword **PRINT** is used to print data on the screen. There are several options of the print function which will be discussed later in this chapter. For now we will illustrate only the option used to print a message on the screen. This will tell you what the program will do when it is executed.

General Form: *line number* PRINT *literal*

Example: 90 PRINT "THIS IS A PROGRAM"

BRANCHING WITHIN THE PROGRAM

You may use one of two statements to branch from one location within a program to another. The GOTO statement used to be one of the most popular branching statements. Because of its extensive usage and the difficulty of following logic, the GOTO is now used only when absolutely necessary.

General Form: *line number* GOTO *line number*

Example: 100 GOTO 1000

The following example program will illustrate why the GOTO statement is used very little.

```
10 GOTO 40
20 CLS
30 GOTO 10
40 GOTO 20
```

GOTO statements generally make logic difficult to follow unless the program is very simple. Sometimes programmers find they have created an infinite loop. An infinite loop is where the program continues to process and the computer does not know how to exit the instructions. The example illustrated here shows an infinite loop using GOTO statements. The keyword GOSUB is the more popular means of branching from one location to another. GOSUB allows you to branch to a location, perform some logic and return control to the statement following the branch where you left off. To accomplish this, the keyword RETURN must accompany the keyword GOSUB within the same program. To transfer control from one location to another you would use GOSUB. The general form is constructed as follows:

General Form: *line number* GOSUB *line number*

Example: 70 GOSUB 2000

To return logic control back to the statement following the GOSUB, the RETURN statement is used.

General Form: *line number* RETURN

Example: 2999 RETURN

The following example will illustrate the transfer from the main module to a submodule and return to the main module upon completion of processing the logic in the submodule.

```
10 GOSUB 1000
20 'CONTROL HAS RETURNED
999 END


1000 ' ***** THIS MODULE PERFORMS THE INITIALIZATION
1999 RETURN
```

When programming using the concept of structured programming, you must be careful to include within the main module the BASIC statement, END. This statement causes execution of the program to stop. If the computer does not encounter an END statement, it will sequentially execute one or more of the submodules a second time. The general format of the END statement is given here:

General Form: *line number* END

Example: 999 END

CODING THE MAIN MODULE

With the few BASIC statements discussed, the main module for the utility program may now be written. You will be able to enter the coded lines and the main module will be completed for the billing program. Please refer to the example on page 20.

Lines 10 through 40 are for documentation purposes only in this example. The use of the asterisks (*) is merely to make the lines look more attractive. Line 70 of the example was included to provide vertical spacing. The insertion of vertical spacing such as line 70 helps make the program more readable.

```
10 ' EXC1E1
20 ' CLARK AND LABARRE--CHAPTER 1, EXAMPLE 1
30 ' UTILITY BILL
40 ' ***** MAIN MODULE ****************
50 CLS
60 PRINT "THIS PROGRAM WILL PRODUCE A UTILITY BILL"
70 PRINT
80 GOSUB 1000 'INITIALIZATION MODULE
90 GOSUB 2000 'READ DATA MODULE
100 GOSUB 3000 'CALCULATE CHARGES
110 GOSUB 4000 'PRINT UTILITY BILL
999 END
```

Testing the Main Module

You should generally test the main module by coding the submodules with minimum code and then running the program. To do the minimum code for submodules, each submodule will begin with a REM statement or a (') to identify the module. This will be followed by the PRINT statement to print a literal defining what the module would perform, and the RETURN statement to return control to the main module. The coding of the submodules in this manner is referred to as stubbing in the modules.

```
1000 ' ***** INITIALIZATION ***********
1010 PRINT "INITIALIZE VARIABLES"
1999 RETURN


2000 ' ***** READ INPUT DATA **********
2010 PRINT "READ INPUT DATA"
2999 RETURN


3000 ' ***** CALCULATE CHARGES ********
3010 PRINT "CALCULATE CHARGES"
3999 RETURN


4000 ' ***** PRINT UTILITY BILL *******
4010 PRINT "PRINT UTILITY BILL"
4999 RETURN
```

Once the submodules are stubbed in, run the program. If the main module processes the desired output identified in each of the submodules, you will know that the GOSUB statements are in the correct order. If correct, the submodules would be coded completely. If the output is incorrect, you would debug (correct) the main module's logic and repeat the test. This process would continue until the desired output is obtained. When totally coded, the submodules should produce the desired report.

Writing the Submodule Source Code

After the main module has passed the test, you are ready to begin coding each of the submodules in its complete form. The logic of the program will determine which module to code first, and so on. Looking at the main module will tell you that the initialization submodule should be coded first.

INITIALIZATION OF VARIABLES

The purpose of the initialization module is to set the values of certain variables which will be used in the calculation of other variables to be printed later in the program. These variables are set in this module so they might be easily changed if you desire to do so later. Variables are names used to represent data items. Variables representing alphabetic information generally are referred to as string variables. Variables used to represent numeric information are referred to as numeric variables. Variable names used on the IBM PC and the TRS-80 Model 4 may be as long as 40 characters. This allows you the freedom to fully describe the data used in the program. On the Apple, Commodore, and TRS-80 Model III, variables may be 2 characters long. If longer names are used, only the first two characters are recognized. If you are limited to two characters, you should identify the variable names used in the program and explain what they represent in separate REM statements or on the program documentation sheet.

String Variables.   String variables are identified by adding a dollar sign to the variable name. For example, NAM$ may represent a name. The word NAME$ was not used because NAME is a reserved word. A reserved word is the same thing as a keyword. That is, it is recognized by the computer to perform a unique function. Examine the following examples of string variables.

ADDRESS$ may represent address
AD$ may also represent address

Numeric Variables.   Numeric variables do not need a special identifying character added to their names. For example, ZIP Code may be represented as ZIPCODE. The two words are "run" together because BASIC does not allow the variable name to contain blank spaces between words. On some computers, the variable name may be written as ZIP.CODE. Numeric variables may be used in calculations or to represent a value. Examine the following examples of numeric variable names.

AGE may represent age
AG may also represent age
ZC may represent ZIP Code
RT may represent rate

ASSIGNMENT STATEMENT

The keyword **LET** is used to assign the value to a variable. The syntax for the statement is as follows:

> General Form: *line number* LET *variable name* = *value*
>
> Example: 100 LET A=B+C

The value to be assigned to the variable by a LET statement may be in a constant, literal, or arithmetic computation as shown in the example. When arithmetic is done with the computer, arithmetic operators are used.

The arithmetic operators used in the assignment statement are the same that you use in mathematics classes. They are listed here in the order of hierarchy as performed by the computer.

Symbol	Meaning	
( )	Parentheses	
∧ or ** or ↑	Exponentiation	
*	Multiplication ⎫	Equal priority,
/	Division ⎬	done in order found
+	Addition ⎫	Equal priority,
-	Subtraction ⎬	done in order found

Table 1.1   Arithmetic Operators Used in BASIC

When coding arithmetic statements, you should use the parentheses to enclose the arithmetic functions if uncertain whether they will be performed in the order desired.

The initialization module of our example program is coded as follows. It should then be entered into the computer with the main module and the other stubbed in submodules to determine if the code is correct. If there are any syntax errors, they should be corrected at this time.

```
1000 ' ***** INITIALIZATION MODULE ****
1010 LET CURRENTDATE$="2/10/--"
1020 LET GASRATE=.9963
1030 LET ELECTRICITYRATE=.0372
1040 LET STATETAX=.04
1999 RETURN
```

INPUT THE DATA

The second submodule should now be coded. This will be easily accomplished in this example utility program. Only one line of the stubbed-in submodule needs to be changed. The PRINT statement is replaced with a statement to read data. The keyword READ is used to obtain data from a statement to be included in the program later. Whenever a READ statement is used, the program must also contain one or more DATA statements. The basic format for the READ statement is as follows:

General Form: *line number* READ *variable names*

Example: `2010 READ NAM$, STREETADDRESS$`

The READ statement may contain one or more variable names. In the example given, there are two variable names which are separated by a comma.

The DATA statement may be placed anywhere in the program. However, the general placement is at the end of the code. By placing it here, you will not have placed DATA statements within the logic of the program. DATA statements within the logic make it more difficult to debug the program if errors are present. The DATA statement must contain at least one item of data for each variable name identified within the READ statement.

General Form: *line number* DATA *one or more data elements*

Example: `5010 DATA FLOYD STROMME, 126 CLAIREMONT`

Another BASIC statement sometimes used with the READ and DATA statements is the keyword RESTORE. The RESTORE statement is used to reset the reading pointer to the beginning of the data items in the DATA statements. If there are several DATA statements, the RESTORE will reset the pointer to the first item in the first DATA statement. The general format is as follows:

General Form: *line number* RESTORE

Example: `2020 RESTORE`

The code for the read data module is shown here. The information for the read statement was obtained from the module documentation shown on page 12. Usually all variable names will be placed in the READ statement as shown in line 2010 of the submodule. However, you may use more than one statement if all variable names will not fit on one line.

```
2000 ' ***** READ INPUT DATA **********
2010 READ NAM$, STREETADDRESS$, CITY$, STATE$, ZIPCODE$, GAS, ELECTRICITY
2999 RETURN
```

Here is the DATA line for our utility example. This line must be entered along with the read data source code and must be added to the previously entered code in order to test the read data module. If no syntax errors occur, you may assume that these two modules are correct.

```
5010 DATA FLOYD STROMME, 126 CLAIREMONT, DEVILS LAKE, ND, 58201-8671,33,1092
```

CALCULATE CHARGES

The calculate charges module is coded from the module documentation on page 12.

```
3000 ' ***** CALCULATE CHARGES ********
3010 LET GASTOTAL=GASRATE*GAS
3020 LET ELECTRICITYTOTAL=ELECTRICITYRATE*ELECTRICITY
3040 LET ENERGYCHARGE=GASTOTAL+ELECTRICITYTOTAL
3050 LET TAX=STATETAX*ENERGYCHARGE
3050 LET CURRENTBILL=ENERGYCHARGE+TAX
3999 RETURN
```

The calculation module contains several assignment statements. Generally, the assignment statements may be entered with or without the BASIC statement LET. Notice that lines 3010 through 3050 have been entered without spaces between the variable names and the arithmetic operator. This is one technique of entering the assignment statement. You may also enter the statement with spaces before and after each of the arithmetic operators.

Upon entering the code for the calculate charges module, you may test to check the accuracy of the code. However, no output will be generated because the source code to generate the output is contained in the print utility bill module. Usually, you should go ahead with the coding of the print module before testing to see if the calculation module is correct.

PRINT UTILITY BILL

The coding for the print utility bill module follows. The module documentation sheet on page 13 provided you with the necessary steps to generate the report. The report spacing chart on page 6 provided you with the appropriate placement information. This report will use variables that were given values in the initialization module as well as data from the read input data module. It will also use values computed in the calculate charges module. The print module contains several PRINT statements. Some PRINT statements are similar to those discussed earlier in the chapter. Others are new. Each will be discussed in detail.

The PRINT statement may be used to print various literals. If you do not provide spaces or characters to control the location of printing, the computer will always begin printing at the left side of the output device. The output device may be a printer or VDT (Video Display Terminal). Some computers have 40 column screens, some 64 columns, and others 80 columns. It is necessary for you to know this fact prior to having planned the output of the program.

```
4000 ' ***** PRINT UTILITY BILL *******
4010 PRINT "      NORTH-SOUTH UTILITY COMPANY"
4020 PRINT "          UTILITY BILL"
4030 PRINT
4040 PRINT NAM$
4050 PRINT STREETADDRESS$
4060 PRINT CITY$;" ";STATE$;" ";ZIPCODE$
4070 PRINT
4080 PRINT "RESIDENTIAL GAS CHARGE ";TAB(32) USING "$###.##";GASTOTAL
4090 PRINT
4100 PRINT "RESIDENTIAL ELECTRICITY CHARGE "; TAB(32) USING "$###.##";ELECTRICIT
YTOTAL
4110 PRINT
4120 PRINT "STATE TAX ";TAB(32) USING "$###.##";TAX
4130 PRINT
4140 PRINT CURRENTDATE$, "AMOUNT DUE ";TAB(32) USING "$###.##";CURRENTBILL
4999 RETURN
```

PRINTING WITH COMMAS

The comma may be inserted between variable names within the PRINT statement. The comma will cause the second variable to be printed in the second print zone. If there was a third variable, it would be printed in the third print zone. Study the examples to determine how the PRINT statement works with the comma.

Example:
```
10 PRINT "CLARK","LABARRE"
20 PRINT 98,89
```

Output:

```
CLARK          LABARRE
  98             89
```

Usually there will be at least 15 spaces in each print zone. However, the print zones do vary from computer to computer. Computers may have three, four, or five print zones. Notice in line 20 of the example, the computer is instructed to print two constants. In the sample output the constants are printed with a space before each one. This space is reserved for a sign. Since each of the numbers were positive, the plus sign (+) was not printed. If the numbers had been negative, the minus sign (-) would have been printed.

PRINTING WITH SEMICOLONS

When the semicolon is used to separate printed literals and data, the results may be different depending upon the sequence of the numeric or string output. Generally you can assume that no spaces occur between the output items. As was stated in the last example, positive numbers may be printed with a space before the number. The example given here illustrates the usage of the semicolon in the PRINT statement.

Example:
```
10 PRINT "WATCH";"FOR";"THE";"SPACE"
20 PRINT "WATCH ";"FOR ";"THE ";"SPACE"
30 PRINT "THE TOTAL IS";98
40 PRINT "THE TOTAL IS ";98
50 PRINT "THE TOTAL IS "; -98
```

Output:
```
WATCHFORTHESPACE
WATCH FOR THE SPACE
THE TOTAL IS 98
THE TOTAL IS  98
THE TOTAL IS -98
```

USING THE TAB OPTION

The TAB option allows the programmer to position the output without providing the actual spaces in the PRINT format. TAB is the abbreviation for tabulate. By placing the TAB option after the PRINT, the program directs the computer to advance the printing position to the designated column before printing.

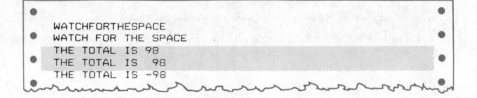

General Form: *line number* PRINT TAB*(column number); item to be printed*

Example: `50 PRINT TAB(40); "BEGIN"`

Remember to use the TAB with the PRINT command. If more than one TAB is used in a statement, be sure to separate items with a semicolon. Also, make sure that each TAB advances the print position beyond the previous printing point. The column number may be expressed as a constant, a numeric variable, or as a numeric expression. On most of the computers the columns begin with 1. However, on some computers the first column is known as 0. Generally you may use 1 as the first column. Study the following examples to determine how the TAB option may be used.

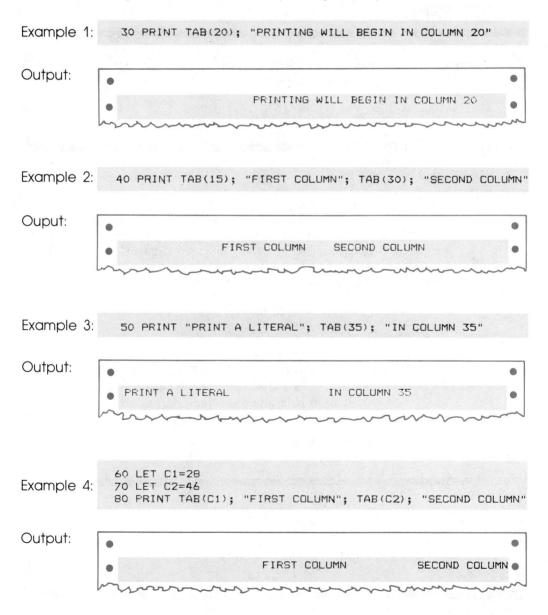

Example 1:
```
30 PRINT TAB(20); "PRINTING WILL BEGIN IN COLUMN 20"
```

Output:
```
                        PRINTING WILL BEGIN IN COLUMN 20
```

Example 2:
```
40 PRINT TAB(15); "FIRST COLUMN"; TAB(30); "SECOND COLUMN"
```

Ouput:
```
              FIRST COLUMN    SECOND COLUMN
```

Example 3:
```
50 PRINT "PRINT A LITERAL"; TAB(35); "IN COLUMN 35"
```

Output:
```
PRINT A LITERAL                   IN COLUMN 35
```

Example 4:
```
60 LET C1=28
70 LET C2=46
80 PRINT TAB(C1); "FIRST COLUMN"; TAB(C2); "SECOND COLUMN"
```

Output:
```
                           FIRST COLUMN       SECOND COLUMN
```

The TAB function must be used with the PRINT command. Remember that the column number contained within the parentheses may not exceed the number of columns on the screen or printer. For example, the IBM may use a number as large as 80 for the screen, whereas the Commodore may use only 40. On the Apple and Commodore, the TAB function does not operate reliably on the printer. On these machines, the SPC function is used when printing on the printer. SPC is an abbreviation of space. The SPC function inserts the designated number of spaces. The general form for SPC is as follows:

General Form: *line number* PRINT *"word";* SPC*(number of columns); "word"*

Example: `60 PRINT "HI";SPC(10);"THERE"`

PRINT USING OPTIONS

The formatting statement in BASIC is **PRINT USING**. The functions of the different options of this statement vary greatly from computer to computer. It is not available on the Apple and Commodore. The PRINT USING option is the most easily used feature of BASIC for typical formatting of output data. It may be used to:

1. Truncate output data if a complete string is not wanted.
2. Suppress leading zeros.
3. Round numbers to the right of the decimal.
4. Edit output data to include dollar sign, comma, and decimal.
5. Float the dollar sign over to the most significant digit.
6. Insert the asterisk as a check protector symbol.
7. Edit output to include a plus or minus sign.

The PRINT USING requires a PRINT statement followed by the USING statement which must contain a string of characters or a variable representing a string.

General Form: *line number* PRINT USING *"character string";* *item to print*

Example: `10 PRINT USING "###.###"; 023.4`

or

General Form: *line number* PRINT USING *variable$; item to print*

Example: 20 PRINT USING Z$; 987654.34

Study the following examples to see how several of the options of the PRINT USING might be used in a program.

Example 1:

```
100 PRINT USING "###.##"; 034.5
```

Output:

```
34.50
```

Notice that the leading zero was suppressed to the left of the decimal point. Also, a zero was provided to the right of the decimal point. The three number signs (#) to the left of the decimal point will allow a maximum of three digits to the left of the decimal point. The two number signs to the right of the decimal point will ensure that two numbers will be printed to the right of the decimal point.

In the next example, a variable representing the size of the edited field will be used. In line 150 the variable Z$ will be set up to contain the string representing the edited field. Once set up it may be used over and over. Study the example.

Example 2:

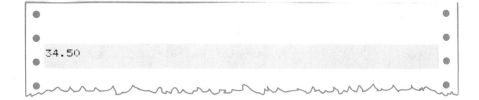

```
150 Z$="##,###.##"
160 PRINT USING Z$; 234.45
170 PRINT USING Z$; 1234.456
180 PRINT USING Z$; 56789.0
```

Output:

```
   234.45
 1,234.46
56,789.00
```

Notice how the comma is suppressed when there are less than four numbers to the left of the decimal. Also, notice how the 5 rounded to a 6 when there were three digits to the right of the decimal.

In Example 3, the dollar sign edits the output to include a sign. Notice that it did not float over to the most significant digit. In order to have the floating dollar sign, you must include two dollar signs in the editing string. Examine Example 4 to see how the dollar sign floated over to the most significant digit. Also notice that the comma was inserted in the correct location.

Example 3:   `30 PRINT USING "$###,###.##"; 1234.56`

Output:

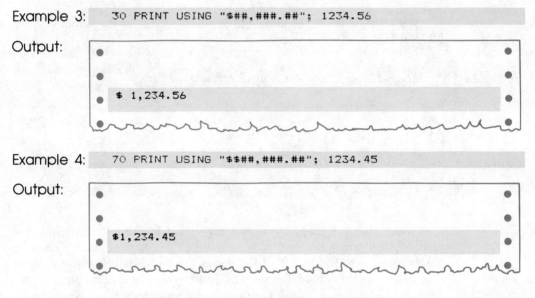

```
$ 1,234.56
```

Example 4:   `70 PRINT USING "$$##,###.##"; 1234.45`

Output:

```
$1,234.45
```

The next example illustrates the use of the check protector symbol or the asterisks (**). Notice how the dollar sign floated over to the most significant digit. The comma was suppressed and asterisks were inserted in front of the dollar sign to fill in the blank spaces.

Example 5:   `80 PRINT USING "**$###,###.##"; 234.56`

Output:

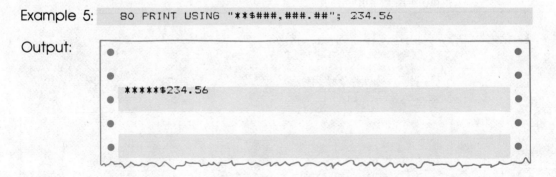

```
*****$234.56
```

Another option of the check protector symbol is shown in Example 6. In this case the dollar sign remained static and the asterisks floated over to the most significant digit.

Example 6:

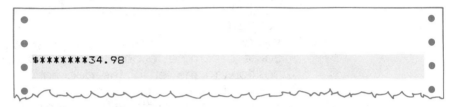

```
90 PRINT USING "$**###,###.##"; 34.98
```

Output:

```
$*******34.98
```

The backslashes (\ \) are used to indicate the length to be used in printing a string. Notice that at least two characters are printed. The number of spaces between the backslashes (in this case two) determine how many additional characters are to be printed. On some computers (for example, the TRS-80), the percent sign (%) is used instead of backslashes.

Example 7:

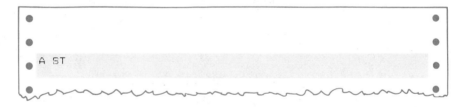

```
200 PRINT USING "\ \"; "A STRING"
```

Output:

```
A ST
```

Look at Example 8. Putting the plus sign in the statement causes the positive number to be printed as usual. However, the negative number is printed with the negative sign to the right. The sign may be placed at either the left or the right. The minus sign may also be used in the editing string as shown in line 60 of Example 8. However, it causes the positive number to be printed with a negative sign and the negative number generally will cause an error or be printed with two negative signs.

Example 8:

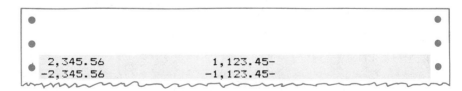

```
50 PRINT USING "###,###.##+"; 2345.56,1123.45-
60 PRINT USING "-###,###.##"; 2345.56,1123.45-
```

Output:

```
 2,345.56          1,123.45-
-2,345.56         -1,123.45-
```

Table 1.2 is a summary of the formatting that can be done with PRINT USING.

Symbol	Function
#	This image is used for numeric output. The number of signs will determine the size of the edited field.
,	The comma is an insertion character which will cause a comma to be printed every three positions to the left of the decimal.
.	The decimal point is also an insertion character. It is used to align numbers with decimals.
$	The dollar sign will place the dollar sign at the beginning of the field of output data.
$$	Two dollar signs will cause the dollar symbol to float over to the most significant digit.
**	Two asterisks will cause the asterisks to float over and fill every position to the most significant digit.
\	The backslash is used to select the length for printing a string. The percent sign is used on the TRS-80.

Table 1.2   Formatting Symbols for PRINT USING

The print module of the utility program contains several of the PRINT statements that have just been discussed. Study the program code for the module to see how each has been used. Lines 4080 through line 4140 illustrate the most commonly used formatting characters when generating output with dollars and cents. Any of the examples could have been used in this module.

The next example shows the entire program. Notice how all of the techniques of structured programming have been used to produce an easy-to-read and understandable program. Look at the data names. Notice how they are sufficiently long to clearly identify what data they represent. Some computers will not allow over two character variable names. If that is the case, the program should define each variable name in the internal documentation at the beginning of the program. Notice the numbering technique. Each module begins with the number in the thousands and ends with 999 of that level. This program will serve as an example to follow as the programs at the end of the chapter are solved.

GETTING THE COMPUTER READY

The first topic of the chapter contained the procedures for solving the problem by using the tools of structured design. The second topic has thus far

```
10 ' EXC1E1
20 ' CLARK AND LABARRE--CHAPTER 1, EXAMPLE 1
30 ' UTILITY BILL
40 ' ***** MAIN MODULE ****************
50 CLS
60 PRINT "THIS PROGRAM WILL PRODUCE A UTILITY BILL"
70 PRINT
80 GOSUB 1000 'INITIALIZATION MODULE
90 GOSUB 2000 'READ DATA MODULE
100 GOSUB 3000 'CALCULATE CHARGES
110 GOSUB 4000 'PRINT UTILITY BILL
999 END
1000 ' ***** INITIALIZATION MODULE ****
1010 LET CURRENTDATE$="2/10/--"
1020 LET GASRATE=.9963
1030 LET ELECTRICITYRATE=.0372
1040 LET STATETAX=.04
1999 RETURN
2000 ' ***** READ INPUT DATA **********
2010 READ NAM$, STREETADDRESS$, CITY$, STATE$, ZIPCODE$, GAS, ELECTRICITY
2999 RETURN
3000 ' ***** CALCULATE CHARGES ********
3010 LET GASTOTAL=GASRATE*GAS
3020 LET ELECTRICITYTOTAL=ELECTRICITYRATE*ELECTRICITY
3030 LET ENERGYCHARGE=GASTOTAL+ELECTRICITYTOTAL
3040 LET TAX=STATETAX*ENERGYCHARGE
3050 LET CURRENTBILL=ENERGYCHARGE+TAX
3999 RETURN
4000 ' ***** PRINT UTILITY BILL *******
4010 PRINT "      NORTH-SOUTH UTILITY COMPANY"
4020 PRINT "            UTILITY BILL"
4030 PRINT
4040 PRINT NAM$
4050 PRINT STREETADDRESS$
4060 PRINT CITY$;" ";STATE$;" ";ZIPCODE$
4070 PRINT
4080 PRINT "RESIDENTIAL GAS CHARGE ";TAB(32) USING "$###.##";GASTOTAL
4090 PRINT
4100 PRINT "RESIDENTIAL ELECTRICITY CHARGE "; TAB(32) USING "$###.##";ELECTRICIT
YTOTAL
4110 PRINT
4120 PRINT "STATE TAX ";TAB(32) USING "$###.##";TAX
4130 PRINT
4140 PRINT CURRENTDATE$, "AMOUNT DUE ";TAB(32) USING "$###.##";CURRENTBILL
4999 RETURN
5000 ' ***** DATA RECORD **************
5010 DATA FLOYD STROMME, 126 CLAIREMONT, DEVILS LAKE, ND, 58201-8671,33,1092
```

provided the background on how to program the problem solution using structured programming techniques. This section will identify the procedures and commands used in entering and running a program on a computer.

Before entering the program, it is important that you make sure that the main memory is clear of any existing program statements. If the computer has just been turned on, it is likely to be clear. To make sure that this is the case, the command NEW may be entered. The command NEW is keyed and the ENTER key or RETURN key is pressed. IBM and Radio Shack use the ENTER key to place data in the memory of the computer. Apple and Commodore use the RETURN key. This book will refer to the keys as the ENTER/RETURN key. In addition to the clearing of memory, the NEW command on most computers clears the VDT and repositions the cursor in the upper left-hand corner. The cursor may be different from computer to computer. However, it is usually an underscore which blinks. On some computers the cursor will be a solid block. It will move to the right as characters are input. You must always press the ENTER/RETURN key after keying a command.

As you begin to enter the program, the line numbers (for example, 10, 20, and so on), may be keyed at the beginning of each line. Another way of getting the line numbers entered on the IBM and TRS-80 is to use the AUTO command. You merely key the command AUTO and press ENTER/RETURN. The computer automatically presents line number 10 on the VDT. If you press ENTER/RETURN, 20 appears. To stop the sequence numbers from appearing, strike the BREAK key.

Executing the Program

The command RUN is keyed to cause the computer to execute the program. This means that the computer will attempt to perform the logic in each of the modules of the program. First the main module statements are performed until a branch to a submodule is identified. The computer performs all of the steps identified in the program until the END statement is encountered. At this point the computer stops execution. As the program is run, one or more errors might be encountered. Most errors will be syntax errors. This generally means that there is a misspelling in a variable name, BASIC keyword, or in the usage of the arithmetic operators. Error messages state the type of error found in the program and on which line it occurs. Execution is stopped at this point and the error must be corrected before the RUN command may be entered again.

Looking at the Program

You are always able to look at the program stored in memory. By keying the command LIST, you may display the program code on the VDT. If the program is too long to be totally displayed on the VDT, it will be necessary to list the program in sections. This may be accomplished by keying the command followed by the range of lines to be printed. For example:

LIST 10-230 would cause the first 23 lines to be displayed. This assumes you have numbered your lines in intervals of 10.
LIST 100 would cause only line 100 to be displayed.

You can also temporarily stop the printing by pressing a designated key.

Inserting Lines into the Program

Lines may be added to the program by entering the line with the appropriate line number between two existing lines. For example, if a line had to be inserted between 40 and 50, you would enter line number 45 and the statement. The computer would automatically insert the line in the appropriate location. The program would then have lines 40, 45, and 50.

Changing Existing Lines

Sometimes it is necessary for you to change the code on a given line. On some computers with full-screen editing like the IBM Personal Computer and the Commodore, you may move the cursor to the location of the change and insert or delete characters. On other computers it will be necessary to key the new line. If the same line number is used, the computer will erase the old line and replace it with the new one.

Eliminating Lines

Once in a while you may key a line that should not have been entered. A single line may be deleted by entering its number and pressing ENTER/RETURN. The DELETE command is used to delete groups of lines. For example, lines 40-100 may be eliminated by keying in DELETE 40-100. Remember, after keying the command, the ENTER/RETURN key must be pressed.

SAVING THE PROGRAM

Upon the completion of the debugging process, you may want to save the program for future use. If the computer was turned off or if the command NEW was entered, the existing program would be destroyed. To keep the program for future use, use the SAVE command. Generally the program will be saved on an auxiliary storage device such as a floppy diskette or a cassette. The SAVE command must be followed by a file name. Usually the file name must be eight characters or less. The name given on the program documentation sheet will be used for the example programs. That name was EXC1E1. The name identified that this was Example Chapter 1, Example 1. It looks like this:

```
SAVE "EXC1E1"
```

Notice that the file name is enclosed in quotation marks. This is true for all computers except the Apple.

LOADING THE PROGRAM

You may want to reload the program into the computer and execute it again. The LOAD command will cause the program to be loaded from storage media. Once the program is loaded, it may be listed or executed again with the use of the LIST and RUN commands.

```
LOAD "EXC1E1"
```

GETTING HARDCOPY OUTPUT

Often you will want to obtain the hardcopy (paper copy) of the program
and the report generated by the execution of the program.

IBM and TRS-80

The hardcopy of the program is obtained by using the **LLIST** command.
Once the program has been loaded into memory, the printer is turned on and
the programmer enters LLIST. The printer then lists each of the program
statements. When the last statement has been printed, the printer will stop.

Obtaining a copy of the report on the IBM and TRS-80 will require you
to convert PRINT statements to **LPRINT**. This process need not be too
difficult if you will load the program into memory and use the editing
features of the computer to insert the L on each line that a PRINT
statement occurs. The print module will look like the following after changes
have been made.

Example:

```
4000 ' ***** PRINT UTILITY BILL *******
4010 LPRINT "          NORTH-SOUTH UTILITY COMPANY"
4020 LPRINT "                   UTILITY BILL."
4030 LPRINT
4040 LPRINT NAM$
4050 LPRINT STREETADDRESS$
4060 LPRINT CITY$;" ";STATE$;" ";ZIPCODE$
4070 LPRINT
4080 LPRINT "RESIDENTIAL GAS CHARGE ";TAB(32) USING "$###.##";GASTOTAL
4090 LPRINT
4100 LPRINT "RESIDENTIAL ELECTRICITY CHARGE "; TAB(32) USING "$###.##";ELECTRICI
TYTOTAL
4110 LPRINT
4120 LPRINT "STATE TAX ";TAB(32) USING "$###.##";TAX
4130 LPRINT
4140 LPRINT CURRENTDATE$, "AMOUNT DUE ";TAB(32) USING "$###.##";CURRENTBILL
4999 RETURN
```

Apple

If hardcopy of the report is desired on the Apple, **PR#1** must be used
before the PRINT statement. This causes the output to be transferred to the
printer. To turn off this transfer, use the **PR#0** command.

```
30 PRINT CHR$(4);"PR#1"
40 PRINT "THIS WILL APPEAR ON THE PRINTER"
50 PRINT CHR$(4);"PR#0"
```

Obtaining a hardcopy list of the program on the Apple requires the use
of PR#1 and PR#0 commands to turn on the transfer to the printer and to
turn it off again. The commands do not contain line numbers because they
are considered commands and are not program lines. On the Apple, the
commands are:

```
PR#1
LIST
PR#0
```

Commodore

To list a report on the Commodore computer, a series of commands must occur. The following example illustrates the statements.

```
40 OPEN 4,4
50 CMD4
60 PRINT "THIS IS TO BE PRINTED ON THE PRINTER"
70 PRINT#4
80 CLOSE 4
```

To obtain a hardcopy of the program on the Commodore, use the commands given in the following example. The commands do not contain line numbers because they are considered to be commands and not program lines.

```
OPEN 4,4
CMD4
LIST
PRINT#4
CLOSE 4
```

REVIEW QUESTIONS

1. Identify the five steps in developing a program. (Obj. 1)
2. Explain the procedures for numbering the modules in a structured program. (Obj. 6)
3. Explain the purpose for documentation within the program. (Obj. 5)
4. Explain the role of the submodules in a structured program. (Obj. 7)
5. Identify two ways to clear the memory of the computer. (Obj. 8)
6. What command is used to place a program on diskette? (Obj. 8)
7. How is the program loaded from diskette and placed in memory? (Obj. 8)
8. Identify ways that a line may be deleted from the program. (Obj. 8)
9. Explain how to place the program on hardcopy. (Obj. 8)

VOCABULARY WORDS

The following terms were introduced in this chapter:

program	hierarchy chart	debug
input data	module	variables
output	subroutines	string variables

machine language	submodules	numeric variables
high-level language	pseudocode	reserved word
interpreter	module documentation	arithmetic operators
compiler	coding	VDT
keywords	internal documentation	leading zero
source document	syntax	floating dollar sign
literal	infinite loop	syntax errors
constants	stubbing in	hardcopy

KEYWORDS AND COMMANDS

The following keywords and commands were introduced in this chapter:

REM	READ	RUN
CLEAR	DATA	LIST
CLS	RESTORE	DELETE
PRINT	TAB	SAVE
GOTO	SPC	LOAD
GOSUB	PRINT USING	LLIST
RETURN	NEW	LPRINT
END	ENTER/RETURN	PR#1
LET	AUTO	PR#0

PROGRAMS TO WRITE

For each of the programs, develop the following:

1. Program documentation sheet.
2. Hierarchy chart.
3. Module documentation sheet for each module.
4. Code the main module. Begin with REM statements and end with the END statement.
5. Test the main module by stubbing in the submodules.
6. Program the submodules one by one and test each.
7. Test the complete program with test data.

Program 1

Write a program to set the advertisement for the annual Spring Festival. This advertisement will be used year after year. Therefore, you are to set up the program using constants for the spring festival, site, date, time, and entrance fee. The advertisement should be centered and spacing between lines should be appropriate to provide easy reading. It might look like the following:

```
                16th Annual

              SPRING FESTIVAL

               CIVIC CENTER

               March 3, 19--

        9:30 a.m. to 5:00 p.m.

         Admittance   $4.50
```

Program 2

Write a program to produce a form for the band instructor to use in keeping track of the students' practice time. This form should contain a column for the activity, a column for each day of the work week, and a column for tallying the total amount of time spent on each activity during the week. If you are creative, you may want to add horizontal and vertical lines between each of the activities and the days of the week. The form may look like the following:

```
                        BAND PRACTICE
                    MONTH ____    WEEK ____
--------------------------------------------------------------------------

                MONDAY    TUESDAY   WEDNESDAY   THURSDAY   FRIDAY   TOTAL

BAND INSTRUCTION

COUNTING

PIANO

CHOIR

OTHER
                                                    WEEKLY TOTAL
```

Program 3

Write a program to calculate the semester grade for one student in Data Processing 101. The student's name, six daily grades, and three test grades are to be read from one DATA statement. The daily work will be worth 40 percent of the grade and test grades will represent the other 60 percent of the grade. Print a report with an appropriate title such as GRADE FOR DATA PROCESSING 101, the student's name, and the calculated percentage grade. Be sure to identify the name and grade with appropriate column headings. Use the following data statement to test your data.

DATA Mary Smith,89,67,78,97,88,86,90,89

Program 4

Your favorite basketball player has had a very good season. The coach would like to determine the average points scored. You are to write a program to read a DATA statement containing the name of the player and the points for the ten conference games (in order). Your program should produce a report showing the date, the year of the season, a listing of points by number of game, the total points labeled, and the average points scored per game with an appropriate label. An example DATA statement is given:

DATA Todd,24,17,31,12,26,23,21,9,30

Program 5

Write a program to produce the monthly budget for a family of four. The data items contained in DATA statements are in the following order: montly income, rent expense, food expense, charge account payments, automobile expenses, clothing expenses, and utility expenses. Develop the program to produce a report with the appropriate title, column headings, listing of income, listing of expenses, total of expenses, and amount available for savings and entertainment. This amount will be obtained by subtracting total expenses from income. Be sure to edit all numeric fields to include dollar signs, commas, and decimal points. An example DATA statement is given:

DATA 1000,300,400,150,75,50,20

Program 6

The Internal Revenue Service allows businesspeople to deduct a mileage cost on their federal tax return. Joseph Bolzonski has been on the road each month for a year. He has kept track of his mileage each month but has not calculated the deduction for mileage for each month or for the year. The IRS allows a deduction of 21 cents per mile. You are to program the solution and produce a report showing the title, monthly mileage, deduction amount, yearly mileage, and yearly deduction amount. An example DATA statement is given:

DATA Joseph Bolzonski, 987,1234,1259,678,987,567,876,432,888,666,987, 1356

Chapter 2

Control Structures

Objectives: 1. Identify the function of a control structure.

2. Identify the four types of control structures.

3. Develop a program using each of the control structures.

4. Develop a program using nested control structures.

5. Explain how different BASIC statements may be used to implement control structures.

6. Explain how repetitive processing may be terminated.

7. List two ways of incrementing a counter while looping.

8. Explain how control may be passed to other programs.

Topic 2.1— CONCEPTS OF PROGRAM CONTROL

An important concept of a BASIC program is the concept of control structure. The control structure of the program is the sequence of steps for executing the instructions. You must develop a structure of program statements when writing a program. If the statements are structured properly, the program will be easy to follow, modify, and debug. A poorly written program will be difficult to read, debug, and modify.

CONTROL STRUCTURES

There are four basic control structures that may be used. They are: sequence, selection, case, and iteration. In a sequence structure, the program statements are executed one after another until all statements have been executed. This structure creates an unconditional branch where statements are executed in order. A review of the example program in Chapter 1 will indicate that it uses a simple sequence control structure. Figure 2.1 shows that in the sequence structure one statement is processed after another.

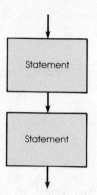

Figure 2.1   Sequence Structure

The second type of structure is called selection. Selection is achieved through the comparison of data to determine which of two program actions will be taken. Each action is based upon a conditional branch, meaning a branch that may or may not be taken. The selection structure in Figure 2.2 illustrates that one or another group of statements is processed based upon the decision statement. A decision statement is one that compares the relationship between two items of data. Usually, the condition represents a true or false situation. Sometimes only one set of statements exists and it is processed when a true situation exists. If a false situation exists, the program continues to process sequentially.

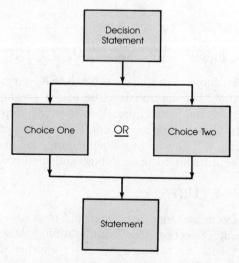

Figure 2.2   Selection Structure

In the selection structure, the program had a choice of one of two possible logic paths. In the case structure, the third type, the program has a choice of several paths. The case structure is sometimes referred to as alternate action and is illustrated in Figure 2.3. It is frequently used in taking one of several choices from a menu.

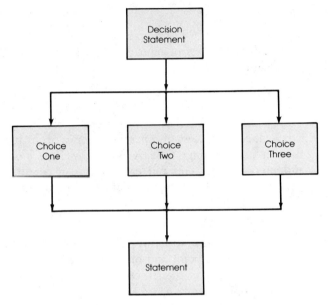

Figure 2.3   Case Structure

The final control structure is the iteration, which is sometimes called the loop or repetition structure. In Figure 2.4 the iteration structure is illustrated. The process of repeating the statements within a loop may continue until some condition becomes true or may continue as long as a condition remains true. Generally, most of the programs written to handle any volume of data will contain at least one iteration structure. Some programs may contain several of each of these structures.

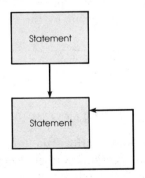

Figure 2.4   Iteration Structure

LOOPS

The power of the computer is best used when you develop a program that uses the same logic over and over by looping. Loops are generally called DO ... UNTIL or DO ... WHILE.

DO ... UNTIL

The DO ... UNTIL loop is based upon the fact that a given condition is false and the process of repeating a series of instructions will continue until the condition is true.

DO ... WHILE

The DO ... WHILE loop is based upon the fact that a given condition is true and the process of repeating a series of instructions will continue until the condition becomes false. A DO ... WHILE loop is generally used to read and process data. You can easily create a condition that is true and will remain true until terminating data or the end of the file is read.

Entering and Exiting a Loop

All four control structures have one common characteristic. They have only one entering point and one exit point. It is not possible to branch into the middle of any of the structures or to branch out at any point other than the exit point.

It is possible to set up structures within a structure. This is known as nesting. Remember that every structure will have only one entering point and one exit point. This concept is also followed when setting up the hierarchy chart for the program.

REVIEW QUESTIONS

1. What is a control structure? (Obj. 1)
2. Identify the four types of control structures. (Obj. 2)
3. Explain how each of the control structures functions. (Obj. 2)
4. Explain what is meant by the term nested control structure. (Obj. 2)

Topic 2.2— BASIC CONTROL STRUCTURES

SEQUENTIAL CONTROL STRUCTURE

The sequence control structure is created without the use of any one specific BASIC keyword. Rather, the statements are coded and the computer executes them in the order that they appear. Study the following example; it illustrates the sequential control structure.

```
10 ' ***** THIS IS AN EXAMPLE OF SEQUENCE
20 GOSUB 1000
30 GOSUB 2000
40 END
```

In this example, the computer executes lines 20, 30, and 40 in sequential order. The fact that control is transferred to another module and returns does not necessarily change this module to another type of control structure.

SELECTION CONTROL STRUCTURE

The selection control structure is developed within the program by using the keywords IF...THEN. This statement is used to tell the computer to make a very simple decision.

General Form: *line number* IF *relationship* THEN *line number or keyword*

Example: 90 IF A=B THEN GOSUB 1000

If the relationship A = B is true, the statements at line 1000 are executed. If the relationship is not true, the statements at line 1000 are not executed. The following example illustrates the use of the IF...THEN in a program.

```
20 ' ***** THIS IS AN EXAMPLE OF SELECTION
30 IF AGE=18 THEN PRINT "AGE IS 18"
40 IF AGE<>18 THEN PRINT "AGE IS NOT 18"
70 END
```

When line 30 of this example is executed, the computer checks to see if the variable AGE is equal to 18. Since AGE was not read or initialized, the condition in line 40 will be true and the "age is 18" message will not be printed sequentially. If we add the statement 10 LET AGE=18, the relationship in line 30 would be true.

Relational Operators

The equal sign used in line 30 of the last example, as well as the not equal sign, are known as relational operators. Relational operators allow the computer to compare one item with another. Six types of relational operators can be used in comparisons. Table 2.1 illustrates the symbols, their meaning, and how they are used in the IF statement.

Relational Operator	Meaning	Example
=	Equal to	20 IF A=B THEN 50
>	Greater than	30 IF A>14 THEN 70
<	Less than	60 IF TOWN$<"NEW YORK" THEN 200
>=	Greater than or equal to	80 IF GRADE>=12 THEN 4000
<=	Less than or equal to	90 IF AGE<=16 THEN 5000
<>	Not equal to	100 IF NAME$<>NAMREAD$ THEN 6000

Table 2.1   Relational Operators

Logical Operators

Logical operators connect two or more relational operators. The most commonly used logical operators are AND, OR, NOT, and XOR (exclusive OR). The meaning of the operators is illustrated here:

IF condition AND condition THEN
IF condition OR condition THEN
IF NOT condition THEN
IF condition XOR condition THEN

The next example shows how the logical operators would be used in a program.

Example:

```
10 A=12
20 B=10
30 C=14
40 IF A=B AND C>B THEN PRINT C
50 IF B<A OR A<C THEN PRINT C
60 IF NOT A THEN PRINT A
```

Another form of the IF ... THEN statement is the IF ... THEN ... ELSE statement. Unlike the IF ... THEN statement where the false condition is ignored and the logic is executed in sequential order, the false condition in the IF ... THEN ... ELSE statement will be handled with the ELSE portion of the statement.

General Form: *line number* IF *relationship* THEN *statement* ELSE *statement*

Example: 40 IF A=B THEN GOSUB 4000 ELSE GOSUB 5000

In this general form, the relationship between A and B is tested. If the relationship is true, control is passed to module 4000. If the test is false, control passes to module 5000. In each case, control is returned to the line following 40 after execution in the submodules. This format allows you to set up separate submodules to perform specific logic depending upon a given data item.

Example:

```
10 ' TEST TO SEE IF MALE OR FEMALE, PRINT NAME
20 GOSUB 1000
30 IF SEX$="F" THEN GOSUB 2000 ELSE GOSUB 3000
999 END
1000 ' ***** READ A RECORD ************
1010 READ NAM$,SEX$
1999 RETURN
2000 ' ***** INDICATE THAT THE PERSON IS FEMALE
2010 PRINT NAM$; " IS FEMALE"
2999 RETURN
3000 ' ***** INDICATE THAT THE PERSON IS MALE
3010 PRINT NAM$; " IS MALE"
3999 RETURN
4000 ' ***** DATA ********************
4010 DATA KATHY,F
```

In this example, control is passed to line 1000 to read a record. Upon return to line 30 the test is made. In this program, the test is true and control passes to line 2000. KATHY IS FEMALE is printed. If we change the DATA statement to 4010 DATA BILL,M line 30 would pass control to line 3000. BILL IS MALE would be printed. In each of the situations, there was only one entry point and one exit point. There was also only one entry point and one exit point in the main module.

Terminating Data

The IF statement allows you to test for terminating data in the DATA statements. Terminating data is data that causes the computer to branch to a statement and end processing. Up to this point each of the programs has contained only a single DATA statement. Usually several items of data will be processed each time a program is executed. The real power of the computer is in its ability to repeat the process over and over without error. The following example illustrates the use of terminating data.

Example:

```
3000 DATA ELLY, A
3010 DATA TOM, B, JENNY, C, JOE, D
3020 DATA STOP, Z
```

CASE STRUCTURE

The case structure is usually written using the ON ... GOSUB statement. The general form for ON ... GOSUB follows:

General Form: *line number* ON *numeric variable* GOSUB *line numbers*

Example: `200 ON X GOSUB 1000,2000,3000`

If a program were written to print out the names and grades of various students and their status (example: freshman, sophomore, junior, or senior) in school, you would need a key field identifying the school year in which the student is currently enrolled. Study the following module from an example program.

```
2000 ' ***** PROCESS DATA *************
2010 READ YR.IN.SCHOOL,NAM$,GRADE
2020 IF YR.IN.SCHOOL=0 THEN 2999
       ELSE ON YR.IN.SCHOOL GOSUB 4000,5000,6000,7000
2030 GOTO 2010
2999 RETURN
```

Notice in the example that the IF statement was used to determine if the YR.IN.SCHOOL read was the termination data. If it was greater than zero, the ELSE option is executed. If YR.IN.SCHOOL is 1, control is passed to line 4000. If YR.IN.SCHOOL is equal to 3, control is passed to line 6000. The status of YR.IN.SCHOOL determines which statement will be branched to in the program.

Assuming that the DATA statement looked like the following, the computer would branch to line 6000 and process whatever statement exists.

```
9000 DATA 3,JERRY JOHNSON,89
```

An alternative to the ON ... GOSUB may be the ON ... GOTO. The format for the statement is as follows:

General Form: *line number* ON *numeric value* GOTO *line numbers*

Example: `150 ON X GOTO 1000,2000,3000`

It is recommended that you not use the ON . . . GOTO in a program for the same reasons that were discussed with the GOTO statement. If control is transferred using the ON . . . GOTO, you will have to use a GOTO to return to a specific location in the program. The use of these two statements together will result in violations of the rules of structured programming and the creation of programs that are difficult to read and debug. Generally the ON . . . GOTO will be used only when transferring control to another program.

USING THE ON KEY STATEMENT

As computers have developed, more and more emphasis has been placed upon writing programs that are easier for the user to utilize. The modern keyboard contains several function keys generally marked, F1, F2, and so on. These function keys may be used within the program to allow the user to select the alternate path of logic that the computer should perform when directed to do so. The ON KEY statement of the IBM allows you to identify the use of the function keys. The format of the ON KEY statement is as follows:

General Form: *line number* ON KEY *BASIC statement*

Example: 100 ON KEY(5) GOSUB 8000

In the example, the ON KEY statement would require the user of the program to press function key 5 in order for the computer to branch to line 8000. The user would have to be prompted to enter the function key 5. Prompting will be discussed in more detail in Chapter 3.

ITERATION CONTROL STRUCTURE

Iteration control may be done by using any of several BASIC statements.

Using FOR . . . NEXT

The FOR . . . NEXT statements may be used to implement the DO . . . UNTIL loop control structure. The beginning of the control structure starts with the statement containing the FOR condition and ends with the statement containing the keyword NEXT. All statements contained between the two statements (FOR . . . NEXT) are executed each time the loop is repeated. The basic format of the FOR statement is illustrated at the top of page 50.

General Form: *line number* FOR *variable = beginning of*
                range TO *end of range*

Example: 3010 FOR X=1 TO 10

The variable following the FOR statement is preferably an integer variable. It represents a counter and is incremented each time the loop is repeated. A counter is a variable that is incremented by a number each time an activity occurs. In the example, the variable X begins counting with 1 and ends counting with 10. This range tells the computer how many times the loop should be repeated.

The NEXT statement uses the same variable as the FOR statement. It causes the variable to be incremented as well as marking the end of the loop.

General Form: *line number* NEXT *variable name*

Example: 3400 NEXT X

Study the following example. Notice that the range identified within the FOR statement is 1 to 10. Therefore, the program counts from 1 to 10.

```
10 'EXC2E1
20 'CLARK AND LABARRE--CHAPTER 2, EXAMPLE 1
30 'FOR...NEXT LOOP EXAMPLE
40 FOR X=1 TO 10
50    PRINT X
60 NEXT X
70 END
```

Using the STEP Option

The previous examples allowed the computer to increment the variable identified in the FOR statement by one on each iteration. The programmer may control the incrementing of the variable by adding the STEP option to the FOR statement.

General Form: *line number* FOR *variable name = beginning*
                of range TO *end of range* STEP *value*

Example: 3020 FOR X=1 TO 10 STEP 3

In the following example, X is set to the value of 1 and is incremented by 3 each time the loop is repeated. In the example, the loop is processed three times. Study the following example:

Example:

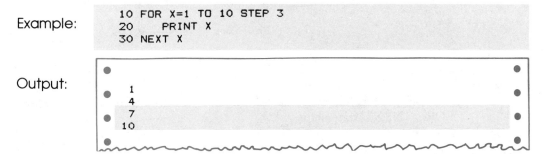

```
10 FOR X=1 TO 10 STEP 3
20     PRINT X
30 NEXT X
```

Output:

```
1
4
7
10
```

Notice how the statement within the FOR . . . NEXT has been indented. The normal convention is to indent all statements which will be executed as a result of the loop. In this case there was only one, the PRINT statement. The STEP option may be incremented by a positive, negative, or a decimal number. If the value is negative, the beginning range must be larger than the ending range.

Using Variables in FOR . . . NEXT Loops

The previous examples have shown the beginning and ending ranges as well as the value of the step as numeric constants. The values may also be expressed as variables.

Writing Nested Loops With FOR . . . NEXT

Some applications require that one process be repeated several times before another process is repeated for the second, third, and so on, times. The first control structure may be referred to as the outer loop and the second control structure may be referred to as the inner loop. The design of the nested loop must be structured so that the outer loop and the inner loop do not overlap. Study the examples shown in Figures 2.5 and 2.6 which illustrate correct and incorrect nested loop design, respectively.

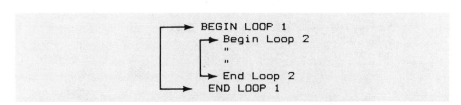

```
BEGIN LOOP 1
  Begin Loop 2
  "
  "
  End Loop 2
END LOOP 1
```

Figure 2.5   Correct Control Structure

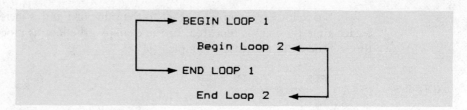

Figure 2.6   Incorrect Control Structure

Look at the following example program illustrating the use of nested FOR . . . NEXT statements.

Example:

```
20   FOR X=1 TO 5
30      TOTAL.GRADE=0
40      READ NAM$
50      PRINT "THE AVERAGE GRADE FOR ";NAM$
60      FOR Y=1 TO 3
70         READ GRADE
80            LET TOTAL.GRADE=TOTAL.GRADE+GRADE
90      NEXT Y
100     LET AVERAGE.GRADE=TOTAL.GRADE/3
110     PRINT TAB(10);AVERAGE.GRADE
120     PRINT
130 NEXT X
140 DATA MARY,89,79,88
150 DATA TOM,98,66,76
160 DATA SONIA,88,85,84
170 DATA JIM,99,68,79
180 DATA SALLY,90,86,79
```

Output:

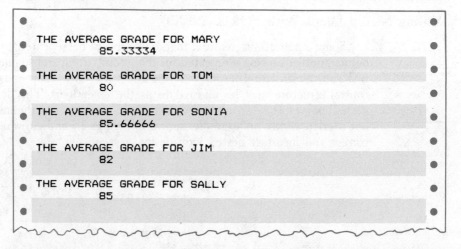

```
THE AVERAGE GRADE FOR MARY
         85.33334

THE AVERAGE GRADE FOR TOM
         80

THE AVERAGE GRADE FOR SONIA
         85.66666

THE AVERAGE GRADE FOR JIM
         82

THE AVERAGE GRADE FOR SALLY
         85
```

Since the variable X has a range of 1 to 5, the outer loop is processed five times. Since the variable Y has a range of 1 to 3, the inner loop is processed three times within the outer loop.

Using the DO . . . WHILE

The WHILE . . . WEND statements allow you to implement a DO . . . WHILE loop. These statements are available on the IBM PC and the TRS-80 Model 4. The WHILE begins the loop and contains a relational statement. As long as the relation is true, the looping through the logic continues. Upon a false condition, control passes to the statement following the WEND. WEND is short for While END.

General Form: *line number* WHILE *relational expression*

Example: `1510 WHILE YR.IN.SCHOOL NOT=0`

General Form: *line number* WEND

Example: `1590 WEND`

When compared to the FOR . . . NEXT statements, there are several differences. The WHILE . . . WEND statements do not incorporate any incrementing features. No variable is increased by any number during the loop. Secondly, the FOR . . . NEXT statements always have a beginning and ending range which control how many times the loop will be repeated. The WHILE . . . WEND statements do not have a built-in range and unless the condition becomes false, the looping will continue. As a result, it is possible to develop a program which may have an infinite loop.

Example:
```
10 WHILE Z<>5
20    PRINT Z
30    LET Z=Z+1
40 WEND
50 END
```

Output:

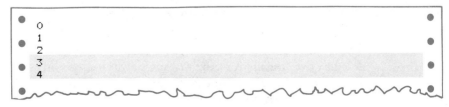

```
0
1
2
3
4
```

CHAINED PROGRAMS

As the applications become more sophisticated and the options more lengthy, the programmer must constantly be thinking of the amount of main memory the program consumes within the computer. If the central processing unit (CPU) has limited memory, you may set up each of the submodules as a separate program. Using the alternate case structure and the BASIC keyword CHAIN, you make the system function as if it were one program. The collection of several programs to carry out the requirements of one application may be referred to as an application system.

The CHAIN statement (available on the IBM and TRS-80 Model 4) is used to transfer control to another program and pass variables to it from the controlling program. The same rules of structured program development are used when developing a system of programs. Each program consisting of a submodule in the system will have one entry point and one exit point.

General Form: *line number* CHAIN *"drive number:program name"*

Example: 100 CHAIN "A:PROGRAM2"

The example instructs the computer to load PROGRAM2 from Drive A (the first drive of the system you are using). The CHAIN command is generally used following a conditional statement such as the IF . . . THEN statement.

The CHAIN statement may direct the computer to transfer control to another program and begin processing at a specific statement. This option is illustrated in the following format.

General Form: *line number* CHAIN *"drive number:program name", line number*

Example: 2000 CHAIN "A:PROGRAM3",8000

In this example, PROGRAM3 is loaded and processing begins with line 8000. The drive number need not be specified. If it is not specified, the default drive (usually A or the first drive) will be accessed to determine if the file is on the diskette. Study the example of the process data module from the example program in this chapter. Notice how the CHAIN statements have replaced the GOSUB statements.

```
3000 ' ***** PROCESS DATA **************
3010 READ YR.IN.SCHOOL,NAM$,GRADE
3020 IF YR.IN.SCHOOL=1 THEN CHAIN "FRESHMAN"
3030 IF YR.IN.SCHOOL=2 THEN CHAIN "SOPHOMORE"
3040 IF YR.IN.SCHOOL=3 THEN CHAIN "JUNIOR"
3050 IF YR.IN.SCHOOL=4 THEN CHAIN "SENIOR"
3060 IF YR.IN.SCHOOL=0 THEN 3999
3070 GOTO 3010
3999 RETURN
```

Each of the submodules is programmed as if it were a program by itself. Each is stored on the storage media and accessed as it is needed by the controlling program.

Using the COMMON Statement

In the program example, three data elements were read and used no matter which year the student was in school. Since the CHAIN statement has replaced the GOSUB and control is passed to a completely new program, it is necessary for you to carry the variables to the new program. The reason for this is because the new program loaded into the memory will erase all variables unless you instruct the computer to carry the variables into it. The process of carrying variables forward to the new program is accomplished by either specifying that all variables are to be carried forward or that common variables are to be carried forward to a new program.

With the ALL option, every variable in the current program is passed to the program loaded as a result of the CHAIN statement. If the ALL option is not included, the current program must contain a COMMON statement. The COMMON statement (available on the IBM and TRS-80 Model 4) must list each of the variables that are passed to the new program. The format for the ALL statement is as follows:

General Form: *line number* CHAIN *"file name"*, *line number*, ALL

Example: `1000 CHAIN "FRESHMAN",4010,ALL`

If the COMMON statement is used, it must appear in both the program passing control and the subprograms.

General Form: *line number* COMMON *variable, variable*

Example: `3010 COMMON YR.IN.SCHOOL,NAM$,GRADE`

The COMMON statement is placed very near the beginning of the program. It must be placed prior to the location of the first statement used to input data into variables.

On the Apple, placing a RUN command on a program line will load and execute another program. All variables are erased when the new program is loaded. For example: 960 RUN PROGRAM2.

On the Commodore, placing a LOAD command on a program line will load and execute another program. No variables are erased when a new program is loaded. For example: 960 LOAD "PROGRAM2",8.

On the TRS-80 Model III, placing a RUN command on a program line will load and execute another program. All variables are erased when the new program is loaded. For example: 960 RUN "PROGRAM2".

EXAMPLE PROGRAM

Assume that you are to write a program to process the grades received on a National General Business Aptitude Test. This test is administered to all students in the freshman, sophomore, junior, and senior classes. The instructor would like you to produce the documentation and program to read several data statements and produce a listing of students, the grade received, and their status in school. In addition, the instructor would like to have a summary of the students from each class that took the exam.

Figure 2.7 is the hierarchy chart for the example program. Notice that the process data module contains submodules. Figure 2.8 contains sample data that might be used in the program. The program documentation sheet is contained in Figure 2.9 and the report spacing chart is shown in Figure 2.10.

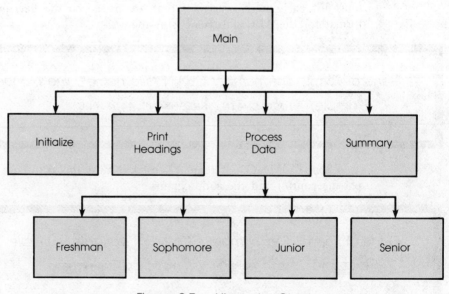

Figure 2.7   Hierarchy Chart

```
2, TOM SALEK, 88
1, MARY BROWN, 98
3, JOHN SMITH, 89
4, ELLEN WALCH, 74
1, ANGELA GRIMALDI, 64
3, CINDY OSOWSKI, 83
0, END, 0
```

Figure 2.8   Sample Data

PROGRAM DOCUMENTATION SHEET		
Program: EXC2E1	Programmer: Clark and LaBarre	Date: 2/20/--
Purpose: This program will process records of students taking the NGBA test. It prints a list of students and a summary of how many in each grade took the test.		
Input: Information data will be from DATA lines	**Output:** List of students on screen	
Data Terminator: 0, EOD, 00		
Variables Used:		

Variables Used:

YR.IN.SCHOOL	=	Year in School
NAM$	=	Name
GRADE	=	Grade Received on Test
NO.OF.FR	=	Number of Freshmen
NO.OF.SO	=	Number of Sophomores
NO.OF.JR	=	Number of Juniors
NO.OF.SR	=	Number of Seniors

Figure 2.9   Program Documentation Sheet

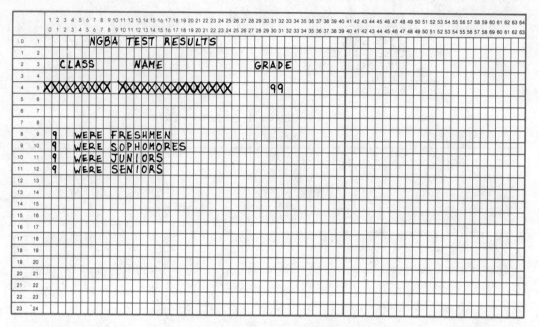

Figure 2.10   Report Spacing Chart

Module documentation sheets are shown in Figures 2.11 through 2.19. Following each of the module documentation sheets is the program code for the module. Figure 2.20 contains the entire program.

MODULE DOCUMENTATION	Program: EXC2E1	Module: MAIN Lines: 10-999

Module Description:

This is the main module.

Module Function (Program Design):

1. Clear memory, if necessary (TRS-80).
2. Initialize variables.
3. Print headings.
4. Process records.
5. Print summary totals.

```
10 ' EXC2E1
20 ' CLARK AND LABARRE--CHAPTER 2, EXAMPLE 1
30 ' SELECTION PROCESS WITH MODULES
40 ' ***** MAIN MODULE ****************
50 GOSUB 1000 'INITIALIZE VARIABLES
60 GOSUB 2000 'PRINT HEADINGS
70 GOSUB 3000 'PROCESS DATA
80 GOSUB 4000 'SUMMARY ROUTINE
999 END
```

Figure 2.11   Main Module Documentation Sheet and Code

MODULE DOCUMENTATION	Program: ___EXC2E1___	Module: __INITIALIZE VARIABLES__ Lines: __1000-1999__

Module Description:

Initialize the variables.

Module Function (Program Design):

1. Set NO.OF.FR = 0.
2. Set NO.OF.SO = 0.
3. Set NO.OF.JR = 0.
4. Set NO.OF.SR = 0.

```
1000 ' ***** INITIALIZE VARIABLES *****
1010 LET NO.OF.FR=0
1020 LET NO.OF.SO=0
1030 LET NO.OF.JR=0
1040 LET NO.OF.SR=0
1999 RETURN
```

Figure 2.12   Initialize Module Documentation Sheet and Code

MODULE DOCUMENTATION	Program: EXC2E1	Module: PRINT HEADINGS Lines: 2000-2999

Module Description:

Print the title and column headings.

Module Function (Program Design):

1. Print the title.
2. Print the column headings.

```
2000 ' ***** PRINT HEADINGS ***********
2010 PRINT
2020 PRINT TAB(6);"NGBA TEST RESULTS"
2030 PRINT
2040 PRINT TAB(3);"CLASS";TAB(13);"NAME";TAB(28);"GRADE"
2050 PRINT
2999 RETURN
```

Figure 2.13   Print Headings Module Documentation Sheet and Code

MODULE DOCUMENTATION	Program: EXC2E1	Module: PROCESS DATA Lines: 3000-3999

Module Description:

Process the data statements.

Module Function (Program Design):

While there is still data:
1. Read a data statement.
2. Check to determine year in school status.
3. Branch to submodule for the year in school.

```
3000 ' ***** PROCESS DATA *************
3010 READ YR.IN.SCHOOL,NAM$,GRADE
3020 IF YR.IN.SCHOOL=1 THEN GOSUB 5000
3030 IF YR.IN.SCHOOL=2 THEN GOSUB 6000
3040 IF YR.IN.SCHOOL=3 THEN GOSUB 7000
3050 IF YR.IN.SCHOOL=4 THEN GOSUB 8000
3060 IF YR.IN.SCHOOL=0 THEN 3999
3070 GOTO 3010
3999 RETURN
```

Figure 2.14   Process Data Module Documentation Sheet and Code

MODULE DOCUMENTATION	Program: __EXC2E1__	Module: __SUMMARY ROUTINE__ Lines: __4000-4999__

Module Description:

Print the summary lines.

Module Function (Program Design):

1. Print the summary line for Freshmen.
2. Print the summary line for Sophomores.
3. Print the summary line for Juniors.
4. Print the summary line for Seniors.

```
4000 ' ***** SUMMARY ROUTINE **********
4010 PRINT
4020 PRINT NO.OF.FR;" WERE FRESHMEN"
4030 PRINT NO.OF.SO;" WERE SOPHOMORES"
4040 PRINT NO.OF.JR;" WERE JUNIORS"
4050 PRINT NO.OF.SR;" WERE SENIORS"
4999 RETURN
```

Figure 2.15   Summary Module Documentation Sheet and Code

MODULE DOCUMENTATION	Program: EXC2E1	Module: <u>FRESHMAN ROUTINE</u> Lines: <u>5000-5999</u>

Module Description:

Print the detail line for Freshmen.

Module Function (Program Design):

1. Print the detail line with the Freshman class designation.

```
5000 ' ***** FRESHMAN ROUTINE *********
5010 PRINT "FRESHMAN";TAB(11);NAM$;TAB(29);GRADE
5020 LET NO.OF.FR=NO.OF.FR+1
5999 RETURN
```

Figure 2.16   Freshman Module Documentation Sheet and Code

MODULE DOCUMENTATION	Program: EXC2E1	Module: <u>SOPHOMORE ROUTINE</u> Lines: <u>6000-6999</u>

Module Description:

Print the detail line for Sophomores.

Module Function (Program Design):

1. Print the detail line with the Sophomore class designation.

```
6000 ' ***** SOPHOMORE ROUTINE ********
6010 PRINT "SOPHOMORE";TAB(11);NAM$;TAB(29);GRADE
6020 LET NO.OF.SO=NO.OF.SO+1
6999 RETURN
```

Figure 2.17   Sophomore Module Documentation Sheet and Code

MODULE DOCUMENTATION	Program: EXC2E1	Module: JUNIOR ROUTINE Lines: 7000-7999

Module Description:

Print the detail line for Juniors.

Module Function (Program Design):

1. Print the detail line with the Junior class designation.

```
7000 ' ***** JUNIOR ROUTINE ***********
7010 PRINT "JUNIOR";TAB(11);NAM$;TAB(29);GRADE
7020 LET NO.OF.JR=NO.OF.JR+1
7999 RETURN
```

Figure 2.18   Junior Module Documentation Sheet and Code

MODULE DOCUMENTATION	Program: EXC2E1	Module: SENIOR ROUTINE Lines: 8000-8999

Module Description:

Print the detail line for Seniors.

Module Function (Program Design):

1. Print the detail line with Senior class designation.

```
8000 ' ***** SENIOR ROUTINE ***********
8010 PRINT "SENIOR";TAB(11);NAM$;TAB(29);GRADE
8020 LET NO.OF.SR=NO.OF.SR+1
8999 RETURN
```

Figure 2.19   Senior Module Documentation Sheet and Code

```
10 ' EXC2E1
20 ' CLARK AND LABARRE--CHAPTER 2, EXAMPLE 1
30 ' SELECTION PROCESS WITH MODULES
40 ' ***** MAIN MODULE ***************
50 GOSUB 1000 'INITIALIZE VARIABLES
60 GOSUB 2000 'PRINT HEADINGS
70 GOSUB 3000 'PROCESS DATA
80 GOSUB 4000 'SUMMARY ROUTINE
999 END
1000 ' ***** INITIALIZE VARIABLES *****
1010 LET NO.OF.FR=0
1020 LET NO.OF.SO=0
1030 LET NO.OF.JR=0
1040 LET NO.OF.SR=0
1999 RETURN
2000 ' ***** PRINT HEADINGS ***********
2010 PRINT
2020 PRINT TAB(6);"NGBA TEST RESULTS"
2030 PRINT
2040 PRINT TAB(3);"CLASS";TAB(13);"NAME";TAB(28);"GRADE"
2050 PRINT
2999 RETURN
3000 ' ***** PROCESS DATA *************
3010 READ YR.IN.SCHOOL,NAM$,GRADE
3020 IF YR.IN.SCHOOL=1 THEN GOSUB 5000
3030 IF YR.IN.SCHOOL=2 THEN GOSUB 6000
3040 IF YR.IN.SCHOOL=3 THEN GOSUB 7000
3050 IF YR.IN.SCHOOL=4 THEN GOSUB 8000
3060 IF YR.IN.SCHOOL=0 THEN 3999
3070 GOTO 3010
3999 RETURN
4000 ' ***** SUMMARY ROUTINE **********
4010 PRINT
4020 PRINT NO.OF.FR;" WERE FRESHMEN"
4030 PRINT NO.OF.SO;" WERE SOPHOMORES"
4040 PRINT NO.OF.JR;" WERE JUNIORS"
4050 PRINT NO.OF.SR;" WERE SENIORS"
4999 RETURN
5000 ' ***** FRESHMAN ROUTINE *********
5010 PRINT "FRESHMAN";TAB(11);NAM$;TAB(29);GRADE
5020 LET NO.OF.FR=NO.OF.FR+1
5999 RETURN
6000 ' ***** SOPHOMORE ROUTINE ********
6010 PRINT "SOPHOMORE";TAB(11);NAM$;TAB(29);GRADE
6020 LET NO.OF.SO=NO.OF.SO+1
6999 RETURN
7000 ' ***** JUNIOR ROUTINE ***********
7010 PRINT "JUNIOR";TAB(11);NAM$;TAB(29);GRADE
7020 LET NO.OF.JR=NO.OF.JR+1
7999 RETURN
8000 ' ***** SENIOR ROUTINE ***********
8010 PRINT "SENIOR";TAB(11);NAM$;TAB(29);GRADE
8020 LET NO.OF.SR=NO.OF.SR+1
8999 RETURN
9000 ' ***** DATA ********************
9010 DATA 2,TOM SALEK,88
9020 DATA 1,MARY BROWN,98
9030 DATA 3,JOHN SMITH,89
9040 DATA 4,ELLEN WALCH,74
9050 DATA 1,ANGELA GRIMALDI,64
9060 DATA 3,CINDY OSOWSKI,83
9070 DATA 0,END,0
```

```
        NGBA TEST RESULTS

   CLASS        NAME              GRADE

 SOPHOMORE   TOM SALEK            88
 FRESHMAN    MARY BROWN           98
 JUNIOR      JOHN SMITH           89
 SENIOR      ELLEN WALCH          74
 FRESHMAN    ANGELA GRIMALDI      64
 JUNIOR      CINDY OSOWSKI        83

   2  WERE FRESHMEN
   1  WERE SOPHOMORES
   2  WERE JUNIORS
   1  WERE SENIORS
```

Figure 2.20   Code for Entire Program with Output

The previous example program has been rewritten to include the CHAIN statement and the COMMON statement. The COMMON statement is included in line 40. Notice that instead of one program, there are now five different programs. Basically the system still functions in the same manner as the first program.

```
10 ' EXC2E1
20 ' CLARK AND LABARRE--CHAPTER 2, EXAMPLE 1
30 ' SELECTION PROCESS WITH CHAINING TO MODULES
40 COMMON NO.OF.FR,NO.OF.SO,NO.OF.JR,NO.OF.SR
50 ' THE COMMON ALLOWS THE VALUES OF
60 ' THE VARIABLES TO BE PASSED
70 ' BETWEEN THE PROGRAMS WITHOUT
80 ' LOSING THEIR VALUES.
90 ' ***** MAIN MODULE ***************
100 CHAIN "INITIAL.SUB"    'INITIALIZE VARIABLES
110 CHAIN "HEADING.SUB"    'PRINT HEADINGS
120 CHAIN "PROCESS.SUB"    'PROCESS DATA
130 CHAIN "SUMMARY.SUB"    'SUMMARY ROUTINE
999 END
```

Figure 2.21   Main Module Program Code

```
10 COMMON NO.OF.FR,NO.OF.SO,NO.OF.JR,NO.OF.SR
20 ' SUBPROGRAM TO INITIALIZE VARIABLES
1000 ' ***** INITIALIZE VARIABLES *****
1010 LET NO.OF.FR=0
1020 LET NO.OF.SO=0
1030 LET NO.OF.JR=0
1040 LET NO.OF.SR=0
1999 CHAIN "MAIN.MOD",110
```

Figure 2.22   Initialize Variables Module Program Code

```
10 COMMON NO.OF.FR,NO.OF.SO,NO.OF.JR,NO.OF.SR
20 'SUBPROGRAM TO PRINT HEADINGS
2000 ' ***** PRINT HEADINGS **********
2010 PRINT
2020 PRINT TAB(6);"NGBA TEST RESULTS"
2030 PRINT
2040 PRINT TAB(3);"CLASS";TAB(13);"NAME";TAB(28);"GRADE"
2050 PRINT
2999 CHAIN "MAIN.MOD",120
```

Figure 2.23   Print Headings Module Program Code

```
10 COMMON NO.OF.FR,NO.OF.SO,NO.OF.JR,NO.OF.SR
3000 ' ***** PROCESS DATA *************
3010 READ YR.IN.SCHOOL,NAM$,GRADE
3020 IF YR.IN.SCHOOL=1 THEN GOSUB 5000
3030 IF YR.IN.SCHOOL=2 THEN GOSUB 6000
3040 IF YR.IN.SCHOOL=3 THEN GOSUB 7000
3050 IF YR.IN.SCHOOL=4 THEN GOSUB 8000
3060 IF YR.IN.SCHOOL=0 THEN 3999
3070 GOTO 3010
3999 CHAIN "MAIN.MOD",130
```

Figure 2.24   Process Data Module Program Code

```
10 COMMON NO.OF.FR,NO.OF.SO,NO.OF.JR,NO.OF.SR
20 ' THIS SUBPROGRAM PRINTS THE
30 ' SUMMARY OF THE STUDENT
40 ' CLASSIFICATION AND THEN
50 ' PASSES CONTROL BACK TO THE
60 ' MAIN PROGRAM.
4000 ' ***** SUMMARY ROUTINE **********
4010 PRINT
4020 PRINT NO.OF.FR;" WERE FRESHMEN"
4030 PRINT NO.OF.SO;" WERE SOPHOMORES"
4040 PRINT NO.OF.JR;" WERE JUNIORS"
4050 PRINT NO.OF.SR;" WERE SENIORS"
4999 CHAIN "MAIN.MOD",999
```

Figure 2.25   Summary Routine Module Program Code

REVIEW QUESTIONS

1. Explain which BASIC statements are used to implement the selection control structure. (Obj. 1)
2. Define each of the control structures. (Obj. 2)
3. Define the term unconditional branch. (Obj. 2)
4. Define the term conditional branch. (Obj. 2)
5. Explain what is meant by relational operators. (Obj. 3)
6. Why might a person want to use an IF...THEN rather than a GOTO to branch to another part of the program? (Obj. 7)
7. Explain the difference between a FOR...NEXT loop and a WHILE ...WEND loop. (Obj. 5)
8. How can the counter in a FOR...NEXT be incremented by a number other than 1? (Obj. 4)
9. Identify the difference between GOSUB and RETURN and the CHAIN statement. (Obj. 8)
10. Explain why terminating data may be needed. (Obj. 6)

VOCABULARY WORDS

The following terms were introduced in this chapter:

sequence	alternate action	nesting
unconditional branch	iteration	relational operator
selection	loop	counter
conditional branch	repetition	application system
case		

KEYWORDS AND COMMANDS

The following keywords and commands were introduced in this chapter:

DO ... UNTIL	ON GOTO	WHILE ... WEND
DO ... WHILE	ON KEY	CHAIN
IF ... THEN	FOR ... NEXT	ALL
IF ... THEN ... ELSE	STEP	COMMON
ON ... GOSUB		

PROGRAMS TO WRITE

For each of the programs, prepare the necessary documentation prior to writing the BASIC code.

Program 1

Write a program to calculate the area and perimeter of various sizes of rectangles. Read the data from DATA statements. Calculate the perimeter and print the results, then calculate the area and print the results. Each output should be presented in a simple report.

Equations: Area = Length * Width
Perimeter = 2 * (Length + Width)

Program 2

Write a program to show how much money will accumulate if you deposit an amount in a bank account for three years. Show the results if the interest is compounded and paid daily, weekly, monthly, quarterly, and yearly.

Print a report showing the amount deposited and the amounts at the end of the three-year period for each of the calculations.

Equation: New Principal = Old Principal + Old Principal * (Interest/ Periods Per Year)

Daily = 360
Weekly = 52
Monthly = 12
Quarterly = 4
Yearly = 1

Program 3

Write a program to read DATA statements containing name, age, and completion time for a race (example: 1:28). The report should print out the results based upon the age group. The groups will consist of those 10-19 years of age, 20-29 years of age, 30-39 years of age, 40-49 years of age, and 50 and over. Each age group will have three participants. Each person will win first, second, or third within their respective group. Be sure to include a title and column headings in the report. Remember to include terminating data.

Program 4

Write a program to calculate the grade point average for a group of students for the semester. Each student will have five classes and a grade based on the following scale: A = 4, B = 3, C = 2, D = 1, F = 0. Calculate the total points and divide by the number of classes. Present the output in a neatly designed report.

Program 5

Write a program to compute the scores for three teams participating in a cross-country race. Each team may have up to seven runners. The team with the lowest accumulated score will win first place, second lowest score will win second place, and so on. Print a report listing which team took first, second, and so on. The report should include title, column headings, team name, total score, and respective position.

Program 6

Write a program to accumulate the sales income from four products sold in five territories. You are interested in the sales income by territory as well as sales income for each of the products. Produce a report with the appropriate title, column headings, and listing of data and totals. Your report should contain dollar signs, commas, and decimal points for each of the dollar amounts.

## Chapter 3

Data Storage and Modification

Objectives:
1. Describe procedures for inputting and storing data.
2. Identify the differences in the storing of numeric and alphabetic character data.
3. Use arithmetic operators in expressions.
4. Use relational operators in conditional statements.
5. Explain techniques of data modification.
6. Use data modification techniques in programs.

Topic 3.1— CONCEPTS OF STORING AND MODIFYING DATA

The computer's ability to process data rapidly has enabled people to apply the computer to many tasks. Because some of the applications require the input of numeric data and other applications require the input of alphabetic data, the computer had to be designed to work with all types of information. In some cases the computer is called upon to handle large volumes of numeric data consisting of extremely long numbers. In other cases, such as the business office, the computer is called upon to handle large volumes of words. Some applications such as those performed in engineering require the use of special characters. The BASIC character set consists of alphabetic characters, numeric characters, and special characters. The ASCII (American Standard Code for Information Interchange) character set contains 256 different characters. (See Appendix A for the ASCII character set.)

The alphabetic characters contain both uppercase and lowercase letters. The numeric characters contain the digits 0 through 9. Several special characters have a specific meaning and will be discussed later in this chapter.

INPUTTING NUMERIC AND CHARACTER DATA

In an earlier chapter, variables were identified as either string variables or numeric variables. Inputting data into these variables may be accomplished in basically three ways: (a) the variables may be set up as a constant; (b) data may be read into the variable; and (c) data entry may be interactive (placed into the variable by entering data from the keyboard while the program is running). There are two types of data: string (or character) and numeric. A string is a number of characters up to 255, enclosed in double quotation marks if set. up as a constant. Some examples of string constants are shown below:

> "THIS IS A CONSTANT"
> "$1000.00"
> "12345.55"
> "NAME OF STUDENT"

Numeric data consists of positive and negative numbers. Numbers are not enclosed in quotation marks and cannot contain commas. There are several ways to store numbers.

> *Integer:* A whole number between -32768 and +32767. Integers may not have decimal points. For example, 126 and 1487 are integers.
> *Real Number:* A real number is one that may contain a decimal point. For example, 14.87 and 1.86 are real numbers.

Real numbers may be stored internally as either single precision or double precision numbers. Numbers stored as single precision may contain up to seven digits, although only six digits will be accurate (nine digits on Apple and Commodore). When numbers are stored as double precision, up to 17 digits will be stored and up to 16 digits are printed with accuracy on the IBM and TRS-80 only.

HIERARCHY OF OPERATORS AND FUNCTIONS

An expression may be as simple as a numeric constant or variable, or it may be combined with operators to produce a value that will be stored in a variable.

Arithmetic Operators

The arithmetic operators perform the typical mathematical options usually incorporated into an equation (formula). They are listed in order of hierarchy in the following table.

Operator	Operation	Example
$\wedge$ or $\uparrow$ or **	Exponentiation	$A \wedge B$
-	Negation	-A
*, /	Multiplication, Floating Point Division	A*B, A/B
\	Integer Division	A\B
MOD	Modulo Arithmetic	A MOD Y
+, -	Addition, Subtraction	A+B, A-B

Table 3.1   Arithmetic Operators

This is the standard order followed in all mathematical calculations. With the exception of integer division and modulo arithmetic, the operators should be familiar to you. In integer division, the quotient is truncated (decimal portion is dropped) before being printed or stored. In modulo arithmetic, the result is the remainder of a division.

Numeric Functions

Numeric functions are performed on numeric values. A function is a keyword used in an expression to perform a predetermined operation on one or more sets of data. BASIC contains several functions that are contained within the interpreter. You may also define functions. Functions are always evaluated first within an expression. To change that order of evaluation within the expression, you may use parentheses to enclose those operations to be performed first, second, and so on.

TABLES

Up to this point we have used a separate constant or variable to store each value. Frequently, it is beneficial to set up tables to handle the data. A table is a list of data elements. The organization of a table is shown in Figure 3.1. The purpose of tables is to make the programming task easier. Without tables, you either handle the data immediately after input into the program or you must define enough variable names to store each of the data items as it is entered into the process. For example, if you need to utilize seven scores in different calculations, you would have to set up seven variable names to store the scores. With the use of a table, you could set up a table to handle seven data elements. This table would be referred to as a one-dimensional table. One-dimensional means that there will be only rows or columns, but not both.

SCORES

Row 0	1111
Row 1	2222
Row 2	3333
Row 3	4444
Row 4	5555
Row 5	6666
Row 6	7777

Figure 3.1   Organization of a Table

Referencing Data in a Table

Each data element in a one-dimensional table is stored in a row. In Figure 3.1, the first data element is stored in row 0. The data element stored in row 3 would be accessed by SCORE(3). Many people refer to a table as an array and some refer to a table as a matrix. Even though these two words mean something different in mathematics, they are used interchangeably in data processing.

Subscripts

The number of the row is referred to as the subscript. The subscript is enclosed in parentheses and must always be a whole number. The value of SCORE(5) is 6666. A subscript used to reference a data element within a table may be a constant, a variable, or an arithmetic expression. Subscripts may not have negative values.

Two-Dimensional Tables

The one-dimensional table will save you valuable time. However, much of the information processed in everyday life is made up of data elements related to each other. For example, if you wanted to determine the average heating bill per month for each house located on a given block, you would have to store the heating bill for each of the twelve months for each of the houses. Each house and monthly bill could be stored in separate tables as illustrated in Figure 3.2, one for each of the months. By using a two-dimensional table (table with rows and columns) you could combine all the data into one table as shown in Figure 3.3.

TABLE NAMES:	House No.	Jan.	Feb.	Mar.	•••	Dec.
Row 0	223	123.50	50.23	23.45	•••	119.45
Row 1	225	111.33	78.56	34.56	•••	112.33

Figure 3.2   One-Dimensional Tables

	M(0)	M(1)	M(2)	M(3)	• • •	M(12)
Row 0	223	123.45	50.23	23.45	• • •	119.45
Row 1	225	111.33	78.56	34.56	• • •	112.33

Figure 3.3   Two-Dimensional Table

The two-dimensional table saves valuable time when information may be arranged into rows and columns. Each of the monthly bills identified by M(1), M(2), M(3) ... M(12) is stored in a column. To access the data in the first row, you would address the first monthly bill as M(0,1). The zero represents the first row (labeled as 0) in the table and the one represents the second column (labeled as 1).

GETTING DATA FROM THE KEYBOARD

In the programs you have been asked to write up to this point, you have either used constants to provide the value for the data element or read DATA statements to obtain the value of the variable. By processing data in this manner, the programs have had little flexibility to handle changing data. The reading of DATA statements can be known as batch processing. Batches of the data are gathered together and processed at one time in batch processing. Today most information systems allow you to interact with the program. As you run an interactive program, you will be asked to respond to questions. These questions are known as prompts. The more specific the prompts, the easier it is to use the program. For example, you write a program to allow for interactive input of test scores. You program the computer to ask for such items as student number and test score. This information is stored in a table. After you have entered all the data, the rows of information in the table may be processed just like DATA statements. If the table has been set up to handle more than one test score, you may be asked to input the test number. In other words, test 1 would be stored in column 1 of the test data elements and test 2 would be stored in column 2. Figure 3.4 illustrates the input and storage of a student's number and test scores.

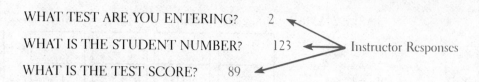

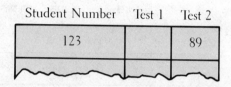

Figure 3.4   Input and Storage of a Student's Number and Test Scores

If another student is entered into the table illustrated in Figure 3.4, the row subscript must be incremented and the questions repeated. This process would continue until the table is full or all responses have been entered. Interactive input allows you to make decisions, change data, add data to the program, and control the sequence of events such as telling the computer when to stop execution.

DATA MODIFICATION

Because many programs written today will be interactive, you may be called on to modify data. **Data modification** is the process of selecting a portion of a variable for comparison purposes or changing the contents of a variable. It may be the process of checking the left or right characters to determine if they meet certain specifications. It may be to check for the middle characters or to determine the length of a data element. In each of the cases identified, the computer would be expected to select, compare, or modify the value of the variable in order to complete the process.

Left-Hand Characters

In an interactive program, you are often asked whether you want to continue the process. You are expected to answer with either a yes or no response. Depending on the response, the computer will perform one conditional branch or another. In responding to the question, the user may key YES, Yes, or Y to indicate continued processing. Because this is a logical comparison, the IF . . . THEN statement is used. By checking for only the left-most character, all three responses can be treated alike. Figure 3.5 shows this relationship.

Right-Hand Characters

The comparison of right-hand characters may be accomplished in the same manner as the left-hand characters. Frequently, inventory numbers will have either letters or numbers on the right that identify a given category of

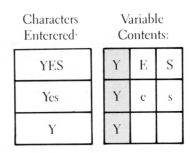

Figure 3.5   Comparing the Left-Most Character

products. Assume that all diskettes in stock are identified with the letters DT. A check of the right two characters of a variable stored in a table would allow you to access those items classified as a diskette. Table 3.2 illustrates an inventory table containing products identified by the two right-most characters.

Variables	Products
123DT	5.25 Diskettes
234DT	8.00 Diskettes
001DT	3.25 Diskettes
909DT	3.50 Diskettes

Table 3.2   Inventory Table Identified by Right-Most Characters

Middle Characters

The examination of the middle characters of a variable commonly occurs in checking for the day within a given date. Data is often entered into a variable as MM/DD/YY (04/07/85 would represent a date). Figure 3.6 illustrates how the day can be determined if we start examining at the fourth character and continue for two characters.

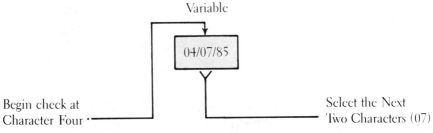

Figure 3.6   Checking for Middle Characters

Length of Data

When data is entered into a program, you may be expected to enter a certain number of characters. For example, suppose that the program expects a five-digit invoice number. If less than the required number of characters is entered, you should be directed to reenter the data. Figure 3.7 illustrates the length of a variable.

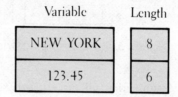

Figure 3.7   Checking the Length of a Variable

Presence of Characters

The presence of characters within a data element may be very important to the processing of data. In an inventory processing program, the inventory number may be made up of numeric and alphabetic characters. The alphabetic characters may be placed at the end of the variable to define the product line. For example, the inventory number may be 12345SKI. The alphabetic characters illustrate that this product is of the SKI line. The 12345 may be the product number. If you were checking the product line to determine the status of skis in inventory, a check could be made to determine if the product was SKI. Sometimes the position of the character is searched for by the computer to allow for a modification. In the use of a text editor or word processing program, the position of a character is located and the character is often deleted, changed, or another is added. In each case the data is modified. Figure 3.8 illustrates the change of a character in a string.

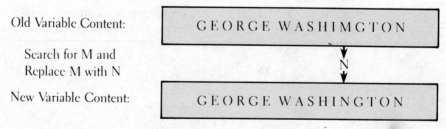

Figure 3.8   Modification of Characters

The form of data may be changed in several ways. Sometimes data will be entered into a string variable and you will want to use the data in a calculation routine. The program is able to determine the value of a string variable. Study the example given in Table 3.3. Notice that the numbers entered were correct. However, they were stored in a string variable. If the string were used in a calculation routine, the computer would return a syntax error. When the variable is modified, the data is correct for usage in an equation. The reverse of this may also be done. Data may be entered as numeric and converted to a string value.

Descriptions	Resulting Data
Data entered into variable N$	12345.56 (string)
Program statement takes the value of N$ and changes it to N	12345.56 (numeric)

Table 3.3   Value of a String

Connecting Data Items

The connection of two or more items is one of the more common data modification techniques. This process is generally referred to as concatenation or catenation. Table 3.4 shows how this is accomplished.

Description	Variables
One variable contains the name of the city	HOUSTON
The next variable contains the state	TX
The last variable contains the ZIP Code	770010001
The three variables as concatenated with the literals, comma, and spaces added to produce:	HOUSTON, TX 77001-0001

Table 3.4   Connection of Data Items

Modifying the Contents of Data

Quite often you may want to modify the contents of data while the program is executing. Perhaps data was entered in lowercase letters and only capital letters are to be printed. Or maybe all characters are in capital letters and you would like to print out the results with only the first letter capitalized and all others in lowercase. It is possible to change the letters. The

ASCII character set assigns a value to each character. The value of the lowercase letter is 32 more than the value of the uppercase letter. By adding 32 to the value of the capital letter, you could replace it with the lowercase letter. Table 3.5 illustrates the changing of the value to represent another letter.

Descriptions	Values
ASCII value of capital letter:	A = 65
ASCII value of lowercase letter:	a = 97
ASCII value of capital letter:	R = 82
ASCII value of lowercase letter:	r = 114

Table 3.5   Changing Values to Another Letter

REVIEW QUESTIONS

1. List the ways in which data may be stored. (Obj. 1)
2. Explain the term interactive program. (Obj. 1)
3. Explain the difference between integers and real numbers. (Obj. 2)

Topic 3.2— STORING AND MODIFYING DATA WITH BASIC

Numeric information is stored internally as either integer or real data. On the IBM and TRS-80, real data is either single precision or double precision. Real numbers (single precision) are used unless a special character is placed at the end of the variable name to identify the variable as one of the other storage formats. Declaring the numeric variable as integer or single precision may result in less accurate computations; however, they do require less storage room within the computer. Also, variables designated as double precision require more time when completing arithmetic computations. If repeat calculations are being performed, a program with integer variables will generally run faster.

Table 3.6 shows the special character to be added to a numeric variable name with the IBM or TRS-80 to designate it as either integer, single precision, or double precision. It also shows the number of memory locations used to store each of the values.

Type	Character	Bytes Used
Integer	%	2
Single Precision	!	4
Double Precision	#	8

Table 3.6   Numeric Variable Designators

If the variable type is not designated, the default will be to single precision. Examples of variable names are shown in Table 3.7.

Variable Name	Meaning
INVENTORY.NUMBER%	Declares an integer value
RECORD.NUMBER!	Declares a single precision value
PLAYER.NUMBER#	Declares a double precision value
AREA#	Declares a double precision value
NO.OF.MILES%	Declares an integer value
SQURE.ROOT#	Declares a double precision value

Table 3.7   Declaration of Numeric Variables

The special character declared the numeric variable as integer, single precision, or double precision.

On the IBM and TRS-80 you may also use the DEF (defined) statement to specify whether the numeric variable is integer, single, or double precision. The keywords DEFINT, DEFSNG, and DEFDBL are used to declare the type of numeric variable that is used in a program.

The DEFINT (define integer) keyword is used to designate that variables beginning with certain letters are integers.

General Form: *line number* DEFINT *letter range*

Example: `10 DEFINT A-Z`

Refer to the following example for the use of DEFINT in a program. The value stored in A will be stored as an integer regardless of the status of the other two variables added together. As a result, the answer will be a whole number. DEFSNG and DEFDBL are used in the same manner.

```
10 DEFINT A
20 B=1.23333
30 C=3.11111
40 LET A=B+C
50 PRINT A
```

DEFINED FUNCTIONS

A function is used like a keyword in an expression to call an operation that is to be completed on one or more variables. BASIC has some functions that reside within the system. Such functions require the use of the keyword to cause the function to be performed. You may also define your functions using the DEF FN statement. The purpose of the DEF FN (define function) statement is to allow you to define a function that will be used within the program. Rather than set up the equation each time it is to be used, you may decide to set it up as a function. The general form of the DEF FN statement is as follows:

General Form: *line number* DEF FN*name (argument list) = expression*

Example: `20 DEF FNAREA(R)=PI*R^2`

In this example, the name is a valid variable name preceded by the letters FN. The function name will be replaced with a value when the function is called. The expression is an operation that will perform the function. The definition of the function is limited to one line. The function type (whether there is a dollar sign at the end of the name) determines whether the function returns a numeric or string value. A DEF FN statement must be executed to define a function before the function is called. The BASIC program shown in the next example shows the use of the defined function in determining the area of a circle.

Example:

```
20 PI=3.141593
30 DEF FNAREA.OF.CIRCLE(R)=PI*R^2
40 INPUT "ENTER THE RADIUS?",RADIUS
50 PRINT "THE RADIUS IS";RADIUS
60 PRINT "THE AREA OF A CIRCLE IS";FNAREA.OF.CIRCLE(RADIUS)
```

The input and output of this program are shown in the following example. Line 30 defines the function. The function was called in line 60. The DEF FN statement may be used to define almost any function that you can imagine.

Input:

```
Enter the Radius?  4 ◀──────── Assume that the user entered 4.
```

Output:

```
●                                                                    ●
 ● THE RADIUS IS 4
   THE AREA OF A CIRCLE IS 50.26549                                 ●
```

ARITHMETIC FUNCTIONS

Several arithmetic functions are supplied with BASIC interpreters. These functions return a numeric value. Table 3.8 lists the numeric functions which are usually available.

Function	Result
ABS(x)	Absolute value of x
COS(x)	Cosine of angle x, where x is in radians
EXP(x)	Raise e to the power of x $(e = 2.718)$
INT(x)	Largest integer less than or equal to x
LOG(x)	Natural logarithm of x
RND(x)	Random number
SIN(x)	Sine of angle x, where x is in radians
SQR(x)	Square root of x
TAN(x)	Tangent of angle x, where x is in radians

Table 3.8   Numeric Functions

Arithmetic functions must be used with some other statement. Generally, they are used with the LET statement or the PRINT statement. The technique of using the functions is shown in the following general form.

General Form: *line number keyword function name (argument expression)*

Example: `10 LET Z=INT(100.12)`

USING A TABLE TO STORE DATA

On most computers, a table of ten elements is automatically created at the time of its first use. If more than ten elements are to be stored under one variable name, you must define the size of the table. When you define the size of the table to store the data elements, you are dimensioning the table. The dimensioning of the table is accomplished by using the DIM statement.

General Form: *line number* DIM *table name(size)*

Example: 10 DIM A(25)

DIM tells the computer that a table is being set up. The number following in parentheses tells the computer the largest number of elements that may be stored in the table. It may be expressed with a constant, numeric variable, or arithmetic expression. For numeric tables, the DIM statement sets all the elements to an initial value of zero. String table elements are set up as variable length with an initial value of null (nothing).

Generally, the DIM statement should be placed near the beginning of the program. It must appear before the table is used in the program. When using the table, the subscript must never be larger than the number used in the DIM statement. Otherwise, an error message will be generated. The error message will be similar to the following: "SUBSCRIPT OUT OF RANGE."

Several tables may be dimensioned in the same statement. For example: 20 DIM NAM$(25),AGE(25) creates two one-dimensional tables. One is a string table for the name and the other a numeric table for the age. Each table is capable of storing 26 elements. The first row in a table is always row zero unless otherwise specified with the OPTION BASE statement. The purpose of the OPTION BASE statement is to declare the minimum value of a subscript. This statement is available on the IBM Personal Computer and TRS-80 Model 4. Even though Apple, Commodore, and TRS-80 Model III do not have the OPTION BASE statement, you may still use a subscript of one as the lowest value. The result will simply be one empty cell at position zero which would not be used. The OPTION BASE statement must be used prior to the DIM statement or the use of any array item in the program.

General Form: *line number* OPTION BASE *minimum array subscript value=*

Example: 10 OPTION BASE 1

Storing Data in a One-Dimensional Table

Once a table has been dimensioned, data may be stored in it with any of the keywords used with regular variables. A subscript must be used following the variable name of the table element to tell the computer the number of the row in which the element should be stored.

Example:

```
10 OPTION BASE 1
20 DIM A(15)
30 FOR X=1 TO 15
40    LET A(X)=X
50 NEXT X
```

Line 10 tells the computer that the minimum subscript will be 1. Line 20 sets up a table named A of 15 elements. Lines 30-50 create a loop and place values in each of the 15 elements of Table A. The contents of the table are shown in Figure 3.9.

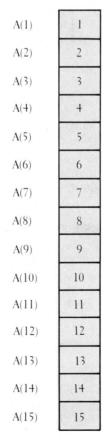

A(1)	1
A(2)	2
A(3)	3
A(4)	4
A(5)	5
A(6)	6
A(7)	7
A(8)	8
A(9)	9
A(10)	10
A(11)	11
A(12)	12
A(13)	13
A(14)	14
A(15)	15

Figure 3.9   One-Dimensional Table with Values

Two-Dimensional Tables

If desired, tables may have two (or more) dimensions. In a two-dimensional table, you must use two subscripts to access data. Figure 13.10 shows the subscripts to use. If you want to access the data in the second column of the third row of a table, for example, you would have to use this subscripted variable: Variable name (3,2).

Columns / Rows	1	2	3	4
1	(1,1)	(1,2)	(1,3)	(1,4)
2	(2,1)	(2,2)	(2,3)	(2,4)
3	(3,1)	(3,2)	(3,3)	(3,4)
4	(4,1)	(4,2)	(4,3)	(4,4)
5	(5,1)	(5,2)	(5,3)	(5,4)

Figure 3.10   Subscripts for Accessing Data in a Two-Dimensional Table

As with a one-dimensional table, you may use either a constant, variable, or arithmetic expression as the subscript. Remember, when accessing data from a two-dimensional table, you must always specify the row number, first, and the column number, second, when identifying the subscript. The following example illustrates the formatting of the statement to obtain data from or place data into a two-dimensional table.

General Form: *line number keyword variable name(row,column)*

Example: `40 LET TABLE.Z(2,5)=10`

As an example, assume that you want to store the average temperature for each month for each of the states of the U.S. You would set up a table with the DIM statement, specifying 50 rows and 12 columns. Each row represents one of the 50 states, and each column represents one of the months. Study the following example program which reads the average temperature for a state for each month and stores it in a table. The loop is repeated 50 times so that each of the state's information is stored in the table. The example shows data for only one state. To actually use the program, you would have to add data for 49 more states.

```
10 OPTION BASE 1
20 DIM TEMPERATURE(50,12)
30 FOR X=1 TO 50
40    FOR Y=1 TO 12
50       READ TEMPERATURE(X,Y)
60    NEXT Y
70 NEXT X
80 END
90 DATA 12,17,23,34,45,56,77,79,74,68,44,32
```

Data may also be put into a table with any of the other regular keywords that assign data to variables. As an example, the following will assign a number to an element within Table A.

```
70 LET A(1)=B*C
```

PRINTING FROM A TABLE

All the keywords and functions used for printing regular variables may also be used with tables. As with the storage of data in a table, the subscript must be used to identify the table element when printing. The following example illustrates the printing of all elements of Table A that was earlier filled with the numbers 1-15.

Example:

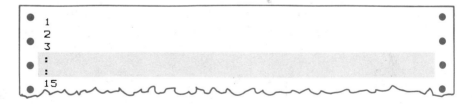

```
110 FOR X=1 TO 15 ◄——————— Creates the loop.
120    PRINT A(X) ◄——————— Prints the element of A with a subscript of X.
130 NEXT X
140 END
```

Output:

```
1
2
3
:
:
15
```

PERFORMING CALCULATIONS WITH TABLE DATA

The table elements may be used in any arithmetic expression. You must always remember to use a subscript to indicate which element is to be used in the expression. If you were to find the average of all fifteen elements of Table A, you might write the following code for the program.

Example:
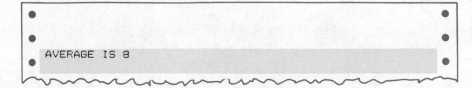

```
210 FOR X=1 TO 15          ←———————— Creates the loop.
220    LET Z=Z+A(X)        ←———————— Adds the value of A to Z.
230 NEXT X
240 LET AVERAGE=Z/15       ←———————— Divides the total value of Z by 15, the
250 PRINT "AVERAGE IS";AVERAGE          number of elements in the table.
```

Output:

```
AVERAGE IS 8
```

EXCHANGING DATA WITHIN TABLE ELEMENTS

When data has been stored in a table, you may want to rearrange it into numeric or alphabetic order. The keyword SWAP may be used to exchange two data items within two table elements if you are using the IBM PC or TRS-80 Model 4.

> General Form: *line number* SWAP *element1,element2*
>
> Example: 150 SWAP A(X),A(Y)
>
> or
>
> Example: 30 IF A(X)>A(Y) THEN SWAP A(X),A(Y)

The following example illustrates the exchanging of the contents of a table element without using the SWAP statement.

Example:
```
30 IF A(X)>A(Y) THEN Z=A(X):A(X)=A(Y):A(Y)=Z
```
If A(X) is greater than A(Y), then A(X) is moved to the temporary area Z and A(X) is assigned the value of A(Y). The swap is then completed by assigning A(Y) the value stored in Z.

In Chapter 7 you will be taught several techniques on how to arrange data, exchange data, and sort data.

INTERACTIVE INPUT INTO THE PROGRAM

The INPUT statement requests data from the keyboard. This request requires you to interact with the program. As a result, it is known as interactive processing

Using the INPUT Statement

The keyword used for assigning a value entered from the keyboard to a variable is INPUT. The INPUT statement causes the computer to stop execution until data is entered from the keyboard. Once the ENTER/ RETURN key is pressed, execution continues.

General Form: *line number* INPUT *variable name(s)*

Example:
```
50 INPUT CUSTOMER.NUMBER
60 INPUT CUSTOMER.NAME$,CUSTOMER.ADDRESS$,ZIP.CODE
```

INPUT is followed by one or more variable names. The data entered will be placed in the variables in the sequence in which it is entered. If you entered one number in response to line 50 of the example, it would be placed in the variable named CUSTOMER.NUMBER. If two numbers were entered, the first would be placed in the variable and the second would be ignored. Line 60 illustrates the entering of multiple data with one INPUT statement. When several data items are requested, you must key all data items, separating them with commas. If the INPUT statement requests string information, such as does line 60, you must not enter a comma within the string unless the string is enclosed in quotes. If a name such as REARDON, EILEEN were to be entered, it would have to be entered with quotation marks. Therefore, the data would be entered as: "REARDON, EILEEN". The input data for line 60 would be similiar to the following:

```
?"REARDON, EILEEN", "EAU CLAIRE, WI",54701  ◄── Press
                                                ENTER/RETURN.
```

If you fail to enter at least the same number of data items as requested by the INPUT statement, the computer will display another question mark or a message to indicate that more data must be entered.

Just as was indicated with the READ and LET statements, the data entered must be the same type as called for in the INPUT statement. For example, a numeric value may be entered and the number will be recognized as a string if the variable name ends with a dollar sign. However, if the variable name represents a numeric variable, you could not enter alphabetic information. If you do, the computer will respond with ?REDO or a similiar message. If you enter too much data, some computers respond with a message such as ?EXTRA IGNORED.

Using Prompts

A prompt is a literal that is printed to tell the user what data is to be entered. This prompt may be included in the INPUT statement or printed with a separate PRINT statement. The following example illustrates how INPUT statements with prompts may be used in a program.

Example:

```
10 OPTION BASE 1
20 DIM STUDENT.LIST$(30)
30 LET PROCEED$="Y": X=1
40 WHILE PROCEED$="Y"
50    INPUT "ENTER A NAME: ";STUDENT.LIST$(X)
60    LET X=X+1
70    IF X>30 THEN PROCEED$="N"
         ELSE INPUT "DO YOU HAVE MORE DATA?  ENTER Y OR N";PROCEED$
80 WEND
90 END
```

When the program is run, line 50 would request that data be entered. You enter a student name. The first name is to be stored in STU-DENT.LIST$(1). Line 60 increments the subscript. Line 70 checks to determine if the subscript is greater than 30, the largest possible for the table. If it is, PROCEED$ is changed to "N" and the WEND is executed. If it is not, the ELSE option is executed and you are requested to input either a Y or N. If Y is entered, the process continues. If N is entered, execution stops.

Using LINE INPUT

LINE INPUT is available on the IBM and the TRS-80. LINE INPUT is a convenient way to input character strings that may contain blanks, commas, and colons. These would otherwise need to be enclosed in quotation marks when used with the regular INPUT statement.

General Form: *line number* LINE INPUT *variable name$*

Example: `100 LINE INPUT "Enter City and State:";CITY.STATE$`

When the line is executed and the computer is waiting for a response from the keyboard, no question mark appears. Any character may be entered and accepted regardless of whether it is preceded by spaces, a minus sign, quotes, or a comma. Any data entered will be stored in the variable when ENTER/RETURN is pressed. With LINE INPUT, only one variable may be included in the statement.

Interactive Input Without Using ENTER/RETURN

Often you may like to give the user the opportunity to interact with the program without requiring that ENTER/RETURN be pressed or without any data being displayed on the screen. For example, if the program required that the user enter data interactively, the program could be directed to print the entered data on the screen and provide the user with an opportunity to read the data to check the validity of information entered. When the data has been read, the user may be directed to strike any key on the keyboard. This character will not be printed and will change the status of a given variable. If the character is to be printed, the program must contain a PRINT statement. As the given character is entered, execution will continue. The user will not need to press the ENTER/RETURN.

The three statements which allow the user to interact without ENTER/RETURN are GET (used on Apple and Commodore), INKEY$ (used in IBM and TRS-80), and INPUT$ (used on IBM and TRS-80 Model 4). String variables should be used with these statements.

GET

The GET statement varies from Apple to Commodore. Also, in later chapters the GET will be used when processing data files.

General Form: *line number* GET *variable*

Example: 40 GET C$

The GET statement is used to get one character from the keyboard and assign it to a variable. On the Apple, the GET statement causes execution to stop until a key is pressed. It then places the value in the variable and execution continues. When used on the Commodore, the GET statement does not cause the execution to pause. Rather, the computer continues to scan the keyboard. If no key has been struck, execution continues. Generally the GET statement will be placed in a loop when it is used on the Commodore. This allows the computer to continue to scan the keyboard waiting for a character. An example of a loop used in a program on the Commodore is shown here:

```
80 PRINT "STRIKE ANY KEY TO CONTINUE"
90 GET C$: IF C$="" THEN 90
```

INKEY$

The INKEY$ function may be used on the IBM or TRS-80 to get one character from the keyboard and assign it to a variable.

General Form: *line number character variable* = INKEY$

Example: 150 A$=INKEY$

INKEY$ functions identically to the GET statement on the Commodore. When a statement with the INKEY$ function appears, the keyboard is scanned. If a key had been struck, a character will be stored in the variable. If no key has been struck, a null string is placed in the variable. While INKEY$ is being used, no characters are displayed on the screen. Because execution continues regardless of whether a key is struck, INKEY$ is generally placed in a loop similiar to the one shown for the Commodore.

INPUT$

The INPUT$ function is the most sophisticated of all the statements for entering data without the use of the ENTER/RETURN.

General Form: *line number character variable =*
             INPUT$(number of characters)

Example: 150 A$=INPUT$(2)

When the computer is executing a program containing an INPUT$ statement, it will pause when the INPUT$ is encountered. The computer will wait until the number of characters specified has been entered. The fact that more than one character may be entered makes the statement more sophisticated. INPUT$ will accept all keyboard characters including the ENTER. It will not allow you to correct any characters entered. Study the following example of INPUT$.

Example:
```
10 PRINT "TYPE C TO CONTINUE OR S TO STOP"
20 A$=INPUT$(1)
30 IF A$="C" THEN 10 ELSE IF A$<>"S" THEN 20
40 END
```

DATA MODIFICATION

As data is entered or compared, it is often necessary to examine it to determine the validity of the information. Sometimes it is necessary to modify the variable in order to make valid comparisons. Several functions are available to accomplish these tasks. Each of the functions discussed in this section must be used along with one or more BASIC keywords. Each function is frequently used as part of an IF ... THEN statement or as part of a LET statement. Wherever a constant is used in the example, it may be replaced by a variable or an expression.

LEFT$

The LEFT$ function is used to examine the left portion of a variable string. It begins with the left-most character and returns one or more characters as specified in the statement.

General Form: LEFT$*(character variable,number of characters)*

Example: LEFT$(NAM$,8)

This example identified that the left eight characters of the variable NAM$ are to be examined. Study the following example:

```
60 INPUT "ENTER YOUR NAME";NAM$
70 INPUT "WHAT IS YOUR GRADE?  (i.e. SOPHOMORE)"; GRADE$
80 IF LEFT$(GRADE$,2)="SO" THEN PRINT NAM$
```

In this example, you were asked to enter name and grade. If you wanted to print out only those classified as sophomores, it would be necessary to examine only the left two characters to tell seniors from sophomores. The left two characters of sophomores would be SO and the left two characters of seniors would be SE. Since they both start with the letter S, we could not have the students enter only one letter to indicate their grade.

RIGHT$

The RIGHT$ function works in the same manner as the LEFT$ function. The RIGHT$ function begins with the right-most character and proceeds to the left depending upon how many characters have been identified.

General Form: RIGHT$*(character variable,number of characters)*

Example: RIGHT$(WORDS$,4)

If you were given a long list of words and told to examine the list and print out all words that end with "tion," you would be able to read the word and examine it for the right four characters. Study the following portion of program:

```
10 'Read the words and examine for "tion"
20 'If the word has tion as an ending
30 'print the word.
40 READ WORDS$
50 IF RIGHT$(WORDS$,4)="tion" THEN PRINT WORDS$
```

In the example shown, several assumptions have been made. First we must assume that the words were entered in lowercase characters. If they were entered in uppercase letters, the computer would never find a match for the literal "tion." The literal "TION" is not equal to "tion." The example also illustrates the usage of uppercase and lowercase characters as remarks. It is assumed that your computer would allow you to use uppercase and lowercase characters. However, you could easily use all uppercase characters. To make use of the example, you would have to add data lines and set up a loop to repeat the examination process for all data.

MID$

The MID$ function starts the examination of a variable at a specified character number and continues for the number of characters also specified.

General Form: MID$*(character variable,start location,number of characters)*

Example: MID$(SSN$,4,2)

The number of characters to be examined may be omitted. In that case, all characters from the beginning location to the end of the string would be used. For example, suppose we have a list of names and addresses of persons living in the city of Atlanta. We want to count all persons who live in the Old National neighborhood. Since all persons living there have fourth and fifth characters of 49, we can find them. Assuming that the ZIP Codes were entered into a table named as ZIP$, we may examine the data to determine how many have 49 in the fourth and fifth positions. The following example would examine the existing data.

Example:
```
150 FOR X=1 TO 100
160    IF MID$(ZIP$(X),4,2)="49" THEN NUMBER=NUMBER+1
170 NEXT X
```

The LEFT\$, RIGHT\$, and MID\$ functions allow you to extract characters from a variable as well as examine them. The LEFT\$ and RIGHT\$ may not be used to the left of the equal sign in an assignment statement. The MID\$ may be used on either side of the equal sign. When the MID\$ function is on the left, it serves as part of a LET statement and inserts different characters into the variable on the left of the equal sign.

Concatenation

Often you may want to have the user input information in one manner and handle it differently once in the computer. An example of this is inputting the birthdate. The month, day, and year may be input separately. Once stored in the computer, you may want to treat the information as one total field of information. Concatenation allows you to "add" fields together.

General Form: *string variable + string variable + string variable*

Example: `A$=MONTH$+DAY$+YEAR$`

In the general form, the variable may be replaced by any string literal. Study the following example to see how concatenation may be used in a program. Remember that you are able to concatenate only string variables or literals.

Example:
```
10 'PRINT CONCATENATION IN A PROGRAM
20 INPUT "ENTER THE MONTH IN WHICH YOU WERE BORN";MONTH$
30 INPUT "ENTER THE DAY ON WHICH YOU WERE BORN";DAY$
40 INPUT "ENTER THE YEAR IN WHICH YOU WERE BORN";YEAR$
50 LET Z$=MONTH$+" "+DAY$+" "+YEAR$        'Concatenation
60 PRINT Z$
70 END
```

Output:

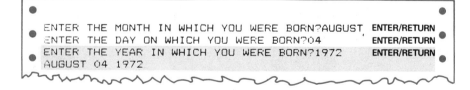

```
ENTER THE MONTH IN WHICH YOU WERE BORN?AUGUST  ENTER/RETURN
ENTER THE DAY ON WHICH YOU WERE BORN?04              ENTER/RETURN
ENTER THE YEAR IN WHICH YOU WERE BORN?1972       ENTER/RETURN
AUGUST 04 1972
```

LEN

The **LEN** (length) function counts the number of characters in a data item. Blanks are also counted as characters. The result of the count of the number of characters may be used directly in an IF...THEN statement or other operation as shown in the example following the general form.

General Form: LEN*(character string)*

Example: 150 LENGTH=LEN(ADDRESS$)

Example:
```
40 INPUT "ADDRESS";ADDRESS$
50 IF LEN(ADDRESS$)>20 THEN PRINT "PLEASE REENTER MAXIMUM OF
   20 CHARACTERS":GOTO 40
```

The LEN function is very valuable in data validation. It enables you to limit the length of the data entered that the program is intended to handle.

ASC

The ASC (ASCII) function returns the ASCII code for the first character of the string identified.

General Form: ASC*(string)*

Example: 190 X=ASC(ADDRESS$)

In this example, the result of the ASC function is a numeric value that is the ASCII code of the first character in the variable ADDRESS$. If ADDRESS$ did not contain a character, the results would be null and an "ILLEGAL FUNCTION CALL" error would occur. In the following example, notice the results.

Example:
```
40 INPUT "ENTER YOUR CITY";ADDRESS$
50 PRINT ASC(ADDRESS$)
60 END
```

Output:

```
ENTER YOUR CITY?TOLEDO     ENTER/RETURN
84
```

The output from the screen illustrates that the city "TOLEDO, OHIO" was entered as data into the variable ADDRESS$. The numeric value returned was 84, which is the ASCII value for the letter T. If the letter T had been lowercase, the numeric value 116 would have been returned.

CHR$

The **CHR$** (character string) function is the opposite of the ASC function and is used to convert from an ASCII code to a character.

General Form: CHR$*(number)*

Example: `250 X$=CHR$(84)`

In the example, the character whose ASCII code is 84 is stored in variable X$. The range of the number must be from 0 to 255. Each number represents a given ASCII character. See Appendix A for all of the ASCII codes.

STR$

The **STR$** (string) function returns the string representation of the value of a variable or number.

General Form: STR$*(numeric value)*

Example: `150 Y$=STR$(X)`

In this example, Y$ is assigned the string representation of the variable X. Study the following example. A space is placed to the left of the number for the sign of the number.

Example:
```
40 INPUT X
50 Y$=STR$(X)
60 PRINT Y$
```

Output:
```
?234.56
 234.56
```
This represents the string "234.56".

VAL

The **VAL** (value function) is the opposite of the STR$ function. It returns the numeric value of a string variable or literal.

General Form: VAL*(character variable)*

Example: 150 X=VAL(Y$)

The VAL function will strip all leading blanks from the string. If the character variable contains any nonnumeric characters (alphabetic or special characters), most computers consider only the characters before the nonnumeric one. Line 320 of the following example illustrates this.

Example:

```
310 S$="123C"
320 X=VAL(S$)
330 PRINT X
350 END
```

Output:

```
123
```

INSTR

The **INSTR** (in string) function (used on the IBM and TRS-80 Model 4) is used to find the location of one character string within another character string.

General Form: *line number numeric variable=INSTR(start position,string to search,string to find)*

Example: 70 X=INSTR(1,X$,Y$)

The INSTR searches for the first occurrence of one string in the other and returns the position at which the match is found. The start position is optional. If it is not specified, the search will begin with the first character in the string. If the string being searched for is not found, a zero is returned. Study the example using the INSTR to determine how the first and last names may be reversed.

Example:

```
40 N$="MACDONALD, CAROL"
50 P=INSTR(N$,",")
60 PRINT MID$(N$, P+2); " "; LEFT$(N$, P-1)
```

Output:

```
CAROL MACDONALD
```

STRING$

The **STRING$** function (available on the IBM and TRS-80) produces a string made of any desired characters. For example, it can produce a string of hyphens or underline characters.

General Form: STRING$*(how long,character)*

Example: `150 X$=STRING$(80,"-")`

In this example, the variable X$ would contain 80 hyphens. If X$ were printed, the output would be a line of hyphens.

SPACE$

The SPACE$ function returns a string of spaces. The SPACE$ function shown in the following general form would produce 40 spaces. If line 90 were executed, X$ would be equal to 40 spaces. This could be printed to blank out 40 spaces on the screen. This function may be used in formatting the screen by inserting a specified number of spaces before printing a variable or literal.

General Form: SPACE$*(number)*

Example: `90 X$=SPACE$(40)`

SPC

The SPC (space) function is similiar to the TAB function. The only difference is that the SPC function moves the printing point a specified number of spaces while the TAB moves the printing point to a specified column.

General Form: *line number* PRINT SPC*(number of spaces);data to print*

Example: 100 PRINT SPC(10);"WORD"

The number used in parentheses may not exceed the number of characters of width on the device to which printing is taking place. In other words, the number could not exceed 80 if you were printing on an 80-column screen. Study the following example:

Example:
```
50 PRINT "THIS STARTED IN POSITION ONE";SPC(20);"AND THIS WILL
   END IN POSITION 80"
```

Output:

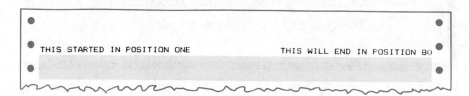

```
THIS STARTED IN POSITION ONE                    THIS WILL END IN POSITION 80
```

By using one or more of the functions, it is possible to present, examine, or compare data to obtain the desired results. Your reports will appear more professional and the task of modifying and examining data will be made easier.

REVIEW QUESTIONS

1. Identify three characters, each of which may be added to a numeric variable name to designate the level of precision with which a number will be stored. (Obj. 2)
2. Define the keywords DEFINT, DEFSNG, and DEFDBL. (Obj. 2)
3. Define the term arithmetic function. Identify several arithmetic functions, and explain their purpose. (Obj. 4)
4. Define the term table and explain how it may be used to store data. (Obj. 1)

5. Explain how GET, INKEY$, and INPUT$ are alike. How are they different? (Obj. 1)
6. Identify three keywords that allow for the examination of portions of a string variable. Identify what they will do. (Obj. 5)
7. Explain the term concatenation. (Obj. 6)
8. What functions may be used to change numeric variables to strings and string variables to numeric? Explain how each performs. (Obj. 6)
9. Identify how the STRING$ might be used in a program to help the programmer save coding time. (Obj. 6)

VOCABULARY WORDS

The following terms were introduced in this chapter:

arithmetic operator	subscript	data modification
truncated	matrix	concatenation
numeric functions	array	catenation
function	two-dimensional table	dimensioning
table	batch processing	null
one-dimensional table	prompts	interactive processing

KEYWORDS AND COMMANDS

The following keywords and commands were introduced in this chapter:

DEF	SQR	RIGHT$
DEFINT	TAN	MID$
DEFSNG	DIM	LEN
DEFDBL	OPTION BASE	ASC
DEF FN	SWAP	CHR$
ABS	INPUT	STR$
COS	LINE INPUT	VAL
EXP	GET	INSTR
INT	INKEY$	STRING$
LOG	INPUT$	SPACE$
RND	LEFT$	SPC
SIN		

PROGRAMS TO WRITE

Complete the appropriate documentation for each of the programs before writing the code.

Program 1

The instructor of Data Processing 101 would like you to develop a program to determine the average score for the first test given this semester. The output report should list the students' names and scores. The program should allow the instructor to input up to 30 names. If there are less than 30 students, the instructor should be able to indicate that there is no more data and the report will be generated giving the listing and the average score. The report should look similar to the following:

```
                    FIRST TEST SCORE REPORT

        STUDENT                                SCORE

        Mary Smith                              89
        Tom Jones                               78
         "       "                               "
         "       "                               "
        Volanda Thompson                        96

                    AVERAGE SCORE IS            87
```

Program 2

The instructor of Data Processing 101 was pleased with the program you developed for Program 1. As a result, you have been asked to develop a program using a two-dimensional array to allow for the input of three test grades for each student. Again, the program should allow for up to 30 students' data to be inputted. If there are less than 30 students, the instructor should be able to terminate the interactive input of the data. The report will be generated giving the title, student name, test score for each student, and the average for each test. The report will be very similar to the one shown in Program 1 with the exception of the title and three columns. There will be one column for each of the three tests.

Program 3

You are to prepare a monthly accounts receivable report. Each record to be inputted interactively contains the customer number, discount rate, and the sales amount. The program you develop should allow for the interactive input of all data before any calculations or printing of the report take place.

Your output should include the appropriate title and column headings. The report should list the customer's name, discount rate, sales amount, the amount of the discount, and the total amount due. (Because all of the accounts are due immediately, every customer will receive the discount). After all records have been processed, the results are printed. The total of all sales, discounts, and amount due should be printed. The input data follows:

Customer Name	Discount	Sales Amount
Arnie Arnold	.05	$1000.00
Carlota Lamas	.10	9800.00
Harry Hollerith	.05	1600.00
Marie Murray	.05	3568.00
Sally Smith	.10	5600.00
Enid Schwartz	.07	4575.00

Program 4

The basketball coach would like you to develop a program which would allow the coach to enter the statistics for the 12 players on the team. At this time the coach is only interested in recording and determining the averages for each player for the ten conference games as well as determining the average points scored per game. Write a program using a two-dimensional table to allow the coach to enter the data for each of the players for the game. After all data has been entered, you are to calculate the per game average for each player and store the average within the table.

As the report is being generated, you are to add up the score for each player for each of the games played and divide by the number of players to obtain the average points scored by a player per game. Print out a report that contains a title, column headings, data lines, and a summary line. The report should look similiar to the following:

Yearly Conference Statistics

Player Name	Basketball Game Number										Average
	1	2	3	4	5	6	7	8	9	10	
Tom Smith	11	9	6	14	0	17	8	13	11	9	8.8
"	"	"	"	"	"	"	"	"	"	"	"
Per Game Ave.	6.6	5.4	4.5	2.3	8.8	9.9	9.8	7.8	8.8	8.8	7.8

Program 5

The workers in a plastic cup factory have been assigned pay classifications ranging from 1 to 5 according to their skills and knowledge required for the job they are performing. Recently the management of the firm approved salary increases for the workers. The new pay scales are to be determined from their old salary. The information concerning the pay classifications and percentage of increase is shown at the top of page 102.

Pay Classification	Increase Percentage
1	4%
2	5%
3	6%
4	7%
5	8%

You are to write a program that will store the information for pay classification and percentage of increase in a table. Then you are to read and process the following data. A report is to be generated that will give the employee report title, column headings, detail lines for employee number, name, pay classification, monthly salary, and new monthly salary.

1234 Toby Tobias 1 1245.56
2345 Mary Johnson 3 1344.66
3456 Cindy Zahn 5 2100.00
4321 Willard Korn 4 1987.54
5436 Bart Stone 2 1234.78

Program 6

The local tax assessor would like to have you develop a program that would summarize the taxes collected. The county has been divided into seven districts. The taxes are collected from each of the taxpayers and recorded on data records. Some taxpayers own property in several districts and therefore must pay taxes in each of those districts. You are to set up a table. Initialize the values of each element in the table to zero. As each data record is read, you are to add the taxes paid to the table element. After all records have been read, you are to print out the summary of the table in a neat report. It should contain a title, column headings representing each of the districts, and the amount of taxes for each district. Use the following data:

Taxpayer	District	1	2	3	4	5	6	7
John Shillak		123.45	23.45	33.99	89.88	777.77	987.90	123.80
Joan McHenry		000.00	00.00	00.00	00.00	998.08	000.00	000.00
Lorraine Missling		890.00	00.00	00.00	23.78	098.22	000.00	000.00
Tom Halaychik		000.00	00.00	00.00	00.00	000.00	789.56	000.00
Fuji Akita		986.50	25.00	12.50	78.80	000.00	000.00	000.00
Craig Brenholt		000.00	99.99	99.99	99.99	189.90	000.00	080.60

## Chapter 4

Simple Data Files

Objectives:
1. Explain the purpose of data files.
2. Explain how data is stored in sequential files.
3. Describe the technique of accessing information in sequential files.
4. Write a program using a sequential file.
5. Explain how data is stored in random files.
6. Describe the technique of accessing information in random files.
7. Write a program using random files.
8. Identify three ways of determining record numbers.

Topic 4.1— PRINCIPLES OF DATA FILES

You have learned to read data into the computer from DATA statements. You have set up variables for input when programs required the user to interact with the computer. Each of these provided the computer with information to process. In each case, it was possible to process only fairly small amounts of data. You have stored information in tables and then processed the data. This gave you an opportunity to store moderate amounts of data. Most applications processed in business and industry, however, require the processing of large volumes of data. Usually the data processed must be retained for future use. If such data is simply stored in tables, it will be destroyed when you turn off the computer or run another program. To solve this problem, large amounts of data are generally stored on magnetic media such as tape or disk.

DISK FILES

You are familiar with the file cabinets used in offices and schools. Perhaps there is a file cabinet in your home. Each file cabinet contains several drawers. For example, one file drawer in the school office may contain the information with the students' names, addresses, phone numbers, and several other items of information. This collection of information about the students is known as a file.

The information pertaining to one specific student is known as a record. Perhaps you have written down the names and phone numbers of your friends. Each name and phone number is known as a record. Records contain fields of information. Each data item, such as a name, is known as a field. Usually a file will be made up of several records. However, a file may be as small as one record or as large as millions of records. Records may contain one field or many fields of information. Fields may be as small as one character or as large as the entire record. Figure 4.1 illustrates the typical data that would be stored in a record containing information about students enrolled in a given course.

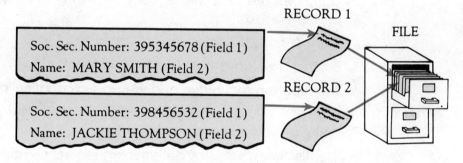

Figure 4.1   Fields, Records, and Files

DISK STORAGE

Data stored on a disk is stored on tracks. The tracks are concentric circles on the disk. Tracks are divided into sectors. Each sector may store one or more records. Figure 4.2 illustrates the data from two records as it might be stored on a disk. Files may also be stored on magnetic tape. Since most files are stored on disks, however, only disks will be discussed in this text.

SEQUENTIAL DATA FILES

A sequential file stores and reads records one after another. A sequential file may be written to, read from, or appended. When records are written to a sequential file, they are written one after another without any space between records. Generally, a return character is inserted between the records

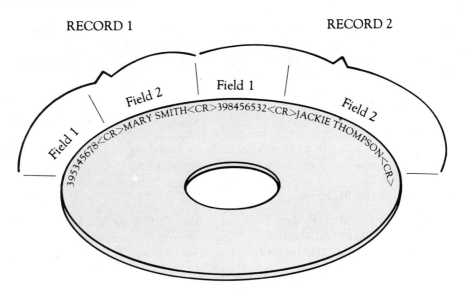

RECORD 1   RECORD 2

Figure 4.2   File of Social Security Numbers and Names Stored on Disk

by the computer. Just as sequential records are written one after another, they are read in the same manner. If you want to use the data stored in the second record, you have to read the first record to get to the second. This is called sequential processing and is the simplest method of file handling. Files may be opened for reading as many times as desired. Each time the records are read the data remains the same. Sequential files may also be appended. This means that once the file is created by writing records to it, the file may be opened again and records may be added to the end of the file.

Writing a Sequential File

The writing of data to a sequential file requires you to complete the following steps: (1) the file must be opened; (2) data must be written to the file; and (3) the file must be closed.

OPENING THE FILE

Opening a file on the computer is somewhat like opening a file drawer. Before anything may be stored in a file cabinet, the drawer must be opened. Prior to writing on a diskette, a file must be opened for output or to be appended. If the file is opened as output (for writing to it) or as input (for reading it) the file pointer will be set at the beginning of the file. A pointer is a technique used by the computer to remember which record is to be written or read. As a record is written or read, the pointer is advanced to the next record. If a file contains records and is opened for output the second time, the records already stored will be destroyed. As records are written to the file it is recreated with new data. When a file is opened to be appended, the file pointer is set to the end of the file. The name given to a file must correspond to the rules that you have used in naming programs stored on a disk.

WRITING THE DATA

After a file is opened for output, the file is available to receive data. Writing to a file on disk is similar to writing to the screen or the printer; only small changes are required in the process.

CLOSING THE FILE

After all data has been written to the file, the file must be closed. This means that the file has been stored on disk and may not be accessed without opening the file again. This operation is similar to the closing of the file cabinet drawer.

Reading a Sequential File

Reading data previously stored in a file and placing it in variables for use requires several steps. The file must be opened, read, and (upon completion of the process) closed.

OPENING THE FILE

Opening a file for reading is almost identical to opening a file for writing. The name given to the file when it is opened for output will be used when opening the file for input into the computer.

READING THE DATA

Once a file is opened for input, records may be read from the disk. The data is placed in variables identified in the special statement that is used to read data from a file. Each field in a record will have to be read in the order in which it was earlier written.

CLOSING THE FILE

Closing the file after reading is identical to closing the file after data has been written to it.

RANDOM DATA FILES

Random data files are files that can be written and read in any order. As you are aware, records in a sequential file must be written or read one after another. In a random file, the records may be written or read in any order desired. The program must direct the computer to place the file pointer at the desired record. If you want to read data stored in record 13, you tell the computer to go to that location in the file. It is not necessary to read records 1 through 12 before reading record 13. Another benefit of random files is the ability to read and write during the same processing activity. In other words, you may access (read) a random record, make some changes, and write the record back to the file in a series of steps.

Designating Record Lengths

Random files usually require that all records be of the same length. This is in contrast to a sequential file, where the data is separated by return characters and uses only the amount of space required. For example, if a name contains 11 characters, only 11 storage spaces are required in a sequential file. In a random file, each field must have a specified length. For example, a name may be specified as 20 characters. If a name entered from the keyboard contains only 11 characters, it still takes 20 characters of space on disk. At first this may make you believe that sequential files are better than random files, but do not be too hasty in making your judgment. The ability to access records randomly permits more rapid access to the records. The random access allows access to data over and over without opening and closing the file several times during the processing of records. Often, data from small files will be read and stored in tables prior to the manipulation of the data. However, if the file is very large, the tables would consume all of the RAM (random-access memory) and make it impossible to process the records. Random processing allows you to leave the records on disk and only access the specific record needed for processing at a given time. Figure 4.3 illustrates the storage of records in locations one and four in a random file. If desired, records stored in a random file may also be processed sequentially.

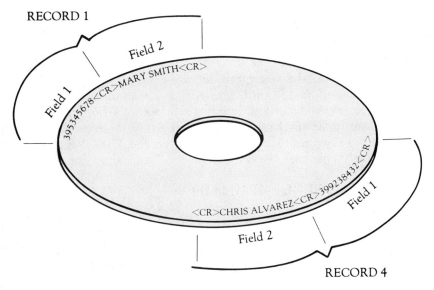

Figure 4.3   Random File on Disk

Creating and Using Random Files

Random files must be opened before reading and writing and must be closed after use. Once the file is opened, it is possible to read and write to it. The methods of performing these steps vary considerably from one computer to another. They will be explained in detail in Topic 4.2.

REVIEW QUESTIONS

1. What is a file? (Obj. 1)
2. Identify three reasons why data files are necessary. (Obj. 2)
3. Explain the following terms: file, record, and field. (Obj. 2)
4. Explain the procedure for reading the third record in a sequential file. (Obj. 3)
5. Identify the three steps involved in creating a sequential file. (Obj. 3)
6. Identify the three steps involved in reading a sequential file. (Obj. 3)
7. Identify two differences between sequential and random files. (Obj. 5)
8. Identify two benefits of using random files. (Obj. 5)
9. Identify the steps necessary to create and access random files. (Obj. 6)
10. Explain how the storage of data differs between random and sequential files. (Obj. 2)

Topic 4.2— IMPLEMENTING FILES IN BASIC

Even though the processing of sequential files varies from computer to computer, the concept is the same on all computers. The processing of random files also varies greatly from computer to computer. Therefore, this section will be divided into two main sections: Implementing Sequential Files and Implementing Random Files. Each of those two sections will be divided into three sections. One section covers the TRS-80 and IBM, another covers the Apple, and the last one covers the Commodore.

IMPLEMENTING SEQUENTIAL FILES

Figure 4.4 shows the program documentation sheet for a program to create a sequential file. Figure 4.5 shows the program documentation sheet for a program to access the file and print a report on a printer. Following the documentation sheets, the code for each computer is shown.

PROGRAM DOCUMENTATION SHEET		
Program: EXC4E1	Programmer: Clark and LaBarre	Date: 4/23/--

Purpose:

To write a program to input students' names and social security numbers. As the data is entered, it will be written to a file called "STUDENT".

Input: Name and social security number are input from the keyboard	Output: A file named STUDENT

Data Terminator:

Variables Used:

```
STUDENT$   =   Student Name
SSN$       =   Student Social Security Number
ANSWER$    =   Yes or No Response to see Whether Data is Correct
```

Figure 4.4   Program Documentation Sheet for Creating a File

PROGRAM DOCUMENTATION SHEET

Program:	Programmer:	Date:
EXC4E2	Clark and LaBarre	4/23/--

Purpose:

The purpose of this program is to read a file and print the results on paper.

Input:	Output:
Names and social security number are read from the file	A report showing names and social security numbers

Data Terminator:

End-of-file condition check

Variables Used:

STUDENT$ = Student Name
SSN$ = Student Social Security Number

Figure 4.5 Program Documentation Sheet for Accessing a File

IBM AND TRS-80

The processing of sequential files on the IBM and TRS-80 requires you to become familiar with several new statements. Each of these statements will be discussed fully in the following paragraphs.

Opening the File

A file used for sequential processing may be opened for output, input, or to be appended. The **OPEN** statement is used for all three operations. The general form of the statement is shown below:

General Form: *line number* OPEN "*filename*" FOR *mode* AS
#*file number*

Example: 20 OPEN "STUDENT.FIL" FOR OUTPUT AS #1

The mode specifies how the file is to be opened. It may be either **OUTPUT, INPUT,** or **APPEND** The file number has nothing to do with the data stored in the file. The number is used later to refer to the file when using the PRINT, WRITE, and INPUT statements accessing the file.

An alternate form for opening files may be used on the IBM. It must be used with the TRS-80 Model III and Model 4. The APPEND mode may not be used with the alternate form. The mode should be entered as an O for output or an I for input.

General Form: line number OPEN "mode",file number,"file
name"

Example: 20 OPEN "O",1,"STUDENT.FIL"

Writing to a Sequential File

After a file has been opened for output, you may enter data to be written to the disk. Either the **PRINT #** or the **WRITE #** statement may be used to place data on the disk. Each of the statements is different and will be discussed in the following paragraphs.

General Form: *line number* PRINT# *file number,variable name*

Example: 70 PRINT#1,STUDENT$

The number following PRINT# is always the same as the number used in the OPEN statement. When writing several variables to disk, each should be written by a separate PRINT# statement. The computer may temporarily store data in memory locations known as a **buffer** before writing it to the disk. Therefore, the disk drive may not turn on each time a PRINT# or WRITE# statement is executed. It is faster to use the WRITE# statement to write data to a sequential file.

General Form: *line number* WRITE# *file number,variable name(s)*

Example: 70 WRITE#1,STUDENT$;SSN$

The file number is the number of the opened file. The variables may be separated by either commas or semicolons. The WRITE# statement automatically inserts commas between items as they are written to disk and puts strings inside quotation marks. A return character is inserted after the last item when the list is written. Because of the commas and quotation marks, files created with WRITE# are slightly longer than those created with PRINT#.

Reading a Sequential File

When a file has been opened for input, either the **INPUT#** or **LINE INPUT#** statement may be used to read information from the disk into variables. The number of the open file is written after the keyword INPUT#. The number tells the computer to get the information from the referenced file rather than from the keyboard.

General Form: *line number* INPUT# *file number,variable name(s)*

Example: 170 INPUT#1,STUDENT$,SSN$

Checking for the End of the File

If the exact number of records in a file is known, you can create a loop to read the file that many times. Since you usually do not know the number, the program must be written to detect when the end of the file is reached. This is done with the EOF function. The EOF (End Of File) function may be used with either an IF . . . THEN statement or a WHILE . . . WEND loop.

General Form: *line number* IF EOF*(file number)* THEN *action*

Example: 140 IF EOF(1) THEN 210

or

General Form: *line number* WHILE NOT EOF*(file number)*

Example: 140 WHILE NOT EOF(1)

The EOF function will automatically be true or false, depending on whether the end of the file has been reached on the specified file. When using a WHILE . . . WEND loop, as long as the end of the file function is not true, the statements between the WHILE . . . WEND will be executed. When using any other kind of loop, the EOF function should be checked with an IF . . . THEN immediately before each input from a file.

Closing the File

Files should be closed as quickly as possible after processing all of the data. This will help protect the file from such disasters as power failures and possibly avoid the destruction of the data. Using CLOSE without a file number closes all files that are open.

General Form: *line number* CLOSE # *file number*

Example: 300 CLOSE#1

In all of the file processing statements, you may use variables for file names and numbers. For example:

```
20 A$="STUDENT.FIL"
30 OPEN "A$" FOR OUTPUT AS #1
```

The following example program will get information from the keyboard and write the information to the disk. Note that this program follows the documentation from Figure 4.4.

Example 1:

```
10 ' EXC4E1
20 ' CLARK AND LABARRE--CHAPTER 4, EXAMPLE 1
30 ' INPUTS INFORMATION FROM THE KEYBOARD
40 ' AND STORES IT IN A SEQUENTIAL FILE
50 OPEN "O",1,"STUDENT.FIL"
60 CLS
70 INPUT "Please enter the number of students";X
80 FOR N=1 TO X
90      INPUT "Student's name";STUDENT$
100     INPUT "Social security number";SSN$
110     PRINT
120     PRINT
130     INPUT "Is this information correct? (Y/N)";ANSWER$
140     IF ANSWER$="N" THEN GOTO 90
150     WRITE#1,STUDENT$,SSN$
160 NEXT N
170 CLOSE#1
999 END
```

The following example program will read the data from the disk file and print the results. Review the documentation in Figure 4.5 as you study this program.

Example 2:

```
10 ' EXC4E2
20 ' CLARK AND LABARRE--CHAPTER 4, EXAMPLE 2
30 ' READS FROM A SEQUENTIAL FILE AND PRINTS RESULTS
40 OPEN "I",1,"STUDENT.FIL"
50 CLS
60 PRINT TAB(8);"STUDENTS ENROLLED IN CLASS"
70 PRINT "NAME";TAB(29);"SS NUMBER"
80 PRINT
90   WHILE NOT EOF(1)
100     INPUT#1,STUDENT$,SSN$
110     PRINT STUDENT$;TAB(29);SSN$
120 WEND
130 CLOSE#1
999 END
```

Output:

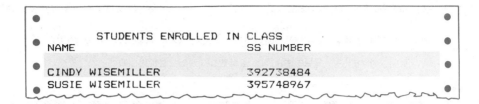

```
          STUDENTS ENROLLED IN CLASS
NAME                          SS NUMBER

CINDY WISEMILLER              392738484
SUSIE WISEMILLER              395748967
```

APPLE

All statements controlling the use of data files on the Apple use PRINT. This keyword is used in opening, writing, reading, or closing the file. The computer must be told that the PRINT statements are directed to the disk system. To do this, the first character printed on a line must be a Control-D character. You may assign this character to a variable to assist in file handling. Here is an example of how it is done: 50 D$=CHR$(4). The ASCII 4 is a Control-D character. By using the CHR$ function we are able to convert it to a string and store it in variable D$. When printing the D$ for disk operations, never end the previous PRINT statement with a semicolon. The Control-D is not recognized unless it is the first character printed following a return character. All of the following illustrations assume the D$ has been given the value of Control-D.

Opening the File

When the OPEN statement is used, the file pointer is placed at the beginning of the file. From this point, the file may be either written or read, depending on the file command given after the OPEN. It may not be both written and read following the OPEN statement.

General Form: *line number* PRINT D$;"OPEN *file name*"

Example: 30 PRINT D$;"OPEN STUDENT"

Deleting Old Data

If you are using a file name that has been previously used, you should delete the old file before recreating the new data file. The DELETE statement is used to delete an existing file. You must open, delete, and then reopen the file.

General Form: *line number* PRINT. D$;"DELETE *file name*"

Example: 80 PRINT D$;"DELETE STUDENT"

The proper sequence for deleting an existing file and reusing its name for output is given in this example:

```
70 PRINT D$;"OPEN STUDENT"
80 PRINT D$;"DELETE STUDENT"
90 PRINT D$;"OPEN STUDENT"
```

Adding Data to a Sequential File

If a file has already been created and you want to add information to the existing file, you must use the APPEND rather than the OPEN statement.

General Form: *line number* PRINT D$;"APPEND *file name*"

Example: 100 PRINT D$;"APPEND STUDENT"

Writing to a Sequential File

Once a file is opened on the Apple, the **WRITE** statement is used to tell the computer that data is being written to the disk.

General Form: line number PRINT D$;"WRITE file name"

Example: 150 PRINT D$;"WRITE STUDENT"

After the WRITE statement has been executed, all PRINT statements will send their output to the file on disk rather than to the screen. When printing to a disk file, print only one value with each print statement to ensure that a return is printed to the disk after each item to separate it from the following item. For example, use PRINT X$:PRINT Y$ rather than PRINT X$,Y$.

Output will continue to be written on disk until you cause the computer to print another Control-D character. The easy way to do this is to print variable D$, which had the character assigned to it earlier. The following example illustrates the command to return the printing to the screen: 200 PRINT D$.

Generally, the printing of the Control-D and the WRITE will occur many times while the file is open. When getting data from the keyboard, the sequence will basically be (1) print the prompt for data and input the data, (2) print the WRITE, (3) print the data to disk, and (4) print Control-D to return print to the screen for the next prompt.

Reading a Sequential File

To read data from a file, the READ statement is used. This READ is different from the one used with DATA lines.

General Form: *line number* PRINT D$;"READ *file name*"

Example: `80 PRINT D$;"READ STUDENT"`

Upon execution of the READ statement, the input will come from the disk rather than from the keyboard. The INPUT statement is then used to input information just as it has been used in the past. If the inputted information is to be printed on the screen, a Control-D must be printed before attempting to print the data. Another READ statement must then be printed to get the next data from the disk. This cycle must continue until all data is read and printed.

Checking for the End of the File

If the exact number of records in the file is known, you can set up a loop to handle that many inputs of data. Since this is not usually the case, you must write the code to detect when the end of the file is reached. On the Apple this is done with the ONERR GOTO statement.

General Form: *line number* ONERR GOTO *line number*

Example: `90 ONERR GOTO 250`

The ONERR GOTO statement may be placed anywhere in the program before beginning the read of the file. When the end of the file is reached, the program will branch to the number following the GOTO. At that number should be a statement to close the file. This check is for general purposes and will cause a branch to that location regardless of the error encountered. If you want to check to ensure that the end of the file has been reached rather than some other error, the PEEK function may be used.

General Form: *line number number variable =PEEK(memory location)*

Example: 160 E=PEEK(222)

The PEEK allows you to determine what value is stored in a given memory location. Memory location 222 is the location where Apple stores the error code. By assigning the value of the error location to a variable, we are able to use the IF . . . THEN to determine if it contains a 5, which indicates that the end of the file has been reached.

Closing the File

The file should be closed as quickly as possible after using it. The file is closed with the CLOSE statement.

General Form: *line number* PRINT D$;"CLOSE *file name"*

Example: 190 PRINT D$;"CLOSE STUDENT"

To facilitate programming, the file name may be assigned to a string variable. The string variable may be used with the OPEN, WRITE, READ, and CLOSE statements. The following example illustrates the use of the variable:

Example:
```
80 F$="STUDENT"
90 PRINT D$;"OPEN ";F$
```

The first program of two examples inputs information from the keyboard and writes it to the disk file. This program follows the documentation from Figure 4.4.

Example 1:

```
10 REM EXC4E3
20 REM CLARK AND LABARRE--CHAPTER 4, EXAMPLE 3
30 REM INPUTS INFORMATION FROM THE KEYBOARD
40 REM THEN WRITES TO DISK FILE
50 D$=CHR$(4)
60 PRINT D$;"OPEN STUDENT"
70 HOME
80 INPUT "PLEASE ENTER THE NUMBER OF STUDENTS ";X
90  FOR N=1 TO X
100    INPUT "STUDENT'S NAME? ";STUDENT$
110    INPUT "SOCIAL SECURITY NUMBER? ";SSN$
120    PRINT
130    PRINT
140    INPUT "IS THIS INFORMATION CORRECT? (Y/N) ";ANSWER$
150    IF ANSWER$="N" THEN GOTO 100
160    PRINT D$;"WRITE STUDENT"
170    PRINT STUDENT$:PRINT SSN$
180    PRINT D$
190 NEXT N
200 PRINT D$;"CLOSE STUDENT"
999 END
```

The second program of the two examples illustrates the input of information from the disk file and prints it to the screen. It follows the documentation from Figure 4.5.

Example 2:

```
20 REM EXC4E4
30 REM CLARK AND LABARRE--CHAPTER 4, EXAMPLE 4
40 REM INPUTS FROM DISK AND PRINTS TO SCREEN
50 D$=CHR$(4)
60 ONERR GOTO 170
70 PRINT D$;"OPEN STUDENT"
80 HOME
90 PRINT TAB(8)"STUDENTS ENROLLED IN CLASS"
100 PRINT "NAME";TAB(29)"SS NUMBER"
110 PRINT
120 PRINT D$;"READ STUDENT"
130 INPUT STUDENT$,SSN$
140 PRINT D$
150 PRINT STUDENT$;TAB(29)SSN$
160 GOTO 120
170 PRINT D$;"CLOSE STUDENT"
999 END
```

COMMODORE

Several new statements are used to process sequential files on the Commodore. These statements are discussed fully in the following paragraphs.

Opening the File

The OPEN statement is used to open a file for either input or output.

General Form: *line number OPEN file number,device
number,channel number,"drive number: file
name,file type,read with command"*

Example: 50 OPEN 1,8,3,"0:STUDENT,S,W"

The number following the OPEN is the number by which the file will be addressed in later PRINT statements. Generally, the number 1 will be used unless you have more than one file open, in which case you could use 1 for the first file, 2 for the second, and 3 for the third. The device number will usually be 8. The channel number is a number used in setting up the hardware and may be any number from 2 through 14. The drive number and file name identifies the file. The S and W at the end of the statement tells the computer that a sequential file is to be written. To read a file, the W is replaced with an R. When the file is opened for writing, data previously written to the file will be erased and new information will be written beginning at the start of the file.

Writing to a Sequential File

After the file has been opened for writing, the PRINT# statement is used to write data to the disk.

General Form: *line number PRINT# file number,variable*

Example: 100 PRINT#1,A$

The PRINT# is followed by a number that identifies the file which has been previously opened. This statement tells the computer to write the data to the file identified.

When writing to disk, write only one value with each print statement. This will ensure that a return is written after each item on disk. This will also permit you to access each of the data items later when the file is inputted. For example, use PRINT X: PRINT Y rather than PRINT X,Y.

Reading a Sequential File

After a file is opened for reading, the INPUT# statement is used to input information from the disk into variables. As with PRINT#, the file number is identified after the keyword INPUT#. The number references the file on disk that has been previously opened.

General Form: *line number* INPUT# *file number,variable name(s)*

Example: 150 INPUT#1,X,Y

Checking for the End of the File

If the number of items stored in the file is known, you can set up a loop to read the exact number. However, since this is rarely the case, you must usually write the code to detect when the end of the file is reached. On the Commodore this is done with the STATUS variable and the IF...THEN statement.

General Form: *line number* IF STATUS=64 THEN *action*

Example: 90 IF STATUS=64 THEN 170

STATUS is a special variable that is automatically set up by the computer. When the end of the file is reached, the value stored in STATUS will be 64. The IF...THEN statement may be used to examine the STATUS variable to determine if it is equal to 64. If it is equal to 64, a branch is made to the statement to close the file. The examination of the STATUS variable should be within the loop inputting data from the disk. It should appear after each input statement from the file.

Closing the File

A file should be closed as soon as possible after its use. It is closed on the Commodore with the CLOSE statement.

General Form: *line number* CLOSE *file number*

Example: 280 CLOSE 1

The first of two example programs obtains information inputted from the keyboard and writes it to disk. Refer to the documentation in Figure 4.4 as you study the program.

Example 1:

```
10 REM EXC4E5
20 REM CLARK AND LABARRE--CHAPTER 4, EXAMPLE 5
30 REM INPUTS FROM THE KEYBOARD AND WRITES TO DISK
40 OPEN 1,8,3,"0:STUDENT,S,W"
50 PRINT "⊐";:REM "SHIFT CLR-HOME"
60 INPUT "ENTER THE NUMBER OF STUDENTS";X
70 FOR N=1 TO X
80 PRINT "STUDENT'S NAME";
90 INPUT S$
100 PRINT "SOCIAL SECURITY NUMBER";
110 INPUT SSN$
120 PRINT
130 PRINT
140 INPUT "IS THIS INFORMATION CORRECT? (Y/N)";ANS$
150 IF ANS$="N" THEN GOTO 80
160 R$=CHR$(44):REM A COMMA SEPARATES THE FIELDS ON DISK
170 PRINT#1,S$;R$;SSN$
180 NEXT N
190 CLOSE 1
999 END
```

The second example program inputs information from the disk and prints it on the screen. Refer to the documentation in Figure 4.5 as you study this program.

Example 2:

```
10 REM EXC4E6
20 REM CLARK AND LABARRE--CHAPTER 4, EXAMPLE 6
30 REM INPUTS FROM DISK AND PRINTS ON SCREEN
40 OPEN 1,8,3,"0:STUDENT,S,R"
50 PRINT "⊐";:REM "SHIFT CLR-HOME"
60 PRINT TAB(7)"STUDENTS ENROLLED IN CLASS"
70 PRINT "NAME";SPC(24)"SS NUMBER"
80 PRINT
90 INPUT#1,S$,SSN$
100 PRINT S$;SPC(20-LEN(S$))SSN$
110 IF STATUS=64 THEN 130
120 GOTO 90
130 CLOSE 1
999 END
```

IMPLEMENTING RANDOM FILES

IBM AND TRS-80

Random file operations on the IBM and TRS-80 require the use of several new keywords. These keywords make up the statements that allow for the reading and writing of records to disk. The steps involved in creating and accessing random files are more complex, but they are offset by the convenience of reading any record stored on disk without reading all of the preceding records. With the most sophisticated form of random file (the one discussed here), numbers are stored in a "shrunken" form. Therefore, in many cases a random file will consume less space than a comparable sequential file.

Determining Record Length

Before first using a random file, you must decide the length of the records to be stored. To determine the length of the record to be used for a file, you must decide how long each of the fields of data will be, then add their lengths together. When records are stored in a random file, it is not necessary to have a return character or space between fields. Therefore, you first count the number of characters in each field and add them together to get the length of the record. Remember, always count the longest item likely to be stored in a field as the length of that particular field. However, if only an occasional item may be longer than the rest, consider abbreviating those long items to conserve disk space. Table 4.1 illustrates the processing, using data for a simple program.

Variable Used	Variable Meaning and Length
NAM$	Name of student - maximum length is 20
SS$	Social Security Number - maximum length is 9

Table 4.1   Example of Variables Used with a Random File

Using the numbers from Table 4.1, we assume that no name will exceed 20 characters. The social security number will be entered without the hyphens, so it will be 9 characters long. We add up the two field lengths to find that the record length is going to be 29 characters.

To use a random file, you must open the file, then use the FIELD statement to assign memory space to the random file buffer. The random file buffer is a series of memory locations that the data is temporarily placed in on its way to or from the disk. To write data to a random file, the program places data in the buffer, then writes the contents of the buffer to disk. When reading data, the program gives a command to read a record, whose contents are placed in the buffer. From the buffer, the data is available for use by the program.

Opening and Closing the File

Opening a random file is similar to opening a sequential file. Closing the file is identical to closing a sequential file. The **OPEN** statement may be used to open a random file.

General Form: *line number* OPEN *"file name"* AS *#file number*
              LEN = *record length*

Example: 40 OPEN "STUDENT" AS #1 LEN=29

An alternate method of opening a file (required on the TRS-80 Models III and 4) is shown in the following example. The mode must be specified as R to designate that the file is being opened as a random file.

Example:

    40 OPEN "R",1,"STUDENT",29

Fielding a Random File

After a random file is opened, its buffer (which is created by the OPEN statement) must be fielded. That is, variable names must be assigned to it. The variables to be used with the buffer are identified using the FIELD statement.

General Form: *line number* FIELD# *file number, number* AS
              character variable

Example: 50 FIELD #1,20 AS BNAM$,9 AS BSS$

The field statement must contain unique character variable names. For example, the variables used with the FIELD statement cannot have the same names as the variables used to input data from the keyboard. It is a good idea to give buffer variables those names related to their functions. For example, BNAM$ (short for BUFFERNAME) might represent a student's name, BSS$ (short for BUFFER SOCIAL SECURITY) might represent a student's social security number in the buffer. Before data may be written to the disk, it must be placed in the variables identified for the buffer. When you get information from the disk, it is automatically placed in the buffer. Then you may use it from the buffer or assign it to another variable. The following example illustrates the OPEN and FIELD statements for the example program.

Example:

```
110 OPEN "R",1,"STUDENT",29
120 FIELD #1,20 AS BNAM$,9 AS BSS$
```

Writing to a Random File

After opening a file as random and describing the buffer, you are ready to place data to the buffer fields. The keyword **LSET** is used to place data into the buffered fields.

General Form: *line number* LSET *buffer field variable name = variable name*

Example: `180 LSET BNAM$=NAM$`

LSET places characters in the buffer field starting at the left. Blanks are placed in the remaining spaces if the data is shorter than the length of the field. Data may also be placed in the buffer field using the **RSET** keyword. If RSET is used, the data is right justified and blanks are placed in the spaces to the left of the data if it is shorter than the field length. Since all data must be stored in the buffer as string variables, the LSET keyword is generally used. The following example illustrates that portion of the program when data is placed in the buffer.

Example:

```
360 LSET BNAM$=NAM$
370 LSET BSS$=SS$
```

After placing all data in the buffer, the contents of the buffer may be written to the disk. The entire record stored in the buffer is written with the PUT# statement.

General Form: *line number* PUT # *file number,record number*

Example: 430 PUT#1,RECORD.NO

The record number tells the computer where to place the record in relationship to the positions in the file. Records in a random file are stored in their relative position. In other words, record number one is stored in the first record position, record number two is stored in the second position, record number 10 is stored in the tenth position, and record number 29 is stored in the 29th position. If no record number is specified, the record will be written to the position following the previously accessed record. If this were the first record and no other records had been accessed, it would be written in record number one if you did not specify a record number.

Identifying the record number is the responsibility of the programmer. Three of the possible ways of doing this are:

1. The records can be written to a random file in sequential order (for example, record 1, record 2, and so on).
2. You may input a record number from the keyboard. The first student could be given the number 1, the second student gets the number 2, and so on.
3. The last method is for the program to calculate a record number. In Chapter 10 the concepts of calculating record numbers will be discussed in more detail.

The following example illustrates the inputting of the record number prior to the writing of the record on disk.

Example:

```
2000 INPUT "NAME OF STUDENT";NAM$
2010 INPUT "SOCIAL SECURITY NUMBER";SS$
2020 INPUT "RECORD NUMBER";RECORD.NO
2030 LSET BNAM$=NAM$
2040 LSET BSS$=SS$
2050 PUT#1,RECORD.NO
```

In order to read the record written to a random file in the previous example, you must remember what the record number was for the record you wish to access. As an alternate, you may read all of the records in sequential order.

Reading a Random File

Reading a random file is the reverse of writing it. First the data is read from the disk into the buffer with the keyword GET #

General Form: *line number* GET #*file number,record number*

Example: 300 GET#1,RECORD.NO

When the GET is executed, the computer reads the given record number to retrieve the data and place it in the buffer. Once the data is in the buffer, it may be addressed by the variable name given to it in the field statement. The variable name used in the field statement may be used with statements such as the PRINT BNAM$ or LET NAM$ = BNAM$. It may not be used to the left of the equal sign in a LET statement. The following example illustrates getting data from a random file.

Example:

```
4010 OPEN "R",1,"STUDENT",29
4020 FIELD #1,20 AS BNAM$,9 AS BSS$
4030 INPUT "ENTER RECORD NUMBER";RECORD.NO
4040 GET#1,RECORD.NO
4050 PRINT BNAM$,BSS$,
```

Storing Numeric Data in Random Files

Numeric data must be made into string data before writing it to random files. To do this, you use the "make" functions. Depending on the data, it may be stored as integer, single precision, or double precision. The "make" function is used as the numeric data is LSET to the buffer. This function causes the number to be compressed to fit into less disk space. The three options available use the keywords MKI$, MKS$, and MKD$. The MKI$ means MaKe Integer, the MKS$ means MaKe Single precision, and the MKD$ means MaKe Double precision.

General Form: *line number* LSET *buffer field* =MKI$*(number)* or MKS$*(number)* or MKD$*(number)*

Example: 200 LSET NUM$=MKS$(X)

Any number must be made into a string variable using one of the three "make" functions prior to setting it to the buffer. Which "make" function to use depends on the kind of number being stored. If the number is in an integer variable, the MKI$ function is used. For single precision variables (including all those not defined as a particular type), use MKS$. For long numbers stored in double precision variables, use MKD$. When storing numbers, you must use the proper number of characters in the field statement. If storing an integer number with the MKI$ function, be sure to set up the field length as 2. A MKS$ needs a field length of 4, and a MKD$ requires a field length of 8.

Once numbers have been stored in a random file and you wish to retrieve them, they must be converted back to numeric form from the buffer. This is accomplished by using one of three "convert" functions. The purpose of the "convert" functions is to change the contents of the buffer (string variables) back to numeric. If the number was stored using the MKI$, it must be converted back using the **CVI** function. If the number was stored using the MKS$, it must be converted back using the **CVS** function. Likewise, the number stored with MKD$ must be converted using the **CVD** function. The following example illustrates the general form of the statement.

General Form: *line number numeric variable =CVI(buffer variable) or CVS(buffer variable) or CVD(buffer variable)*

Example: `1600 LET NUMBER=CVS(NUM$)`

When a number is uncompressed, it is usually assigned to a variable. However, it may be printed directly or used in a computation if desired.

Checking for End of File

The **LOF** (length of file) function gives the number size of a random file. For files created under version 2.x of IBM BASIC, LOF gives the actual number of characters in the file. For files created by IBM BASIC 1.x, LOF will return a multiple of 128. For example, if the actual data in the file is 180 characters, the number 256 (128 x 2 = 256) is returned. With the TRS-80, LOF returns the record number of the last record in the file.

General Form: *line number numeric variable =LOF(file number)*

Example: `60 FILESIZE=LOF(1)`

On the IBM, the number returned by LOF may be divided by the record length to determine how many records have been written to the file. Study the following example:

Example:

```
150 OPEN "DATAFILE" AS #1, LEN=29
160 GET #1, LOF(1)/29    ' (Would get the last record)
```

The example would access the last record in the file. Note that this method will not work accurately in version 1.x of IBM BASIC. Therefore, it is recommended that you not rely on it if you are using this version of BASIC.

The following example illustrates the entering of data from the keyboard and writing it to a random file. The example also illustrates the reading of data from the disk and writing the information on the screen.

Example:

```
10 ' FXC4E7
20 ' CLARK AND LABARRE--CHAPTER 4, EXAMPLE 7
30 ' THIS PROGRAM WILL CREATE A RANDOM FILE
40 ' AND ALLOWS THE ACCESS OF RECORDS STORED
50 UNFINISHED$="Y"
60 INCORRECT$="N"
70 ANSWER$="Y"
80 OPEN "R",1,"STUDENT",29
90 FIELD #1,20 AS ST$,9 AS SS$
100 ' ***** MAIN MODULE ***************
110 CLS
120 PRINT "          MENU"
130 PRINT
140 PRINT "<1> ENTER A RECORD"
150 PRINT
160 PRINT "<2> ACCESS A RECORD"
170 PRINT
180 PRINT "<3> END PROCESSING"
190 INPUT CHOICE
200 IF CHOICE=1 THEN GOSUB 1000
210 IF CHOICE=2 THEN GOSUB 2000
220 IF CHOICE=3 THEN 240
230 GOTO 110
240 CLOSE#1
999 END
1000 ' ***** ADD A RECORD TO THE FILE *
1010 ANSWER$="Y"
1020 WHILE ANSWER$=UNFINISHED$
1030     CLS:PRINT "ENTER RECORD NUMBER"
1040     INPUT RECORD.NO%
1050     PRINT
1060     PRINT TAB(6)"STUDENT";RECORD.NO%;" GRADE INFORMATION"
1070     PRINT
1080     PRINT
1090     PRINT "STUDENT'S NAME"
1100     INPUT "  (MAX. 20 LETTERS)  ";STUDENT$
1110     PRINT
1120     PRINT "SOCIAL SECURITY NUMBER"
1130     INPUT "  (MAX. 9 NUMBERS)   ";SSN$
1140     PRINT
1150     PRINT
1160     INPUT "IS THIS INFORMATION CORRECT (Y/N)  ";ANSWER$
1170     ANSWER$=LEFT$(ANSWER$,1)
```

Continued

```
1180    IF ANSWER$=INCORRECT$ THEN 1020
1190    LSET ST$=STUDENT$
1200    LSET SS$=SSN$
1210    PUT#1, RECORD.NO%
1220    PRINT
1230    INPUT "DO YOU WISH TO ENTER ANOTHER STUDENT (Y/N)   ";ANSWER$
1240    ANSWER$=LEFT$(ANSWER$,1)
1250 WEND
1999 RETURN
2000 ' ***** ACCESS A RECORD **********
2010 GOSUB 3000     ' INPUT RECORD NUMBER
2020 GOSUB 4000     ' READ STUDENT RECORD FROM DISK
2030 GOSUB 5000     ' PRINT STUDENT INFORMATION
2040 INPUT "WOULD YOU LIKE TO ACCESS ANOTHER (Y/N)   ";N$
2050 IF N$="N" THEN 2999 ELSE 2010
2999 RETURN
3000 ' ***** ENTER THE RECORD NUMBER **
3010 PRINT
3020 CLS
3030 INPUT "          ENTER THE RECORD NUMBER";RECORD.NO%
3999 RETURN
4000 ' ***** INPUT STUDENT RECORD FROM DISK
4010 GET#1,RECORD.NO%
4999 RETURN
5000 ' ***** PRINT STUDENT REPORT *****
5010 CLS
5020 PRINT TAB(23);"STUDENT INFORMATION REPORT"
5030 PRINT
5040 PRINT TAB(8);"STUDENT NAME";SPC(7);"SOC SEC NUMBER"
5050 PRINT
5060 PRINT TAB(4);ST$;
5070 PRINT SPC(6);SS$
5080 PRINT:PRINT:PRINT
5999 RETURN
```

APPLE

Random file operations on the Apple are adaptations of those used for sequential files. Each of the following paragraphs will explain the differences.

Opening and Closing the File

The basic differences between opening a sequential file and a random file on the Apple is the addition of the length (L) option. The record length must be determined and the number must follow the file name when opened. Study the following example:

Example:
```
50 D$=CHR$(4)
60 PRINT D$;"OPEN STUDENT,L31"
```

In deciding the record length, you must look at the data to be entered into each of the variables and decide what will be the longest item for each. Then the length of the fields will be added together. When each field is stored on diskette, it must be separated from other fields with a return. Therefore, one return character must be added for each field. Study the following example to determine the length of the record.

Variable Used	Length	Comments
NAM$	20 characters	Assume the longest name to be 20 characters
SS$	9 characters	Assume a social security number without hyphens

Table 4.2   Record Length

The numbers (20 and 9) are added together to give 29. We add 2 for the return character after each field to arrive at a length of 31. This is the number given as the length when the file is opened. Closing random files on the Apple is identical to the closing of a sequential file.

Writing to a Random File

After a random file is opened on the Apple, records may be written to it. The WRITE statement is used to tell the computer to write a record to the disk. The WRITE statement is used in the same manner as it was used in writing to sequential files. The only difference is the addition of a record number. The following example illustrates the statement as it is used with random files.

```
500 PRINT D$;"WRITE STUDENT,R";RECNBR$
```

The R identifies that it is a record and RECNBR$ is the actual number of the record. The statement could also be written using catenation as follows:

```
500 PRINT D$;"WRITE STUDENT,R"+RECNBR$
```

Note that record numbers are given as character data. When the WRITE statement is executed, the disk drive is positioned to write to the proper location on the disk. PRINT statements are used to record the data on the disk. After all of the variables are written to disk, the Control-D character must be printed to return printing to the screen. On page 132 is an example of the inputting and writing of data to the disk.

Example:
```
2000 INPUT "NAME OF STUDENT ";NAM$
2010 INPUT "SOCIAL SECURITY NUMBER ";SS$
2020 INPUT "RECORD NUMBER ";RECNBR$
2030 PRINT D$;"WRITE STUDENT,R"+RECNBR$
2040 PRINT NAM$:PRINT SS$
2050 PRINT D$
```

Identifying the record number is your responsibility. Three of the possible ways of doing this are:

1. The records can be written in sequential order. A counter can be incremented each time a record is written (for example, record 1, record 2, and so on).
2. The record number may be inputted from the keyboard.
3. The third method is to have the program calculate the record number.

Calculation of record numbers will be explained in detail in Chapter 10.

Reading a Random File

The READ statement is used to tell the Apple that data is to be inputted from the disk. The statement is used in the same manner as it was used with sequential files. The exception is that the record number is added to the statement. The following statement illustrates the use of the READ statement:

Example:
```
1000 PRINT D$;"READ STUDENT,R";RECNBR$
```

When the READ statement is executed, it positions the disk drive at the location for the specified record number. The INPUT statement is used to read data from the disk. The Control-D character must be printed after information has been inputted if control is to return to the screen or the keyboard. The following example illustrates the input of data from the disk on the Apple.

Example:
```
4000 INPUT "ENTER RECORD NUMBER TO READ ";RECNBR$
4010 PRINT D$;"READ STUDENT,R";RECNBR$
4020 INPUT NAM$,SS$
4030 PRINT D$
4040 PRINT NAM$,SS$
```

COMMODORE

Random file operations on the Commodore are adaptations of those used for sequential files. The following paragraphs will explain the differences.

Opening and Closing the File

The basic differences between opening a sequential file and a random file on the Commodore are the addition of a command channel and the use of the length (L) option. The record length must be determined and the number of characters in the record must be identified when the file is opened. Study the following example:

```
50 OPEN 15,8,15
60 OPEN 1,8,2,"0:STUDENT,L,"+CHR$(42)
```

Data stored in the random file on the Commodore requires a delimiter between data fields and at the end of the record. Therefore, as you look at the data to be entered into each of the variables and decide what the longest item for each will be, then you must add on a comma for each of the fields and a return for the end of the record. Adding them together gives the record length. Study the following example:

Variable Used	Length	Comments
NAM$	20 characters	Assume the longest name to be 20 characters
SS$	9 characters	Enter it without hyphens

Table 4.3   Record Lengths

The numbers (20 + 1 and 9 + 1) are added together to give 31. We therefore open the file with a record length of 31. Closing a random file on the Commodore is identical to closing a sequential file.

Writing to a Random File

After a random file on the Commodore is opened, it is ready to have records written to it. The PRINT statement is used to write data to the disk. Prior to writing data to the file, you must identify which record is to be written. A PRINT statement to the command channel sets the record number.

General Form: *line number* PRINT #*file number,* "P"*CHR$ (channel number + 96); CHR$(low record); CHR$ (high record); CHR$ (position in record)*

Example:
```
480 INPUT RN$:RN=VAL(RN$)
490 HI=INT(RN/256):LO=RN-HI*256
500 PRINT#15, "P"CHR$(2+96);CHR$(LO);CHR$(HI);CHR$(1)
```

The high record should be 0 until the low record reaches 255. At that time, the high record should be changed to 1 and the low record should start over at 0. The execution of this will position the disk drive in the proper place for data to be written to the disk. After positioning the drive, write the data. The following example illustrates the writing of data to the diskette.

Example:

```
2000 INPUT "NAME OF STUDENT";NAM$
2010 INPUT "SOCIAL SECURITY NUMBER";SS$
2020 INPUT "RECORD NUMBER";RN$
2030 RN=VAL(RN$)
2040 HI=INT(RN/256):LO=RN-HI*256
2050 PRINT#15,"P"CHR$(2+96);CHR$(LO);CHR$(HI);CHR$(1)
2060 PRINT#1,NAM$;CHR$(44);SS$
```

Identifying the record number is your responsibility. Three of the possible ways of doing this are:

1. The records may be written in sequential order. A counter can be incremented each time a record is written (for example, record 1, record 2, and so on.
2. You may enter the record number from the keyboard.
3. The record number may be calculated by the program. Calculation of record numbers will be explained in detail in Chapter 10.

Reading a Random File

The INPUT# statement is used to read data from a random file on the Commodore as it was used to read from a sequential file. The PRINT to the command channel is used to position the disk drive prior to reading data from the file. The following example illustrates the use of these statements to read data.

Example:

```
2000 PRINT#15,"P";CHR$(2+96);CHR$(LO);CHR$(HI);CHR$(1)
2010 INPUT#1,NAM$,SS$
```

The following example illustrates the accessing of a random file on the Commodore.

```
4000 INPUT "ENTER RECORD NUMBER TO READ";RN$
4010 RN=VAL(RN$)
4020 HI=INT(RN/256):LO=RN-HI*256
4030 PRINT#15,"P";CHR$(2+96);CHR$(LO);CHR$(HI);CHR$(1)
4040 INPUT#1,NAM$,SS$
4050 PRINT NAM$,SS$
```

REVIEW QUESTIONS

1. Identify the differences between opening a sequential file and opening a random file. (Obj. 2)
2. Identify the differences between writing to a sequential file and writing to a random file. (Objs. 2, 5)
3. Identify how the computer understands which record should be written or read on a sequential file and on a random file. (Objs. 2, 5)
4. Identify the differences between reading a sequential file and a random file. (Objs. 3, 6)
5. Explain how the record length is determined. Why is it necessary to know the length for random files? (Obj. 7)
6. What are delimiter characters and how are they used between fields for a random file if they are necessary? (Obj. 7)
7. Describe the difference, if any, in closing a sequential and random file. (Objs. 3, 6)
8. Explain how the end of file may be determined when processing a sequential file. (Obj. 4)
9. Explain how data in an existing file may be deleted prior to writing new data. (Obj. 4)
10. Explain three ways of determining the record number in a random file. (Obj. 8)

VOCABULARY WORDS

The following terms were introduced in this chapter:

file	sector	pointer
record	sequential file	random data files
field	sequential processing	buffer
tracks		

KEYWORDS AND COMMANDS

The following keywords and commands were introduced in this chapter:

For Apple:

OPEN	WRITE	PEEK
DELETE	READ	CLOSE
APPEND	ONERR GOTO	

For Commodore:

| OPEN | INPUT# | CLOSE |
| PRINT# | STATUS | |

For IBM and TRS-80:

OPEN	EOF	MKS$
OUTPUT	CLOSE	MKD$
INPUT	OPEN...AS	CVI
APPEND	LSET	CVS
PRINT#	RSET	CVD
WRITE#	PUT#	LOF
INPUT#	GET#	
LINE INPUT#	MKI$	

PROGRAMS TO WRITE

Complete the appropriate documentation for each of the programs before writing the code.

Program 1

Write a program to create a sequential file of the inventory items for a sporting goods store. The file should contain fields for a stock number, product description, quantity on hand, and unit cost. The program should provide the user the opportunity to input the inventory items from the keyboard. Make sure that you prompt the user prior to entry of data items. Use the following data.

```
3364D Men's Light Hiking Boots 103 $68.75
3435D Wilderness Oxford         141  32.75
4812D Women's Camp Moccasin      78  32.75
3121D Hunting Shoe               45  46.00
8771F Duffle Bag                241  14.50
6474F Canoe Chair                23  16.00
6467F Life Vest                  89  39.50
```

Continued

```
5142F Backpack                     233  13.75
8361K Universal Bike Rack          781  25.00
5725K Sleeping Bag                 121  92.00
5859K Camper Mattress               86  35.00
7472K Comforter                     78  60.00
8789K Cargo Duffle Bag              37  26.00
8758K Camera Bag                   276  25.60
8822K Mini Camera Bag              123  16.75
```

Program 2

Write a program to access the sequential file created by Program 1 and print a report. Use a title and appropriate column headings. As the detail lines are written, you should multiply the quantity by the unit cost to determine the value of each item in inventory. Also, add each total to an accumulator so that you may print the total value of the inventory at the end of the report.

Program 3

Modify Program 1 to store the data in a random file. As the programmer, you are to provide the record numbers by creating a counter to increment each time a record is written. Use the same data as Program 1.

Program 4

Modify Program 2 to access the random file for the data and print a report with the same information. Remember to use the same technique in arriving at the record number you used when the file was created.

Program 5

Your boss has asked you to write a program that would place the store inventory records on a file. Your boss would like to be able to add records to the file at any time and also would like the ability to look at the contents of a record at any time. Using the random file organization, write a program for the menu driven system which will allow your boss to do these activities. The record layout is given following this program. You are to use the item number as the record number when writing the data to a random file.

```
10 Apple Cat II Modem $589.99
06 Amdek 300 Amber    $299.00
21 FX-80 Epson        $529.00
01 Smith Corona TP2   $449.00
04 Prowriter II       $649.00
14 Bank Street Writer $049.95
03 Hayes Smart Modem  $389.00
17 NEC PC-8200        $699.00
09 Blank Diskettes    $025.98
08 Dust Cover         $003.99
```

Program 6

As the designated convention registration chairperson, you recognize that it will be quite a task keeping track of people registering. Therefore, you have decided to write a program for convention registration. This program must allow the input of records to the attendance file at any time. Also, you must be able to access records in the file at any time. (Usually during the convention, people will want to know the room number of another participant staying at the hotel.) After registration has been completed, you must be able to print a complete listing of all participants in attendance of the convention. Develop a menu-driven system.

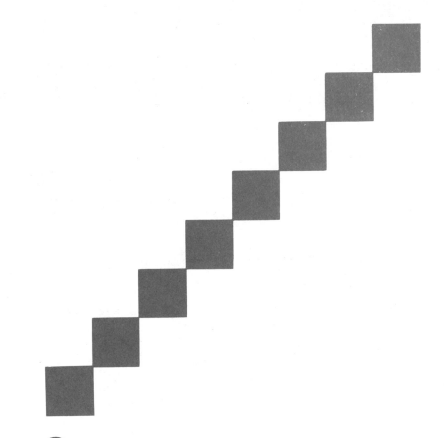

Unit 2 • User Interfacing

## Chapter 5

Display Control

Objectives: 1. Give the advantages of effective screen displays.
2. Describe the elements of effective screen displays.
3. Describe the procedures for implementing effective screen displays using the BASIC language.
4. Plan and code programs using effective screen displays.

Topic 5.1— PRINCIPLES OF EFFECTIVE SCREEN DISPLAYS

Effective screen displays are important whether the screen is just displaying output or is being used to get input. Let's take a look at some of the advantages of good displays and some of the techniques used to produce them.

THE IMPORTANCE OF EFFECTIVE SCREEN DISPLAYS

The importance of effective screen displays can be categorized into three areas that are discussed in the following paragraphs.

Greater Accuracy in Screen Displays

Displays should be arranged so that they are easy to read. This can lead to greater accuracy on the part of the person reading the display. As an example, suppose that we have a computer keeping watch on a chemical manufacturing process in which the temperature must be maintained within a normal range. We want the computer to produce a log of the temperature, with a measurement taken once each minute. The trends in the temperature should be easily visible to the operator on the line. First, look at the temperature printouts in Figure 5.1. In this figure, note that the computer simply printed one value after another. This makes the trend of temperatures very hard to follow. For example, did you become aware that the temperature exceeded it's maximum limit at 10:22? Unless you had known this already, there is no way you could have been aware of it.

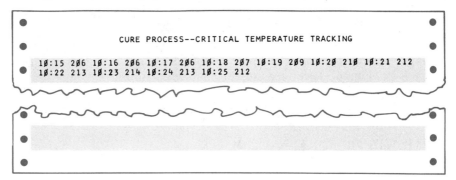

Figure 5.1   A Hard-to-Follow Display That May Lead to Errors

Now look at Figure 5.2. This time, the computer has printed a lower and an upper limit of temperatures and is plotting readings within those bounds. Notice how much easier it is to detect the temperature trends.

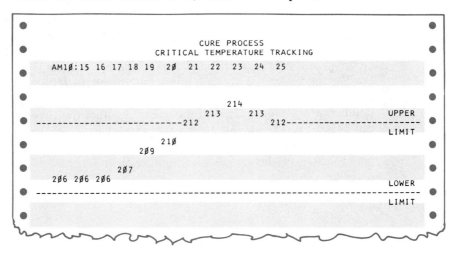

Figure 5.2   An Easy-to-Follow Display Designed to Reduce Errors

Less Fatigue With Screen Displays

Properly designed displays also lead to less fatigue on the part of the operator. If a display is hard-to-read, the operator may suffer eyestrain from trying to see what is on the screen. To reduce fatigue, displays should have adequate blank space to make reading them easy. Also, certain items may be highlighted (emphasized) in some fashion. Look back at Figure 5.2 to see how the temperatures above the maximum have been highlighted. Using colors that contrast enough but not too much is also important.

Faster Operation With Screen Displays

Easy-to-follow displays also increase the speed of operations. This can be seen by again examining Figures 5.1 and 5.2. In referring to the display in Figure 5.1, you read several times and temperatures and form a mental image of the trend that is happening. With the display in Figure 5.2, the trend is immediately visible, perhaps saving valuable seconds.

ELEMENTS OF SCREEN DISPLAYS

There are several techniques programmers can use to improve the effectiveness of displays. Among them are the use of direct cursor positioning, inverse video, and various colors.

Direct Cursor Positioning

When using the PRINT statement to place information on the screen, printing takes place in the next available space on the screen. This means that when large amounts of information are printed, each new line is printed on the bottom of the screen as the oldest line of information scrolls off the top of the screen. In contrast, direct cursor positioning enables you to place the cursor in any desired point on the screen before printing. For example, the readings in Figure 5.2 are not printed from top to bottom in the normal manner. Therefore, you would use direct cursor positioning to place the numbers in the proper place on the screen. Another time when this technique can be used is when asking the user to reenter incorrect data. As the cursor can be positioned in the same place on the screen, correct data can then be keyed on top of the incorrect data rather than repeating the entire prompt sequence.

Inverse Video

Inverse means backwards. Therefore, inverse video means that the normal display colors are reversed. If the normal characters are white on black, for example, inverse characters would be black on white. Inverse video is also frequently called reverse video. Inverse video is used for highlighting information on the screen. Things to be highlighted may include titles, menu choices, or important information. Refer to Figure 5.3 for an example.

In this example, the name of the company and the menu selection are shown in inverse video. The menu selection is made by striking the first letter of the desired choice, at which time the choice changes into inverse video.

Once the desired option is in inverse video, the ENTER/RETURN key is pressed to select the item. Note that the second menu item has been chosen in the example.

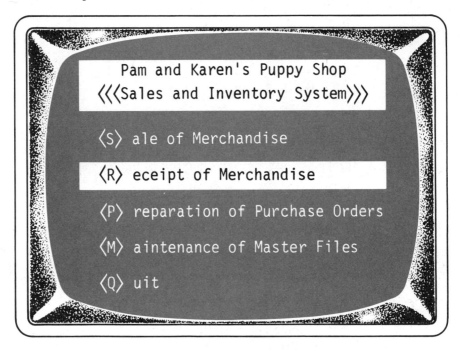

Figure 5.3   Menu Using Inverse Video

Colors on the Screen

Color can also make a display more readable. Almost any kind of highlighting can be done effectively with color. For example, in the menu given in Figure 5.3, the text might change colors to indicate which choice has been selected. Or, suppose a program displays a budget on the screen. It would be nice if the program would display unfavorable items in red and others in green. For example, if you had planned to spend $400 on the telephone and instead spent $450, the $450 could show up in red to indicate that you spent more than you had planned.

Screen Clears

Every new screen display should always start out on a clean screen. Frequently, at least part of the screen needs to be cleared during an operation. For example, if you are looking at the record of credits and grades earned by a student, it would be good for the student's name, grade, and major to remain at the top of the screen while the actual courses and grades appear in several sequences at the bottom of the screen.

REVIEW QUESTIONS

1. Describe the advantages of using effective video displays. (Obj. 1)
2. How can effective displays increase accuracy? (Obj. 1)
3. How can effective displays lead to less fatigue? (Obj. 1)
4. How can effective displays save time? (Obj. 1)
5. What is meant by direct cursor positioning? (Obj. 2)
6. How can inverse video, colors, and screen clears enhance the effectiveness of a video display? (Obj. 2)

Topic 5.2— TECHNIQUES FOR BASIC SCREEN DISPLAYS

The techniques for controlling screen displays are given in the following sections. Since all four of the machines discussed in this text are different, the methods for each will be presented.

IBM

DIRECT CURSOR POSITIONING ON THE IBM

The cursor can be directly positioned to any row and column on the screen. Since the display of the IBM PC can be set to either 40 columns or 80 columns, the maximum column number to which the cursor can be positioned will be either 40 or 80, depending on the width. The width is set by using the **WIDTH** statement:

General Form: *line number* WIDTH *40 or 80*

Example: `100 WIDTH 80`

A mode is a way of operating. On the IBM, there are three modes: text (characters only; no graphics), high-resolution monochrome graphics, and medium-resolution color graphics. With the color graphics mode, the 80-column width is not available. If you have trouble setting the 80-column width, use the **SCREEN** 0 statement before the WIDTH statement. This will change the screen into text mode. You will learn more about the SCREEN statement later.

Direct cursor positioning is done by using the **LOCATE** statement before the PRINT statement that is to place the data on the screen.

> General Form: *line number* LOCATE *row number, column number*
>
> Example: 310 LOCATE 10,5
>   320 PRINT "This is Row 10, Column 5"

The two numbers following LOCATE specify first the row number, then the column number at which the cursor is to be positioned. The row number may be any number from 1 through 25. As indicated earlier, the maximum column number will be either 40 or 80. Entering values that are too large or too small can cause an error.

Here is an example showing how to print the time on the screen in a position of your choice. Since the computer automatically keeps track of the time in a variable called TIME$, we will use that variable to print the time. Note that we have followed the PRINT statement with a semicolon. This is to keep the cursor from going to the next line at the end of the statement. Since we are printing on the last line on the screen, the time would scroll up if we allowed the cursor to move to the following line. In general, it is good practice to follow each PRINT with a semicolon any time you are controlling printing with the LOCATE statement.

```
10 ' EXC5E1
20 ' CLARK AND LABARRE--CHAPTER 5, EXAMPLE 1
30 ' ILLUSTRATION OF DIRECT CURSOR POSITIONING ON THE IBM PC
40 CLS                    'Clear the screen
50 LOCATE 24,70           'Send the cursor to Row 24, Column 70
60 PRINT TIME$;           'Print the time
70 GOTO 50                'Repeat the process
```

INVERSE VIDEO AND TEXT COLOR ON THE IBM

Inverse video and text colors are both discussed in this section since inverse video is achieved by reversing the background and foreground colors of the screen. The background is the color the screen surface will be, while the foreground is the color of the characters on the screen. Remember that the text mode is selected by using a statement of SCREEN 0. There are a couple of additional things that can also be accomplished with this statement. If your computer has a Color/Graphics Monitor Adaptor, you can use the SCREEN statement to turn the color on or off. This is done by adding either a 0 or 1 to the end of the statement. A zero turns the color off; a one turns it on.

Example 1: 200 SCREEN 0,0 puts the computer in text mode and turns off color.

Example 2: 200 SCREEN 0,1 puts the computer in text mode and turns on color.

Remember, when dealing with the screen, that anything you do not change remains just like it was. Therefore, if the screen was already in text mode, you can use a statement such as 200 SCREEN,1 to turn on color. Color is normally on unless you turn it off.

Also, if your IBM has the Color/Graphics Monitor Adaptor, you can use SCREEN 1 or SCREEN 2 instead of SCREEN 0. SCREEN 2 puts the computer in high-resolution graphics mode, which allows the use of monochrome graphics. Using this mode has no effect on printing text on the screen except that no colors may be specified. SCREEN 1 puts the computer in medium-resolution graphics mode. In medium-resolution graphics mode, color graphics can be displayed, but only 40 text characters can be printed on a line. With only 40 characters on a line, each character is larger. There are many occasions when the larger text is preferable. In medium-resolution graphics mode, the use of color is different. These differences will be discussed in the section in Chapter 13 on pixel graphics. Using graphics mode makes partial screen clears and scrolling easier, as will be discussed in the sections on those operations.

Now, we will get back to colors. In text mode, the IBM PC can display any of 16 colors if the Color/Graphics Monitor Adaptor is installed. These colors are numbered 0-15 as shown in Table 5.1.

No./Color	No./Color	No./Color
0 Black	6 Brown	12 Light Red
1 Blue	7 White	13 Light Magenta
2 Green	8 Gray	14 Yellow
3 Cyan	9 Light Blue	15 High-Intensity White
4 Red	10 Light Green	
5 Magenta	11 Light Cyan	

Table 5.1   Text Colors on the IBM PC

The selection of colors to use is made through the use of the **COLOR** statement. Once a COLOR statement is executed, any items printed appear in the designated color. Here is the form of the COLOR statement:

General Form: *line number* COLOR *foreground, background*

Example: 300 COLOR 2,0

This example sets the foreground color to 2 (green) and the background color to 0 (black). Therefore, anything printed will appear as green characters on a black background. If you want to switch to inverse video, the color combination should be turned around. For example, to print black characters on a green background, you include a color statement such as 400 COLOR 0,2.

Characters on the IBM may be made to blink or flash by adding 16 to the foreground color number. Once printed in blinking mode, characters will continue to blink until they scroll off the screen or are erased. Using the color statement again, without the 16 added to the color number, will turn off blinking mode for characters printed. Characters already blinking, however, will continue to blink as long as they are on the screen.

Now look at an example using colors and flashing characters. This program, which simply prints randomly colored words in randomly chosen locations on the screen until the user strikes a key, is not of practical value. However, it shows the application of the concept. Direct cursor positioning is also used.

```
10 ' EXC5E2
20 ' CLARK AND LABARRE--CHAPTER 5, EXAMPLE 2
30 ' ILLUSTRATES COLOR CHARACTERS ON IBM PC
40 SCREEN 0              'Make sure the computer is in text mode
50 WIDTH 80              'Make sure the computer is in 80-column width
60 CLS                   'Clear the screen
70 WHILE INKEY$=""       'Set up loop to run until a key is struck
80     ROW=RND*23+1      'Randomly choose a row
90     COLUMN=RND*74+1   'Randomly choose a column
100    PRINTCOLOR=RND*16 'Randomly choose a color
110    LOCATE ROW,COLUMN 'Move the cursor to chosen position
120    COLOR PRINTCOLOR  'Set chosen color
130    PRINT "HELLO";    'Print HELLO
140 WEND                 'End loop
150 COLOR 7              'Restore color to white
160 CLS                  'Clear screen
170 END
```

SCREEN CLEARS ON THE IBM

Screen clears may be either complete or partial. In other words, the entire screen or just a part of it may be erased. As you learned in Chapter 1, the keyword CLS is used to clear the entire screen. The following paragraphs describe how to partially clear the screen.

Some versions of IBM BASIC do not provide a keyword that can be used to simplify clearing a section of the screen. Therefore, when only part of the screen needs to be cleared, you must use a combination of other statements. One of the best ways to clear a few lines on the screen is to set up a character variable containing either 40 or 80 blanks. The number of blanks will depend on which screen width you are using. Then print this line of blanks on each line of the screen to be erased. On page 148 is an example showing how you would clear rows 7-24 of the screen.

```
10 ' EXC5E3
20 ' CLARK AND LABARRE--CHAPTER 5, EXAMPLE 3
30 ' ILLUSTRATES PARTIAL SCREEN CLEARS ON THE IBM PC
40 FOR ROW=1 TO 24              'Lines 40-60 print on each row so there
50    PRINT "THIS IS ROW";ROW   'will be something to erase.
60 NEXT ROW
70 BLANKLINE$=STRING$(80," ")   'Set up a variable of 80 blanks.
80 FOR ROW =7 TO 24
90    LOCATE ROW,1              'Lines 80-110 print blanks over rows
100   PRINT BLANKLINE$;         '7-24, thereby erasing them.
110 NEXT ROW
```

This same technique can be used to erase only a partial width of the screen. Just make the length of the blanks shorter and position the cursor to the proper horizontal as well as vertical position before printing the blanks. To erase the entire right half of the screen, for example, you could use the following steps:

```
10 ' EXC5E4
20 ' CLARK AND LABARRE--CHAPTER 5, EXAMPLE 4
30 ' ILLUSTRATES ERASING RIGHT HALF OF SCREEN ON THE IBM PC
40 FOR ROW=1 TO 24              'Lines 40-60 print lines of X's to ensure
50    PRINT STRING$(75,"X")     'there will be something to erase.
60 NEXT ROW
70 BLANKHALF$=STRING$(40," ")   'Set up a variable of 40 blanks.
80 FOR ROW=1 TO 24
90    LOCATE ROW,41             'Lines 80-110 print blanks over the right
100   PRINT BLANKHALF$;         'half of each line.
110 NEXT ROW
```

Later versions of IBM BASICA allow the creation of viewports on the screen provided you set the computer to graphics mode by using the SCREEN statement. A viewport is simply a defined area of the screen. Look at Figure 5.4 to see the layout of the screen and a viewport in graphics mode.

After using the SCREEN statement to set the computer to graphics mode (SCREEN 1 or SCREEN 2), the viewport is set up by using the keyword VIEW.

Here's how:

General Form: *line number* VIEW *(x1,y1)-(x2,y2)*

Example: 300 VIEW (0,0)-(160,100)

After creating a viewport, the contents of that viewport can be erased by using the keyword CLS. Note that clearing a part of the screen in this manner does not return the cursor to the top left screen position.

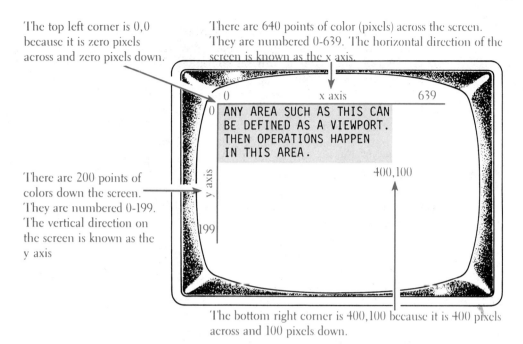

The top left corner is 0,0 because it is zero pixels across and zero pixels down.

There are 640 points of color (pixels) across the screen. They are numbered 0-639. The horizontal direction of the screen is known as the x axis.

0   x axis   639

0

ANY AREA SUCH AS THIS CAN
BE DEFINED AS A VIEWPORT.
THEN OPERATIONS HAPPEN
IN THIS AREA.

400,100

There are 200 points of colors down the screen. They are numbered 0-199. The vertical direction on the screen is known as the y axis

y axis

199

The bottom right corner is 400,100 because it is 400 pixels across and 100 pixels down.

Figure 5.4   Layout of High-Resolution Graphics Screen (SCREEN 2)

SCROLLING WITH THE IBM

Scrolling refers to the movement of text up the screen as successive printing is done. For example, if you print enough lines on the screen, the first line printed will eventually go off the top. If you have printed headings on the screen, they will usually be scrolled off before the data being printed. Frequently, however, you want the headings to remain. As an example, suppose that we want to print a table of numbers, their square roots, and their squares. The numbers will range from 1 through 50. We want a heading line to stay on the screen at all times. The easiest way to do this is to put the headings at the bottom of the screen on row 25, since normal BASIC scrolling does not affect row 25. Here is an example program of how it may be done.

```
10 ' EXC5E5
20 ' CLARK AND LABARRE-CHAPTER 5, EXAMPLE 5
30 ' ILLUSTRATES NONSCROLLING 25TH LINE ON THE IBM PC
40 CLS:KEY OFF                          'Clear screen, erase function keys
50 COLOR 0,7                            'Inverse video
60 LOCATE 25,1                          'Cursor to Row 25, Column 1
70 PRINT "NUMBER    SQUARE ROOT    SQUARE"; 'Print footer
80 IMAGE$="   ##        #.#####       ####" 'Create PRINT USING image
90 COLOR 7,0                            'Normal video
100 LOCATE 24,1                         'Cursor to Row 24, Column 1
110 FOR NUMBER=1 TO 50                  'Count from 1 to 50
120    PRINT USING IMAGE$;NUMBER,SQR(NUMBER),NUMBER^2 'Print detail line
130 NEXT NUMBER                         'Next count
```

When scrolling, it is frequently desirable to stop the scroll at almost a screenful of new information so that the information can be studied. Then by striking a key, the scrolling can be continued. This kind of action can be added to a program by including a test to see whether the desired number of lines have been printed. If, for example, you want the scroll to pause after each 20 lines, you can examine the value of the counter variable after each print statement. If the counter contains 20, 40, 60, or any other multiple of 20, you want to pause. In mathematical terms, if the counter is evenly divisible by 20, it is time to pause. In the next example, we have added such a statement to the previous example. In line 130 NUMBER/20 gives a decimal result, while NUMBER\20 gives an integer result. If the two answers are the same, then the number was equally divisible by 20, and we need to pause. The pause lasts until the user strikes any key. Here is the modified program:

```
10 ' EXC5E6
20 ' CLARK AND LABARRE-CHAPTER 5, EXAMPLE 6
30 ' ILLUSTRATES SCROLL-STOP ON THE IBM PC
40 CLS:KEY OFF
50 COLOR 0,7
60 LOCATE 25,1
70 PRINT "NUMBER    SQUARE ROOT    SQUARE";
80 IMAGE$="   ##        #.#####      ####"
90 COLOR 7,0
100 LOCATE 24,1
110 FOR NUMBER=1 TO 50
120    PRINT USING IMAGE$;NUMBER,SQR(NUMBER),NUMBER^2
130    IF NUMBER/20=NUMBER\20 THEN PRINT"Press Any Key to Continue";:
                               Z$=INPUT$(1):
                               PRINT
```

TRS-80

DIRECT CURSOR POSITIONING ON THE TRS-80

Direct cursor positioning can be done to any position on the screen. Each print position is numbered sequentially beginning with 0. On the Model III, there are 64 positions on each row. The first row (called row 0) contains cursor positions 0-63; the second row (called row 1) contains positions 64-127. This numbering continues until the end of the screen is reached. Usually, you will be thinking in terms of row and column rather than a single position number. You can convert the row and column to the single position number with the formula ROW*64 + COLUMN, remembering to start numbering the rows and columns with 0. Direct cursor positioning is done by using the PRINT@ statement.

General Form: *line number* PRINT@*position,data to print*

Example: 320 PRINT@260,"This is Position 260"

Here is an example showing how to print the date and time on the screen in a position of your choice. Since the computer automatically keeps track of the date and time in a variable called TIME$, we will use that variable to print the time. Note that we have followed the PRINT@ statement with a semicolon. This is to keep the cursor from going to the next line at the end of the statement. Since we are printing on the last line on the screen, the time would scroll up if we allowed the cursor to move to the following line. In general, it is good practice to follow each PRINT@ statement with a semicolon.

```
10 ' EXC5E7
20 ' CLARK AND LABARRE--CHAPTER 5, EXAMPLE 7
30 ' ILLUSTRATES CURSOR POSITIONING ON THE TRS-80 MODEL III
40 CLS                       'Clear the screen
50 PRINT@1000,TIME$;         'Print the date and time on the last row
60 GOTO 50                   'Repeat the process
```

The TRS-80 Model 4 can display 24 rows of 80 columns each. The PRINT@ statement on the Model 4 may be used with row and column numbers. For example, 60 PRINT@(4,12),"This is Row 4, Column 12".

INVERSE VIDEO ON THE TRS-80

The TRS-80 Model III has no way to switch to inverse video under BASIC. On the Model 4, PRINT CHR$(16) will switch the computer to inverse video. PRINT CHR$(17) will switch back to normal video.

SCREEN CLEARS ON THE TRS-80

As you learned in Chapter 1, complete screen clears are done by using the keyword CLS. The following paragraphs describe how to clear a partial screen.

TRS-80 BASIC does not provide a keyword for clearing only part of the screen. Therefore, when part of the screen needs to be cleared, you must use a combination of other statements. One of the best ways is to set up a character variable containing a number of blanks equal to the width of your screen. Then print this line of blanks on each line of the screen to be erased. On page 150 is an example showing how you would clear the first four rows of the screen.

```
10 ' EXC5E8
20 ' CLARK AND LABARRE--CHAPTER 5, EXAMPLE 8
30 ' ILLUSTRATES PARTIAL SCREEN CLEAR ON THE TRS-80 MODEL III
40 CLEAR 200
50 FOR ROW=0 TO 1000 STEP 64
60   PRINT "THIS IS POSITION";ROW      'Print something to ensure there is
70 NEXT ROW                            'text to erase
80 BL$=STRING$(64," ")                 'Set up variable of 64 blanks
90   FOR ROW=0 TO 192 STEP 64          'Loop from Row 0 to Row 5 (64 positions each)
100    PRINT@ROW,BL$;                   'Print blanks on the row
110 NEXT ROW                           'Go to next row
```

This same technique can be used to erase only a partial width of the screen. To erase the entire right half of the screen, for example, you could use the following steps:

```
10 ' EXC5E9
20 ' CLARK AND LABARRE--CHAPTER 5, EXAMPLE 9
30 ' ILLUSTRATES CLEARING OF PARTIAL WIDTH OF THE SCREEN ON TRS-80 MOD III
40 FOR ROW=0 TO 1000 STEP 64
50   PRINT STRING$(60,"X")             'Print something to ensure there is
60 NEXT ROW                            'text to erase
70 BLH$=STRING$(32," ")                'Set up variable of 32 blanks
80   FOR ROW=32 TO 992 STEP 64         'Loop from mid-Row 0 to mid-Row 15
90     PRINT@ROW,BLH$;                  'Locate to mid-Row and print blanks
100 NEXT ROW
```

Remember if you are using a Model 4, half of the screen width is 40 columns, and you can use row and column designators rather than the position designator.

SCROLLING WITH THE TRS-80 MODEL III

Scrolling refers to the movement of text up the screen as successive printing is done. For example, if you print enough lines on the screen, the first line printed will eventually go off the top. If you have printed headings on the screen, they will usually be scrolled off before the data being printed. Frequently, however, you want the headings to remain. As an example, suppose that we want to print a table of numbers, their square roots, and their squares. The numbers will range from 1 through 50. We want a heading line to stay on the screen at all times. The TRS-80 provides that as many as seven lines at the top of the screen can be protected from scrolling. This is done by placing a number into a special memory location. The number tells how many lines we want protected. The keyword POKE is used to place the number, as shown in the following example. Note: Poking values into memory can be very dangerous. Poking into the wrong places or using the wrong values has the potential of damaging programs and data, both in memory and on the diskette. Therefore, when using POKE, make sure that you are doing it correctly.

```
10 ' EXC5E10
20 ' CLARK AND LABARRE--CHAPTER 5, EXAMPLE 10
30 ' ILLUSTRATES SCROLLING ON THE TRS-80 MODEL III WITHOUT DESTROYING HEADINGS
40 CLS                                       'Clear the screen
50 POKE 16916,2  'Put a 2 in memory location 16916, protecting two lines
60 IMG$=" ##         #.#####         ####"   'Create PRINT USING image
70 PRINT "NUMBER   SQUARE ROOT    SQUARE"    'Print heading (this line protected)
80 PRINT "==============================="   'Print rule (this line protected)
90  FOR NUM=1 TO 50                          'Count from 1 to 50
100     PRINT USING IMG$;NUM,SQR(NUM),NUM[2  'Print detail line
110 NEXT NUM
```

Note that the procedure was to designate how many lines to protect. Then print those lines on the screen. Lines printed after the protected lines will scroll, but the protected lines will not.

When scrolling, it is frequently desirable to stop the scroll at almost a screenful of new information so that the information can be studied. Then by striking a key, the scrolling can be continued. This kind of action can be added to a program by including a test to see whether the desired number of lines has been printed. If, for example, you want the scroll to pause after each 12 lines, you can examine the value of the counter variable after each print statement. If the counter contains 12, 24, 36, or any other multiple of 12, you want to pause. In mathematical terms, if the counter is evenly divisible by 12, it is time to pause. In the following program, we have added such a statement to the previous example. In line 110 the NUM/12 gives a decimal result, while INT(NUM/12) gives an integer result. If the two answers are the same, then the number was equally divisible by 12 and a pause is called for. The pause lasts until the user presses ENTER. Here is the modified program:

```
10 ' EXC5E11
20 ' CLARK AND LABARRE--CHAPTER 5, EXAMPLE 11
30 ' ILLUSTRATES SCROLL-STOP ON THE TRS-80 MODEL III
40 CLS
50 POKE 16916,2
60 IMG$="  ##         #.#####         ####"
70 PRINT "NUMBER    SQUARE ROOT     SQUARE"
80 PRINT "==============================="
90  FOR NUM=1 TO 50
100     PRINT USING IMG$;NUM,SQR(NUM),NUM[2
110     IF NUM/12=INT(NUM/12) THEN LINE INPUT "Press ENTER to Continue";Z$
120 NEXT NUM
```

APPLE

DIRECT CURSOR POSITIONING ON THE APPLE

Direct cursor positioning can be done to any row and column on the screen. Since the display of the Apple may be either 80 columns or 40 columns, the maximum column number to which the cursor can be positioned will be either 80 or 40, depending on the width. If you have an 80-column card installed in your computer, the width is set to 80 by using the following statement:

General Form: *line number* PRINT CHR$(4);"PR#3"

Example: `40 PRINT CHR$(13);CHR$(4);"PR#3"`

Direct cursor positioning is usually done by using the VTAB and HTAB statements before the PRINT statement that is to place the data on the screen.

General Form: *line number* VTAB *row number.*HTAB *column number*

Example: `310 VTAB 10:HTAB 5`
              `320 PRINT "This is Row 10, Column 5"`

The numbers following VTAB and HTAB specify the row number and the column number at which the cursor is to be positioned. The row number may be any number from 1 through 24. The maximum column number is 40, even with the 80-column card installed; HTAB simply does not work beyond 40. To position the cursor to columns beyond 40, you must poke the column number into memory location 1403. For example, to position the cursor to column 63, you use the statement 100 POKE 1403, 63. When using this method, the columns are numbered 0-79. Note: Poking values into memory can be very dangerous. Poking into the wrong places or using the wrong values has the potential of damaging programs and data or crashing the computer system. Therefore, when using POKE, make sure that you are doing it correctly.

Here is an example showing how to make the computer count on the screen, placing each number on the screen in a position of your choice. We will use a FOR . . . NEXT loop to do the counting. Note that we have followed the PRINT statement with a semicolon. This is to keep the cursor from going to the next line at the end of the statement. Since we are printing on the last line on the screen, the number would scroll up if we allowed the cursor to move to the following line. In general, it is good practice to follow each PRINT with a semicolon any time you are controlling printing with the VTAB and HTAB statements.

```
40 HOME                :REM Clear the screen
50 FOR CT=1 TO 500     :REM Count from 1 to 500
60    VTAB 24:HTAB 32   :REM Send the cursor to Row 24, Column 32
70    PRINT CT;         :REM Print the count
80 NEXT CT             :REM Next count
```

INVERSE VIDEO ON THE APPLE

Inverse video on the Apple is selected by using the keyword INVERSE

General Form: *line number* INVERSE

Example: 100 INVERSE

All characters printed after the INVERSE statement will be in inverse video. To return to normal characters, the keyword NORMAL is used.

General Form: *line number* NORMAL

Example: 200 NORMAL

Here is an example showing the entire process:

```
40 PRINT "THIS LINE IS PRINTED NORMALLY."
50 INVERSE
60 PRINT "THIS LINE IS PRINTED IN INVERSE VIDEO."
70 NORMAL
80 PRINT "THIS LINE IS PRINTED NORMALLY."
```

If you are using a 40-column display, characters can also be set to flash. This is done by using the keyword FLASH before printing.

General Form: *line number* FLASH

Example: 90 FLASH
           100 PRINT "HELLO"

Everything printed after the use of FLASH will flash. To stop flashing, use the keyword NORMAL. Remember that all three of the commands INVERSE, FLASH, and NORMAL only affect text printed after the use of the keyword. In other words, text that is in reverse video or flashing will remain in that condition after using the keyword NORMAL, but newly printed text will be normal.

SCREEN CLEARS ON THE APPLE

Screen clears may be either complete or partial. In other words, the entire screen or just a part of it may be erased. As you learned in Chapter 1, the Apple uses the keyword HOME to clear the entire screen. The following paragraphs describe how to clear part of the screen.

Apple BASIC does not provide a keyword for clearing only part of the screen. However, by placing numbers into special memory locations by using the keyword POKE, the Apple can be made to set margins on the screen. In effect, we are allowed to define a smaller screen or window on the screen surface. Anything already on the screen but outside the window is unaffected by the keyword HOME. The margins of the window are set by poking the desired numbers into special memory locations. Here are the commands:

To set the Line Width: POKE 33,*number of columns* (maximum 40 or 80)
To set the Left Margin: POKE 32,*column number* (the left edge is 0)
To set the Top Margin: POKE 34,*number of lines* (possible values 0-23)
To set the Bottom Margin: POKE 35,*line number* (possible values 0-24)

Only the top margin is changed in the following example, even though the other margins may also be changed.

```
30 HOME
40 PRINT "THIS IS ON LINE 1"
50 PRINT "THIS IS ON LINE 2"
60 PRINT "THIS IS ON LINE 3"
70 PRINT "THIS IS ON LINE 4"
80 POKE 34,2  :REM Remove first two lines from the screen "window"
90 HOME :REM Everything on the screen is erased except the first two lines
```

A word of caution is in order. If you are using an 80-column display and set a screen window, the VTAB statement does not act in its normal manner. Instead, you must VTAB to the row above the desired row, then use a PRINT statement to get to the desired row. For example, to print a word on line 12, you could use the following statements:

```
200 VTAB 11          :REM VTAB to line above the desired location
210 PRINT            :REM Use PRINT to go one line lower on the screen
220 PRINT "COMPUTER" :REM Print the desired word
```

If you prefer, you can clear part of the screen by using methods that do not involve poking values into memory locations. One of the best ways is to set up a character variable containing either 40 or 80 blanks. The number of blanks will depend on which screen width you are using. Then print this line of blanks on each line of the screen to be erased. Here is an example showing how you would clear only rows 7-24 of the screen:

```
100 BL$="                         ":REM 40 blanks
110 FOR ROW=7 TO 24      :REM Loop from Row 7 to Row 24
120    VTAB ROW:HTAB 1   :REM Locate to the first column of the row
130      PRINT BL$;      :REM Print 40 blanks
140 NEXT ROW             :REM Do the next count
```

This same technique can be used to erase only a partial width of the screen. To erase the entire right half of the screen, for example, you could use the following steps:

```
100 BL$="          "     :REM Variable of 20 blanks
110 FOR ROW=1 TO 24      :REM Loop from Row 1 to Row 24
120    VTAB ROW:HTAB 21  :REM Locate to Column 21 of the row
130      PRINT BL$;      :REM Print 20 blanks
140 NEXT ROW
```

SCROLLING WITH THE APPLE

Scrolling refers to the movement of text up the screen as successive printing is done. For example, if you print enough lines on the screen, the first line printed will eventually go off the top. If you have printed headings on the screen, they will usually be scrolled off before the data being printed. Frequently, however, you want the headings to remain. As an example, suppose that we want to print a table of numbers, their square roots, and their squares. The numbers will range from 1 through 50. We want a heading line to stay on the screen at all times. To accomplish this, we change the top margin just as we did in the previous example on clearing part of the screen. Just as changing the top margin protected lines from erasing, it also protects them from scrolling.

```
40 HOME                                      :REM Clear the screen
50 PRINT "NUMBER   SQUARE ROOT    SQUARE"    :REM Print heading
60 PRINT "================================"  :REM Print rule
70 POKE 34,2   :REM Sets top margin, protecting top two lines from scroll
80 FOR NUM=1 TO 50                           :REM Counts from 1 to 50
90    PRINT NUM;TAB(10);SQR(NUM);TAB(25);INT(NUM^2) :REM Print detail line
100 NEXT NUM                                 :REM Next count
```

Note that the procedure is to print the headings, then designate where the top of the text window is to be located. Since the headings are located above the newly defined window, the headings will remain while the data scrolls beneath them.

COMMODORE 64

CURSOR POSITIONING ON THE COMMODORE 64

Cursor positioning can be done to any row and column on the screen. The display of the Commodore 64 is 80 columns, but only 40 columns appear on one line. Therefore, if you position the cursor beyond column 40, it will go to the next line. It is recommended, therefore, that you not position the cursor beyond the fortieth column.

Cursor positioning is done by using the PRINT statement to print a literal containing the cursor control keys. For example, to position the cursor to row 3 and column 5 and print the word, you send the cursor home, then down 2 times and across 4 times, followed by the word to print. Here is a statement to print these commands. Remember, you do not key in the words describing the cursor movement; you strike the cursor control keys on the keyboard. Various shapes will be printed on the screen as you strike the cursor keys.

10 PRINT "HOME CURSORDOWN CURSORDOWN CURSOR-RIGHT CURSORRIGHT CURSORRIGHT CURSORRIGHT HELLO"

Here is what the line looks like as actually keyed into the Commodore 64:

```
10 PRINT "▒◙◙◙▌▌▌HELLO"
```

If desired, you may print the CHR$ function of the ASCII code that makes the desired movement. For example, to move the cursor down one line, you could PRINT CHR$(17). Here are the codes:

Cursor Home: 19
Cursor Left: 157
Cursor Right: 29
Cursor Up: 145
Cursor Down: 17

Here is an example showing how to make the computer count on the screen, placing each number on the screen in a position of your choice. We will use a FOR...NEXT loop to do the counting. Note that we have followed the PRINT statement with a semicolon. This is to keep the cursor from going to the next line at the end of the statement. Since we are printing on the last line on the screen, the number would scroll up if we allowed the cursor to move to the following line. In general, it is good practice to follow each PRINT with a semicolon any time you are controlling cursor positions.

```
40 PRINT "⊡";          :REM CLEAR THE SCREEN
50 FOR R=1 TO 24
60 PRINT                :REM GET CURSOR TO BOTTOM OF SCREEN
70 NEXT R
80 FOR CT=1 TO 500      :REM COUNT FROM 1 TO 500
90 PRINT TAB(32);CT;    :REM PRINT THE COUNT
100 PRINT "▮▮▮▮▮";      :REM BACK UP THE CURSOR ON THE SAME LINE
110 NEXT CT             :REM NEXT COUNT
```

REVERSE VIDEO AND COLOR ON THE COMMODORE 64

Reverse video on the Commodore 64 is selected by printing a CTRL-9. The CTRL-9 is placed inside quotes as a literal. When you key it, you will get a reverse video R. Everything from that character to a RETURN (which will occur automatically at the end of a PRINT statement that does not end with a comma or semicolon) will be in reverse video. If you want to turn off reverse video before the RETURN character, print a CTRL-0 inside quotes, which will appear on the screen as a symbol when you type it.

Text color on the Commodore is changed by printing the desired color control key as a literal enclosed in quotes. Here are the available colors. By way of example, CTRL-1 means that you hold down the CTRL key while striking the 1 key. COMM-1 means that you hold down the Commodore key while striking the 1 key. A different symbol will appear on the screen for each of the color commands you enter inside quotes.

Key Combination	Color	Key Combination	Color
CTRL-1	Black	COMM-1	Orange
CTRL-2	White	COMM-2	Brown
CTRL-3	Red	COMM-3	Lt. Red
CTRL-4	Cyan	COMM-4	Gray 1
CTRL-5	Purple	COMM-5	Gray 2
CTRL-6	Green	COMM-6	Lt. Green
CTRL-7	Blue	COMM-7	Lt. Blue
CTRL-8	Yellow	COMM-8	Gray 3

Table 5.2   Text Colors on the Commodore 64

Here is a short example program showing inverse video and the use of color.

```
40 PRINT "THIS LINE IS PRINTED NORMALLY"
50 PRINT "▮THIS LINE IS PRINTED IN REVERSE VIDEO"
60 PRINT "THIS LINE IS PRINTED NORMALLY"
70 PRINT "▮THIS LINE IS PRINTED IN RED"
```

SCREEN CLEARS ON THE COMMODORE 64

Screen clears may be either complete or partial. As you learned in Chapter 1, the Commodore 64 uses the shifted version of the CLR/HOME key to clear the screen. The following paragraphs describe how to erase just part of the screen.

Commodore 64 BASIC does not provide a keyword for clearing only part of the screen. Therefore, when only part of the screen needs to be cleared, you must use a combination of other statements. One way to do this is to poke the code for a blank into each memory location representing the part of the screen to be erased. The top left corner of the screen is normally location 1024. Each row begins 40 locations after the previous one. Here is an example showing how you would clear only rows 7-24 of the screen:

```
100 FOR R=1264 TO 2024        :REM MEMORY LOCATIONS FOR
110 POKE R,32                 :REM ROWS 7-24, POKED WITH
120 NEXT R                    :REM THE CODE FOR A BLANK
```

This same technique can be used to erase only a partial width of the screen. To erase the entire right half of the screen, for example, you could use the following steps:

```
100 FOR R=1024 TO 1984 STEP 40    :REM BEGINNING OF ROWS
110 FOR C=19 TO 39                :REM COLUMNS TO CLEAR
120 POKE R+C,32                   :REM BLANK INTO MEMORY
130 NEXT C
140 NEXT R
```

SCROLLING ON THE COMMODORE 64

When scrolling, it is frequently desirable to stop the scroll at almost a screenful of new information so that the information can be studied. Then by striking a key, the scrolling can be continued. This kind of action can be added to a program by including a test to see whether the desired number of lines has been printed. If, for example, you want the scroll to pause after each 20 lines, you can examine the value of the counter variable after each print statement. If the counter contains 20, 40, 60, or any other multiple of 20, you want to pause. In mathematical terms, if the counter is evenly divisible by 20, it is time to pause. The following printout is an example of such a statement. In line 90 the NUM/20 gives a decimal result, while INT(NUM/20) gives an integer result. If the two answers are the same, then the number was equally divisible by 20 and we need to pause. The pause lasts until the user presses ENTER. Here is the program:

```
40 PRINT "⌂";
50 PRINT "NUMBER    SQ ROOT    SQUARE"
60 PRINT "========================="
70 FOR NUM=1 TO 50
80 PRINT NUM,INT(SQR(NUM)*100)/100,INT(NUM↑2)
90 IF NUM/20=INT(NUM/20) THEN INPUT "PRESS ENTER TO CONTINUE";Z$
100 NEXT NUM
```

REVIEW QUESTIONS

Answer the following questions for the computer you are using.
1. Describe the procedure for moving the cursor to any desired position on the screen. (Obj. 3)
2. Describe the procedure for printing in inverse video. (Obj. 3)
3. Describe the procedure for printing in colors. (Obj. 3)
4. Describe how to erase a portion of the display. (Obj. 3)
5. Describe how to keep headings on the screen while data scrolls. (Obj. 3)
6. Describe how to temporarily stop scrolling at the end of each screen of data. (Obj. 3)

VOCABULARY WORDS

The following terms were introduced in this chapter:

highlighted	mode	medium-resolution graphics mode
direct cursor positioning	high-resolution graphics mode	
inverse video		viewports
reverse video		scrolling

KEYWORDS

The following keywords were introduced in this chapter:

WIDTH	PRINT@	NORMAL
LOCATE	POKE	FLASH
SCREEN	VTAB	CTRL-9
COLOR	HTAB	CTRL-0
VIEW	INVERSE	

PROGRAMS TO WRITE

For each of the programs, prepare the necessary documentation before writing the BASIC code.

Program 1

Clear the screen. Then use direct cursor positioning to print the following data in the specified locations on the screen.

Print your name at row 1, column 1 in reverse video.
Print your phone number at row 1, column 30 in normal video.
Print your birthdate at row 5, column 10 in normal video.

Program 2

The scores made by eight students on a standardized test were as follows: Michelle Barth, 300; Frankie Jones, 381; Buttons Tunicliff, 412; Robbie Brown, 289; Ramsey Richards, 402; Michael Marcus, 363; Sharon Csinisek, 303; and Jo Delaney, 401. This data is to be placed in DATA statements in a program. The program should print a report showing the scores. The names of those students who scored above the average are to be highlighted by a different color or reverse video.

Program 3

You want to make a nice-looking opening screen for a program you have written. The screen should be bordered on all four sides by a reverse video box. The name of the program and your name as programmer should appear inside the box in reverse video or a different color.

Program 4

The computer is to be set up as a system to give information on various airline flights. At the top of the screen should be lines identifying the airline, along with a numbered list of cities the airline serves. Instructions tell the user to enter the number of the city to see information about the flights to that city. When the user enters a city, the bottom part of the screen should be erased and the data for that city displayed. To make programming easy, set up a separate module for each city, with print statements giving the desired information. Information should include the names of the departure and arrival cities, as well as flight numbers and times of departure and arrival.

Program 5

As part of their testing program, a soft drink company randomly measures the contents of drinks to make sure that equipment is working within the normal range of weights. Here are the weights of a sample of drinks: 3 drinks weighed 11.8 ounces, 5 drinks weighed 11.9 ounces, 6 drinks weighed 12 ounces, 5 drinks weighed 12.1 ounces, and 6 drinks weighed 12.2 ounces. These values may be put in a program as DATA statements. Your program should produce output in the form of a graph showing the number of drinks per weight. The output should resemble the following:

```
                          SAMPLE WEIGHTS

      NUMBER OF  6                  X         X
      DRINKS:    5          X              X
                 4
                 3          X
                 2
                 1
                 0
                    --------------------------------
      WEIGHT:         11.8 11.9 12.0 12.1 12.2
```

Program 6

The main module of a program is to consist of the menu illustrated in Figure 5.3. Plan and code the main module. Stub in submodules and test the main module.

CONTINUING PROJECT

This chapter begins two continuing projects. These projects are information processing systems that will grow with each chapter. As you progress through the text, your projects will become more and more complete. Your teacher may require one or both of the projects from you.

Before writing any program of the continuing project, be sure to complete all appropriate documentation. Documentation is especially important for a project such as this that will be rather complex when it is completed. The documentation you do at this time will be modified as the project progresses. For example, each time a new module is added in subsequent chapters, you will need to modify the hierarchy chart.

For this chapter you will prepare a sign-on program for your project. This is a separate program that will always be run first when using the system. It should print on the screen information about the name of the business, the name of the system being run, the author of the system, and the revision number of the system. For this chapter the revision number should be 1.0. Each time you add features for the other chapters, increment the revision number by 1. For example, after you add to the project in Chapter 6, the revision number will be 2.0. As you work on the programs and make changes in them, increment the decimal part of the number. For example, if you go back after completing the program for this chapter and make a change in it, you can change the revision number to 1.1. The sign-on program's only function for this chapter is to print the opening screen. Later it will be modified to run other programs necessary for completing the desired work.

Project 1

For Project 1 you will plan and write a personnel records system for a business that you name. A personnel records system keeps up with important information about the employees of a business. Some of the kinds of data stored are employee's name, social security number, work department, pay rate, number of income tax withholding exemptions, and records of earnings. At the end of each pay period, the system calculates and prints paychecks. These functions will be developed as the project progresses. For this chapter, plan and write the sign-on program described earlier. You should use techniques such as inverse video or color to make the opening screen look impressive.

Project 2

For Project 2 you will plan and write a merchandising system for a business that you name. A merchandising system includes several major functions including point of sale (checkout), inventory, sales analysis, and reordering of merchandise. These functions will be developed as the project progresses. For this chapter, plan and write a sign-on program described earlier. You should use techniques such as inverse video or color to make the opening screen look impressive.

## Chapter 6

Input Control

Objectives: 1. Describe the importance of accurate data.

2. Explain how the accuracy of input data can be increased.

3. Describe the error traps that may be used to help ensure the accuracy of data.

4. Describe the abilities and inabilities of INPUT and LINE INPUT.

5. Describe an algorithm for most reliably accepting input.

6. Code an algorithm for most reliably accepting input.

Topic 6.1— PRINCIPLES OF DATA INPUT

Writing a program to accept input from the keyboard is very easy. However, writing a program to reliably handle any character that may be keyed is more difficult. Also, writing the program so that it will do as much checking of the inputted data as possible can be quite difficult. This chapter explains how such improved methods of inputting data may be accomplished.

IMPORTANCE OF ACCURATE DATA

Since the early days of the computer, the expression "garbage in, garbage out" has been heard. This statement means that if you enter incorrect data into the computer, incorrect processed information comes out. If the incorrect information is put into a bank's computer, an incorrect balance in a person's checking account may be the result. If incorrect data is entered for scheduling a student, the student may end up in the wrong class. Incorrect data fed into the computer of an airplane may cause the craft to follow the wrong flight path.

METHODS OF INCREASING ACCURACY

The computer itself cannot automatically correct wrong data. However, by paying attention to detail, the programmer can write a program in such a way that many common data entry errors can be caught and pointed out to the user. The user can then reenter the data correctly. Some of the methods that can be used are discussed in the following paragraphs.

Use Good Prompts

If the user of a program is unsure about the kind of data to be entered, errors are likely to result. By using good prompts, the programmer helps ensure that the user knows what to enter. As an example, suppose that the following prompt appears on the screen all by itself:

```
ENTER YOUR COMMAND:
```

Unless you are very familiar with the program, you will have no idea what to enter unless you take the time to search the pages of the program's reference manual (assuming that one was prepared). By making a simple change in the prompt, however, it becomes much more meaningful. Here is how a much better version might appear:

```
ENTER YOUR COMMAND (UPDATE, PRINT, OR QUIT):
```

By showing the user what commands are available, response to the prompt is much more likely to be accurate.

As another example, assume that we have a program to calculate the interest paid on loans. At one point, the program must ask the user to enter the interest rate. Look at this possibility:

```
WHAT IS THE INTEREST RATE?
```

If the rate is 14.5 percent, does the user key in 14.5 or .145? With the prompt as shown, it is impossible to tell which way of entering the number is necessary for the program to properly operate. A simple change in the prompt makes the intent much clearer:

```
WHAT IS THE INTEREST RATE IN PERCENT?
```

Prevent System-Generated Error Messages

The computer's operating system and the high-level language in which a program is written are both capable of producing many error messages. As a matter of fact, there are several hundred possible error messages with some versions of BASIC. Usually a program stops executing whenever the system detects an error condition and prints one of these error messages. While meaningful to a programmer, these messages frequently mean nothing to the user when the program stops executing or waits for the input of corrected data. Here are some real error messages produced by popular microcomputers and operating systems. If you did not know BASIC, would you understand them?

```
RE-DO FROM START

BS ERROR IN 9873

TYPE MISMATCH IN 198

OD ERROR IN 3810

SYSTEM ERROR NO. 417
```

The occurrence of many of these error messages can be prevented by requiring a program to carefully screen (examine) all input. While such screening can require substantial amounts of coding, it can make programs much easier to use and can prevent program failures. For example, with a poorly written program, it would be possible for a user to enter thousands of pieces of data, then lose it all because the program could not correctly handle a particular incorrect data item. Some of the items that can be checked by the program to help ensure accuracy are discussed in the following paragraphs.

Require Appropriate Character or Numeric Data

To do arithmetic, the computer must have numeric data. Therefore, in all cases where numeric data is to be input, the program should check to make sure that the items keyed in are numeric. If a number keyed in has an alphabet letter accidentally placed in the middle of it, inaccurate data will result.

While any data can be considered to be character data, a check should still be made to ensure that keyed in data is either all alphabetic or a combination of alphabetic and numeric, whichever is required by the program. For example, if the program asks a person to enter his or her first and last names, there should be no digits or punctuation marks keyed in. The program can check to ensure that this is the case.

Limit the Length of Data

If you are filling out an application form, you should not write more than that which will fit into the space on the form. Neither should a computer program allow a user to enter a longer item of data than that which the program can handle. For example, names entered on the keyboard may be going to a random file on the disk. If the file has been set up for a maximum name length of 25 characters, the program should not allow entry of more than 25 characters when the name is keyed in.

Range Check the Data

Frequently, the data to be input into the computer can be defined as belonging to a certain range. For example, student grades on examinations might range from 0-100. Months of the year range from 1-12. When selling tickets to a concert, the sections in which seats are located may range from 1-25. It is simple to have the program check such data to ensure that it is within the acceptable range. Out-of-range data should be rejected and the user should be requested to enter acceptable data.

Validate the Data by Table Lookups

There are times when the range check described in the previous paragraph is not effective. For example, suppose that the computer is being used to assign classes to classrooms. The lowest numbered room in the building is 101, while the highest numbered room is 240. It would seem a simple matter to ask the user the number of the room they wish to assign to a class, then check to see if the number is between 101 and 240. However, if the particular building has no room numbers between 108 and 201, and if rooms 206 and 218 do not exist, a range check will not work very well. The existence of rooms with names rather than numbers, such as gymnasium or cafeteria, would also make the range check ineffective. In cases such as this, the only accurate way to determine the validity of a data item is to look it up in a table of all the valid items. Other examples in which data entered might be looked up in a table of valid numbers are customer numbers, stock numbers, flight numbers, and ZIP Codes.

Validate the Data by Using a Consistency Check

Where most of the items discussed in previous paragraphs involve the use of only one data item at a time, a consistency check involves two or more data items. Such a consistency check compares the items in some way to see if the relationship is correct. Here are some examples:

1. A student, in registering for courses for next semester, enters a request to take Weight Training 402. The computer might check the student's record to make sure that the course has not already been passed. That is, retaking a course that has already been passed is inconsistent and should not be allowed.
2. In purchasing a ticket for a concert, a fan requests a ticket for October 15. The computer checks to see whether the concert is being held on that date. If it is not, the data is inconsistent and should not be accepted.

REVIEW QUESTIONS

1. Why is it important to have accurate data input into the computer system? (Obj. 1)
2. How can a computer program help ensure the accuracy of input data? (Obj. 2)
3. What are some of the things to consider in planning a prompt that should appear on the screen? (Obj. 2)
4. Why should you avoid the occurrence of system-generated error messages? (Obj. 2)
5. Describe the functions of different kinds of error traps. (Obj. 3)
6. How can you decide what kind of error traps a program should use? (Obj. 3)

Topic 6.2— DATA INPUT WITH BASIC

In earlier chapters you have learned how to do simple input with BASIC. In the following sections you will learn how to accomplish more advanced data input.

THE STRONG AND WEAK POINTS OF INPUT AND LINE INPUT

As you are aware, the simplest way to accomplish entering data is to use the INPUT statement. There are a couple of weak points when using this statement, however. First of all, suppose that we have a statement such as:

```
100 INPUT "ENTER THE QUANTITY:   ";C
```

If the user enters a number in response to this line, all is well. Suppose, however, that a nonnumeric character is entered by mistake. The computer will usually respond with a brief error message that may or may not be understood by the operator. Here is an example of how such a program run might proceed:

```
RUN

ENTER THE QUANTITY:   Y

Re-do from start?_
```

It is extremely unlikely that the new user will know what to do in response to the "redo" message. An experienced user might know that it means to reenter the data, making sure to enter a number rather than a character.

When using INPUT, it is also difficult to enter data that contains a comma. Suppose that the user is to enter a last name, a comma, and a first name. If using INPUT, the entire name must be enclosed in quotation marks if it is to be accepted. If it is not in quotes, only the letters appearing before the comma will be stored in the variable.

The keyword LINE INPUT solves most of the problems of INPUT. No matter what the user enters, it will be stored in the variable. Then the program may analyze what was entered and decide what kind of action to take. LINE INPUT also solves the problem of input being cut off when a comma is encountered. With LINE INPUT, everything keyed before pressing the ENTER/RETURN key is stored in the variable.

With LINE INPUT, as well as INPUT, there are still some problems remaining in data input. For example, neither of these statements has the ability to limit the number of characters entered by the user. Thus, a user would be allowed to type more characters than space that may have been set aside on the disk, printer, or screen. Also, with these keywords, no checking of the input can be done until the user presses the ENTER/RETURN key. Until that point, the data keyed in is not available to the program. By writing your own data entry subroutine, however, all the problems of the INPUT and LINE INPUT statements can be solved. How you can do that is discussed in the following paragraphs.

AN ALGORITHM FOR IMPROVED DATA INPUT

In considering how a data entry routine should function, think about the kinds of data checks that were discussed earlier in this chapter. Think, too, about the items for good displays that were discussed in Chapter 5. With those items in mind, several features of an improved data entry routine can be listed. They are:

1. The prompt and the actual entry of the data should be done at whatever point on the screen is desired by the programmer.
2. The user should not be allowed to enter data longer than the maximum length that has been established. For example, if you decide that the maximum length of a name should be 20 characters, the user should not be allowed to enter more than that. This check can be implemented by not allowing the entry of any character after the maximum. Alternately, it may be done by checking the length of the data after the user presses ENTER/RETURN.
3. The user should be allowed to change the data as desired before it is accepted by the program. The best solution of all is to allow the user to freely move the cursor around the screen, changing any data item on the screen until all items are as desired. Then by striking one key, the computer can accept the entire screen of information. As an alternate, a much easier to program method is to allow the user to

change a data item as much as desired before pressing ENTER/
RETURN. When ENTER/RETURN is pressed, the program pro-
ceeds to the next item.

4. The program should refuse to accept character data when numeric
   data is needed. Similar to the previous item, the program may either
   refuse to accept nonnumeric characters or it may look for them after
   the user has pressed ENTER/RETURN.

The four items just discussed are things the data entry routine itself can
do. Once data has been entered, it is up to other parts of the program to
perform such checks as looking up the data in a table or performing a
consistency check to see if the data is valid.

IMPLEMENTATION OF ALGORITHMS FOR IMPROVED DATA INPUT

In this section, we will look at three different methods for accepting
input from the keyboard. The first will accept the data by use of the INPUT
or LINE INPUT statement. The program will then do some checking of the
data. The second method will check the data one character at a time as it is
entered, preventing the entry of undesired characters. The third method will
allow the operator to make changes anywhere on a data entry screen before
the data is made available to the program.

Checking Data After Standard Input

Checking the data immediately after it is entered is the easiest method
to code. Remembering the earlier discussion about the desirable characteristics of a data entry routine, the following program design can be developed:

1. Locate the cursor to the desired screen location.
2. Use a standard INPUT or LINE INPUT statement to get input from
   the keyboard. LINE INPUT is preferred if it is available.
3. Use IF . . . THEN statements to check the validity of the data. If data
   is invalid, print an appropriate error message in a standard location on
   the screen (such as the bottom line). Then send program control back
   to Step 1 for reentry of the data.

Here is an example showing how this method may be used to get a name
and an amount from the keyboard. After the data is checked and accepted,
the name and amount are printed as verification. Note that this program only
demonstrates the data entry process. It does not do anything useful. The
program is coded for the IBM. To use it with the TRS-80, change each
LOCATE to PRINT@; if using a Model III, shorten the variable names as
necessary and insert a CLEAR statement as Line 35. To use the program
with the Apple, replace each LOCATE with VTAB and HTAB, replace
LINE INPUT with INPUT, shorten variable names as necessary, and delete
line 160. On the Commodore, replace each LOCATE with a PRINT

statement to position the cursor. Then replace LINE INPUT with INPUT, shorten the variable names as necessary, and delete line 160. When using this program on a computer without LINE INPUT, remember that you must enclose in quotation marks any input that contains a comma. Following the program is a detailed description of how it works.

```
10 ' EXC6E1
20 ' CLARK AND LABARRE--CHAPTER 6, EXAMPLE 1
30 ' A SIMPLE DATA ENTRY EXAMPLE
40 CLS
50 LOCATE 8,1
60 LINE INPUT "NAME:     ";NAM$
70 LOCATE 24,1
80 PRINT STRING$(39," ");
90 IF LEN(NAM$)>20 THEN LOCATE 24,1:
                      PRINT ">>NAME IS TOO LONG.   REENTER.<<";:
                      GOTO 50
100 LOCATE 10,1
110 LINE INPUT "AMOUNT:   ";AMOUNT$
120 LOCATE 24,1
130 PRINT STRING$(39," ");
140 AMOUNT=VAL(AMOUNT$)
150 CHECK$=STR$(AMOUNT)
160 IF LEFT$(CHECK$,1)=" " THEN CHECK$=MID$(CHECK$,2)
170 IF AMOUNT$<>CHECK$ THEN LOCATE 24,1: PRINT "MUST BE NUMERIC":
                      GOTO 100
180 LOCATE 12,5
190 PRINT "RESULT:   ";NAM$,AMOUNT
999 END
```

The coding of the program is done according to the program design. To check to see that the entered name does not exceed the desired number of characters, the LEN function is used. If the name is too long, an error message is printed on line 24 and control is sent back to line 50 for reentry of the data. Note that immediately following the LINE INPUT statement is a statement that prints 39 blank spaces on line 24 of the screen. This statement will erase any error message that may have been at the bottom of the screen.

After the amount is input, it is necessary to check to see whether any nonnumeric characters were entered. Any nonnumeric character makes the number invalid, resulting in the printing of an error message and the return of control to the statement that gets the input. Here's how the checking algorithm works:

1. Note that the amount entered by the user was stored as a character string in a variable known as AMOUNT$.
2. Convert the character string to a numeric value and store it in a variable known as AMOUNT.
3. Next, convert the numeric value back into a string value and store it in a variable known as CHECK$.

4. Remember that the IBM and TRS-80 versions of BASIC put a blank in front of all numbers unless they are negative. If you are using one of these types of BASIC, and the first character of CHECK$ is a blank, strip the blank off by using the MID$ function.

5. Compare AMOUNT$ and CHECK$. If they are the same, all the characters are numeric; otherwise, at least one nonnumeric character was entered.

Here is an example of the analysis of a valid number. The user keys in 987.31, which is stored in AMOUNT$. The VAL function returns 987.31, which looks the same except for the blank in front, and stores it in AMOUNT. AMOUNT is now converted back to character data, giving 987.31, which is stored in CHECK$. Since 987.31 has a blank in front, the blank is taken off. Now AMOUNT$ and CHECK$ are compared. Since they are the same, all the characters were numeric.

Here is an example of the analysis of an entry containing a nonnumeric character. The user keys in 98U.31, which is stored in AMOUNT$. The VAL functions returns 98 (remember that the conversion goes until the first nonnumeric character is encountered), which is stored in AMOUNT. AMOUNT is now converted back to character data, giving 98, which is stored in CHECK$. Since 98 has a blank in front, the blank is taken off. Now AMOUNT$ and CHECK$ are compared. Since they are not the same, the error message is printed and control is sent back for reentry of the data.

Checking Data During Input

When you want to check data during input, it is best to create a data entry routine as a separate module or subroutine in a program. Then a GOSUB statement can be used to send control to that module each time data from the keyboard is needed. Then, the design of data input looks like this:

1. Set up parameters for the input of data. This refers to setting up a prompt, setting the row and column position, and specifying such things as the maximum length and whether the data is to be numeric.

2. Send program control to the data entry routine to get the data.

3. Perform any additional error trapping needed on the data.

4. Copy the data from the input variable to the variable where it will be stored. This is necessary since the same variable is always used for input.

With a design such as this, the amount of work done by the data entry routine can be tailored to the needs of the program. For some programs, it may be rather simple, while for others it may be quite complex. In the following sections, we will first illustrate a simple data entry routine. This will be followed by a routine that accomplishes additional checking functions on the data.

MOST SIMPLE MODULE

When using a separate data entry module, a hierarchy chart can be drawn as shown in Figure 6.1. Note that the data entry module can be called by any other module of the program. That is, it can be called by the main module or by any of the submodules of the program. This makes the data entry module a service module to all of the others. We have used dotted lines in the chart to reflect this relationship.

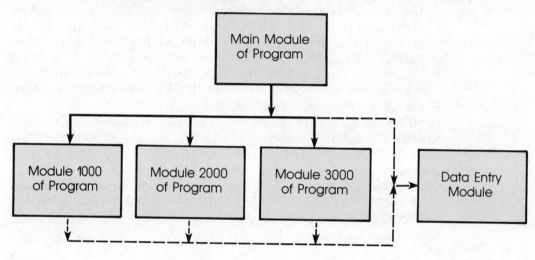

Figure 6.1   Hierarchy Chart

The simplest version of the data input routine simulates the action of the LINE INPUT statement. First, look at the main module of the program and compare it with the program design. Note that in this simple program no additional error checking is done after the data is input from the keyboard. Also, we will illustrate only the main module and the data entry module. To run the program on the Apple, Commodore, or TRS-80, replace each LOCATE with the appropriate statement and shorten the variable names as necessary.

```
10 ' EXC6E2
20 ' CLARK AND LABARRE--CHAPTER 6, EXAMPLE 2
30 ' DATA INPUT ROUTINE THAT SIMULATES LINE INPUT
40 CLS
50 LOCATE 10,5                'POSITION THE CURSOR
60 PRINT "ENTER A NAME:   ";  'PRINT THE PROMPT
70 GOSUB 65000               'GO GET THE DATA
80 LOCATE 14,5               'POSITION THE CURSOR
90 NAM$=ITEM$                'COPY THE VARIABLE TO STORAGE VARIABLE
100 PRINT NAM$               'PRINT THE STORAGE VARIABLE
999 END
```

Now look at the program design for the data entry module or subroutine:

1. Initialize the variables to be used for data input. Since we will be accepting data one character at a time in order to check it, we will need a variable to hold each character. We will also need a variable to hold the accumulation of all the valid characters that are entered. We will use CHAR$ to hold individual characters and ITEM$ to hold the accumulated characters. When control is returned from the subroutine to the main module, ITEM$ will always contain the valid characters that have been entered. By placing a null (the "nothing" character, ASCII code 0) in each variable at the start of the routine, we ensure that no leftover characters contaminate the new data.

2. As long as the user has not pressed ENTER/RETURN to signify the end of the data, do the following:
    a. Subject the character to any desired filters. A filter in a computer program is somewhat like any other filter; it traps certain things. For example, we will be trapping backspace characters in this first program. Later we will also be trapping such things as unwanted nonnumeric characters. All characters that survive the filters are valid input characters. To make the organization of the data input routine easier to understand, we will set up each filter as a separate module. The following program has only one filter, designed to trap the backspace key.
    b. Catenate (attach) the new character to the accumulating string of characters.
    c. Print the new character on the screen.
    d. Get another character from the keyboard for processing.

Since we are setting up each filter as a separate submodule, the hierarchy chart for the entire program needs to be expanded by adding the filters. For this program, since it contains only a backspace filter, the new module is added under the data entry module as shown in Figure 6.2.

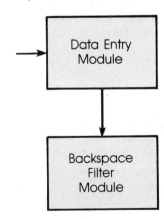

Figure 6.2   Addition to Hierarchy Chart

Converting the program design to BASIC code gives the following module. Note the IF...THEN that checks for the backspace character (ASCII code of 8) and sends control to the filter subroutine. Refer to the program design and the remarks in the program as you study how the module operates. If you are using a computer that does not have WHILE... WEND capability, it is necessary to construct the loop with a GOTO. To do that, change line 65040 to a remark statement. Then change line 65120 to read IF CHAR\$<>CHR\$(13) THEN GOTO 65040.

```
65000 ' ***** DATA INPUT MODULE *******
65010 ITEM$=""                'SET ITEM$ TO NULL
65020 CHAR$=""                'SET CHAR$ TO NULL
65040 WHILE CHAR$<>CHR$(13)   'REPEAT THE FOLLOWING UNTIL ENTER/RETURN
65050    IF CHAR$=CHR$(8) THEN GOSUB 65200    'BACKSPACE FILTER
65090       ITEM$=ITEM$+CHAR$  'CATENATE CHARACTER TO ACCUMULATION
65100       PRINT CHAR$;       'PRINT THE CHARACTER
65110       CHAR$=INPUT$(1)    'GET A NEW CHARACTER FOR PROCESSING
65120 WEND                     'END OF THE LOOP
65199 RETURN                   'RETURN TO THE CALLING MODULE
```

Now think about what should happen when the backspace key has been struck. If at least one character of input remains, the backspace should back up the cursor and erase one character from both the screen and the accumulated character variable. However, if no characters of input exist, the backspace character should do nothing. That is how the backspace filter module works. Here is its program design:

1. Check to see how many characters of input exist.
2. If more than zero characters exist; remove the last character from the accumulated character variable and backspace the cursor on the screen (which also erases the last character on the screen).
3. Set the character variable to **null** (nothing). This is to prevent an unwanted backspace from happening when the calling module prints the character that was entered.
4. Return to the calling module.

Compare the following coding to see how each of the program design steps is translated into BASIC.

```
65200 ' ***** BACKSPACE FILTER ********
65210 ITEMLEN=LEN(ITEM$)
65220 IF ITEMLEN>0 THEN ITEM$=LEFT$(ITEM$,ITEMLEN-1):
                        PRINT CHR$(29);"_";CHR$(29);
65230 CHAR$=""
65299 RETURN
```

A MORE CAPABLE MODULE

The more capable data entry module described in the following paragraphs is based on the most simple version discussed in the previous section. The following capabilities have been added to it:

1. An underline is drawn to indicate the maximum permissible length of input. The user is not allowed to enter more characters than designated by the underline. The maximum length feature is done by using an additional filter.

2. If numeric input is desired, the module will not accept any nonnumeric character. Instead, the computer will beep to request entry of correct data. The numeric check feature is also implemented as an additional filter.

With the two new filters, the hierarchy chart for the data entry part of the program is drawn as shown in Figure 6.3.

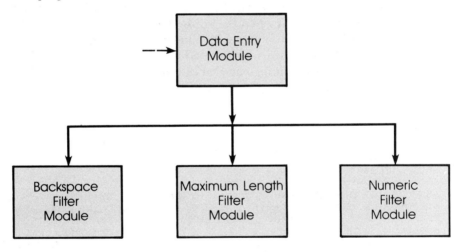

Figure 6.3   Addition to Hierarchy Chart

Now look at the modules and how they are coded. The main module, which follows immediately, is almost identical to its form under the most simple data entry. However, two LET statements have been added. The variable MAXLEN contains the maximum number of characters that may be entered. The variable NUMERIC contains a 1 if the data is to be numeric, or a 0 if it is to be character data. After control is returned from the data entry module, the value in ITEM$ is converted to a numeric value with the VAL function. This is essentially the same step as in the simpler program in that the data is copied from ITEM$ into the variable where it is to be stored.

```
10 ' EXC6E3
20 ' CLARK AND LABARRE--CHAPTER 6, EXAMPLE 3
30 ' DATA INPUT WITH UNDERLINE, BACKSPACE; NUMERIC, & MAXIMUM LENGTH FILTERS
40 CLS
50 NUMERIC=1
60 LOCATE 10,5
70 PRINT "ENTER A NUMBER:  ";
80 MAXLEN=6                     'MAXIMUM NUMBER OF CHARACTERS TO BE ENTERED
90 NUMERIC=1                    'A 1 INDICATES NUMERIC, 0 INDICATES CHARACTER
100  GOSUB 65000
110  LOCATE 14,5
120  NUMBER=VAL(ITEM$)          'CONVERT ITEM$ TO NUMERIC AND STORE IT
130  PRINT NUMBER
999  END
```

There are two changes in main data input module. One is the addition of a line (Line 65030) to print underline characters to indicate the maximum length. Once the underlines are printed, the cursor must be backed up to the beginning of the input area. This is done by printing a series of cursor left characters (ASCII 29 on the IBM). The backspace character (ASCII 8) is not used because it would erase the underline characters as it backs up. If using a computer that does not have STRING$ capability, FOR...NEXT loops may be used, printing one character on each iteration. The second change in the module is the addition of lines to send control to the new filter subroutines.

```
65000 ' ***** DATA INPUT MODULE *******
65005 LOCATE,,1
65010 ITEM$=""
65020 CHAR$=""
65030 PRINT STRING$(MAXLEN,"_");STRING$(MAXLEN,29);
65040 WHILE CHAR$<>CHR$(13)      'REPEAT THE FOLLOWING UNTIL ENTER/RETURN
65050    IF CHAR$=CHR$(8) THEN GOSUB 65200      'BACKSPACE FILTER
65060    GOSUB 65300                            'MAXIMUM LENGTH FILTER
65070    IF NUMERIC THEN GOSUB 65400           'NONNUMERIC FILTER
65080 '   SPACE FOR ANOTHER FILTER LATER IF DESIRED
65090    ITEM$=ITEM$+CHAR$
65100    PRINT CHAR$;
65110    CHAR$=INPUT$(1)
65120 WEND
65199 RETURN
```

The backspace filter replaces the use of the ASCII 8 to move the cursor back and erase the last character on the screen. This is done because we now want to replace the erased character with an underline rather than a blank. This is accomplished by printing a cursor left character, then printing an underscore. This effectively erases the last character. Now, another cursor left character is printed to bring the cursor back into position over the newly printed underscore.

```
65200 ' ***** BACKSPACE FILTER ********
65210 ITEMLEN=LEN(ITEM$)
65220 CHAR$="":IF ITEMLEN>0 THEN ITEM$=LEFT$(ITEM$,ITEMLEN-1):
            PRINT CHR$(29);" ";CHR$(29);    'DO THE BACKSPACE
65230 CHAR$=""
65299 RETURN
```

The maximum length filter simply compares the length of the accumulated ITEM$ to the maximum permissible length. If ITEM$ has grown as long as permitted, a null is placed in CHAR$, preventing any further growth of ITEM$. A beep alerts the user to an error condition.

```
65300 ' ***** MAXIMUM LENGTH FILTER ***
65310 IF LEN(ITEM$)=MAXLEN THEN BEEP:
                        CHAR$=""
65399 RETURN
```

The nonnumeric filter only allows the entry of the digits 0-9, the minus sign (-), and the decimal point (.). The ASCII code of the entered character is examined to see if it is numeric. If it is not, a null is placed in CHAR$ to replace the invalid character. A beep alerts the user to an error condition.

```
65400 ' ***** NONNUMERIC FILTER *******
65410 IF CHAR$>"" THEN ASCII=ASC(CHAR$)
                ELSE ASCII=0
65420 IF ASCII>0 THEN IF (ASCII<45 OR ASCII>57) OR ASCII=47 THEN BEEP:
                        CHAR$=""
65499 RETURN
```

Coding Methods for Increasing Accuracy

Think back for a moment to the methods explained in Topic 6.1 for increasing the accuracy of data. Look at how the items have been addressed in our improved data entry modules.

1. The use of good prompts is really not a matter of coding. It is a matter of composing prompts that are meaningful to the user and then making sure those prompts are printed at the appropriate time. With our data entry module, either good or bad prompts can be used. It is up to the programmer to supply good prompts.

2. Preventing the occurrence of system-generated error messages is handled by our data entry module. Those messages generally deal with entering string data when numeric was being requested, or with entering too many or too few values. Since all characters are initially accepted into a character variable, all characters entered will be successfully captured. Then our numeric filter can make sure only

numeric values are entered. Since we have written the routine to always accept one item of data at a time, there is no problem with the user entering too many or too few items.

3. Requiring the data to be numeric or nonnumeric is handled as discussed in the previous paragraph.

4. Limiting the length of input data to the maximum that can be handled by the program is done by the maximum length filter of the data entry routine.

5. Range checking of data is one kind of error trap that must be done by the program after control is returned from the data entry module. In other words, the data entry module as we have written it will not do range checking.

6. Validation of data by table lookup is another kind of error trap that must be done by the main program; it is not handled by the data entry module.

7. Validation of data by use of a consistency check must also be performed by the main program after the value is accepted by the data input module.

REVIEW QUESTIONS

1. What are the advantages and disadvantages of using the INPUT statement? (Obj. 4)
2. What are the advantages and disadvantages of using the LINE INPUT statement? (Obj. 4)
3. If a program is to use INPUT or LINE INPUT for accepting data, how can you code the program to ensure against data items that are too long? (Obj. 5)
4. If a program is to use INPUT or LINE INPUT for accepting data, how can you code the program to ensure that the wrong entry of nonnumeric data will not cause the printing of a system-generated error message? (Obj. 5)
5. Is it more desirable to check each character of data as it is input or to wait until an entire item is input before doing any checking? Why? (Obj. 3)
6. Describe the algorithm for a data input method that shows the maximum input length on the screen and checks each character as it is entered. (Obj. 5)

VOCABULARY WORDS

The following terms were introduced in this chapter.

filter   catenate   null

KEYWORDS

No new keywords were introduced in this chapter.

PROGRAMS TO WRITE

Program 1

You want to use the computer to prepare name tags for the persons who will be exhibiting their products at a convention. You are using continuous-form name tags that are 3.5 inches wide and 2 inches long. The exhibitor's name will be on one line, with the name of the company on another line. Your printer is set up to print at 10 characters per inch. For the name, you will command the printer to expand each character to double width. For each person for whom a name tag is needed, the program should accept data, verify that it is within the maximum allowed width, and then print the name tag. To expand the width of the name on the printer, you will print a special control code just before printing the name. Check with your teacher or look in the printer manual to find the correct code.

Program 2

The county tax collector uses a very simple program for logging in tax payments. When a payment is made, the operator enters the taxpayer's social security number (no hyphens) and the amount of the payment. These two numbers are then printed on the printer as a permanent record. At the end of the day, the total amount collected is printed at the bottom of the report. Even though the program does what it is supposed to do, the operator has become frustrated by the many occasions on which system-generated errors appear. Therefore, the tax collector has employed you to rewrite the program in such a way that no system-generated error is likely to appear during use of the program.

Program 3

You want to use the computer to sort the membership list of a civic club of which you are a member. The names need to be entered as last name, comma, first name. The computer you are using does not have a LINE INPUT statement. (If it does, assume that it does not.) Write a program to do the job in such a way that the LINE INPUT is simulated and the names do not have to be enclosed in quotation marks.

Program 4

Modify Program 3 so that no name may be over 25 characters in length including the comma.

Program 5

Modify Program 2 so that the data input routine will automatically place hyphens in the social security number as it is entered. The hyphens will then also appear when the number is printed.

Program 6

A program is needed for creating a file of merchandise orders. Each order received is to be entered into the computer, with the data being added to a sequential file on disk. Each order stored on disk must begin with a diagonal line (/), which has been chosen to represent the beginning of an order. The diagonal is followed by the customer number of the customer placing the order. This is followed by a series of stock numbers and quantities. The customer number and the quantities are numeric. The stock numbers all consist of two alphabetic characters followed by four digits. Your program should ensure that all numbers really are numbers and should assure that each stock number is in the proper format. Use the most advanced form of data entry you can.

CONTINUING PROJECTS

Before writing any program on the continuing projects, be sure to complete all appropriate documentation.

Project 1

Write a menu program for your project. The menu program, which you should name P1MENU, will be run by the sign-on procedure you wrote in Chapter 5. The menu printed on the screen should be easy to read. Selections should be made by entering a number or letter of the desired choice. Once the desired choice is entered, the menu program should run a separate program that executes the chosen task. In writing your program, use an advanced data entry routine that can be continued in use throughout the project. For testing your program, stub in each of the programs the menu needs to execute. The names for the stubbed-in programs for testing are P1MAINT, P1PAY, and P1REP. The following choices should be on the menu:

1. Maintain Master File
2. Prepare Payroll
3. Print Reports
4. Quit

Project 2

Write a menu program for your project. The menu program, which you should name P2MENU will be run by the sign-on procedure you wrote in Chapter 5. The first thing the program should do is execute a logging process that requests the user to enter his or her name. This name should then be recorded in a sequential file known as LOGONS. If the computer being used has the capability to do so, the name should be appended to any other names that may already be in the file. If the computer being used has system variables for the date and time, these should also be written to the file.

Once the operator has logged on, the main menu of the program should be printed. The menu on the screen should be easy to read. Selections should be made by entering the first letter of the desired choice. The selected item should be highlighted in some way. The user should be able to change his or her mind about the selection by making a different choice. Once the user is sure that the highlighted item is the desired one, pressing the ENTER/ RETURN key should execute the selection. The menu program should run a separate program that executes the chosen task. In writing your program, use an advanced data entry routine that can be continued in use throughout the project. For testing your program, stub in each of the programs the menu needs to execute. The names for the stubbed-in programs for testing are P2SELL, P2MAINT, P2ANAL, and P2REORD. The following choices should be on the menu:

1. Point of Sale
2. Inventory Maintenance
3. Sales Analysis
4. Merchandise Reorder
5. Quit

Unit 3 • Sorts and Searches

## Chapter 7

Sorts

Objectives: 1. Define sorting.

2. Name two applications that require sorting.

3. Describe the algorithm for a delayed replacement sort.

4. Describe the algorithm for the Shell-Metzner sort.

5. Describe a pointer-based sort and tell when it should be used.

6. Write programs containing sort routines.

Topic 7.1— PRINCIPLES OF SORTING

Many computer applications require that data be arranged in order. This arranging is known as sorting. Both numeric and character data may be sorted. Numeric data may be arranged in ascending order (smallest to largest) or in descending order (largest to smallest). Alphabetic data is usually arranged in alphabetic order. One of the most common applications for sorting is in the production of all kinds of directories. These may include telephone directories and membership lists of organizations. Another example is in the preparation of large mailings, where the Postal Service gives a postage discount to mailers who have sorted letters into groups by ZIP Code. By arranging the addresses in order before printing the envelopes, the envelopes will be grouped when they are printed rather than requiring a time-consuming hand sort.

METHODS FOR ORDERING DATA

When data needs to be in order, there are several points at which that order can be established. The first is to require the user to enter the data in proper sequence. This means that the user must most likely sort the data by hand before entering it, which is not a good use of the user's time. A second method is to let the computer arrange the data in proper sequence as it is being entered. When using this method, the first item that is input is stored in the first row of a table. Then the next item is input. If the second item is larger than the first, it is stored in the second position in the table. If the second item is smaller, the first item is moved to row two of the table and the new item is stored in row one. For items beyond the second one, the same general procedure is followed. If the new item is larger than any other item in the table, it is stored in the next empty row. If there are larger items already in the table, they are all moved down one row in the table to make room for the new item.

Frequently, however, data is ordered by sorting all of the data after it has been entered. There are many algorithms that can be used to sort data. Generally, data is placed in a table and is then rearranged by the steps of the chosen algorithm. However, in the case of random data files too large to fit into memory, the sort can be done on the disk. The same algorithms used for sorting data in tables can be used for sorting the records of a random file on disk; record numbers are used rather than row numbers. Sorting a file while it remains on disk, however, is very slow compared to sorting data that is in memory.

You are probably familiar with the simple bubble sort. In the following sections we will examine two additional sort algorithms. We will then examine how to sort data without physically rearranging it.

Delayed Replacement Sort

A method known as the delayed replacement sort will be discussed first. It is easy to understand but, like the bubble sort, is suitable only for sorting small numbers of items. The delayed replacement sort is based on the same concept you would probably use to sort items. It finds the smallest item (or largest, if you are doing a descending sort) in the table and places it in the first row. Then it finds the second smallest item and places it in the second row. This process continues until all the items are in their proper positions. Here is a detailed explanation of how this process can be done with the computer. Assume that a table has been filled with numbers. Place a one (for row one) in a compare variable that designates the row of the smallest value yet found. Then make comparisons with all other items in the table. Whenever a value is found that is less than the one indicated by the compare variable, immediately put the row of the newly found small value in the compare variable. The result of this process is that, when you get to the end of the table, the row number of the smallest item in the entire table will be contained in the compare variable. At this point, swap the contents of row one and the contents of the compare variable's row. This will place the smallest value in the first row of the table. This process accomplishes the results shown in Figure 7.1.

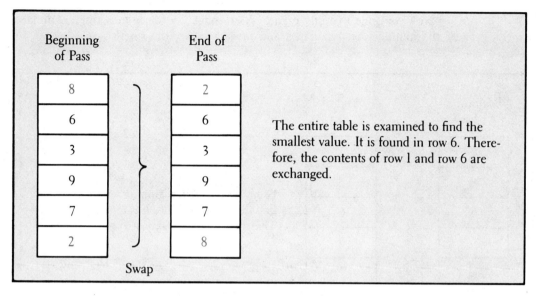

Figure 7.1   Placing the Smallest Item in Sorting Six Numbers

At this point, you have been through the entire table one time. You have placed the first item in its proper position. Therefore, you do not need to deal with the first item in the second pass. Start this time with the second element of the table and find the smallest value from there to the end of the table. When you reach the end of the table, swap the item in the second row with the smallest item found. This gives the result shown in Figure 7.2, with the first and second items now in their proper positions.

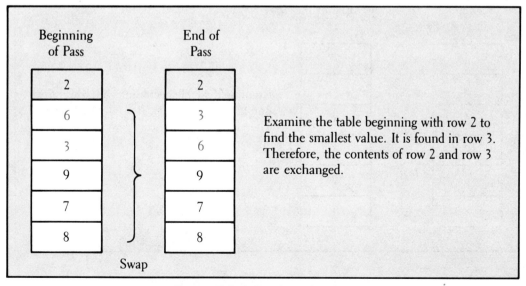

Figure 7.2   Placing the Second Number

Now continue to study Figures 7.3 through 7.5 to see how the remainder of the numbers are compared and moved during the sort.

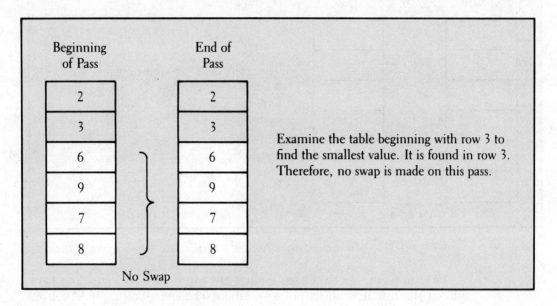

Figure 7.3   Placing the Third Number

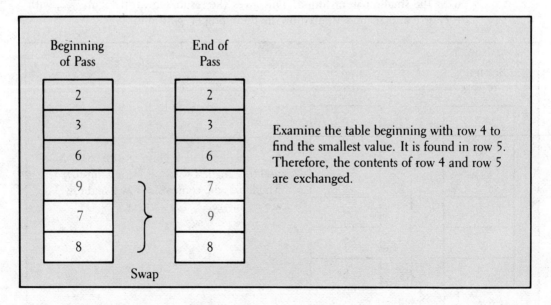

Figure 7.4   Placing the Fourth Number

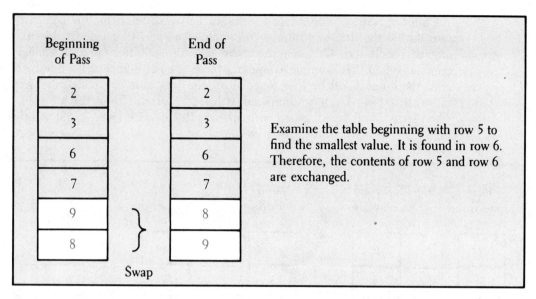

Figure 7.5   Placing the Fifth Number

Shell-Metzner Sort

The Shell-Metzner sort is one of several more advanced sort algorithms suitable for use in sorting larger numbers of items. It works much faster than the bubble sort and delayed replacement sort. The Shell-Metzner algorithm takes its name from two persons who developed it. A sort known as the Shell sort was first described by D. L. Shell. The method was later modified by Marlene Metzner of Pratt and Whitney Aircraft Company. The modified method became known as the Shell-Metzner sort.

From your study of the bubble sort and delayed replacement sort, you should realize that each item in a table is compared with all other items in the table. This leads to a very large number of comparisons, which slows down the operation of the sort. Also, the bubble sort performs very large numbers of swaps, further slowing its operation. These shortcomings are handled in the Shell-Metzner sort by using an algorithm that "understands" that if Number A is less than Number B and Number B is less than Number C, there is no need to compare Numbers A and C. An example would be if 16 is less than 27 and 27 is less than 48, there is no need to compare 16 and 48. This is accomplished by roughly dividing all the data items into halves, then successively refining the arrangement into fourths, eighths, and so on. Once an item is into its proper part of the table it is no longer routinely compared with items that belong in other parts of the table. For example, once an item is properly placed in the first quarter of the table, no further comparisons are routinely made between it and items that belong in other quarters of the table.

Starting with a wide interval (distance between items) for the comparisons during the first pass through the table, the Shell-Metzner sort does its original rough sort. On each successive pass through the table, a smaller interval is used. For example, consider a table of eight numbers. For the first pass, the interval will be four (one-half of the total number of items). This means that Item 1 will be compared with Item 5 (Item 1 plus the interval). Then Item 2 will be compared with Item 6, Item 3 with Item 7, and so on. Figure 7.6 shows how the first pass looks.

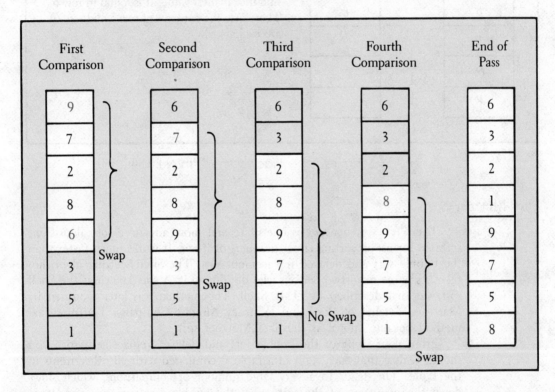

Figure 7.6   First Pass Using Shell-Metzner Algorithm

In Figure 7.7, examine the movement that has taken place. The first column shows the original order. The second column shows the order after one pass. Note that the pass involved only four comparisons as compared to many more in the bubble sort's first comparison. Note also that each number, if it moved, moved four rows. This large movement is in comparison to the one-row-at-a-time movement with the bubble sort.

The first pass is, in effect, a rough sort that gives the items a big move toward the right location. Most of the numbers are in the correct half of the table. Now it is necessary to do a finer sort to get items closer to their exact positions. This is accomplished by dividing the interval by two and making

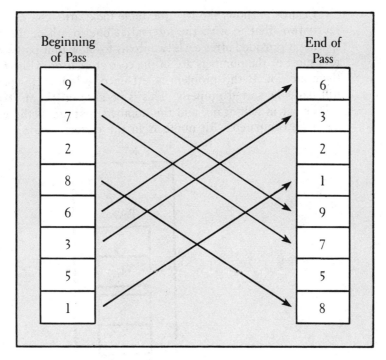

Figure 7.7   Data Items Move Large Distances on the First Pass

another pass through the table. Study Figure 7.8 for an illustration of what happens when we make the same kind of pass through the table, except that the interval is cut to two.

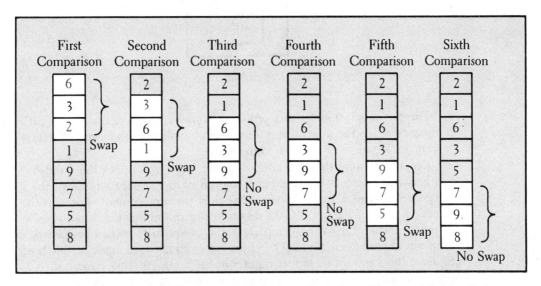

Figure 7.8   Pass With Interval at One Fourth of Table Size

Figure 7.9 shows the way the table looks after the pass with the interval set at two—that is, with the interval at one fourth of the table size. Wider spacing is provided after each two items to show four parts to the table. Note that most of the numbers are in the correct quarter of the table, but some of them are not. If this problem is left uncorrected at this point, the numbers will never be sorted properly. This is because on the next pass, the interval will be cut in half again, and the numbers that are in the wrong quarter will never be compared with numbers in the correct quarter.

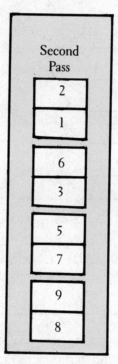

Figure 7.9   Data After the Second Pass

There is a solution to this problem, however. Look again at the fifth comparison when the interval was four. This column is reproduced as the first column of Figure 7.10 for your convenience.

Keeping in mind that the interval is four, note that earlier the number 9 had been compared to the number 6, and no swap was necessary. Now the 9 and 5 are compared and swapped. This gives the arrangement shown in the second column of Figure 7.10. As shown in this column, if the 5 had been in its position when the earlier comparison of this row to the 6 had happened, a swap would have been made. Therefore, the swap must be made at this time to move the 5 toward its proper quarter of the table. Anytime a swap such as this is made, you continue backing up an interval at a time until no swap is

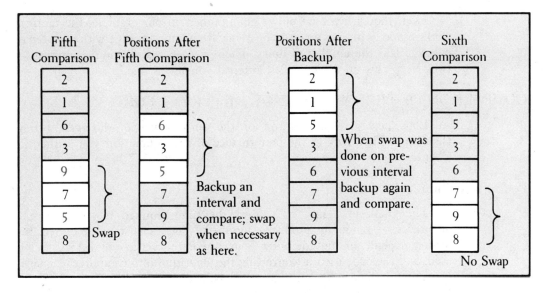

Figure 7.10   Solving the "Wrong Quarter" Problem

made. This ensures that the number gets all the way to its proper quarter. Once the backing up is done, proceed to the next comparison as normal. As you will note in the last column of the Figure 7.10, all the numbers are in the correct quarter of the table.

Next, divide the interval by two again. This brings it to one in our example. Do another pass through the table with the interval set at one. Again, you must do the backup whenever a swap is made. Figure 7.11 shows how the pass is done. Upon the completion of this pass, the table will be in order.

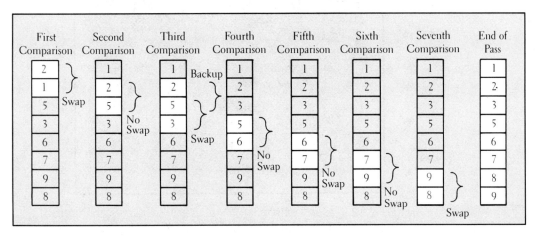

Figure 7.11   Operation of the Final Pass

Even though we used only eight numbers in our example, the method works properly for any quantity of items. Remember to start with an interval equal to half the number of items. Then on each pass divide the interval by two. Keep this up until the last interval you use is one.

COMPARISON OF PERFORMANCE OF DIFFERENT SORTS

Look now at a comparison of the performance of different sorting algorithms. First, look at the performance of the bubble sort you learned in Chapter 3.

Performance of the Bubble Sort

The graph in Figure 7.12 shows the time required to sort different quantities of randomly produced numbers. The exact times required for sorting depend on the computer being used, the version of BASIC being used, and the code used in converting the algorithm into computer language. However, the general relationships will hold true.

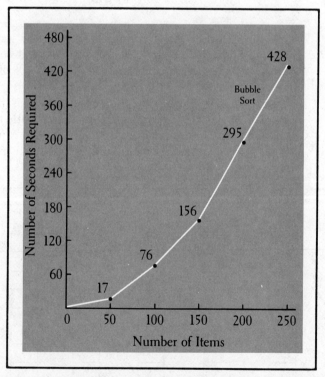

Figure 7.12   Comparison of Times Required to Sort Different Numbers of Items Using a Bubble Sort

In the chart, note that 17 seconds were required for sorting 50 numbers. You might expect that sorting twice as many numbers would take about twice as long. The actual number of seconds to sort 100 numbers, though, is shown as 76—more than four times as long. As you can see from the chart, this performance trend continues. The more items you are sorting, the slower the sort runs. When you note that more than seven minutes were required for sorting 250 items, you realize that this kind of sort is suitable only for use with very small numbers of items.

Performance of the Delayed Replacement Sort

The performance of the delayed replacement sort is shown in Figure 7.13. The line for the bubble sort is also shown to make comparisons easier. Note that the sorting time required is less than with the bubble sort. Also, performance does not slow down quite as quickly. For sorting 250 items, however, almost four minutes were required. This means that the delayed replacement sort is suitable for use only with small numbers of items.

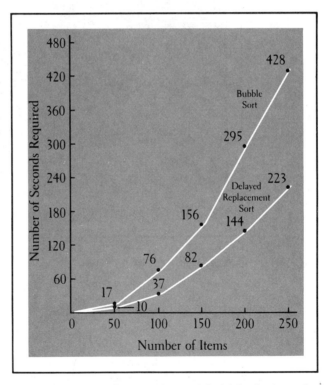

Figure 7.13   Comparison of Bubble Sort and
               Delayed Replacement Sort

Performance of the Shell-Metzner Sort

You can see the advantage of the Shell-Metzner sort over the bubble sort and the delayed replacement sort by looking at Figure 7.14. This figure repeats the bubble sort and delayed replacement sort speeds from Figure 7.13. It also adds the speeds for the Shell-Metzner sort done on the same computer with the same data. Note that although the Shell-Metzner sort does slow down as the number of items increases, the increase in time is not nearly so large as with the other sorts. In fact, with 250 items, the Shell-Metzner sort was more than eleven times faster than the bubble sort.

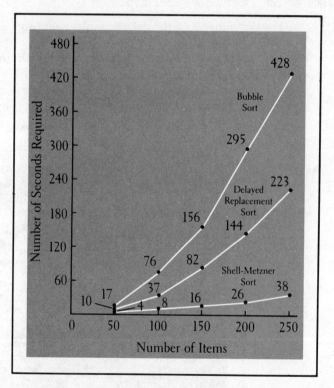

Figure 7.14   Comparison of Sort Times Required by the Bubble Sort, Delayed Replacement Sort, and the Shell-Metzner Sort

ORDERING DATA WITHOUT PHYSICAL REARRANGEMENT

The sort algorithms discussed in the previous sections used physical rearrangement of the data. When sorting tables consisting of only one column of data, this method works nicely. Think about the situation, however, when a multiple-column table needs to be sorted. Suppose a table contains five columns for name, street address, city and state, ZIP Code, and phone number. If you are sorting the table into alphabetic order by name, you compare names to determine when to make a swap. Each time you swap a name, however, you must also swap the street address, the city and state, the ZIP Code, and the phone number. In other words, whenever you would make one swap in a single-column table, you must now make five swaps—one for each column. When making this many swaps, the speed of a sort program slows down tremendously.

There is a good way around this slowdown, however. Regardless of what sort algorithm you are using, you can establish a single-column table of indexes that you move around in sorting. The multiple columns of data can remain in place, and no time will be taken up moving around all those multiple pieces of data. Look at the data table in Figure 7.15. As an example, there are just two columns (Name and Phone) and the rows are numbered (1-3) for easy reference. At the left of the table we have added a single-column that contains index numbers. At the beginning of the sort, these numbers are the same as row numbers of the table.

Index No.		Data Table	
	Row	Name	Phone
1	1.	Smith Hardware Store	987-3987
2	2.	Bryan's Laundromat	323-1938
3	3.	Mario's Restaurant	778-1946

Figure 7.15   Unsorted Index Numbers and the Data Table

Now lets try a delayed replacement sort without actually moving the names or phone numbers. This is called the pointer-based sort. Remembering the sort algorithm, the smallest (closest to the first letter of the alphabet) item is found and placed in row 1. For the pointer-based sort, however, we will not actually move the items, but will move the numbers in the index table. Right now the first index number is one, which means it is pointing at (referring to) the first row of the data (Smith). The second index number is two, referring to the second row of the data (Bryan). The third index number is three, referring to the third row of the data (Mario). Comparing all the data items alphabetically, we find that the smallest is Bryan and that the first row (Smith) should be swapped with Bryan (in the second row). Instead of swapping the data, however, we just swap the two index numbers. This gives the result shown in Figure 7.16.

Index No.	Data Table		
	Row	Name	Phone
2	1.	Smith Hardware Store	987-3987
1	2.	Bryan's Laundromat	323-1938
3	3.	Mario's Restaurant	778-1946

Figure 7.16   Index and Table After One Pass

Now continue to the next pass. Looking at data items beginning with the one pointed at by the second index number, find the smallest value. The second index row contains the number one, pointing at Smith. The third row contains the number three, pointing at Mario. Mario is less than Smith alphabetically, so it should be the second item. Again, instead of swapping items, we swap index numbers. This gives the result shown in Figure 7.17.

Index No.	Data Table		
	Row	Name	Phone
2	1.	Smith Hardware Store	987-3987
3	2.	Bryan's Laundromat	323-1938
1	3.	Mario's Restaurant	778-1946

Figure 7.17   Index and Table After Two Passes

Since the items themselves have not moved, the index must be used to print them in the correct order. The first row of the index contains a two; this means that the second data item (Bryan) is first alphabetically. The second row of the index contains a three; this means that the third data item (Mario) is next alphabetically. The third and last row of the index contains a one, indicating that the first item in the data table (Smith) is the last one in alphabetic order.

REVIEW QUESTIONS

1. What is sorting? (Obj. 1)
2. What are two applications in which sorting is necessary? (Obj. 2)
3. How does a delayed replacement sort work? (Obj. 3)
4. What is the primary disadvantage of a delayed replacement sort? (Obj. 3)
5. How does the Shell-Metzner sort work? (Obj. 4)
6. What are the advantages of the Shell-Metzner sort? (Obj. 4)
7. How is a sort algorithm modified to make it a pointer-based sort? (Obj. 5)
8. When is the use of a pointer-based sort most advantageous? (Obj. 5)

Topic 7.2— SORTING WITH BASIC

This topic explains how to code sorting algorithms in BASIC. The delayed replacement sort, a pointer-based replacement sort, and the Shell-Metzner sort will all be coded and explained.

CODING A DELAYED REPLACEMENT SORT

For the explanation of the delayed replacement sort, randomly generated numbers will be sorted. In an actual application, the items to be sorted would be input from the keyboard or some other input device, or read from auxiliary storage. The three steps in the program are: (1) generate a table of random numbers, (2) sort the numbers, and (3) print the numbers. Each of these steps can be a module as shown in the hierarchy chart in Figure 7.18. We will do a module documentation sheet for each module and then code that module.

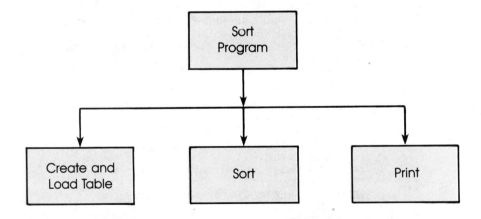

Figure 7.18   Hierarchy Chart for a Sort Program

Figure 7.19 shows the module documentation sheet and code for the generation of the table of numbers.

MODULE DOCUMENTATION	Program: __EXC7E1__	Module: __CREATE & LOAD__ Lines: __1000-1999__

Module Description:

This module creates a table and fills it with randomly generated numbers.

Module Function (Program Design):

1. Define all variables as integers, if appropriate to your computer.
2. Find out from the user how many numbers are desired.
3. Dimension the table to the size desired by the user.
4. Randomize if your computer requires it.
5. Run a loop from one to the desired table size, placing a newly generated random number in the next row of the table on each loop.

```
10 ' EXC7E1
20 ' CLARK AND LABARRE--CHAPTER 7, EXAMPLE 1
30 ' DELAYED REPLACEMENT SORT
40 GOSUB 1000          'CREATE AND LOAD TABLE
50 GOSUB 2000          'SORT
60 GOSUB 3000          'PRINT
999 END

1000 ' ***** CREATE AND LOAD TABLE MODULE
1010 DEFINT A-Z
1020 CLS
1030 INPUT "HOW MANY NUMBERS";N
1040 DIM TABLE(N)
1050 RANDOMIZE VAL(RIGHT$(TIME$,2))
1060 FOR ROW=1 TO N
1070     TABLE(ROW)=INT(RND*1000)
1080 NEXT ROW
1999 RETURN
```

Figure 7.19   Creating the Table of Random Numbers

Figure 7.20 shows the module documentation sheet and code for the sorting process.

MODULE DOCUMENTATION	Program: EXC7E1	Module: SORT Lines: 2000-2999

Module Description:

This module sorts the numbers in a table using the delayed replacement sort algorithm.

Module Function (Program Design):

1. Repeatedly go through the table, varying the starting point from one to the size of the table. On each pass through the table do the following:
   a. Record the starting point row as the smallest item.
   b. For each row from the starting point to the table size:
      If the name in the table row being examined is smaller than the smallest previously found name, record the row number of the new smallest name.
   c. Swap the item in the starting row with the smallest item found.

```
2000 ' ***** SORT MODULE **************
2010 PRINT "SORTING . . ."
2020 START=1
2030 SMALL=START
2040 FOR ROW=START+1 TO N
2050    IF TABLE(ROW)<TABLE(SMALL) THEN SMALL=ROW
2060 NEXT ROW
2070 SWAP TABLE(START),TABLE(SMALL)
2080 START=START+1
2090 IF START<N THEN 2030
2999 RETURN
```

Figure 7.20   Sorting the Table of Random Numbers

Figure 7.21 shows the module documentation sheet and code for the printing of the numbers.

MODULE DOCUMENTATION	Program: EXC7E1	Module: PRINT
		Lines: 3000-3999

Module Description:

This module prints the sorted lines from the table.

Module Function (Program Design):

1. Loop through the table, printing the item from the next row on each loop.

```
3000 ' ***** PRINT MODULE *************
3010 CLS
3020 FOR ROW=1 TO N
3030    PRINT TABLE(ROW);
3040 NEXT ROW
3999 RETURN
```

Figure 7.21   Printing the Sorted Table of Numbers

CODING A POINTER-BASED SORT

Now, look at an example showing the application of a pointer-based delayed replacement sort. We will use a three-column table giving last names, first names, and horoscope signs. The data will be read from DATA statements. The program is divided into three modules: (1) create and fill the table, (2) sort the data, and (3) print the sorted data.

The module documentation sheet and program code for the module that creates and fills the table are shown in Figure 7.22. Note in this figure that an index table is created and filled at the same time the data table is created and filled.

MODULE DOCUMENTATION	Program: <u>EXC7E2</u>	Module: <u>CREATE & FILL</u> Lines: <u>1000-1999</u>

Module Description:

This module creates a table and fills it with data read from data lines.

Module Function (Program Design):

1. Define variables as integers if appropriate to your computer.
2. Set the variable for table size to 20.
3. Dimension a table for the data and one for the index pointers.
4. Loop through the table, reading data into the data table and placing row numbers into the index pointer table.

```
10 ' EXC7E2
20 ' CLARK AND LABARRE--CHAPTER 7, EXAMPLE 2
30 ' POINTER-BASED DELAYED REPLACEMENT SORT
40 GOSUB 1000          'CREATE AND FILL TABLE
50 GOSUB 2000          'SORT
60 GOSUB 3000          'PRINT
999 END

1000 ' ***** CREATE AND FILL TABLE ****
1010 DEFINT A-Z
1020 N=20
1030 DIM NAM$(N,3),PT(N)
1040 FOR ROW=1 TO N
1050     READ NAM$(ROW,1),NAM$(ROW,2),NAM$(ROW,3)
1060     PT(ROW)=ROW
1070 NEXT ROW
1999 RETURN
```

Figure 7.22   Creating and Filling a Three-Column Alphabetic Table

In Figure 7.23, the data is sorted. In the code, notice how the index numbers are moved rather than moving the data.

MODULE DOCUMENTATION	Program: __EXC7E2__	Module: __SORT__ Lines: __2000-2999__

Module Description:

This module sorts the data using a pointer-based sort.

Module Function (Program Design):

1. Repeatedly go through the table, varying the starting point from one to the size of the table. On each pass through the table do the following:
   a. Record the starting point row as the row of the smallest item.
   b. For table items referenced by each row of the pointer table from the starting point to the table size:
      If the name in the referenced row is smaller than the smallest previously found item, record the row number of the new and smallest item.
   c. In the pointer table, swap the item in the starting row with the smallest item found.

```
2000 ' ***** SORT MODULE **************
2010 CLS
2020 PRINT "SORTING . . ."
2030 START=1
2040 SMALL=START
2050 FOR ROW=START+1 TO N
2060     IF NAM$(PT(ROW),1)<NAM$(PT(SMALL),1) THEN SMALL=ROW
2070 NEXT ROW
2080 SWAP PT(START),PT(SMALL)
2090 START=START+1
2100 IF START<N THEN 2040
2999 RETURN
```

Figure 7.23   Sorting a Three-Column Alphabetic Table

Once the data is sorted, it is printed out using the code as shown in Figure 7.24. Note that the numbers from the index table are used to control the order of the printout.

MODULE DOCUMENTATION	Program: EXC7E2	Module: PRINT Lines: 3000-3999

Module Description:

This module prints out the contents of the data table, using the pointers in the index table to control the order of printout.

Module Function (Program Design):

1. Loop through the index table. For each row in the index table, print the data table items at which the pointer points.

```
3000 ' ***** PRINT MODULE *************
3010 CLS
3020 FOR ROW=1 TO N
3030    PRINT NAM$(PT(ROW),1);", ";NAM$(PT(ROW),2);TAB(25);NAM$(PT(ROW),3)
3040 NEXT ROW
3999 RETURN

4000 DATA STARR,KATHY,ARIES,SHENG,YANG,SCORPIO,FISK,JASON,VIRGO,TRUED,DAVE,LEO
4010 DATA LOCKWOOD,JOYCE,PISCES,GONZALEZ,JOSE,LIBRA,TURNER,BETY,CAPRICORN
4020 DATA BARBER,PAT,TAURUS,GARNER,ED,AQUARIUS,GORDON,LEE,LEO
4030 DATA HUDDLESTON,KEITH,CANCER,BRUCE,AL,GEMINI,REICHERT,BILLY,LIBRA
4040 DATA SCULLEY,JOYCE,PISCES,GAUSE,V.J.,LEO,ALLEN,I.N.,CAPRICORN
4050 DATA MOODY,DARLENE,SAGITTARIUS,DAVIS,DELORES,ARIES,KNIGHT,REBECCA,ARIES
4060 DATA KAVOUKLIS,NICHOLAS,TAURUS
```

Figure 7.24   Printing a Sorted Three-Column Alphabetic Table

CODING A SHELL-METZNER SORT

For the explanation of the Shell-Metzner sort, randomly generated numbers will be sorted. In an actual application, the items to be sorted would be input from the keyboard or some other input device or read from auxiliary storage. The three steps in the program are: (1) generate a table of random numbers, (2) sort the numbers, and (3) print the numbers. Each of these steps can be a module as shown earlier in the hierarchy chart in Figure 7.18. We will do a module documentation sheet for each module and then code that module. Figure 7.25 shows the module documentation sheet and code for the generation of the table of numbers.

MODULE DOCUMENTATION	Program: EXC7E3	Module: CREATE & FILL. Lines: 1000-1999

Module Description:

This module creates a table and fills it with randomly generated numbers.

Module Function (Program Design):

1. Define all variables as integers if appropriate to your computer.
2. Find out from the user how many numbers are desired.
3. Dimension the table to the size desired by the user.
4. Randomize if your computer requires it.
5. Run a loop from one to the desired table size, placing a newly generated random number in the next row of the table on each loop.

```
10 ' EXC7E3
20 ' CLARK AND LABARRE--CHAPTER 7, EXAMPLE 3
30 ' SHELL-METZNER SORT
40 GOSUB 1000        'CREATE AND FILL TABLE
50 GOSUB 2000        'SORT
60 GOSUB 3000        'PRINT RESULTS
999 END

1000 ' ***** CREATE AND FILL TABLE ****
1010 DEFINT A-Z
1020 CLS
1030 INPUT "HOW MANY NUMBERS";N
1040 RANDOMIZE VAL(RIGHT$(TIME$,2))
1050 DIM TABLE(N)
1060 FOR ROW=1 TO N
1070     TABLE(ROW)=INT(RND*1000)
1080 NEXT ROW
1999 RETURN
```

Figure 7.25   Creating the Table of Random Numbers

Figure 7.26 shows the module documentation sheet and code for the sorting process.

MODULE DOCUMENTATION	Program: EXC7E3	Module: SORT Lines: 2000-2999

Module Description:

This module sorts the numbers in a table using the Shell-Metzner sort algorithm.

Module Function (Program Design):

1. Set the interval size to the number of items in the table.
2. Until the interval size is reduced below one, repeatedly go through the table doing the following:
   a. Divide the interval size by two.
   b. For each row from the first to the table size less the interval:
      Compare the contents of the row to the contents of the row one interval below in the table; if they are greater then (1) swap the two items and (2) remake earlier comparisons whose outcome has been effected by the swap, swapping these earlier items where necessary.

```
2000 ' ***** SORT MODULE **************
2010 PRINT "SORTING . . ."
2020 INTERVAL=N     'INITIALIZE INTERVAL TO SIZE N VALUE
2030 INTERVAL=INTERVAL\2
2040    FOR ROWA=1 TO N-INTERVAL
2050       ROWB=ROWA+INTERVAL
2060       IF TABLE(ROWA)>TABLE(ROWB) THEN GOSUB 20000   'SWAP DATA
2070    NEXT ROWA
2080 IF INTERVAL>1 THEN 2030
2999 RETURN

20000 ' ***** SWAP MODULE *************
20010 SWAP TABLE(ROWA),TABLE(ROWB)
20020 TEMP=ROWA
20030 IF TEMP>INTERVAL THEN IF TABLE(TEMP-INTERVAL)>TABLE(TEMP) THEN
           SWAP TABLE(TEMP-INTERVAL),TABLE(TEMP):
           TEMP=TEMP-INTERVAL:GOTO 20030
20999 RETURN
```

Figure 7.26   Sorting the Table of Random Numbers

Figure 7.27 shows the module documentation sheet and code for the printing of the numbers.

MODULE DOCUMENTATION	Program: EXC7E3	Module: PRINT Lines: 3000-3999
Module Description: This module prints the sorted items from the table.		
Module Function (Program Design): 1. Loop through the table, printing the item from the next row on each loop.		

```
3000 ' ***** PRINT THE RESULTS ********
3010 CLS
3020 FOR ROW=1 TO N
3030    PRINT TABLE(ROW);
3040 NEXT ROW
3999 RETURN
```

Figure 7.27   Printing the Sorted Table of Numbers

REVIEW QUESTIONS

1. What are the steps in creating and filling a table with randomly generated numbers? (Obj. 6)
2. Describe the control structures used to set up a delayed replacement sort? (Obj. 6)
3. What is the difference in coding the sort for a one-column table and the sort for a multicolumn table? (Obj. 6)
4. What is the difference in coding a physical sort and a pointer-based sort? (Obj. 6)
5. Describe the control structures used to set up a Shell-Metzner sort? (Obj. 6)
6. How does the computer determine when it has finished a Shell-Metzner sort? (Obj. 6)

VOCABULARY WORDS

The following terms were introduced in this chapter:

ascending order   delayed replacement sort   pointer-based sort

descending order   Shell-Metzner sort

KEYWORDS AND COMMANDS

No new keywords or commands were introduced in this chapter.

PROGRAMS TO WRITE

For each of the programs, prepare the necessary documentation prior to writing the BASIC code.

Program 1

Write a program that uses a delayed replacement sort to sort a list of names into alphabetic order and then print the alphabetized list. Input the names from the keyboard.

Program 2

Write a program that uses a delayed replacement sort to sort a list of names, automobile models, and license plate numbers into alphabetic order based on the name. The program should get the data from DATA lines. This will allow comparison with later programs.

Program 3

Convert program 2 to a pointer-based sort. Time the performance of your program both before and after this change.

Program 4

Convert program 2 to a Shell-Metzner sort. Time its performance and compare it to previous versions of the program.

Program 5

Convert program 4 to a pointer-based Shell-Metzner sort. Time its performance and compare it to previous versions of the program.

Program 6

Modify program 5 so that the data can be sorted on the basis of either the name, the automobile make, or the license plate number. The program should ask the user for the field upon which sorting should take place.

CONTINUING PROJECTS

Before writing any program of the continuing projects, be sure to complete all appropriate documentation.

Project 1

You are now ready to create the master file maintenance program (P1MAINT) of your payroll system. When this option is chosen from the main menu, the user should be presented with another menu. The choices on the new menu, each of which will be written as a separate module, are:

1. Add an Employee
2. Change Information About an Employee
3. Return to the Main Menu

For this chapter, you will only be preparing the module for adding an employee. The module to change information will be prepared later. Whenever one or more employees is added, the program should sort the data so that all employees are arranged in order by their names. While the program is operating, data should be stored in one or more tables. Between program runs, the data should be stored in a sequential file on disk. Before being stored, the data should be sorted by employees' social security numbers. The data to be stored about each employee includes:

1. Name
2. Street Address
3. City, State
4. ZIP Code
5. Social Security Number
6. Work Department
7. Emergency Phone Number

Project 2

You are now ready to create the inventory maintenance program (P2MAINT) of your merchandising system. When this option is chosen from the main menu, the user should be presented with another menu. The choices on the new menu, each of which will be programmed as a separate module, are:

1. Add an Inventory Item
2. Change Information About An Inventory Item
3. Return to the Main Menu

For this chapter, you will only be preparing the module for adding an inventory item. The module to change information will be prepared later. Inventory items should be stored in a random file. Before the program exits after one or more items is added, the data must be sorted so that all items are arranged in order by their stock numbers. This sort may happen as each item is entered or after they are all entered. Do not use a bubble sort. Note that the data must be rearranged on the disk, not just in memory. The data to be stored about each inventory item includes:

1. Stock Number (alphanumeric, 8 character maximum)
2. Description (25 character maximum)
3. Selling Price (what you sell the item for)
4. Price Paid (what you paid for the item)
5. Reorder Level (order more when you get down to this quantity)
6. Reorder Quantity (how many should be reordered each time)
7. Source (where you buy the product; 4-digit numeric code)
8. Quantity on Hand at the Beginning of the Year
9. Current Quantity on Hand
10. Quantity Sold Today
11. Quantity Sold This Week
12. Quantity Sold This Quarter
13. Quantity Sold This Year

Fields 1-9 should be entered when adding a new item to inventory. Fields 10-13 are computed as later parts of the program execute.

Chapter 8

Searches

Objectives:
1. Describe applications in which searches are necessary.
2. Explain how a sequential search works.
3. List the advantages and disadvantages of a sequential search.
4. Explain how a binary search works.
5. List the advantages and disadvantages of a binary search.
6. Write programs using searches.

Many computer applications require searches. A **search** is the process of finding a desired data item within a larger group of data items. Consider the following examples:

1. A student wants to know his or her gradepoint average. Before the computer can supply the information, a program must locate the records of this particular student among those of all the students.
2. A telephone number needs to be looked up. In a computerized phone directory, the program must locate the one number among the thousands that may be in the directory.
3. A person wants to make a flight reservation. Information on flights between the two desired cities must be located among the information about hundreds of flights.
4. Computerized records of license plates need to be searched to find out whether a particular automobile has been reported stolen.

Topic 8.1— PRINCIPLES OF SEARCHING

For some applications that require the location of particular data, a set of computer programs known as a data base system is used. A **data base system** is specially designed software for storing data with the computer, processing it as required, and retrieving required information. Searching for required information is one of the built-in functions of a data base system. Each data base system has its own set of rules to be followed. However, the user of such a system is not required to write program steps to search for data.

When a programmer is writing a program to search for desired data, one of two methods is used. One of these methods is the sequential search. The other is the binary search. These two methods are discussed in the following sections.

SEQUENTIAL SEARCH

The simplest method for locating desired data is the sequential search. Sequential means one after another. Therefore, a sequential search looks at items one after another in trying to locate the desired one. Suppose that you have a list naming the kinds of wild animals found in your area. To find the desired animal, you can simply start at the beginning of the list and look at each name until you come to the one for which you are searching. If you get to the end of the list and have not found the desired animal, you know it is not on the list. This method can be used by the computer as well as by a person.

Advantages of a Sequential Search

The biggest advantage of a sequential search is that the data does not have to be arranged in any particular order. Going back to the animal example, you can find the desired name regardless of what order was used in writing the list. It makes no difference whether the list is arranged alphabetically, by animal family, or is totally unarranged. The sequential search also allows duplicate items to be found. For example, if HORSE is on your list of animals in two different places, both of the listings can be found. Another advantage of the sequential sort is that it is very easy to code in a computer language.

Disadvantages of a Sequential Search

The sequential search has one big disadvantage. As the number of items of data increases, more and more time is required. To illustrate this, assume that you have a list containing ten data items. On average, the computer has to examine five items (halfway through the list) to find the desired one. When an item is not on the list, ten comparisons are necessary. Compare this to a list containing 4,000 names. With the longer list, an average of 2,000 comparisons must be made to find the desired data. When the desired item is not on the list, 4,000 comparisons are necessary to verify this fact. In spite of the speed of the computer, thousands of comparisons take time—especially on a microcomputer.

BINARY SEARCH

The binary search can be understood by thinking about a person looking for a phone number in a large directory. Study those steps in Figure 8.1.

LOOK FOR KAREN RYAN'S PHONE NUMBER:

<u>Step 1:</u>Open the directory and see what name is on that page. Since the name you are searching for (Ryan) comes after the name that you have found (Miller), all entries in the first part of the directory can be disregarded. The remainder of the search uses only the second part.

<u>Step 2:</u>Open the directory to a page in the middle of the second part. Examine the names there (Wyman). Since Wyman comes after Ryan, you can disregard all entries from Wyman to the end of the directory. Combined with the action from Step 1, this means that the third quarter of the directory must contain the name that you are searching for.

<u>Step 3:</u> Open the directory to the middle of the third quarter to find the name, Ryan, Karen. If Karen had not been found at this point, you could continue searching smaller and smaller parts of the directory until her name was found.

Figure 8.1   Searching a Phone Directory

The main difference between the human-powered search in Figure 8.1 and a computer search is that the computer is accurate in picking the middle of each part of the data. The binary search gets its name from the fact that after each comparison the number of items still under consideration is divided by two. Remember that the word binary means two.

Advantages of a Binary Search

The big advantage of the binary search is its speed. When searching through only a small number of items, speed is not too important. But with a large number of items, it becomes very important. Think about our two examples from the sequential search section. The first example was searching through ten items. Study the illustration in Figure 8.2 to see how the comparisons are made in locating the desired data.

SEARCH FOR THE NUMBER 64:

Item
No. Value

1	19
2	28
3	32
4	47
5	51
6	63
7	64
8	72
9	85
10	98

Explanation

The first comparison is with the middle item, which is the fifth number. This was found by dividing the number of items by 2. Since the fifth item is smaller than the number you are looking for, you can disregard items 1–5. This leaves items 6–10 for searching.

6	63
7	64
8	72
9	85
10	98

The middle item in the remaining part is found by adding the first and last row numbers (6 and 10) to give a total of 16. This total is divided by 2 to get 8, the number of the middle item. Upon performing this second comparison, you find that the eighth item is larger than the desired number, so you can disregard items 8–10, leaving items six and seven under consideration.

| 6 | 63 |
| 7 | 64 |

The midpoint of the remaining items is found by adding the first and last row numbers (6 and 7), giving a total of 13. Dividing by 2 gives 6.5, which you will truncate to 6. Examining the sixth item (this is the third comparison of all) shows that it is smaller than the one for which you are searching, so item number six is disregarded—leaving only number seven.

| 7 | 64 |

As a human, you can tell that there is only one number left to compare. The computer, however, can go through its normal routine by finding the center point. For the fourth comparison, 7 plus 7 divided by 2 gives 7. So, you compare the seventh item; it is the one you are looking for.

Figure 8.2   Maximum Comparisons of Binary Search on Ten Items

Note from Figure 8.2 that four comparisons were made in finding the desired item. Also note that this is the worst possible case. With ten items in the list, it is impossible to make more than four comparisons. Therefore, the worst performance of the binary search is better than the average performance of the sequential search, which required five comparisons on average.

Disadvantages of a Binary Search

The biggest disadvantage of the binary search is that the items to be searched must be in order. That is, character data must be alphabetized and numeric data must be in either ascending or descending sequence. For examples in this chapter, we will put numbers in ascending sequence. Another disadvantage is that each data item should be unique. That is, if the same data item is recorded more than once, only one of them will be found. This disadvantage can be overcome by extra coding if there must be data items that are the same as other items.

REVIEW QUESTIONS

1. What are some of the applications in which searching is required? (Obj. 1)
2. How does a sequential search work? (Obj. 2)
3. What are the advantages and disadvantages of a sequential search? (Obj. 3)
4. How does a binary search work? (Obj. 4)
5. What are the advantages and disadvantages of a binary search? (Obj. 5)
6. Under what circumstances is a sequential search acceptable for use? (Objs. 3, 5)

Topic 8.2— SEARCHING WITH BASIC

Searching with BASIC is done using keywords with which you are already familiar. We'll look at a sequential search, then a binary search.

SEQUENTIAL SEARCH

To illustrate how a sequential search is done, we will develop a program for use by the Sun and Ski Resort. This hotel would like a guest directory program. When a room number is entered, the program should print the names of the guests staying in that room. If a guest's name is entered, the program should print the room number to which that guest has been assigned. If only the first part of a name (SMITH, for example) is entered, the program should print the names of all guests whose names begin with those letters. For this example program, the data tables will be filled from data lines. For actual use, the data would be entered from the keyboard and stored in a file.

Hierarchy Chart

Analysis of the problem indicates that two functions must be performed in this program. One is the creation and filling of the data tables, the other is the searching procedure itself. Therefore, a hierarchy chart is prepared as shown in Figure 8.3.

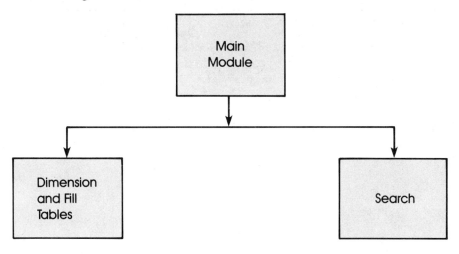

Figure 8.3   Hierarchy Chart for Guest Directory Program

Module Design and Coding

The modules of the program are designed and coded as described in the following paragraphs.

MAIN MODULE

The main module must first call the submodule that dimensions and fills the data table. The table, which will hold a maximum of 100 rows of information, stores guests' names in its first column and their assigned room numbers in the second column. After the table is filled, the main module enters an infinite loop of asking for the desired data and then calling on the search module to find it. Note that the operator of the program may enter either a name or a room number as input. When called, the search module will determine which was entered. Study the module documentation sheet and code for the main module in Figure 8.4.

MODULE DOCUMENTATION	Program: EXC8E1	Module: __MAIN__ Lines: __10-999__

Module Description:

This is the main module. It causes the table to be dimensioned and filled. Then, as long as the user wants to continue, it asks for input of a guest name or room number and performs the search module.

Module Function (Program Design):

1. Perform the dimension and fill table module.
2. As long as the user wants to continue, do the following:
   a. Get the user's input of the guest's name or room number.
   b. Perform the search module.

```
10 ' EXC8E1
20 ' CLARK AND LABARRE--CHAPTER 8, EXAMPLE 1
30 ' SEQUENTIAL SEARCH PROGRAM
40 GOSUB 1000        'DIM AND FILL TABLES
50 CLS
60 PRINT "SUN AND SKI RESORT--GUEST DIRECTORY"
70 PRINT
80 PRINT"ENTER NAME OR ROOM TO SEARCH FOR:"
90 LINE INPUT LOOK$
100 PRINT
110 GOSUB 2000        'SEARCH
120 PRINT
130 LOCATE 24,1
140 PRINT "HIT Q TO QUIT, ANY OTHER KEY TO CONTINUE . . .";
150 Z$=INPUT$(1)
160 IF Z$<>"Q" THEN 50
999 END
```

Figure 8.4   Main Module Documentation Sheet and Code

DIMENSION AND FILL MODULE

The dimension and fill module must create the data table and fill it with data. Study the module documentation and code for this module as shown in Figure 8.5.

MODULE DOCUMENTATION	Program: EXC8E1	Module: DIMENSION AND FILL TABLE Lines: 1000-1999

Module Description:

This module dimensions the data table and fills it with data.

Module Function (Program Design):

1. Dimension the data table as 100 rows by 2 columns.
2. Read names and room numbers into the table from data lines.

```
1000 ' ***** DIM AND FILL TABLES ******
1010 DIM GUEST$(100,2)
1020 FOR N=1 TO 100
1030    READ GUEST$(N,1),GUEST$(N,2)
1040    IF GUEST$(N,1)="EOD" THEN N=N-1:GOTO 1999
1050 NEXT N
1999 RETURN
```

Figure 8.5   Documentation Sheet and Code for Dimension and Fill Module

SEARCH MODULE

The search module does the real work of the program in finding the desired information. Its documentation and code are shown in Figure 8.6. Study this figure carefully to see how the search module works. The data lines used are also shown in Figure 8.6.

MODULE DOCUMENTATION	Program: __EXC8E1__	Module: __SEARCH__ Lines: __2000-2999__

Module Description:

This module decides whether the user entered a guest's name or room number. It then searches the appropriate column of the data column and prints the desired information for each match that is found. If the guest or room is not found, a message is then printed.

Module Function (Program Design):

1. Convert the data input by the user into numeric form. Remember that the first nonnumeric character causes the conversion process to end.
2. Find the number of characters on which the user wants to base the search. Do this by checking the length of the data input by the user.
3. If the numeric conversion of the user's input is greater than 100, it is a room number and set the search column to 2. Otherwise, set the search column to 1 for guests' names.
4. Place a zero in the hit flag variable. This is a variable that always starts a search with a zero in it. Whenever a match is found during the search, a one is placed in the variable.
5. Sequentially examine the data table, looking at the number of characters from each row that has been specified by the length of the user's input. Whenever a match is found, place a one in the hit flag variable. Also, print the guest's name and room number.
6. If the hit variable still contains a zero, print a not found message.

```
2000 ' ***** SEARCH MODULE ************
2010 NUMBER=VAL(LOOK$)
2020 COMLEN=LEN(LOOK$)
2030 IF NUMBER>100 THEN COL=2 ELSE COL=1          'SET ROOM NUMBER
2040 HIT=0
2050 FOR ROW=1 TO N
2060    IF LEFT$(GUEST$(ROW,COL),COMLEN)=LOOK$ THEN HIT=1:
                               PRINT GUEST$(ROW,1);TAB(25);GUEST$(ROW,2)
2070 NEXT ROW
2080 IF HIT=0 THEN PRINT "NOT FOUND"
2999 RETURN
60000 ' ***** DATA ********************
60010 DATA JONES FRED,103,RICO SALLY,107,MARTIN WALTER,101
60020 DATA MCNALLY CLYDE,108,MARSHAL HARRIET,129
60030 DATA NELSON HUBERT,137,ABEL HANK,184,MILES JANE,173
60040 DATA JONES MIRIAM,189,SINGLETARY VICKEY,143
60050 DATA STACY HAL,169
60060 DATA ARIENS SUSAN,198
60070 DATA MARSHALL BRAD,129
60999 DATA EOD,0
```

Figure 8.6   Documentation Sheet and Code for Search Module

BINARY SEARCH

To illustrate a binary search, we will use the Mud Bog Raceway. The Mud Bog Raceway is a sea of red mud. Racing on it has become a favorite form of recreation for many persons in the area, however. As with other races, the goal of the mud bog races is to be the first racer to get a vehicle from the starting line to the finish line. Each vehicle is assigned a unique identification number to make recognizing it easier.

To help the public address announcer, the raceway wants to install a computerized system to immediately print out statistics about each racer. The announcer simply enters the number of the car and the information is shown on the screen for the announcer to relay to the spectators. The facts to be stored include the number of the racer, the driver's name, the type of vehicle, the vehicle's horsepower, and any earlier wins by the racer. By putting the data in data lines, adding new racers is easy to do.

Hierarchy Chart

The program must be able to fill the data table, then find items in it. Therefore, a hierarchy chart with two submodules can be developed as shown in Figure 8.7.

Module Design and Coding

The modules of the program are designed and coded as described in the following paragraphs.

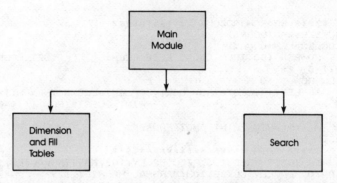

Figure 8.7   Hierarchy Chart for Mud Bog Raceway Program

MAIN MODULE

The main module must first call the submodule that dimensions and fills two data tables, which will hold information about a maximum of 100 racers. One table will contain the racers' numbers. The other table stores data in four columns as follows:

Column 1: Driver's Name
Column 2: Type of Vehicle
Column 3: Vehicle Horsepower
Column 4: Previous Wins

After the tables are filled, the main module enters an infinite loop of asking for the racer number, then calling on the binary module to find the data about it. The main module then prints the data. Study the module documentation sheet and code for the main module in Figure 8.8.

MODULE DOCUMENTATION	Program: ___EXC8E2___	Module: __MAIN_____ Lines: __10-999_____
Module Description:		
This is the main module. It first calls on the module that dimensions and fills the tables. Then, it repeatedly calls on the binary search module to find data, which it then prints.		
Module Function (Program Design):		

1. Perform the dimension and fill submodule.
2. As long as the user wants to continue, do the following:
   a. Get a racer number from the user.
   b. Perform the binary search module to find the row number of the desired data.
   c. Print the data from the located row.		

```
10 ' EXC8E2
20 ' CLARK AND LABARRE--CHAPTER 8, EXAMPLE 2
30 ' BINARY SEARCH PROGRAM
40 GOSUB 1000              'DIM AND FILL TABLES
50 CLS
60    PRINT "MUD BOG RACEWAY--INSTANT STATISTICS SYSTEM"
70    PRINT
80    PRINT "ENTER RACER NUMBER TO SEARCH FOR: "
90    LINE INPUT LOOK$
100   LOOK=VAL(LOOK$)
110   GOSUB 2000           'SEARCH
120   PRINT
130   FOR COL=1 TO 4
140      PRINT STAT$(HIT,COL)
150   NEXT COL
160   LOCATE 24,1
170   PRINT "HIT Q TO QUIT, ANY OTHER KEY TO CONTINUE . . .";
180   Z$=INPUT$(1)
190 IF Z$<>"Q" THEN 50
200 CLS
999 END
```

Figure 8.8   Main Module Documentation Sheet and Code

DIMENSION AND FILL MODULE

The dimension and fill module must create two tables and fill them. One table contains racer numbers. The other contains statistics. Since the binary search module will return a row number of zero if a racer is not found, this module will place a not found message in row zero of the statistics table. This message will then be printed by the main module whenever a racer is not found. Study the documentation sheet and coding of this module in Figure 8.9.

MODULE DOCUMENTATION	Program: EXC8E2	Module: DIMENSION AND FILL TABLE Lines: 1000-1999

Module Description:

This module dimensions and fills the racer number table and the racer statistics table to hold information on a maximum of 100 racers. The statistics column holds the driver's name, vehicle type, vehicle horsepower, and previous wins in that order.

Module Function (Program Design):

1. Dimension the racer number table to 100 rows and the racer statistics table to 100 rows and 4 columns.
2. Put a not found message in Row 0, Column 1 of the statistics table.
3. Fill the remaining table rows from data lines.

```
1000 ' ***** DIM AND FILL TABLES ******
1010 DIM ID(100),STAT$(100,4)
1020 STAT$(0,1)="NOT FOUND"
1030 FOR N=1 TO 100
1040    READ ID(N),STAT$(N,1),STAT$(N,2),STAT$(N,3),STAT$(N,4)
1050    IF STAT$(N,1)="EOD" THEN N=N-1:GOTO 1999
1060 NEXT N
1999 RETURN
```

Figure 8.9   Documentation Sheet and Coding of the Dimension
and Fill Module

SEARCH MODULE

In this program the binary search module does not print. Therefore, it simply places the row number in which the racer is found in a variable. The main module uses this variable to print out statistics from the correct row. As you study the documentation sheet and coding of this module, remember that smaller and smaller parts of the table are looked at until the item is found or the table part being examined diminishes to nothing. Note that variables are used to keep up with the beginning and ending points for the section from which the examination row will be chosen. Figure 8.10 shows this module.

REVIEW QUESTIONS

1. Describe the steps that must be followed in a sequential search. (Obj. 6)
2. What must a binary search do when the desired data is located? (Obj. 6)
3. In a binary search, how do you determine which part of the table to "abandon" in setting up the next comparison? (Obj. 6)
4. In a binary search, how do you calculate the row number with which the next comparison should be made? (Obj. 6)

VOCABULARY WORDS

The following terms were introduced in this chapter:

data base system   sequential search   binary search

KEYWORDS AND COMMANDS

No new keywords or commands were introduced in this chapter.

| MODULE DOCUMENTATION | Program: EXC8E2 | Module: BINARY SEARCH |
| | | Lines: 2000-2999 |

Module Description:

This module uses a binary search to find the row number of the desired racer. The row number is placed in a variable for reference by the main module. If the racer number is not found, a zero is in the variable.

Module Function (Program Design):

1. Set to zero the variable (hit) that will be used to store the row in which the racer is found.
2. Set to zero the three variables that will be used to keep up the following data: the row with which the next comparison is to be made (target), the smallest row number of the table part currently being searched (low boundary), and the largest row number of the table part currently being searched (high boundary).
3. As long as the high boundary is greater than or equal to the low boundary, repeat the following steps. That is, until the portion of the table being examined diminishes to nothing, continue doing these steps.
   a. Compare the desired racer number to the number stored in the target row of the racer number table. If a match is found, place the target row number in the hit variable and exit the binary search routine.
   b. If the number being searched for is larger than the number being stored in the target row, all numbers from row 1 through the target row can be disregarded. This is done by setting the low boundary variable to the target row plus 1.
   c. If the number being searched for is less than the number stored in the target row, all numbers from the target row through the end of the table can be disregarded. This is done by setting the high boundary variable to the target row minus 1.
   d. Select a new target row. This is done by adding the low boundary and high boundary numbers and dividing by two. Use the integer part of the quotient of this division.

```
2000 ' ***** BINARY SEARCH MODULE *****
2010 HIT=0
2020 TARGET=0
2030 LOBOUND=1
2040 HIBOUND=N
2050 WHILE HIBOUND>=LOBOUND
2060     IF ID(TARGET)=LOOK THEN HIT=TARGET:GOTO 2999
2070     IF LOOK>ID(TARGET) THEN LOBOUND=TARGET+1
2080     IF LOOK<ID(TARGET) THEN HIBOUND=TARGET-1
2090     TARGET=(HIBOUND+LOBOUND)\2
2100 WEND
2999 RETURN
60000 ' ***** DATA ********************
60010 DATA 32,JOHN ABLES,65 JEEP,398 HP,WINNER OF 1984 MUD RUN
60020 DATA 47,SUSAN COX,84 TOYOTA,321 HP,NO WINNINGS
60030 DATA 51,DUB COX,83 FORD,612 HP,1985 GRAND CHAMPION
60040 DATA 63,MORTIMER HUNT,65 DODGE,147 HP,NO WINNINGS
60050 DATA 64,MERLE MARSH,84 GMC,418 HP,1984 CALIF OPEN
60060 DATA 85,BURT RUSSELL,73 NISSAN,183 HP,NO WINNINGS
60999 DATA 0,EOD,EOD,EOD,EOD
```

Figure 8.10   Documentation Sheet and Coding of Binary Search Module

PROGRAMS TO WRITE

For each of the programs, prepare the necessary documentation prior to writing the BASIC code.

Program 1

Assume that you are the credit manager in a department store that has its own brand of credit card. Whenever a customer presents a credit card, the sales person must enter the card number into the computer to see whether the customer is behind in payment of the account. Only the card numbers of persons who are behind in their payments are entered into the computer. Therefore, if a card number is not found, the program should print an "account okay" message. If the card number is found, the program should print a message that the customer must go to the credit department and talk to a representative about the overdue account. In writing the program, use a sequential search. Place the account numbers in data lines.

Program 2

Modify Program 1 to use a binary search.

Program 3

You operate a lawn mower manufacturing business on the sunny shores of the Gulf of Mexico. In the parts list for your mowers, you have assigned each part your own part number. However, in purchasing the parts from their manufacturers, many of the parts have manufacturer's numbers that are different from your numbers. For example, the gasoline shutoff valve that you have labeled as part number 16-3987 is known by its manufacturer as part number KX3-4YA. To keep up with all this, you need a computer program that will give the manufacturer's number when your number is entered. To do this, it will use a table with two columns. The first column will contain your part number. The second column will contain the manufacturer's number for the same part. When your part number is entered, the program should print the manufacturer's number. Use a sequential search. Use data lines.

Program 4

Modify Program 3 to use a binary search.

Program 5

You are planning to have a garage sale. Since you are so organized, you decide to give each item a stock number and use your computer to make all the sales. Therefore, you write a program that stores the stock numbers in one column of a table, and the price of the items in the second column of the table. A companion character table should contain a brief description of the items. When an item is being sold, you enter its stock number and the computer looks it up to get the price. The program then marks the item as sold. At the end of the sale, the program should print out two reports. One report should list the items sold and the amount of money taken in. The other report should list all the items not sold. Invent your own way for the program to mark the items as sold. Use a sequential search.

Program 6

Modify Program 5 to use a binary search.

CONTINUING PROJECT

Before writing any program of the continuing projects, be sure to complete all appropriate documentation.

Project 1

For this chapter's work on your project, you will again be working with the master file maintenance program. You will now create the module used to change information about an employee. Remember that the module is the second choice from the master file maintenance menu. The user should be able to make changes by entering the social security number of the employee for whom a change is to be made. The program must then search the table for that employee and print the current information on the screen. The user can then input the new information and replace the old. When the user has made all the desired changes, the module should return control to the master file maintenance menu.

Project 2

For this chapter's work on your project, you will again be working with the inventory maintenance program. You will be adding the module that provides for changing information about an inventory item. Remember that this module is the second choice from the inventory maintenance menu. The user should be able to make changes by entering the stock number of the item for which a change is to be made. The program must then search for that item and print the current information on the screen. The user can then input the new information to replace the old. Remember to rewrite the updated information to disk after each record is changed. When the user has made all the desired changes, the module should return control to the master file maintenance menu.

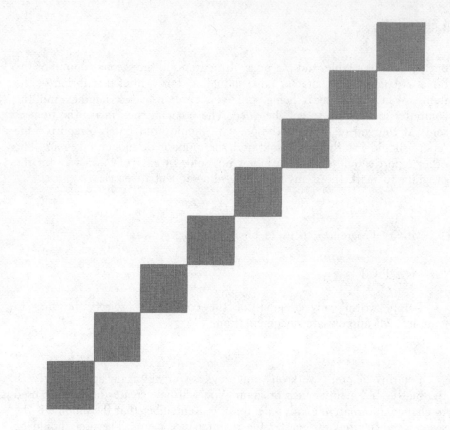

Unit 4 • Advanced Data Files

Chapter 9

Multiple Files

Objectives: 1. Describe how multiple files are used in file processing systems.

2. Identify factors to consider when selecting file organization.

3. Describe the differences between master and detail files.

4. Explain the procedures for file maintenance of sequential files.

5. Explain the importance of record design.

6. Write programs using multiple files.

Topic 9.1— PRINCIPLES OF USING MULTIPLE FILES

Applications in business and industry usually require the use of more than one data file. Generally, these files will be related and more than likely will result in the upgrade of one specific file. Applications using one or more files may be referred to as **file processing systems**. You must make the decisions concerning the file organization for each of the files used in the file processing systems. Several factors must be considered when determining whether a file should be sequential or random. Consideration should be given to the design of the file processing system and the volume of records to be processed. The volume of records in a file is referred to as **file size**. You must keep in mind how many records make up the file when deciding on the organization. You must also consider the storage media and the volume of records that may be stored on selected media. You must keep in mind how much activity will take place within each file. **Activity** refers to the number of transactions that may be processed or how many updates may be made to a specific file. Many files are large in size and low in activity. A file organized in this manner is slow to process sequentially because every record is read in order to update a very few. A typical payroll application, on the other hand, is a good example of a file that is generally large in size with high activity. Every time a payroll period ends, the main file containing the information about the employee is updated using the current pay period information. Each of the records is updated. Therefore, sequential file organization is most appropriate for this application.

Another consideration in file organization is the frequency of change to the existing data within the file. The addition and deletion of records from a file is known as volatility. A file whose activity contains a large number of additions of records and deletions of records would be recognized as being very volatile. A file with low activity concerning additions and deletions is referred to as a static file.

Files are usually classified as different types. The file organization (for example: sequential and random) is definitive; the type is merely a means of referring to different kinds of files. Files may be classified as master files, detail files, and related files. Quite often a file may serve in many categories because of multiple file processing activities.

MASTER FILES

A master file contains the most permanent data concerning the records used in the given application. It usually contains summary information that reflects the current status of the given application. For example, the master file from the accounts receivable application contains the permanent information about the customer such as the customer number and name. It also contains information that may be considered to be volatile because it may change readily. For example, it contains the address which may change at any time. It also may contain the credit limit which may be changed. The master record may also contain cumulative information such as an account balance. This account balance would be updated every time the accounts receivable application is processed. Figure 9.1 illustrates a typical layout for the master file record for an accounts receivable application.

Customer Number	Customer Name	Address	City	State	ZIP Code	Account Balance
99999	xxxxxxxxxxxxxxxxxxx	xxxxxxxxxxxxxx	xxxxxxxxx	xx	xxxxxxxx	99999.99

Figure 9.1   Master Record Layout

DETAIL FILES

Master file records may be designed to contain all of the transaction activity concerning a given application. However, the record soon becomes quite lengthy and cumbersome to work with in the program. To facilitate the recording of transaction information, a detail file may be developed to store current information concerning each transaction processed. A transaction stored on the detail record may consist of such fields of data as the product number, product description, unit price, quantity, and total price. An illustration of a detail record is shown in Figure 9.2.

Product Number	Product Description	Unit Price	Quantity	Total Price
99999	XXXXXXXXXXXXXXXXXXXXXXXX	99999.99	999	999999.99

Figure 9.2   Detail Record Layout

The detail records are processed against their respective master file records to provide invoices, summary reports, and updated master files.

RELATED FILES

Related files are files that contain related information concerning either the master or detail files. For example, the accounts receivable detail file contains records relating to the transactions. These transactions will usually reflect the sale of an item of merchandise. When the detail file is created, the detail record may contain only specific information concerning the customer number, product number, and quantity. The related file may contain the product number, product description, and unit price. Figure 9.3 illustrates a layout of a related detail record.

Product Number	Product Description	Unit Price
99999	XXXXXXXXXXXXXXXXXXXXXXXX	999999.99

Figure 9.3   Related Detail Record Layout

When the transactions are processed, the detail records are processed against the master records. When the master and detail records have been matched, the remaining information concerning the product description and unit price would be taken from the related detail file. Study the system design in Figure 9.4 to see how three files may be used in the accounts receivable application to generate an invoice statement.

Related files may serve many purposes. As was illustrated in Figure 9.4, the related file provided important descriptive and pricing information for the application. Related detail files may be used to store tables of information that are needed in the application. For example, in the payroll

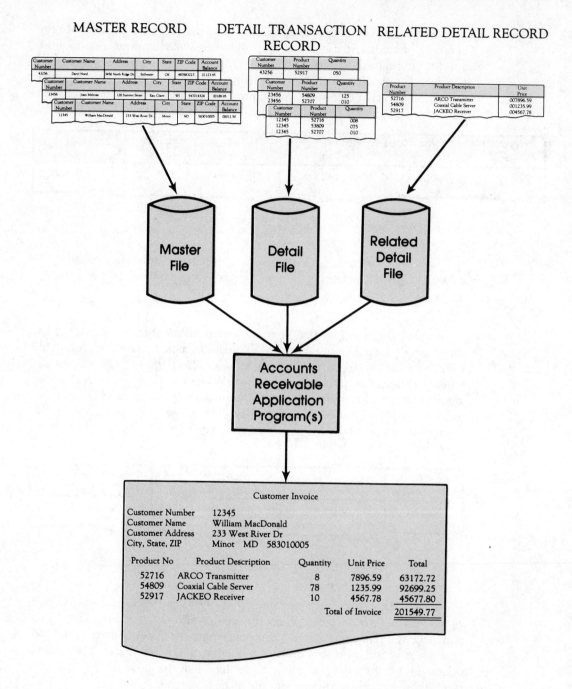

Figure 9.4   File Processing System

application, the state and federal tax tables need to be stored. When the number of dependents is input, the application must look up the appropriate tax rate to be applied to the computation of the payroll. Detail files are also used to store control information. In many of the larger businesses and schools having a mainframe computer, the user is given a user number. This is a number that helps the computer to identify whether or not the user is an authorized user of the computer. This number is compared to the numbers stored in a related file to determine whether or not the user is allowed to use the computer. These types of files are sometimes referred to as control files.

In business, it is very important that records of all daily activity be kept. Since the transaction detail file for accounts receivable would be used over and over, the transactions for a given day would have to be erased. This is because a customer may make an inquiry later concerning the activities of a given day. Rather than destroying the data, it is placed in a history file. A history file is nothing more than a sequential storage of each and every record making up the past transaction file. Another type of related file that is built into most transaction or interactive systems is an audit file. Audit files record the chronological activities of all processing completed within a file processing system. The audit file is sometimes used to reconstruct a given day's activity for accounting auditing purposes or for federal tax auditing purposes. The built-in control of an audit file also provides the company with some backup in case active files are destroyed. Most companies will store audit files in fire-proof vaults or off site.

FILE MAINTENANCE

File maintenance is an important activity within any file processing system. The maintenance of the master file allows the user to keep the permanent and semipermanent data up-to-date. File maintenance must be performed on sequential and random files. File maintenance on random files is actually easier than performing maintenance on the sequential file. The reason for this is that the random file may be accessed, updated, and rewritten to the same location. As each record is read in a sequential file maintenance procedure, it must be written to a new sequential file. When the record to be changed is located, it is changed and also written to the new file. After reading and changing all of the records in the file and writing them to the new file, the new file must be renamed using the name of the old file. Figure 9.5 illustrates the system of updating a sequential master file.

File maintenance on sequential files may be either batch or interactive. Generally file maintenance of random files will be interactive. However, interactive processing of adding, changing, and deleting transactions to a sequential file could conceivably require several passes through the file. To avoid this, you would either have to sort the transactions, manually putting them into the same order as the records in the master file, or create a detail

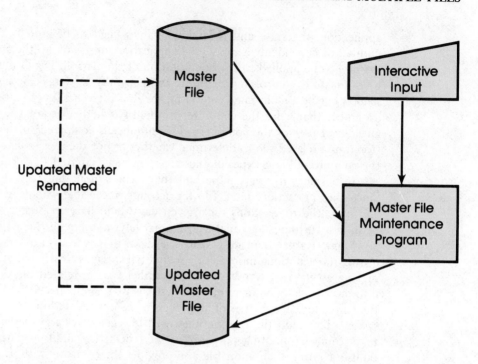

Figure 9.5   Sequential Update of Master File

file of transaction records that would be sorted. The master file should have been sorted previously. Each of the transaction records would have to contain a code identifying whether it was an addition, change, or deletion. For example, the record could contain a 1 for add, 2 for change, and 3 for delete. In an interactive system, you have to prompt the user to indicate what activity the user wishes to perform on the current record illustrated on the screen. It is possible that no changes would be made and the record would have to be written to the updated master file. If new records were added to the master file, it would have to be reordered (sorted) to make sure that it would be ready for future transaction processing.

RECORD DESIGN

When designing records for use in multiple file processing systems, it is a good practice to locate important access fields at the beginning of the record and consistently in the same location if possible. This field will be used to compare the master to the detail or the detail to the related detail. Figure 9.6 illustrates the location to be compared during the file processing.

If transaction records are to be used in updating files, the update code could be located either in the first position of the record or immediately following the record identifying fields such as customer number or product number.

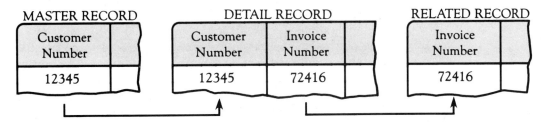

Figure 9.6   Master, Detail, and Related Records to be Compared

EXCEPTION OR AUDIT REPORTS

Often when the maintenance of a file is processed, the system will be designed to produce either an exception report or an audit report. The exception report will print a detail line of any exceptions encountered when processing the maintenance transactions. For example, maybe a change is attempted on a master record that has been previously deleted. This would be an exception and would be printed in the report. The audit report, on the other hand, may be a report that shows the original record accessed, any changes made to the record, and the record after changes have been made. This type of report is stored for a period of time and is used to provide control for the system. Usually this type of report will also show who made the changes. This again ensures that authorized personnel are the only people making changes to the file.

REVIEW QUESTIONS

1. Explain what is meant by the term file processing system. (Obj. 1)
2. Identify several factors to consider when determining which file organization should be used for a given file. (Obj. 2)
3. Explain what is meant by the term activity. (Obj. 2)
4. Explain what is meant by the term volatility. (Obj. 2)
5. What are master files used for in file processing? (Obj. 3)
6. What is a detail file? (Obj. 3)
7. What is a related file? (Obj. 3)
8. Identify several types of related files and the purpose of each. (Obj. 3)
9. Explain the purpose of file maintenance. (Obj. 4)
10. Why is record design important when using records from several files? (Obj. 5)

Topic 9.2— MULTIPLE FILES WITH BASIC

Multiple files are used in most business applications. Some of the standard applications in business are related to the accounting functions such as accounts receivable, accounts payable, inventory, payroll, and purchasing. Many of these applications use files that are interrelated. In other words, a file used in the purchasing application system would be used to update the inventory file. Information used in purchasing files would be used to update accounts payable. Information used in a sales application system would be used to update accounts receivable. Information pertaining to the items sold would be used to update inventory files. Some of the interrelationships are illustrated in Figures 9.7, 9.8, and 9.9. Figure 9.7 is a system flowchart of a sales processing system; the OLD.YTD.SALES file is the master file. The transactions are stored in the sales transactions file. The detail records in the transactions file contain information concerning the individual daily sales. The program for processing the master and detail files is illustrated in the middle of Figure 9.7. The output to be produced is a sales report and an updated sales file. Upon completing the updating of the sales file, it would be transformed into a master file for the next processing period. Most of the computers allow you to use a system command in the program to do this. For example, the IBM PC would use the NAME statement to change the update to the master file.

General Form: *line number* NAME *"old master file" "new master file"*

Example: `1990 NAME "UPDATED.SALES" "OLD.YTD.SALES"`

If the master file OLD.YTD.SALES had been a random file, it could have been updated in the original file as the detail records are being processed.

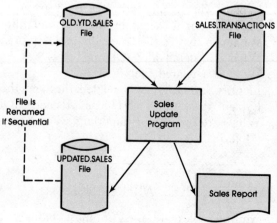

Figure 9.7   Sales Processing

The sales report would be a summary report illustrating the important information concerning the daily sales.

Figure 9.8 illustrates the system flow for a payroll processing system. Again, the system utilizes two files: the master and detail files. Study the flowchart to determine what processing would be completed and how the files would be used in the application.

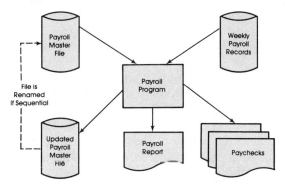

Figure 9.8   Payroll Processing

The interrelated file processing system illustrated in Figure 9.9 shows how several detail files may be used in one application to develop a detail file that will be used in the second application. In this system flowchart, the grades from each of the courses (DP 101 and MATH 201) were used to compile the STUDENT.GRADE file. The STUDENT.GRADE file is used as the detail file to process against the STUDENT.MASTER file to produce report cards and an updated STUDENT.MASTER.

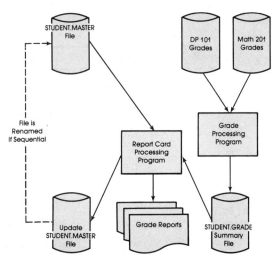

Figure 9.9   Interrelated File Processing System

PROGRAMMING THE EXAMPLE APPLICATION

The following documentation and program illustrates a typical multiple file processing system. As the hierarchy chart illustrates in Figure 9.10, the system will consist of a main menu which will control four major submodules. The major submodules are designed to permit you to create a master file, a product description file, and a detail transaction file. The fourth module permits you to process the records stored in the detail transaction file and update the master file account balance as well as generate invoice reports. The master file menu module controls all elements of the file maintenance system for the master file. File maintenance after the file is created consists of adding new records, changing existing records, and deleting records no longer valid. In addition, you will have the ability to list the file to determine its contents.

Figures 9.11 through 9.20 illustrate the module documentation for each of the major modules. The data for the application is shown in Figure 9.21. The report spacing chart is shown in Figure 9.22. This illustrates the invoice to be produced when the records are processed.

The program for the menu driven application system using multiple files is shown in the sections that follow. Study the one that is similar to the computer you are using. Because of the length of the program, not all of the elements of an actual file processing system are included. Inquiry and the maintenance capability for each product description file and the transaction file would also be included in the system. Sample output generated by the system is shown in Figure 9.24 at the end of the application program.

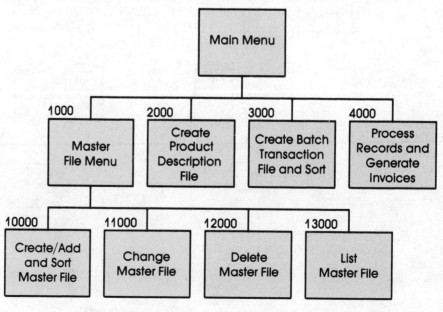

Figure 9.10   Hierarchy Chart

PROGRAM DOCUMENTATION		
Program: EXC9E1	Programmer: Clark and LaBarre	Date: 5/23/--

Purpose:

The purpose of the multiple file application is to handle sales invoices for the Down-Under Printer Supply Company. Three major sequential files are used in the system. The master file contains the customer information. The product description file contains data concerning inventory. The detail file contains data related to each transaction.

Input:	Output:
Interactive input into the master file. Read data records for the product description file. Interactive input into the detail transaction file.	Individual invoices for each of the customers. Ability to list content of the master file.

Data Terminator:

Variables Used:

Varies from computer to computer.

Figure 9.11   Program Documentation

MODULE DOCUMENTATION	Program: __EXC9E1__	Module: __MAIN__ Lines: __10-999__

Module Description:

The main module contains the menu which allows the user to access any one of the four major submodules.

Module Function (Program Design):

1. Get the user's choice.
2. If the user's choice is to stop, the program ends and control is returned to the main menu.
3. If the user's choice is one of the acceptable options, that option is performed.
4. After choice is processed, control returns to the main menu.

Figure 9.12   Main Module

MODULE DOCUMENTATION	Program: __EXC9E1__	Module: __MASTER__ Lines: __1000-1999__

Module Description:

The master submodule contains the master file menu with its options. The master submodule is made up of four submodules.

Module Function (Program Design):

1. The master file menu is displayed.
2. If the user enters 5, then the process ends and processing returns to the main menu.
3. On the user's choice, perform:
    a. Create a master file or add a record to the master file.
    b. Change a record in the master file.
    c. Delete a record from the master file.
    d. List the contents of the master file.

Figure 9.13   Master File Menu

MODULE DOCUMENTATION	Program: __EXC9E1__	Module: __PRODUCT DESCRIPTION__ Lines: __2000-2999__

Module Description:

This module creates a related data file containing product description information. The data in this file is used to supplement the data stored in the master file and the current data in the detail transaction file.

Module Function (Program Design):

1. Open the product description file.
2. Read the data records then write them to the file.
3. Close the file.
4. Return control to the main menu.

Figure 9.14   Create Product Description File

MODULE DOCUMENTATION	Program: __EXC9E1__	Module: __TRANSACTION FILE__ Lines: __3000-3999__

Module Description:

This module allows for the entry of the correct purchase transactions. All transactions are inputted into a table and sorted prior to writing them to a file.

Module Function (Program Design):

1. Enter the data.
2. Sort the table.
3. Open the transaction file.
4. Write the sorted table to the disk file.
5. Close the file.
6. Return control to the main menu.

Figure 9.15   Create Batch Transaction File

MODULE DOCUMENTATION	Program: __EXC9E1__	Module: __PROCESS RECORDS__ Lines: __4000-4999__

Module Description:

This module processes the transaction records and generates an invoice for each of the customers. Each master record is updated after all transactions have been processed for each specific customer.

Module Function (Program Design):

1. Open the product description file and load data into a table.
2. Open the master file and the new master file.
3. While not at the end of the master file, read a master record.
4. Print heading lines for the invoice.
5. Perform processing of the detail lines until the next customer number is read.
6. Advance the paper, read the next master file, and continue the process until all transactions have been processed.
7. Control is returned to the main menu after closing the file.

NOTE: At this point the new master file would have to be renamed to the old master file if it is to be used for the next file updating routine. (If this cannot be done in BASIC, return to the operating system mode.)

Figure 9.16   Process Records

MODULE DOCUMENTATION	Program: __EXC9E1__	Module: __CREATE/ADD MASTER__ Lines: __10000-10999__

Module Description:

This module allows the user to create a master file or add a record to the master file.

Module Function (Program Design):

1. Existing data is loaded into a table.
2. Add new data to table.
3. The table is sorted into sequential order.
4. Data is written to a sequential file.
5. The file is closed.
6. Control is returned to the master menu.

Figure 9.17   Create/Add to the Master File

MODULE DOCUMENTATION	Program: <u>EXC9E1</u>	Module: <u>CHANGE MASTER</u> Lines: <u>11000-11999</u>

Module Description:

This module allows for the records within a master file to be changed.

Module Function (Program Design):

1. The file is opened.
2. The contents of the file are placed in a table.
3. The record to be changed is accessed in the table (search).
4. Changes are made to the data.
5. Data in the table is rewritten to the master file and the file is closed.
6. Return to the master menu.

Figure 9.18   Changing Records in a Sequential File

MODULE DOCUMENTATION	Program: <u>EXC9E1</u>	Module: <u>DELETE MASTER</u> Lines: <u>12000-12999</u>

Module Description:

This module allows the user to delete a record from the master file.

Module Function (Program Design):

1. The file is opened.
2. The contents are placed in a table and the file is closed.
3. The record to be deleted is identified.
4. The key value is zeroed out.
5. The file is opened again.
6. The contents of the table (other than the deleted record) are rewritten to the master file.
7. The file is closed.
8. Control returns to the master menu.

Figure 9.19   Deleting Records in a Sequential File

MODULE DOCUMENTATION	Program: __EXC9E1__	Module: __LIST MASTER__ Lines: __13000-13999__

Module Description:

The purpose of this module is to list the contents of the master file.

Module Function (Program Design):

1. The file is opened.
2. The headings are printed.
3. Read a record and write the detail line until all records have been read.
4. Close the file.
5. Return to the master file menu.

Figure 9.20   List Records from a Master File

DATA FOR MASTER FILE

Customer Number	Customer Name	Address	City	State	ZIP Code	Account Balance
34562	Eiko Okana	4501 Maple Dr	Kokomo	IN	469018954	0100.00

Customer Number	Customer Name	Address	City	State	ZIP Code	Account Balance
45678	Harry Zimmerman	3315 S Solano	Las Cruces	NM	880012334	0000.00

Customer Number	Customer Name	Address	City	State	ZIP Code	Account Balance
08434	Al Abrahamsom	7221 S 180th St	Kent	WA	980516772	0058.00

Customer Number	Customer Name	Address	City	State	ZIP Code	Account Balance
23456	Michael Rutter	151 Earl Street	Portland	OR	972109618	0000.00

Customer Number	Customer Name	Address	City	State	ZIP Code	Account Balance
12345	Antonia Garcia	123 East Grant	New Milford	CT	956081323	0087.00

DATA FOR DETAIL TRANSACTION FILE OF PURCHASES

Customer Number	Product Number	Quantity
45678	11111	2
45678	22222	2

Customer Number	Product Number	Quantity
34562	33333	1

Customer Number	Product Number	Quantity
23456	11111	1
23456	33333	2
23456	44444	1

Customer Number	Product Number	Quantity
12345	55555	1

Customer Number	Product Number	Quantity
08434	11111	2
08434	33333	1
08434	44444	1

DATA FOR PRODUCT DESCRIPTION FILE

Product Number	Product Description	Unit Price
11111	Top Print 80 Column Printer	799.99
22222	Quick Print 132 Column Printer	989.95
33333	Perfect Print Letter Quality	1995.00
44444	Laser Print 3000	8995.00
55555	Multiple Copy Impact Printer	2795.00

Figure 9.21   Data for Master File, Product Description File, and Detail Transaction File

CUSTOMER INVOICE

SOLD TO: NAME
ADDRESS
CITY, STATE, ZIP CODE

PRODUCT NUMBER	PRODUCT DESCRIPTION	QUANTITY	UNIT PRICE	TOTAL
99999	XXXXXXXXXXXXXXXXXXXXXXXX	999	9999.99	$99999.99

TOTAL INVOICE $99999.99

Figure 9.22 Report Spacing Chart

```
10 ' EXC9E1
20 ' CLARK AND LABARRE--CHAPTER 9, EXAMPLE 1
30 ' ***** PURCHASING APPLICATION MAIN MENU
40 DIM CUSTOMER.NO$(15), CUSTOMER.NAME$(15), ADDRESS$(15), CITY$(15),
      STATE$(15), ZIP$(15), AMOUNT(15)
50   WHILE X$<>"N"
60      CLS
70      LOCATE 8,15
80      PRINT "DOWN UNDER PRINTER SUPPLY CO."
90      LOCATE 9,15
100     PRINT TAB(15);"    PURCHASING APPLICATION"
110     PRINT TAB(15);"         MAIN MENU"
120     PRINT
130     PRINT
140     PRINT TAB(15);"MASTER FILE MENU......................1"
150     PRINT TAB(15);"CREATE PRODUCT DESC FILE..............2"
160     PRINT TAB(15);"CREATE TRANSACTION FILE...............3"
170     PRINT TAB(15);"PROCESS TRANSACTIONS..................4"
180     PRINT TAB(15);"END...................................5"
190     PRINT
200     PRINT
210     INPUT "ENTER YOUR CHOICE........";CHOICE
220     IF CHOICE<1 OR CHOICE>5 THEN PRINT "BAD CHOICE":GOTO 60
230     ON CHOICE GOSUB 1000, 2000, 3000, 4000, 999
240     INPUT "     DO YOU WANT TO CONTINUE (Y/N)";X$
250 WEND
999 END
1000 ' ***** MASTER FILE MENU *********
1010 LET CONTINUE$="Y"
1020 WHILE CONTINUE$<>"N"
1030    CLS:LOCATE 8,15
1040    PRINT "MASTER FILE MENU"
1050    PRINT
1060    PRINT TAB(10);"CREATE/ADD TO MASTER..................1"
1070    PRINT TAB(10);"CHANGE MASTER.........................2"
1080    PRINT TAB(10);"DELETE FROM MASTER....................3"
1090    PRINT TAB(10);"LIST MASTER FILE......................4"
1100    PRINT TAB(10);"END...................................5"
1110    PRINT
1120    INPUT "ENTER YOUR CHOICE............";SELECTION
1130    IF SELECTION<1 OR SELECTION>5 THEN PRINT "BAD CHOICE":GOTO 1020
1140    ON SELECTION GOSUB 10000, 11000, 12000, 13000, 1999
1150    INPUT "     DO YOU WANT TO CONTINUE IN THIS MENU (Y/N)";CONTINUE$
1160 WEND
1999 RETURN
2000 ' ***** CREATE THE PRODUCT DESCRIPTION FILE
2010 DATA 11111, "Top Print 80 Column Printer", 799.99
2020 DATA 22222, "Quick Print 132 Column Printer", 989.95
2030 DATA 33333, "Perfect Print Letter Quality", 1995.00
2040 DATA 44444, "Laser Print 3000", 8995.00
2050 DATA 55555, "Multiple Copy Impact Printer", 2795.00
2060 DATA 00000, " ", 0
2070 OPEN "PRODESC" FOR OUTPUT AS #2
2080 READ PRODUCT.NO, PRODUCT.DESC$, UNIT.PRICE$
2090 CLS
2100 WHILE PRODUCT.NO<>0
2110    WRITE #2, PRODUCT.NO, PRODUCT.DESC$, UNIT.PRICE$
2120    READ PRODUCT.NO, PRODUCT.DESC$, UNIT.PRICE$
2130 WEND
2140 CLOSE #2
2999 RETURN
3000 ' ***** CREATE THE TRANSACTION FILE
3010 DIM CUST.NUMB$(10), PROD.NUM$(10), QUANTITY(10)
3020 LET MORE.DATA.SWITCH$="Y"
3030 LET ROW=0
```

Figure 9.23   Program Code for Example Application

```
3040 WHILE MORE.DATA.SWITCH$<>"N"
3050    LET ROW=ROW+1
3060    CLS
3070    LOCATE 10,15
3080    INPUT "ENTER THE CUSTOMER NUMBER";CUST.NUMB$(ROW)
3090    LOCATE 12,15
3100    INPUT "ENTER THE PRODUCT NUMBER";PROD.NUM$(ROW)
3110    LOCATE 14,15
3120    INPUT "ENTER THE QUANTITY";QUANTITY(ROW)
3130    INPUT "        DO YOU HAVE MORE DATA TO ENTER (Y/N)";MORE.DATA.SWITCH$
3140 WEND
3150 '           SORT THE TRANSACTION TABLE
3160 FOR SUB1=1 TO ROW-1
3170    FOR SUB2=SUB1+1 TO ROW
3180       IF CUST.NUMB$(SUB2)>=CUST.NUMB$(SUB1) THEN GOTO 3220
3190       SWAP CUST.NUMB$(SUB1), CUST.NUMB$(SUB2)
3200       SWAP PROD.NUM$(SUB1), PROD.NUM$(SUB2)
3210       SWAP QUANTITY(SUB1), QUANTITY(SUB2)
3220    NEXT SUB2
3230 NEXT SUB1
3240 '              WRITE THE SORTED TRANSACTION FILE
3250 OPEN "TRANS.JPC" FOR OUTPUT AS #3
3260 FOR R=1 TO ROW
3270    WRITE #3, CUST.NUMB$(R), PROD.NUM$(R), QUANTITY(R)
3280 NEXT R
3290 CLOSE #3
3999 RETURN
4000 ' ***** PROCESS TRANSACTIONS AND GENERATE INVOICES
4010 GOSUB 4100 'LOAD PRODUCT DESCRIPTION TABLE
4020 GOSUB 4200 'PRINT INVOICES
4099 RETURN
4100 '              LOAD THE PRODUCT DESCRIPTION TABLE
4110 OPEN "PRODESC" FOR INPUT AS #1
4120 DIM PRODUCT.NO(15), PRODUCT.DESC$(15), UNIT.PRICE$(15)
4130 LET ROW=0
4140 WHILE NOT EOF(1)
4150    LET ROW=ROW+1
4160    INPUT #1, PRODUCT.NO(ROW), PRODUCT.DESC$(ROW), UNIT.PRICE$(ROW)
4170 WEND
4180 CLOSE #1
4199 RETURN
4200 '              PRINT INVOICES
4210 OPEN "MASTER" FOR INPUT AS #2
4220 OPEN "MASTER.NEW" FOR OUTPUT AS #1
4230 WHILE NOT EOF(2)
4240    INPUT #2, CUST.NO$, CUST.NAME$, CUST.ADD$, CUST.CITY$, CUST.STATE$,
                  CUST.ZIP$, AMOUNT.OWED
4250    LPRINT TAB(24);"CUSTOMER INVOICE"
4260    LPRINT
4270    LPRINT TAB(6);"SOLD TO:   ";CUST.NAME$
4280    LPRINT TAB(16);CUST.ADD$
4290    LPRINT TAB(16);CUST.CITY$,CUST.STATE$;"   ";CUST.ZIP$
4300    LPRINT
4310    LPRINT "PRODUCT       PRODUCT DESCRIPTION       QUANTITY   UNIT     TOTAL"
4320    LPRINT "NUMBER";TAB(49);"PRICE"
4330    LPRINT
4340    GOSUB 4500 'PRINT DETAIL LINES AND UPDATE MASTER
4350    LPRINT
4360    LPRINT:LPRINT
4370    LPRINT TAB(41);"TOTAL INVOICE   ";
4380    LPRINT USING "$#####.##";INVOICE.TOTAL
4390    LPRINT
4400    LPRINT
4410    LET INVOICE.TOTAL=0
4420    WRITE #1, CUST.NO$, CUST.NAME$, CUST.ADD$, CUST.CITY$, CUST.STATE$,
                  CUST.ZIP$, AMOUNT.OWED
4430 WEND
4440 CLOSE
```

Figure 9.23   Program Code for Example Application (Continued)

```
4450 PRINT "BE SURE TO RENAME YOUR UPDATED FILE (NEWMASTER) TO THE"
4460 PRINT "OLD MASTER (MASTER)!!!"
4499 RETURN
4500 '              PRINT DETAIL LINES AND UPDATE MASTER
4510 OPEN "TRANS.JPC" FOR INPUT AS #3
4520 WHILE NOT EOF(3)
4530    INPUT #3, C.NUMBER$, P.NUM$, QTY
4540    IF C.NUMBER$<>CUST.NO$ THEN GOTO 4650
4550    FOR ROW1=1 TO ROW
4560       IF VAL(P.NUM$)<>PRODUCT.NO(ROW1) THEN 4620
4570       LET TOTAL=VAL(UNIT.PRICE$(ROW1))*QTY
4580       LPRINT TAB(1);PRODUCT.NO(ROW1);TAB(9);PRODUCT.DESC$(ROW1);
4590       LPRINT TAB(41);QTY;TAB(47);UNIT.PRICE$(ROW1);
4600       LPRINT TAB(56);USING "$#####.##";TOTAL
4610       LET INVOICE.TOTAL=INVOICE.TOTAL+TOTAL
4620    NEXT ROW1
4630 '              UPDATE MASTER
4640    LET AMOUNT.OWED=AMOUNT.OWED+INVOICE.TOTAL
4650 WEND
4660 CLOSE #3
4999 RETURN
10000 ' ***** CREATE/ADD MASTER FILE **
10010 '              ADD THE RECORD TO THE FILE
10020 LET CONTINUE$="Y"
10030 OPEN "MASTER" FOR APPEND AS #1
10040 WHILE CONTINUE$<>"N"
10050    CLS
10060    PRINT
10070    INPUT "ENTER CUSTOMER NUMBER";CUSTOMER.NO$
10080    PRINT
10090    INPUT "ENTER CUSTOMER NAME";CUSTOMER.NAME$
10100    PRINT
10110    INPUT "ENTER CUSTOMER'S ADDRESS";ADDRESS$
10120    PRINT
10130    INPUT "ENTER CUSTOMER'S CITY";CITY$
10140    PRINT
10150    INPUT "ENTER CUSTOMER'S STATE";STATE$
10160    PRINT
10170    INPUT "ENTER CUSTOMER'S ZIP CODE";ZIP$
10180    PRINT
10190    INPUT "ENTER THE AMOUNT OWED";AMOUNT
10200    WRITE #1, CUSTOMER.NO$, CUSTOMER.NAME$, ADDRESS$, CITY$, STATE$, ZIP$,
                   AMOUNT
10210    PRINT
10220    INPUT "     DO YOU HAVE MORE DATA TO ENTER (Y/N)";CONTINUE$
10230 WEND
10240 CLOSE #1
10250 '              LOAD THE TABLE AND SORT
10260 OPEN "MASTER" FOR INPUT AS #1
10270 WHILE NOT EOF(1)
10280    LET SUB=SUB+1
10290    INPUT #1, CUSTOMER.NO$(SUB), CUSTOMER.NAME$(SUB), ADDRESS$(SUB),
                   CITY$(SUB), STATE$(SUB), ZIP$(SUB), AMOUNT(SUB)
10300 WEND
10310 CLOSE #1
10320 FOR SUB1=1 TO SUB-1
10330    FOR SUB2=SUB1+1 TO SUB
10340       IF CUSTOMER.NO$(SUB2)>=CUSTOMER.NO$(SUB1) THEN GOTO 10420
10350       SWAP CUSTOMER.NO$(SUB1), CUSTOMER.NO$(SUB2)
10360       SWAP CUSTOMER.NAME$(SUB1), CUSTOMER.NAME$(SUB2)
10370       SWAP ADDRESS$(SUB1), ADDRESS$(SUB2)
10380       SWAP CITY$(SUB1), CITY$(SUB2)
10390       SWAP STATE$(SUB1), STATE$(SUB2)
10400       SWAP ZIP$(SUB1), ZIP$(SUB2)
10410       SWAP AMOUNT(SUB1), AMOUNT(SUB2)
10420    NEXT SUB2
10430 NEXT SUB1
```

Figure 9.23   Program Code for Example Application (Continued)

```
10440 '                    REWRITE TO THE MASTER FILE
10450 OPEN "MASTER" FOR OUTPUT AS #1
10460 FOR R=1 TO SUB
10470     WRITE #1, CUSTOMER.NO$(R), CUSTOMER.NAME$(R), ADDRESS$(R), CITY$(R),
                   STATE$(R), ZIP$(R), AMOUNT(R)
10480 NEXT R
10490 CLOSE #1
10999 RETURN
11000 ' ***** CHANGE DATA IN THE MASTER FILE
11010 '              LOAD THE MASTER FILE INTO A TABLE
11020 OPEN "MASTER" FOR INPUT AS #1
11030 LET SUB=0
11040 WHILE NOT EOF(1)
11050     LET SUB=SUB+1
11060     INPUT #1, CUSTOMER.NO$(SUB), CUSTOMER.NAME$(SUB), ADDRESS$(SUB),
                   CITY$(SUB), STATE$(SUB), ZIP$(SUB), AMOUNT(SUB)
11070 WEND
11080 CLOSE #1
11090 '              MAKE THE CHANGES
11100 CLS
11110 LET X=0
11120 INPUT "ENTER THE CUSTOMER NUMBER OF THE RECORD YOU WISH TO CHANGE";C.NUM$
11130 WHILE RECORD.FOUND$<>"Y"
11140     LET X=X+1
11150     IF C.NUM$<>CUSTOMER.NO$(X) THEN GOTO 11430
11160     LET RECORD.FOUND$="Y"
11170     CLS
11180     PRINT "THE CUSTOMER NUMBER IS...........";CUSTOMER.NO$(X)
11190     PRINT "THE CUSTOMER NAME IS.............";CUSTOMER.NAME$(X)
11200     PRINT "THE ADDRESS IS..................";ADDRESS$(X)
11210     PRINT "THE CITY IS.....................";CITY$(X)
11220     PRINT "THE STATE IS....................";STATE$(X)
11230     PRINT "THE ZIP CODE IS.................";ZIP$(X)
11240     PRINT "THE AMOUNT OWED IS..............";AMOUNT(X)
11250     PRINT
11260     PRINT
11270     PRINT "IF YOU WISH TO CHANGE ANY OF THE INFORMATION SIMPLY"
11280     PRINT "TYPE IN THE CORRECT DATA.  IF NOT, HIT RETURN.  "
11290     LOCATE 1,34:LINE INPUT C.NO$
11300     LOCATE 2,34:LINE INPUT C.NAME$
11310     LOCATE 3,34:LINE INPUT C.ADD$
11320     LOCATE 4,34:LINE INPUT C.CITY$
11330     LOCATE 5,34:LINE INPUT C.STATE$
11340     LOCATE 6,34:LINE INPUT C.ZIP$
11350     LOCATE 7,33:INPUT NEW.AMOUNT$
11360     IF C.NO$<>"" THEN LET CUSTOMER.NO$(X)=C.NO$
11370     IF C.NAME$<>"" THEN LET CUSTOMER.NAME$(X)=C.NAME$
11380     IF C.ADD$<>"" THEN LET ADDRESS$(X)=C.ADD$
11390     IF C.CITY$<>"" THEN LET CITY$(X)=C.CITY$
11400     IF C.STATE$<>"" THEN LET STATE$(X)=C.STATE$
11410     IF C.ZIP$<>"" THEN LET ZIP$(X)=C.ZIP$
11420     IF NEW.AMOUNT$<>"" THEN LET AMOUNT(X)=VAL(NEW.AMOUNT$)
11430 WEND
11440 '              WRITE THE CHANGED MASTER TO DISK
11450 OPEN "MASTER" FOR OUTPUT AS #1
11460 FOR S=1 TO SUB
11470     WRITE #1, CUSTOMER.NO$(S), CUSTOMER.NAME$(S), ADDRESS$(S), CITY$(S),
                   STATE$(S), ZIP$(S), AMOUNT(S)
11480 NEXT S
11490 CLOSE #1
11500 RETURN
11999 RETURN
12000 ' ***** DELETE A RECORD FROM THE MASTER FILE
12010 '              LOAD THE MASTER FILE INTO A TABLE
12020 OPEN "MASTER" FOR INPUT AS #1
12030 LET SUB=0
12040 WHILE NOT EOF(1)
12050     LET SUB=SUB+1
```

Figure 9.23   Program Code for Example Application (Continued)

```
12060     INPUT #1, CUSTOMER.NO$(SUB), CUSTOMER.NAME$(SUB), ADDRESS$(SUB), CITY$(
SUB), STATE$(SUB), ZIP$(SUB), AMOUNT(SUB)
12070 WEND
12080 CLOSE #1
12090 '               IDENTIFY THE RECORD TO BE DELETED
12100 CLS
12110 INPUT "ENTER THE CUSTOMER NUMBER OF THE RECORD YOU WISH TO DELETE";CN$
12120 LET X=0
12130 WHILE FOUND$<>"N"
12140     LET X=X+1
12150     IF CN$<>CUSTOMER.NO$(X) THEN GOTO 12180
12160     LET FOUND$="N"
12170     LET CUSTOMER.NO$(X)="O"
12180 WEND
12190 '                 REWRITE THE MASTER
12200 OPEN "MASTER" FOR OUTPUT AS #1
12210 FOR X=1 TO SUB
12220     WRITE #1, CUSTOMER.NO$(X), CUSTOMER.NAME$(X), ADDRESS$(X), CITY$(X),
                  STATE$(X), ZIP$(X), AMOUNT(X)
12230 NEXT X
12240 CLOSE #1
12999 RETURN
13000 ' ***** LIST THE MASTER FILE ****
13010 CLS
13020 OPEN "MASTER" FOR INPUT AS #1
13030 LPRINT "CUSTOMER NO  CUSTOMER NAME   ADDRESS        CITY        STATE";
13040 LPRINT " ZIP CODE   AMOUNT"
13050 LPRINT
13060 LPRINT
13070 WHILE NOT EOF(1)
13080     INPUT #1, CUST.NO$, CUST.NAME$, CUST.ADD$, CUST.CITY$, CUST.STATE$,
                  CUST.ZIP$, AMOUNT.OWED
13090     IF CUST.NO$="O" THEN GOTO 13170
13100     LPRINT TAB(2);CUST.NO$;
13110     LPRINT TAB(12);CUST.NAME$;
13120     LPRINT TAB(28);CUST.ADD$;
13130     LPRINT TAB(45);CUST.CITY$;
13140     LPRINT TAB(59);CUST.STATE$;
13150     LPRINT TAB(63);CUST.ZIP$;
13160     LPRINT TAB(74);USING "$###.##";AMOUNT.OWED
13170 WEND
13180 CLOSE #1
13999 RETURN
```

Figure 9.23   Program Code for Example Application (Concluded)

Figure 9.24   Output Generated from Example Application

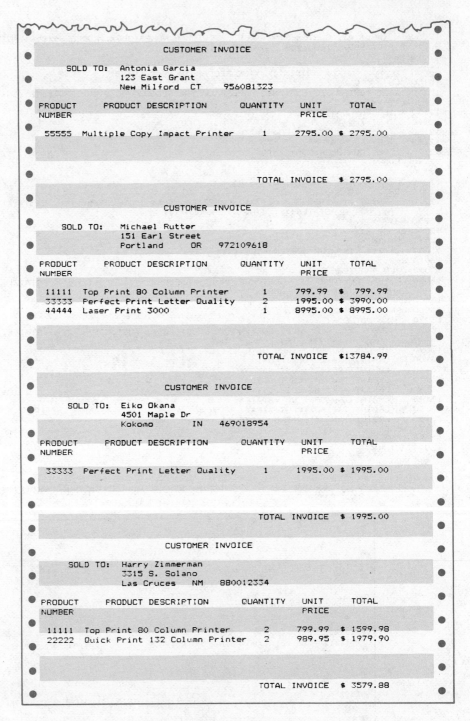

Figure 9.24   Output Generated from Example Application
(Concluded)

CUSTOMER NO	CUSTOMER NAME	ADDRESS	CITY	STATE	ZIP CODE	AMOUNT
08434	Al Abramson	7221 S 180th St	Kent	WA	980516772	$ 58.00
12345	Antonia Garcia	123 East Grant	New Milford	CT	956081323	$ 87.00
23456	Michael Rutter	151 Earl Street	Portland	OR	972109618	$ 0.00
34562	Eiko Okana	4501 Maple Dr	Kokomo	IN	469018954	$100.00
45678	Harry Zimmerman	3315 S. Solano	Las Cruces	NM	880012334	$ 0.00

Figure 9.25 Listing of Master File

REVIEW QUESTIONS

1. Explain the procedure used in the example program to add a record to a sequential master file. (Obj. 4)
2. Why is it necessary to consistently use the same record format when file maintenance is completed on the sequential file? (Obj. 5)
3. Explain what file maintenance procedures were available to the user of the example program. (Obj. 4)
4. Identify which files were used in the sequential file processing system in the example program and identify the purpose of each. (Obj. 6)
5. Identify which file maintenance procedures, if any, were available for the transaction file. (Obj. 4)
6. How many menus were used in the example program and what purpose did they serve? (Obj. 4)

VOCABULARY WORDS

The following words were introduced in this chapter:

file processing system	static	history file
file size	master file	audit file
activity	detail file	exception report
volatility	related file	audit report
volatile		

KEYWORDS AND COMMANDS

The following keywords and commands were introduced in this chapter:

NAME

PROGRAMS TO WRITE

Complete the appropriate documentation for each of the programs before writing the code. The programs may be written using data you create or using the following data.

MASTER FILE DATA

Social Security Number	Name	Street Address	City	State	ZIP Code	Degree	Number of Credits	Number of Dependents
222233344	Larry Honl	3812 Mitcher	Baraboo	WI	567015432	MS	189	3
456678666	Craig Brenholdt	1011 Apple St	Baraboo	WI	567012461	MS	145	2
345678901	Sue Straw	1010 Apple St	Baraboo	WI	567018989	MS	158	0
234567890	Randy Albert	45 Park Ridge	Baraboo	WI	567018934	MA	164	1
123456789	Tammy Halaychik	234 East Tyler	Baraboo	WI	567012348	MB	132	5

UPDATE DATA

Social Security Number	Name	Street Address	City	State	ZIP Code	Degree	Number of Credits	Number of Dependents	Record Code
222233344						DR	194		C
456678666		221 Grant Ave.	Ione		576012334				C
345678901									D
234567890							172		C
123456789		432 Tyler Ave							C
111446666	John Schillak	12 Rim Rock	Baraboo	WI	567013421	DR	198	3	A

Program 1

Write a program to create a master file for the instructors employed by your school. The personnel department would like you to store the person's social security number, name, street address, city, state, ZIP Code, highest educational degree, number of college credits obtained, and number of dependents. This file should be sequential.

Program 2

Write a program to create an update file for the instructors employed by your school district. This file will be used by the personnel department to update the master file that you previously created in Program 1. The file should be created interactively. It should contain the following fields of data: social security number, street address, city, state, ZIP Code, highest degree, number of credits, number of dependents, and record code. The record code will be either an A for add, C for change, or D for delete. When data is input into the update file, if data does not change for an employee, put spaces in the field. If data is to be changed, enter the new data. If a record is to be deleted, it will not be rewritten to a new file.

Program 3

Write a program to allow the personnel department to update the sequential master file by using the update file created in Program 2. Upon completion of the update, print out a copy of the updated master file.

Program 4

Put Programs 1, 2, and 3 together into a menu driven system which will allow the user to access the main menu and branch to either the create master, create update, or process update program. Each activity should return the user to the main menu prior to exiting the program.

Program 5

Rewrite Programs 1 and 2 using random files. The records will be accessed sequentially from the master file and also from the update files. Therefore, it will be necessary that the files be ordered by employee number.

Program 6

Rewrite Programs 3 and 4 to use the random files created for the master and update files to perform the master file update.

CONTINUING PROJECTS

Before writing any program of the continuing projects, be sure to complete all appropriate documentation.

Project 1

The payroll detail files must be constructed. Each of the two files (P1PAYROLL and P1WEEKLY) must be created and maintained in a similar manner as the master file (P1MAINT). When the payroll option is chosen from the main menu, the user should be presented with another menu. The choices on the new menu, each of which will be written as a separate module, are:

1. Prepare individual payroll detail records.
2. Prepare weekly payroll transactions.
3. Prepare tax tables.
4. Return to main menu.

In this chapter you will be preparing the modules for adding and changing an individual payroll detail record. As a second activity, you will be preparing the modules for adding and changing a weekly payroll transaction. Tax tables will be prepared later. Whenever one or more records are added, the program should sort the data in the file so that all employees are arranged in order by their social security number. The data for the individual payroll detail file should include:

1. Social security number.
2. Pay rate.
3. Number of exemptions.
4. Gross earnings to date.
5. Federal tax to date.
6. State tax to date.
7. Net earnings to date.

When data is entered into the detail file, the master file should be accessed to match the name with the name in the master file. The social security number should be selected from the master record used in the detail record. The data for the weekly payroll transaction should include:

1. Social security number.
2. Hours worked.

When data is entered into the weekly payroll transaction file, the master file should be accessed to match the name of the person's record being entered with the master file. The social security number should be read from the master record and used in the detail file. As the user accesses either the choice to prepare the individual payroll detail record or the weekly payroll transactions, another menu should be presented which will permit additions or changes to the record.

Project 2

Now that you have completed the inventory maintenance module, you are ready to prepare the point of sale module. The point of sale module is accessed via the main menu and is stored in a file called P2SELL. This program creates a sales slip for each sale and also creates a transaction file that will be used to access the master inventory file for information. The combined information entered via the keyboard and the information accessed from the master file will be used to produce a report of the transactions with summary information regarding the subtotal, taxes at a rate of five percent, and the total of the purchases. When all transactions have been entered, the master file is updated to reflect the changes for the sales. For example, if two items were sold, the quantity on hand would be decreased by two and the quantity sold for the day, week, quarter, and year would be increased by two.

The two activities described should be accessed via a menu which will give the user a choice of either entering sales transactions or updating. The submenu should include:

1. Process sales transactions.
2. Update master inventory file.
3. Return to main menu.

The sales slip should show the following:

1. Stock number (entered via the keyboard).
2. Description (accessed from the master file).
3. Selling price (accessed from the master file).
4. Quantity (entered via the keyboard).
5. Total of individual sales.
6. Total of all sales.
7. Taxes (total sales multiplied by .05).
8. Total purchases (total sales plus taxes).

## Chapter 10

Linked Files

Objectives:
1. Identify three ways of determining record numbers.
2. Determine the size of the direct file to be created.
3. Describe the makeup of a linked file and the purpose of the parts.
4. Identify the advantages of linked files.
5. Identify the disadvantages of linked files.
6. Identify methods of determining record numbers using hashing schemes.
7. List the steps required to create a linked file.
8. List the steps required to access a linked file.

Topic 10.1— PRINCIPLES OF USING LINKED FILES

In Chapter 4 you were taught to create random files. In Chapter 9 you had an opportunity to work with multiple files. You also learned that the accessing and updating of data in a sequential file required the rewriting of the entire file. File maintenance of random files allowed you the opportunity to read the record, make the change and rewrite the record to the same location. In order to do this, you had to know the random record number. In this chapter you will learn to create random files without knowing the record location. As was pointed out in Chapter 4, a random file may be created in sequential order, by using a record number input as part of the data, or by calculating the record number. A hashing scheme is the term applied to an algorithm created to calculate the record location. The same algorithm used in storing the record must be used to access the record when it is to be read.

DEFINITION OF LINKED FILES

If the random records were physically written in sorted order, it would be easy to access data. However, random files are usually created in random order. This means that the records are not sorted prior to writing. As a result, the location of the record must be obtained by performing some computer logic that will help to locate the record within the file. Random files are of direct organization. This means that they may be accessed directly. In order to do so, it is necessary to know the record number or relative number. It is known as the relative record number because the record is stored in the file in its relative location. That is, the first record is stored in record number one if the relative record number is one. A record with the relative record number of 39 would be stored in location 39. The largest record number identifies the size of the random file. If you had 35 different records with the highest record number of 200, and each record contained 58 characters, you would need at least 11,600 storage positions (bytes) on disk to store the file. The computer would set aside 200 record positions for the file. This is known as sizing the file. Because very few applications lend themselves to being organized for direct access by an identifiable record number, it is necessary for you to develop a hashing scheme that will allow for indirect accessing of the records in the random file. In other words, the user might enter the social security number, the computer would calculate the record number and use it to determine the location. The algorithm used will usually not be perfect and synonyms will then be produced. A synonym results when two records have the same record number location. If a record had been written to a location that was obtained because of the hashing scheme, then it would be necessary to link the second record to the first and create a linked file. A linked file is a file where records are linked to each other by a pointer. Figure 10.1 illustrates a linked file. A pointer is a field in the record that would contain either a null value or the value of the record number of the linked record. In the case of linked files, two areas are set aside in the file. One is called the prime area and the other is known as the overflow area. The overflow area may either be in the same or a different file. Records are written to the first available record in overflow if a record is already present in the prime record location created as a result of the hashing scheme. Figure 10.2 illustrates a file with prime and overflow areas.

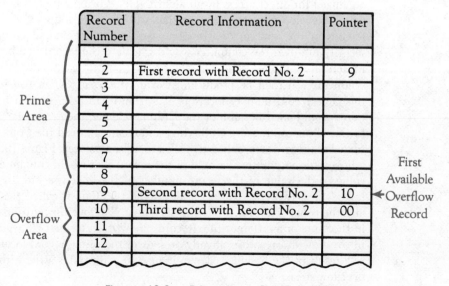

Record Number	Record Information	Pointer
1		
2	First record identified by Record No. 2	6
3		
4		
5		
6	Second record identified by Record No. 2	8
7		
8	Third record identified by Record No. 2	00
n		

Null Value

Figure 10.1   Linked File

Prime Area

Overflow Area

Record Number	Record Information	Pointer
1		
2	First record with Record No. 2	9
3		
4		
5		
6		
7		
8		
9	Second record with Record No. 2	10
10	Third record with Record No. 2	00
11		
12		

First Available Overflow Record

Figure 10.2   Prime and Overflow Areas

ADVANTAGES OF LINKED FILES

Direct file organization has several advantages. Perhaps the biggest advantage would be the ability to access a record directly without reading each of the preceding records. This will save time and computer processing. Another advantage of linking files is the ability to select all records pertaining to one transaction. For example, in an accounts receivable transaction file all records pertaining to a given master record would be linked. The hashing scheme would calculate the same record number and each of these records would be connected to each other. Therefore, by accessing the first record and checking to determine if there is a linkage, we would then access the linked record. The linked record would be checked to determine if there is another linkage, and so on. We would quickly be able to add up the amount of each transaction and give the person an update of the account balance. Figure 10.3 illustrates how an accounts receivable transaction file may be linked.

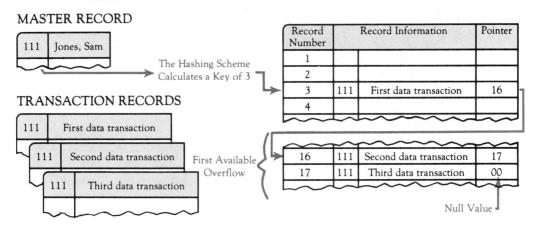

Figure 10.3   Linked List

A third advantage of linked files is the fact that the transactions may be processed without ordering (sorting) the transaction file. This permits us to have lengthy transaction files and to not have to worry about the length of time it will take to sort the file before processing the update routine. Another advantage is the lack of concern you must show for the volume of data to be sorted in the file. Since the data is not going to be placed in a table and sorted, any reasonable amount of data may be stored in a linked file.

Linked files have made online processing feasible for many applications. For example, you are able to call the telephone company and find out the current balance on your bill. If the phone call transaction file was sequential, it would have to be sorted prior to the update. Since it is organized in a linked list, the computer is able to quickly calculate your updated bill. Linked files may be processed sequentially if desired.

DISADVANTAGES OF LINKED FILES

No doubt the biggest disadvantage of linked files in direct file processing is the possibility that two or more records (synonyms) could end up with the same record number. As a result, the records with the duplicate record numbers are written to the overflow area. If the file is highly volatile, the overflow area could end up with more records than the prime area. A second disadvantage is the complication of developing a hashing scheme that will calculate a record key based upon a given field within the record. Another disadvantage has to be the difficulty of updating pointers if one record is deleted. Sometimes the data will be eliminated from the record position and the pointer will remain so as not to interrupt the flow of the linkage. This creates the problem of knowing which records are occupied and which are not. A highly volatile file may result in slower access time even though the file is accessed directly. The slower access time could be the result of deleting the data and flagging the record to indicate that the pointer remained. As a result, many linkages would have to be checked before the desired record is accessed. Perhaps another disadvantage would be the wasted space allocated for the highest record number even though several relative record positions are not used in the file. If all of the record positions were active, this would not be a problem. These are a few of the disadvantages of linking records within a file.

HASHING SCHEMES

Several hashing schemes are available; you could also develop your own. The most popular hashing scheme is known as the prime number division/ remainder procedure . A prime number is a number evenly divisible by 1 or by itself. For example, let's assume that we want to store ten records randomly on a file. We do not know if there will be any synonyms, so we will plan to obtain 75 percent packing of records in the prime area. To determine how many records have to be set aside for the prime area, we complete the following calculation.

$$.75 \ x \ = \ 10$$
$$x \ = \ (10/.75)$$
$$x \ = \ 13.333$$
$$x \ = \ 14 \ \text{prime records}$$

Fourteen records would be set aside for the prime area. Beginning in record location 15, we would store the records for overflow. The prime number selected for division would be 13. It is the closest to the number 14, but not larger. Next, we would divide the key number from the records. Examples would include an employee number or customer number. Assuming that the number was 230, the calculation would be:

$$230/13 = 17 \ \text{with a remainder of 9}$$

The remainder of 9 is added to 1 (remainder plus one). This is done so that no record would ever be stored in location zero. The record would be stored in location number 10. If another record such as customer number 217 were calculated using the same algorithm, the results would be:

217/13 = 16 with a remainder of 9

The remainder of 9 is added to 1, giving 10, which is a synonym of the record for customer number 230. Therefore, the pointer field for record 10 would store the value 15 and the customer number 217 would be written to the first available position in the overflow area. The records written to the file would look similar to the following file example.

Record Number	Data	Pointer
1		
2		
3		
4		
5		
6		
7	Customer No. 161	16
8		
9		
10	Customer No. 230	15
11		
12	Customer No. 115	00
13		
14		
15	Customer No. 217	00
16	Customer No. 084	00
17		
18		
n		

161 / 13 = 12 R 6 + 1   Prime Area

230 / 13 = 17 R 9 + 1

115 / 13 = 8 R 11 + 1

217 / 13 = 16 R 9 + 1 (Synonym) Stored in First Available in Overflow

Overflow Area

In the example, we find that Customer No. 230 was stored in record location 10 because there were no previous records stored in that location. Customer number 217 was a synonym and therefore was stored in the first available overflow area which was location 15. Record numbers 7 and 16 were also synonyms. Because customer number 161 was written before customer number 084, it was placed in the prime area and 084 was placed in the first available overflow location. Records 7 and 16 are linked and records 10 and 15 are linked. When it comes time to access the records, it will be necessary to calculate the record number based upon the customer number entered. Read the record from the file and check to see that the customer number matches the one entered. If not, the pointer position would be checked to determine which overflow record is linked. The linked overflow record is read and the customer number is again checked. If a match is found, the data is manipulated. If it is not found, the linkage is checked again.

Another hashing scheme sometimes used in direct accessing of files is the digit extraction method As the method implies, digits are extracted from a given key field. For example, assume that the assigned key field social security number is used to extract digits to make up the record key. An analysis of the digits in the key field would be made to determine which digits are most evenly dispersed throughout the data sample. These characters within the field would be used for the key. Given the social security number 503467896, we find that digits 9, 7, and 3 are the most distributed. Extracting from right to left, we would find that the record location would be 973. If a small number of records is to be stored, perhaps only two digits will be extracted. Again, you must account for synonyms.

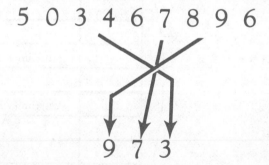

Programmers sometimes use a technique called folding to arrive at a record key. In this technique, the key field is split in two or more parts and the parts are then totaled to form the record value. Study the following example.

Given a Six Digit Field with a Value of 123456:
    Fold in Half: $123 + 456 = 579$
    Fold in Thirds: $12 + 34 + 56 = 102$

Several variations of folding may be used. Some will use alternate digits and fold. Others will select a pattern such as the first two and the last two and the second two and the last two. The purpose is to arrive at a record key that is unique.

CREATING AND MAINTAINING LINKED FILES

Creating linked files requires you to complete a series of steps much like those completed when creating a random file with a programmer-supplied record key. However, linked files require you to complete some additional steps. You must develop an algorithm which will calculate the record number. After calculating the number and before the record is written, you must check for the presence of data in the record position. If data does not exist, the record may be written. If data does exist, the pointer field must be checked to determine the presence of a value or a null. If a value is not present, the first available overflow record number is written to the pointer field and that record number is used to write the data to the overflow record. This process is repeated until all records are written. If the file is to have data added at a later date, the first available overflow record number is usually stored for future use or the first available record has some trailer data written to it so that it may be identified later.

ACCESSING A RECORD

Accessing the records in a linked file means that you must also use the exact same algorithm to calculate the record number for the record to be accessed. Generally, the key field will be entered interactively. The record number would be calculated and the record would be read. If the data in the record matches with the key field input interactively, the correct record has been read. If it does not, the pointer field is checked for a value. That value then becomes the record key for the next record to be read. If the second record read is a match, the data is manipulated. If it is not, the process is repeated until the correct record is accessed. Updating the linked file is not as difficult as updating the sequential file. The file is organized as a direct file. Once the record is accessed, the data may be changed and rewritten to the same location using the same record key.

REVIEW QUESTIONS

1. Identify three ways in which the record location may be identified when creating direct access files. (Obj. 1)
2. Explain what is meant by the term hashing scheme. (Obj. 1)
3. If there were to be 50 records each 34 characters long, written to a linked file and the largest record number was 88, how many characters would have to be allocated for the file? (Obj. 2)

4. Define what is meant by the term linked file. (Obj. 3)
5. Linked files are made up of prime and overflow areas. Define each of those terms. (Obj. 3)
6. Identify four advantages of linked files. (Obj. 4)
7. Identify four disadvantages of linked files. (Obj. 5)
8. Identify three hashing schemes used for creating linked files. (Obj. 6)
9. Identify the steps required to create a linked file. (Obj. 7)
10. Identify the steps required to access records in a linked file. (Obj. 8

Topic 10.2— LINKED FILES WITH BASIC

Throughout business and industry there are several applications that lend themselves to being programmed using linked files. Perhaps the most logical applications are those that are transaction oriented. For example, personnel records stored in a master file using the social security number as the key would create synonyms. Therefore, this program application would have to contain the ability to store synonym records. Usually changes to personnel records will be accomplished interactively. This online processing will require that the application be able to locate any employee record after the user has entered a key data field.

Accounts payable and accounts receivable applications will generally be based upon the concept of linked files. These two applications generally require that the user have the ability to quickly determine the status of the account. By entering the key data field, the record number may be calculated and the record retrieved. If a transaction file exists, the record number may be calculated to locate the first record and the pointer checked to determine if additional transactions exist. Amount fields may be totaled and the master file may be quickly updated to determine the current balance. The creation of a master accounts receivable file using linked files is contained in the following section. Study it carefully to determine the steps for creating the file, accessing the file after creation, and generating the report.

PROGRAMMING A LINKED FILE APPLICATION

The following application system is a menu-driven accounts receivable file system. The application will allow the user to create an accounts receivable master file. Once the file is created, the user would be able to access specific records contained within the file. To save space, the routines to allow for updating the records are not included. The final subsystem allows the user to generate a report of the contents of the file. Figure 10.4 shows the hierarchy chart for the system. Figure 10.5 shows the program documentation sheet and Figures 10.6 through 10.9 show the module documentation sheets.

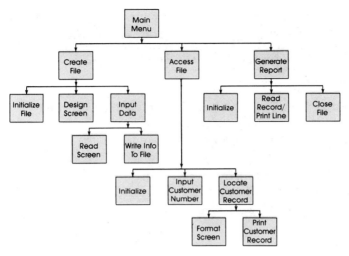

Figure 10.4   Hierarchy Chart

PROGRAM DOCUMENTATION		
Program: EXC10	Programmer: Clark and LaBarre	Date: 5/10/--
Purpose: This application file system creates a random linked file for master records for accounts receivable.		
Input: The user chooses to create a file, access a file, or generate a report of contents of a file. The choice is input via the keyboard.	Output: Write the record to disk; print record contents on the screen; or print the file contents on hard copy.	
Data Terminator:		
Variables Used: Varies from one computer to another.		

Figure 10.5   Program Documentation

MODULE DOCUMENTATION	Program: __EXC10E1__	Module: __MAIN__ Lines: __10-999__

Module Description:

This module prints a menu on the screen. It allows the user to input the choice for creating a file, accessing a file, generating a report or ending the process. Upon getting the user's choice, it calls the appropriate subroutine. The user determines when to stop.

Module Function (Program Design):

1. DO...UNTIL the user chooses to stop:
   a. Print the menu.
   b. Obtain the user's choice.
   c. Process the appropriate subroutine.

Figure 10.6   Main Module Documentation

MODULE DOCUMENTATION	Program: __EXC10E2__	Module: __CREATE FILE__ Lines: __10-7999__

Module Description:

This subroutine creates a random linked file for accounts receivable customers. If synonym records occur, update the pointer and write the record to an overflow area.

Module Function (Program Design):

1. Open the file.
2. Initialize the file.
3. Format the screen.
4. Input the information.
5. Validate the information.
6. Reenter incorrect information.
7. Calculate the record location. Check for the presence of data. Write the record. If data is present, check the linkage. Update the pointer. Write the record to the first available overflow area. Repeat the process.
8. Close the file.

Figure 10.7   Create File Module Documentation

MODULE DOCUMENTATION	Program: EXC10E3	Module: ACCESS FILE
		Lines: 10-6999

Module Description:

This subroutine accesses a linked file that was previously created. Once the record is located, print the contents on the screen.

Module Function (Program Design):

1. Open the file.
2. Input the customer number.
3. Validate the input data.
4. Calculate the record number.
5. Retrieve the record. Match the customer number with the input number. If they are the same, print the contents on the screen. If they are not the same, check the pointer to determine the location of the linked record. Compare the numbers when the record is located. If they are equal, print the contents on the screen. If they are unequal, continue the process.
6. If the record is not located, print a message on the screen.
7. Ask the user if another record is to be retrieved. If not, end the process.
8. Close the file.

Figure 10.8   Access File Module Documentation

MODULE DOCUMENTATION	Program: EXC10E4	Module: REPORT
		Lines: 10-3999

Module Description:

This subroutine will print the contents of the linked file on paper.

Module Function (Program Design):

1. Open the file.
2. Read the records sequentially. If data exists, write it to paper. If data does not exist, read the next record.
3. Close the file.

Figure 10.9   Report Module Documentation

```
10 ' EXC10E1
20 ' CLARK AND LABARRE--CHAPTER 10, EXAMPLE 1
30 ' ***** THIS IS THE MAIN MENU ******
40 CLS
50 LOCATE 5,15:PRINT "MAIN MENU"
60 LOCATE 7,10:PRINT "CREATE THE FILE............1"
70 LOCATE 9,10:PRINT "ACCESS THE FILE............2"
80 LOCATE 11,10:PRINT "GENERATE A REPORT..........3"
90 LOCATE 13,10:PRINT "END APPLICATION............4"
100 LOCATE 16,10:INPUT "ENTER YOUR CHOICE..........",CHOICE
110 IF CHOICE<1 OR CHOICE>4 THEN 100
120 IF CHOICE=1 THEN CHAIN "CREATE FILE"
130 IF CHOICE=2 THEN CHAIN "ACCESS FILE"
140 IF CHOICE=3 THEN CHAIN "REPORT"
150 IF CHOICE=4 THEN GOTO 999
999 END
```

Figure 10.10   Program to Display the Main Menu

```
10 ' EXC10E2
20 ' CLARK AND LABARRE--CHAPTER 10, EXAMPLE 2
30 ' ***** CREATE FILE ****************
40 GOSUB 1000        'INITIALIZE
50 WHILE ANSWER$=UNFINISHED$
60    GOSUB 2000  'FORMAT SCREEN
70    GOSUB 3000  'INPUT INFORMATION
80 WEND
90 GOSUB 7000        'CLOSE FILES
100 CHAIN "MENU"
1000 ' ***** INITIALIZE ***************
1010 PRIME.NUMBER=13
1020 DEF FNRECORD%(CUSTOMER.NO)=(CUSTOMER.NO MOD PRIME.NUMBER)+1'Hashing scheme
1030 NEXT.AVAILABLE=13          'First available overflow record
1040 LAST.OVERFLOW=30           'Last record in the file
1050 ANSWER$="Y"
1060 UNFINISHED$="Y"
1070 DEF FNCHAR$(R,C)=CHR$(SCREEN(R,C))
1080 NULL$=CHR$(0)+CHR$(0)+CHR$(0)
1090 OPEN "CUSTOMER" AS #1 LEN=74
1100 FIELD#1, 20 AS CN$, 5 AS NO$, 20 AS AD$, 15 AS CY$, 2 AS ST$,
        9 AS ZP$, 3 AS LK$
1110 FOR RECORD%=1 TO LAST.OVERFLOW
1120    LSET LK$=NULL$
1130    PUT#1,RECORD%
1140 NEXT RECORD%
1999 RETURN
2000 ' ***** FORMAT SCREEN ************
2010 CLS
2020 LOCATE 2,11
2030 PRINT "CUSTOMER INFORMATION"
2040 LOCATE 5,5
2050 PRINT "NAME:"
2060 LOCATE 7,3
2070 PRINT "NUMBER:"
2080 LOCATE 9,2
2090 PRINT "ADDRESS:"
2100 LOCATE 11,5
2110 PRINT "CITY:"
2120 LOCATE 13,4
2130 PRINT "STATE:"
2140 LOCATE 15,1
2150 PRINT "ZIP CODE:"
2160 LOCATE 18,3
2170 PRINT "IS THIS INFORMATION CORRECT (Y/N)"
2999 RETURN
```

Figure 10.11   Program to Create the File

```
3000 ' ***** INPUT INFORMATION ********
3010 LOCATE 5,11
3020 INPUT CUSTOMER.NAME$
3030 LOCATE 7,11
3040 INPUT CUSTOMER.NO
3050 LOCATE 9,11
3060 INPUT ADDRESS$
3070 LOCATE 11,11
3080 INPUT CITY$
3090 LOCATE 13,11
3100 INPUT STATE$
3110 LOCATE 15,11
3120 INPUT ZIP.CODE$
3130 LOCATE 18,37
3140 INPUT INCORRECT$
3150 INCORRECT$=LEFT$(INCORRECT$,1)
3160 IF INCORRECT$="Y" OR INCORRECT$="y" THEN 3170 ELSE 3010
3170 GOSUB 4000  'SCREENREAD
3180 GOSUB 5000  'WRITE INFORMATION
3190 LOCATE 21,3
3200 INPUT "DO YOU WISH TO ENTER ANOTHER (Y/N)";ANSWER$
3210 ANSWER$=LEFT$(ANSWER$,1)
3999 RETURN
4000 ' ***** SCREENREAD ***************
4010 CUSTOMER.NAME$=""       'Validation
4020 FOR COL=1 TO 20         'Technique
4030    CUSTOMER.NAME$=CUSTOMER.NAME$+FNCHAR$(5,12+COL)
4040 NEXT COL
4050 CUSTOMER.NO$=""
4060 FOR COL=1 TO 5
4070    CUSTOMER.NO$=CUSTOMER.NO$+FNCHAR$(7,12+COL)
4080 NEXT COL
4090 CUSTOMER.NO=VAL(CUSTOMER.NO$)
4100 ADDRESS$=""
4110 FOR COL=1 TO 20
4120    ADDRESS$=ADDRESS$+FNCHAR$(9,12+COL)
4130 NEXT COL
4140 CITY$=""
4150 FOR COL=1 TO 15
4160    CITY$=CITY$+FNCHAR$(11,12+COL)
4170 NEXT COL
4180 STATE$=""
4190 FOR COL=1 TO 2
4200    STATE$=STATE$+FNCHAR$(13,12+COL)
4210 NEXT COL
4220 ZIP.CODE$=""
4230 FOR COL=1 TO 9
4240    ZIP.CODE$=ZIP.CODE$+FNCHAR$(15,12+COL)
4250 NEXT COL
4999 RETURN
5000 ' ***** WRITE INFORMATION ********
5010 RECORD%=FNRECORD%(CUSTOMER.NO)            'Determine the record location
5020 GET#1,RECORD%                             'Get the record
5030 LINK$=LK$
5040 IF LINK$<>NULL$ THEN GOSUB 6000  'FIND END OF LINK Check the pointer field
5050 IF (LINK$=NULL$) OR (NEXT.AVAILABLE<>LAST.OVERFLOW) THEN 5130
5060 'ERROR MESSAGE
5070 CLS
5080 LOCATE 11,12
5090 PRINT "OVERFLOW IS FULL"
5100 LOCATE 12,10
5110 PRINT "RECORD WAS NOT ADDED"
5120 GOTO 5999
5130 'WRITE NEW RECORD
5140 LSET CN$=CUSTOMER.NAME$
5150 LSET NO$=CUSTOMER.NO$
5160 LSET AD$=ADDRESS$
```

Figure 10.11   Program to Create the File (Continued)

```
5170 LSET CY$=CITY$
5180 LSET ST$=STATE$
5190 LSET ZP$=ZIP.CODE$
5200 LSET LK$=STR$(0)
5210 PUT#1,RECORD%            'Write the record to the relative position
5999 RETURN
6000 ' ***** FIND END OF LINK *********
6010 NEXT.AVAILABLE=NEXT.AVAILABLE+1
6020 IF NEXT.AVAILABLE=LAST.OVERFLOW THEN 6999
6030 LAST.RECORD%=RECORD%
6040 RECORD%=VAL(LINK$)
6050 WHILE RECORD%<>0
6060    GET#1,RECORD%
6070    LAST.RECORD%=RECORD%
6080    RECORD%=VAL(LK$)
6090 WEND
6100 'UPDATE POINTER OF CURRENT RECORD
6110 LSET LK$=STR$(NEXT.AVAILABLE)
6120 PUT#1,LAST.RECORD%
6130 RECORD%=NEXT.AVAILABLE
6999 RETURN
7000 ' ***** CLOSE FILES **************
7010 LSET LK$=STR$(NEXT.AVAILABLE)    'Setting up trailer data
7020 LSET CN$="END"
7030 LSET NO$="END"
7040 LSET AD$="END"
7050 LSET CY$="END"
7060 LSET ST$="END"
7070 LSET ZP$="END"
7080 RECORD%=LAST.OVERFLOW
7090 PUT#1,RECORD%               'Writing trailer record for future use
7100 CLOSE#1
7999 RETURN
```

Figure 10.11   Program to Create the File (Concluded)

```
10 ' EXC10E3
20 ' CLARK AND LABARRE--CHAPTER 10, EXAMPLE 3
30 ' ***** ACCESS FILE ****************
40 GOSUB 1000        'INITIALIZE
50   WHILE ANSWER$=UNFINISHED$
60      GOSUB 2000   'INPUT CUSTOMER NUMBER
70      GOSUB 3000   'FIND CUSTOMER
80      LOCATE 21,3
90      INPUT "DO YOU WISH TO ACCESS ANOTHER (Y/N)";ANSWER$
100     ANSWER$=LEFT$(ANSWER$,1)
110 WEND
120 GOSUB 6000       'CLOSE FILES
130 CLS
140 LOCATE 12,12
150 PRINT "SESSION COMPLETED"
160 CHAIN "MENU"
1000 ' ***** INITIALIZE **************
1010 PRIME.NUMBER=13
1020 ERROR.BELL$=CHR$(7)+CHR$(7)
1030 DEF FNRECORD%(CUSTOMER.NO)=(CUSTOMER.NO MOD PRIME.NUMBER)+1   'Setting up
1040 DEF FNCHAR$(R,C)=CHR$(SCREEN(R,C))                'same hashing
1050 ANSWER$="Y"                                       'scheme as used
1060 UNFINISHED$="Y"                                   'in the create
1070 NULL$=CHR$(0)+CHR$(0)+CHR$(0)                     'program
1080 OPEN "CUSTOMER" AS #1 LEN=74
1090 FIELD#1, 20 AS CN$, 5 AS NO$, 20 AS AD$, 15 AS CY$, 2 AS ST$,
        9 AS ZP$, 3 AS LK$
1999 RETURN
```

Figure 10.12   Program to Access Data

```
2000 ' ***** INPUT CUSTOMER NUMBER ****
2010 CLS
2020 LOCATE 8,13
2030 PRINT "CUSTOMER ACCESS"
2040 LOCATE 11,3
2050 PRINT "CUSTOMER NUMBER: "
2060 LOCATE 13,5
2070 PRINT "CUSTOMER NAME:"
2080 LOCATE 16,5
2090 PRINT "IS INFORMATION CORRECT (Y/N)";
2100 LOCATE 11,20
2110 INPUT CUSTOMER.NO
2120 CUSTOMER.NO$=""
2130 FOR COL=22 TO 26
2140    CUSTOMER.NO$=CUSTOMER.NO$+FNCHAR$(11,COL)
2150 NEXT COL
2160 CUSTOMER.NO=VAL(CUSTOMER.NO$)
2170 LOCATE 13,20
2180 INPUT CUSTOMER.NAME$
2190 CUSTOMER.NAME$=""
2200 FOR COL=22 TO 41
2210    CUSTOMER.NAME$=CUSTOMER.NAME$+FNCHAR$(13,COL)
2220 NEXT COL
2230 LOCATE 16,33
2240 INPUT ANSWER$
2250 ANSWER$=LEFT$(ANSWER$,1)
2260 IF ANSWER$="Y" OR ANSWER$="y" THEN 2270 ELSE 2100
2270 LOCATE 18,6
2280 PRINT "*** SEARCHING FOR CUSTOMER ***"
2999 RETURN
3000 ' ***** FIND CUSTOMER ************
3010 GET#1,FNRECORD%(CUSTOMER.NO)
3020 IF LK$=NULL$ THEN 3130
3030 WHILE VAL(LK$)<>0 AND NO$<>CUSTOMER.NO$          'Search for record
3040    RECORD%=VAL(LK$)
3050    GET#1,RECORD%
3060 WEND
3070 IF CN$<>CUSTOMER.NAME$ THEN 3130
3080 'CUSTOMER FOUND
3090 GOSUB 4000 ' FORMAT SCREEN
3100 GOSUB 5000 ' PRINT INFORMATION
3110 GOTO 3999
3120 'NAME OR NUMBER IS INCORRECT
3130 LOCATE 18,2
3140 PRINT ERROR.BELL$;"**** NAME OR NUMBER IS INCORRECT ****"
3999 RETURN
4000 ' ***** FORMAT SCREEN ************
4010 CLS
4020 LOCATE 2,11
4030 PRINT "CUSTOMER INFORMATION"
4040 LOCATE 5,5
4050 PRINT "NAME:"
4060 LOCATE 7,3
4070 PRINT "NUMBER:"
4080 LOCATE 9,2
4090 PRINT "ADDRESS:"
4100 LOCATE 11,5
4110 PRINT "CITY:"
4120 LOCATE 13,4
4130 PRINT "STATE:"
4140 LOCATE 15,1
4150 PRINT "ZIP CODE:"
4999 RETURN
5000 ' ***** PRINT INFORMATION ********
5010 LOCATE 5,11
5020 PRINT CN$
5030 LOCATE 7,11
```

Figure 10.12   Program to Access Data (Continued)

```
5040 PRINT NO$
5050 LOCATE 9,11
5060 PRINT AD$
5070 LOCATE 11,11
5080 PRINT CY$
5090 LOCATE 13,11
5100 PRINT ST$
5110 LOCATE 15,11
5120 PRINT ZP$
5999 RETURN
6000 ' ***** CLOSE FILES **************
6010 CLOSE#1
6999 RETURN
```

Figure 10.12   Program to Access Data (Concluded)

```
10 ' EXC10E4
20 ' CLARK AND LABARRE--CHAPTER 10, EXAMPLE 4
30 ' ***** REPORT *********************
40 GOSUB 1000        'INITIALIZE           'Prints the contents of the
50 FOR RECORD%=1 TO LAST.OVERFLOW-1        'File and record number
60     GOSUB 2000    'READ RANDOM FILE
70                   '& PRINT
80 NEXT RECORD%
90 GOSUB 3000        'CLOSE FILES
100 CLS
110 LOCATE 12,12
120 PRINT "SESSION COMPLETED"
130 CHAIN "MENU"
1000 ' ***** INITIALIZE ***************
1010 LAST.OVERFLOW=30
1020 NULL$=CHR$(0)+CHR$(0)+CHR$(0)
1030 LPRINT TAB(34) "CUSTOMER INDEX"
1040 LPRINT
1050 LPRINT TAB(25) "NUMBER" SPC(14) "NAME"
1060 LPRINT STRING$(79,"=")
1070 OPEN "CUSTOMER" AS #1 LEN=74
1080 FIELD#1, 20 AS CN$, 5 AS NO$, 20 AS AD$, 15 AS CY$, 2 AS ST$,
        9 AS ZP$, 3 AS LK$
1999 RETURN
2000 ' ***** READ RANDOM FILE & PRINT
2010 CLS
2020 LOCATE 12,14
2030 PRINT "PRINTING INDEX"
2040 GET#1,RECORD%
2050 IF LK$=NULL$ THEN 2999
2060 LPRINT TAB(27) NO$ SPC(6) CN$
2999 RETURN
3000 ' ***** CLOSE FILES **************
3010 CLOSE#1
3999 RETURN
```

Figure 10.13   Program to Print the Report

REVIEW QUESTIONS

1. Identify the statement that develops the record numbers for use in the example program. (Obj. 6)
2. Explain the purpose of initializing the file when creating a relative file. (Obj. 7)

3. What is the purpose of the validation technique in statements 4020-4280 in the example program? (Obj. 7)
4. Why was it necessary to use the same hashing scheme to access the records in the example program as was used to write the records in the create program? (Obj. 8)

VOCABULARY WORDS

The following terms were introduced in this chapter:

hashing scheme	linked file	prime number/remainder division procedure
direct organization	pointer	
relative record number	prime area	digit extraction method
sizing	overflow area	folding
synonym		

KEYWORDS AND COMMANDS

No new keywords or commands were introduced in this chapter.

PROGRAMS TO WRITE

Complete the appropriate documentation for each of the programs before writing the code.

Program 1

You are to write a program to store student records in a linked file. The key field will be the social security number and the number of records for the example system will be 30. You are to use the prime number division with remainder technique to arrive at the record location. Hopefully you will be able to achieve the 75 percent prime area capacity. Write a program to create a linked file. The record will contain the social security number, student number, and grade point average based upon a four point scale (for example: 1, 2, 3, 4). The data is to be input interactively. Use the following sample data at the top of page 276.

Student Number	Student Name	GPA
123456789	Johnny Smith	3.09
234567890	Tammy Olson	3.98
123456798	Julie Unferth	2.95
212345678	Jean Julius	4.00
123657890	Wendy Boland	3.62
123548765	Roger Selin	2.08
123658765	Robert Sando	3.66
123653456	Mark Langemo	3.19
234567891	Daryl Nord	2.75
234569603	Randy Denise	3.42

Program 2

Write a program to access the data stored in the file created in Program 1. Display a report showing the social security number, student name, and grade point average. Use the same data as Program 1.

Program 3

Write a program to create a master file for an accounts payable system. The file organization for this file should be random and you should select an appropriate hashing scheme to determine the storage of each record. You may assume that there will be approximately 20 records in the file. The record will contain the fields given here. After creating the file, write the routine that will print the contents of the master file on paper.

Company No.	Company Name	Address	City	State	Zip Code	Account Balance
12345	Southeastern Data	PO Box 582	Santee	CA	920712345	0000.00
23415	Softouch	PO Box 511	Leominster	MA	014533489	1000.00
33344	Aardvark Software	PO Box 265	Milwaukee	WI	532132309	200.00
23451	Basic Software	PO Box 296	Long Beach	CA	908154589	0000.00
45678	Bottom Shelf	PO Box 490	Atlanta	GA	303915498	450.00
38573	Criteron Systems	PO Box 586	Shoreview	MN	551124589	0000.00
11118	Educational Comp	123 Main	Tolland	CT	060842369	0000.00
55556	Easy Software	330 Nie St	Baltimore	MD	212017431	1255.00
43435	Mity Byte	279 E. Glen	Ridgewood	NJ	074505093	0000.00
34234	Low Technology	11 23rd St	Oklahoma City	OK	731068902	0000.00

Program 4

Write a program to create a transaction file for the accounts payable system in Program 3. The transaction file should be random and use the same hashing scheme as was used to create the master file. The record will contain the fields given here. After creating the file, write a routine to place the contents of the file on paper.

Company No.	Transaction Code	Amount
12345	1	11.50
33344	2	100.00
23415	1	1575.90
23451	1	495.00
55556	2	255.00
34234	1	2595.00
55556	2	1000.00
34234	2	1595.00
38573	1	1234.65
45678	2	250.00
45678	1	500.00
11118	1	1200.00
45678	2	25.00
23415	2	2000.00
12345	1	6.50

Transaction Code Explanation:
Purchase = 1
Payment = 2

Program 5

Using the files created in Programs 3 and 4, write the application software to update the account balance in the master file. Print the contents of the master file after updating in report form. Verify the updated master file to make sure that each account is correct.

Program 6

Write the routines to allow the user to maintain the master accounts payable file. The user should be able to add, change, and delete records containing a zero balance. If the account balance is not zero, the user should not be able to delete the record. Place the maintenance routines into a menu driven system. Make some changes to the master file and print out the maintained file contents. On the printed report, highlight the maintenance conducted on the file.

CONTINUING PROJECTS

Before writing any program of the continuing projects, be sure to complete all appropriate documentation.

Project 1

You are now ready to create the tax tables for the payroll program. You will create an index table for the federal taxes and the state taxes. Each of the tables will have exemption tax rates for 0 through 5 or more exemptions. These tables will be accessed to determine the tax percentage when calculating the taxes during the processing of the payroll. The federal tax module (P1FEDTAX) and the state tax module (P1STATAX) should be developed separately. Remember that the tax rates change periodically and therefore the tables must be updated from time to time. When the system is not in use, the tax tables should be stored on disk. When in use with the processing of the payroll program, they will be accessed by searching for the exemption number that matches the payroll detail record. The data for each of the tax tables should include:

1. Exemption number.
2. Tax percentage.

The modules to prepare the tax tables are accessed through the main menu to the preparation of the payroll menu. The menu choice "prepare tax table" should direct the user to yet another menu which would allow a choice of preparing the federal or state tax table.

Project 2

You are to create the merchandise reorder module for the inventory system. This module is accessed via the main menu and should present the user with a submenu which will allow maintenance of a related vendor file or to determine the reorder status of items in inventory. The menu should contain:

1. Maintain related vendor file.
2. Print report or reorder status.
3. Return to main menu.

The related vendor file should be a random file that uses a digit extraction technique to access record locations. Each of the vendors will have a four digit vendor number of which the last two will be extracted to be used as the record number. If duplicates exist, they must be written to the overflow area. The data contained in the file includes:

    1. Vendor number (corresponds to the source number in the master file).
    2. Company name.
    3. Company address.
    4. Company city and state.
    5. Company ZIP code.

The reorder status report should be generated by accessing the master file and checking the quantity on hand with the reorder level. If the quantity on hand is less than the reorder level, the item stock number, description, cost price, reorder quantity, and source number should be printed. This report should be printed with the appropriate title, column headings, and summary calculations.

Chapter **11**

Indexed Files

Objectives: 1. Define indexing.

2. Explain the technique for storing the index and data in an indexed file.

3. List advantages of indexed files.

4. List disadvantages of indexed files.

5. Identify the steps required to create an indexed file.

6. Identify the steps required to access an indexed file.

7. Explain the procedures for maintaining an indexed file.

8. Explain how an index may be sorted and searched.

Topic 11.1— PRINCIPLES OF INDEXED FILES

Creating a simple sequential file is rather easy. You must input the data and write one record after another to the disk file. As you found out in Chapter 10, the creation of a random file may be rather simple if you are using a programmer-supplied record number or more difficult if you are using a hashing scheme to calculate record numbers and linking the synonyms to the overflow area. Since you will not always be afforded the opportunity to use sequential file organization because of the lengthy time of reading each sequential record, you may elect to use random file organization. However, the difficulty of generating a good algorithm for a hashing scheme and the inability of being able to move records around so that they might be sorted in a desired order makes you look for other alternatives. An alternative is to use an indexed file.

DEFINITION OF INDEXED FILES

An indexed file is a file where the records are accessed via an index. It is similiar to accessing a book in the library. If you knew the author's name, you could go to the card catalog in the library and find the name index. A review of the name index cards would permit you to locate the title of the book you want to retrieve. Once the appropriate card has been located, you would write down the Library of Congress or Dewey decimal number pinpointing its location. You would then go to that location to retrieve the book. The card identifying this location information would remain in the card catalog. The card catalog is the index to the files (stacks of books) stored in the library. Libraries have more than one index for each item stored. This is called cross indexing. When two or more indexes occur when working with a computer application, we refer to it as multiple indexing.

Let's assume that we have previously created an indexed random access system for storing employee records. Now we have to locate the data pertaining to a specific employee. The procedure would be as follows. The user would enter the key field of data into the computer. The key field in this example would probably be either the employee number or employee name. Assuming the number was entered, the computer would then search the index table to locate a match for the number. Since the index is stored in RAM (random-access memory), the search is performed at a very high rate of speed. When a match has been found for the number, the record number will also have been located. The record number could be either the subscript for that specific row of the table or it could actually be a value stored as one of the table elements. Using either the subscript as the index or the value stored as the record number, that relative record location would be accessed in the random file. It is easy to provide a simple index for a relative file. By using a table with each entry containing a key value and the record number corresponding to the subscript, we are able to quickly search the table, match key values, use the subscript as the record number, and then read the random record. Upon the creation of the index table and the end of the data entry, the index table is generally stored in a sequential file. The data is stored in a random file.

Indexed files are very usable for any application that is similar to a telephone directory. If you know the telephone number of a person, you are quickly able to look up the phone number in the indexed table of names in the directory. To assist you, the phone company has sorted the index to make your access even more rapid. It would be possible if you knew the number, to search through the phone directory to determine to whom the phone number belongs. However, since the numbers are not in sorted order, the search would take much longer.

Advantages of Indexed Files

Indexed files have several advantages over sequential files or random files created using a hashing scheme. Some of the advantages are:

1. An index table may be quickly searched because it is stored in RAM.
2. Records in an indexed file may be quickly located without knowing the number of the record in the random file. Multiple indexes permit the user to enter one or more key values to be matched with the values in the table.
3. Indexed files allow the user of the application system to better utilize file space. Unlike the linked files, the user could search the index table for the first available location. Then use that subscript number as the record key and to store the key value of the random record. It is possible to eliminate all unused records in an indexed file.
4. Index tables that contain record numbers in addition to keys may be sorted. Therefore, the data stored in a relative file may be ordered by a key value.
5. Indexed files do not require the use of difficult hashing schemes and may be easier to program.

Disadvantages of Indexed Files

Even though it may be rather easy to develop the index table for the storage of key values and record numbers, some disadvantages arise because BASIC does not contain a built-in indexing routine. Some of the disadvantages are listed here:

1. Indexed file organization may require the storage of redundant data. This is especially true when using multiple indexes. The key fields must be stored in the index tables and sequential files as well as being stored as part of the record in the relative file.
2. Two files must be maintained in an indexed file organization. One file is used for the actual data records and another is used to store the index table contents when the application is not being used. As an alternative to this, the entire random file may be read and the index recreated each time the program is run.
3. Indexed files are limited by the number of elements set aside for the index table(s) when the application was first developed. If the index table is filled up, it would be impossible to write more records to the relative file until the table was expanded. This is one of the biggest limitations of data base management systems for small computers. Usually data bases are built on the principle of indexed files. This will allow them to store a certain number of records and they cannot be easily expanded. However, it must be pointed out that usually the number of records that they are designed to store is substantially large enough for most applications.

Creating an Indexed File

The creation of an indexed file requires you to complete the following steps:

1. An index table must be dimensioned to the maximum number of records to be stored in the file. It will be necessary to initialize the table with zeros or nulls depending upon the table elements. One of the data fields is selected as the index field (key field).
2. Data will be input and stored as follows:
   a. Place the value of the key field in the first available location in the index table. Sometimes it is beneficial to store both the key field value and the record number in the table. This is especially true if the index is to be sorted later on the basis of the key value. If storing the record number, it will be the first unused record in the random file.
   b. Using the record number from the index table, the data from the record entered will be written to the random file.
   c. Steps 2, 3, and 4 will be repeated until all data has been entered.
3. After all data has been entered and the index table has been built, you must write the contents of the index table to a sequential file before ending the process. By storing the index table, you may retrieve it for later use in either adding records to the file, maintaining current records, or for producing reports.

Figure 11.1 illustrates the concept of developing an indexed file using a single index. Notice how the key field EMPLOYEE.NO is used as the value to be stored in the index table. The records are then written one by one to the random file. The record for employee number 123 is input into the process. The key field value 123 is placed in the first available table element which would have a subscript of one. Using the number one as the record number, the complete record, "123 Smith Mary 7158349931" would be input. This process would be repeated until all records have been stored. Upon completion of data entry, the index table is written to the sequential file. It is possible to write each row of the table to the sequential file as it is filled. This procedure works well if the data is being created as a batch.

Accessing an Indexed File

Accessing the records in an indexed file previously created requires several steps. These steps are explained here:

1. Both the sequential file containing the index table information and the random file containing the data records must be opened for access. The contents of the sequential file are read record by record and placed into the elements of the table. In other words, the first sequential record is placed in row 1 of the table. (It must be placed in

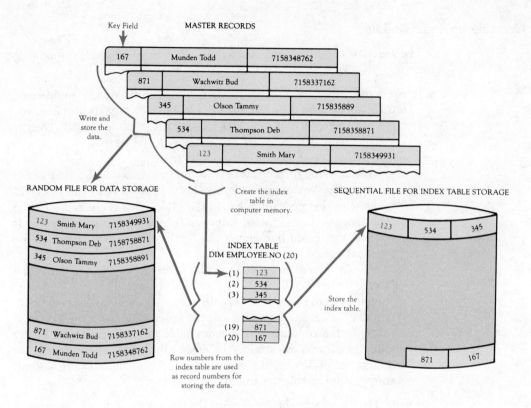

Figure 11.1   Single Index File

row 1 to coincide with the record numbers used to write to the random file. Also, zero is an incorrect record number and will cause an error if used to write or access a random number.)

2. The user would be asked to input a key value corresponding to the key field value previously stored in the index table.

3. A search of the index table should produce a match of the input value and the value stored in the table. When this happens, the subscript number should be assigned to the record number.

4. Using the record number (an index number which will usually be the same as the subscript), the random file is read to obtain desired data.

5. The retrieved data is processed in the desired manner.

The process of accessing information from a file previously created with an index is illustrated in Figure 11.2. Follow through the illustration as you read the following information. After opening the files and loading the contents of the sequential file into the index table, you would input the key value 345. This value would be compared to each element in the index table.

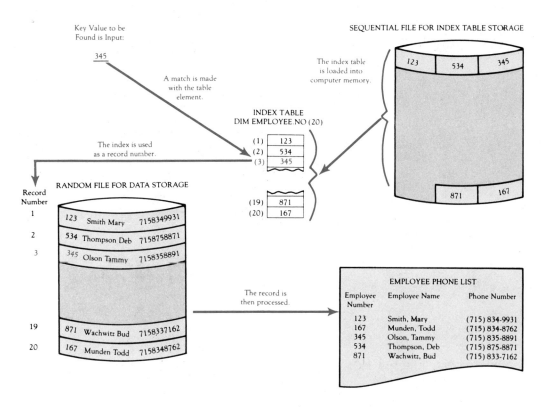

Figure 11.2   Accessing an Indexed File

When it matches with the third element, the number 3 is assigned to the record number. The random file is read to retrieve the third record.

Multiple Indexes

The process of creating an index file with multiple indexes is almost the same as creating an index file with one index. The difference is the placing of two or more key values into the index table(s). All other steps are the same. Figure 11.3 illustrates multiple indexes.

Accessing the records in a file with multiple indexes will also be the same process as accessing records stored in a single index file. The difference will be the ability to input either one or more key values to search for in the index table. Multiple indexes are very usable and generally you will find that most applications require the use of multiple indexes. For example, an employer may not remember the employee number, but can remember the employee name. If both were available as indexes, either could be used to access the file.

INDEX TABLE

DIM N(20), NAM$(20)

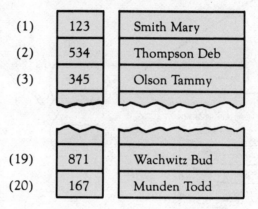

(1)	123	Smith Mary
(2)	534	Thompson Deb
(3)	345	Olson Tammy
(19)	871	Wachwitz Bud
(20)	167	Munden Todd

Index 1: N = Number
Index 2: NAM$ = Name

Figure 11.3   Multiple Index

Maintaining the Indexed File

The process of maintaining the indexed file is slightly different than maintaining the sequential file or relative file. In each of the other two file organizations, you were accessing the records directly. In the indexed file organization, you are accessing the records indirectly. That is, you must maintain the index as well as the file. In the following paragraphs we will discuss the process of adding a record to the index file, the process of deleting a record from an index file, and the process of changing a record in the index file.

Adding a Record to the Indexed File

Adding a record to an indexed file requires you to complete several steps. Assume that the files have been opened and the index table has been filled from the sequential file. You need to complete the following steps to add a record.

1. The new data record to be added must be input into the computer.
2. Make a search of the table to determine where the first available location exists. It is possible that it could be the second table element or it could be the last. A check for a zero or null is then made.
3. Store the key value in the first available table element.
4. Write the data record to the random file using the subscript for the first available table element.

5. Repeat the process if another record is to be added.

6. At the end, the index table must be rewritten to the sequential file.

The sequential file now contains an updated indexed table and the random file contains one or more records than it previously contained.

Deleting a Record From an Indexed File

The steps required to delete a record from the indexed file are as follows:

1. The key value of the record to be deleted would be input into the computer. (The files must be open and the index table loaded prior to this step.)

2. Search the index table to find a match for the key value.

3. After finding the match of the value, a zero or a null value is moved to the table element—eliminating the value previously stored. Since we have removed any index value that will match with the key value, any future searches for the value will result in not finding a match. Therefore, the contents of the record on the relative file need not be removed. Another option would be to remove the information from the relative file also.

If another record is to be deleted, the process continues. If not, the updated index table is rewritten to the sequential file. The location in the index table that was given the value of either zero or null is now available for use in adding a new record if desired.

Changing a Record in an Indexed File

Assuming once again that the files are opened and the index table has been loaded, the following steps must be completed if a record is to be changed in an indexed file.

1. Enter the key value of the record to be changed.

2. Search the table elements to find a match for the key value.

3. Once the match has been found, assign a number to the record number and the random file must be read to obtain the data record.

4. Changes in the data may be made.

5. Rewrite the contents of the record to the random file using the same record number.

6. Repeat the process if other records are to be changed.

Sorting an Indexed File

One of the benefits of organizing a file using an index is the ability to sort the data into the desired order. However, the sort is not actually a sort of the data, but a sort of the index. The process will be identical to the sorts that you previously learned in Chapter 7. However, there are several things you must remember when sorting indexes related to the indexed file. If an indexed file is to be sorted on one or more key values, the table must contain the corresponding record number as one of the elements. Because a key value, such as a name, is moved from one row of the table to another, it will be necessary to take along the number that represents the record number for that specific record. As a result, when creating an index file that is to be sorted, the record number is stored as one of the table elements. Figure 11.4 illustrates the sorting of an index file by number. Figure 11.5 illustrates the sorting by name.

INDEX FILE BEFORE SORT

1	123	Smith
2	534	Thompson
3	345	Olson
19	871	Wachwitz
20	167	Munden

INDEX FILE AFTER SORT

Random Record Number	Data Sorted by Number	
1	123	Smith
20	167	Munden
3	345	Olson
2	534	Thompson
19	871	Wachwitz

Figure 11.4   Sort of Key Value Number

INDEX FILE BEFORE SORT

1	123	Smith
2	534	Thompson
3	345	Olson
19	871	Wachwitz
20	167	Munden

INDEX FILE AFTER SORT

Random Record Number	Data Sorted by Name	
20	167	Munden
3	345	Olson
1	123	Smith
2	534	Thompson
19	871	Wachwitz

Figure 11.5   Sort of Key Value Name

Binary Search of an Indexed File

In each of the procedures discussed in this chapter, you were not told that the search of the index for a given value would be conducted in any manner different than that of starting at the beginning and going row by row searching for the match to a key value. Usually this procedure is rapid enough to locate the desired index if there is a limited number of records. However, when the number of records is very large, it will sometimes take considerable computer time to search the table to find a match of the key value. One way to speed up the process is to conduct a binary search of the index looking for a match to the key value. If we wish to do a binary search of the key value, we would have to sort the values. Once sorted, the index may be searched using the algorithm you learned in Chapter 8.

REVIEW QUESTIONS

1. Explain what is meant by the term indexing. (Obj. 1)
2. Explain how an index may be used to locate information. (Obj. 1)
3. What is meant by the term multiple index? (Obj. 1)
4. Explain where the index table is stored upon completion of use. (Obj. 2)
5. Explain where the data is stored in an indexed file system. (Obj. 2)
6. Identify three advantages of indexed files. (Obj. 3)
7. Identify three disadvantages of indexed files. (Obj. 4)
8. List the steps required to create an indexed file. (Obj. 5)
9. List the steps required to access an indexed file. (Obj. 6)
10. Explain how records are added to an indexed file. (Obj. 7)
11. Explain how records are deleted from an indexed table. (Obj. 7)

Topic 11.2— INDEXED FILES WITH BASIC

Indexed files may be used for many applications in business and industry. They are especially useful for any application that requires frequent inquiry into the file. The use of the index permits the user to access records without knowing the record number. In the application system that is shown in this section, the index is very useful because the visitor to a hospital will know the person's name, but rarely know in which room the person is located. On the other hand, the hospital personnel will have a desire to access the file by room number to determine whether or not it is occupied. The index allows for a rapid search to determine where the random record is stored. Because of the ease of sorting the index, it is a very beneficial manner to use when storing data that must be ordered by either a numeric or alphabetic key field.

PROGRAMMING AN INDEXED FILE APPLICATION

The following application system is a menu-driven hospital occupancy system. The system is designed to allow the receptionist at the hospital to quickly locate the record containing specific information related to a patient. The user has the ability to access the record by either name or room number.

As a result, this is a multiple index system. The application system contains menu options to add records and delete records. The change routine was not included because it does not differ from any other change in a random record. That is, the record would be accessed, the data changed, and the record rewritten. The change does not affect the index unless a key field is changed. The systems flowchart for the patient inquiry system is illustrated in Figure 11.6. It illustrates that the input into the system will be from the keyboard and the files. It illustrates that output will be to the screen and to the files. Figure 11.7 contains the hierarchy chart. The main module controls the other four modules. Entry into the program will be through the main module and the exit from the program will also be through the main module. The program documentation is given in Figure 11.8. The module documentation for each of the modules in the system is illustrated in Figures 11.9 through 11.12. Each of the module documentation sheets identifies the module description and module functions. The functions are defined for each of the specific modules. Read through the module documentation and study the program example for the computer on which you are working.

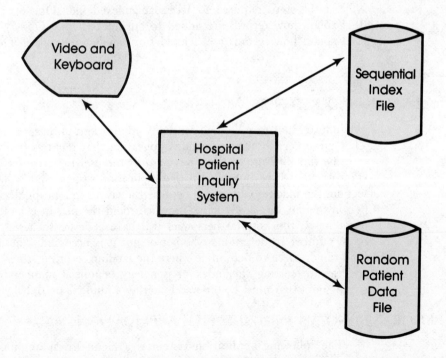

Figure 11.6   Systems Flowchart for Patient Inquiry System

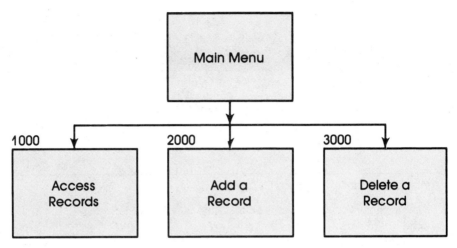

Figure 11.7   Hierarchy Chart

PROGRAM DOCUMENTATION		
Program: EXC11E1	Programmer: Clark and LaBarre	Date: 5/27/--
Purpose: The purpose of this program is to provide for an indexed file processing system that will enable the receptionist at the hospital to inquire into the registration file. The file is created using an index table to point to the random file containing the pertinent information about patients.		
Input: Data records and user commands from the keyboard and from the files during processing	Output: Video display of patient records showing patient name, room number, address, city, state, ZIP code, next of kin, illness, and condition	
Data Terminator:		
Variables Used: Varies from computer to computer.		

Figure 11.8   Program Documentation

MODULE DOCUMENTATION	Program: EXC11E1	Module: MAIN Lines: 10-999

Module Description:

The main module contains the patient menu.

Module Function (Program Design):

1. Dimension and load the index table. If no index file exists, just fill the table with zeros and nulls.
2. Open the random data file.
3. DO...UNTIL the user chooses to stop:
   a. Obtain the user's choice.
   b. Perform the appropriate subroutine.
4. Write the index back to the disk.
5. Close the files.

Figure 11.9   Main Module Documentation

MODULE DOCUMENTATION	Program: EXC11E1	Module: ACCESS RECORDS Lines: 1000-1999

Module Description:

The purpose of this module is to allow the user to access the patient record by either the name or room number.

Module Function (Program Design):

1. Input the name or room number.
2. Search the index table for a match to the input information.
3. Read the random record.
4. Print the random record on the screen.

Figure 11.10   Access Documentation

MODULE DOCUMENTATION	Program: EXC11E1	Module: ADD A RECORD
		Lines: 2000-2999

Module Description:

The purpose of this module is to allow the user to add records to the file.

Module Function (Program Design):

1. While the table is not full:
   a. Permit the data to be entered.
   b. Check the accuracy of the data.
   c. Enter the key values in the index table.
   d. Write the record to the random file.

Figure 11.11   Add a Record Documentation

MODULE DOCUMENTATION	Program: EXC11E1	Module: DELETE A RECORD
		Lines: 3000-3999

Module Description:

The purpose of this module is to permit the user to delete a patient from the index table.

Module Function (Program Design):

1. Enter the name of the patient to be deleted.
2. Search the table for the name.
3. Replace the name and number with spaces and zeros, respectively.

Figure 11.12   Delete a Record Documentation

```
10 ' EXC11E1
20 ' CLARK AND LABARRE--CHAPTER 11, EXAMPLE PROBLEM
30 ' This program creates a sequential and a relative file which contain data
40 ' pertaining to patients in a hospital.  The sequential file contains
50 ' patient names and room numbers which are used to access other information
60 ' about the patient which is contained in the relative file.
70 ' ***** MAIN MODULE ***************
80 LET N=15
90 DIM INDEX.TABLE (N,3)
100 DIM INDEX.TABLE$ (N,3)
110 OPEN "RELFILE" AS #2
120 FIELD #2, 20 AS ADDRESS$, 15 AS CITY$, 2 AS STATE$, 5 AS ZIP.CODE$,
            20 AS NEXT.OF.KIN$, 15 AS ILLNESS$, 10 AS CONDITION$
130 ' LOAD THE INDEX TABLE
140 OPEN "SEQUFILE" FOR OUTPUT AS #1              'ESTABLISH A FILE
150 CLOSE #1
160 OPEN "SEQUFILE" FOR INPUT AS #1
170 WHILE NOT EOF(1)
180    INPUT #1, INDEX, PATIENT.NAME$, ROOM.NUMBER$
190    LET INDEX.TABLE(INDEX,1)=INDEX
200    LET INDEX.TABLE$(INDEX,2)=PATIENT.NAME$
210    LET INDEX.TABLE$(INDEX,3)=ROOM.NUMBER$
220 WEND
230 CLOSE #1
240 ' CREATE INITIAL FILE
250 ' INITIALIZE TABLE VARIABLES
260 FOR INDEX=1 TO N
270    LET INDEX.TABLE(INDEX,1)=INDEX
280    LET INDEX.TABLE$(INDEX,2)="          "
290    LET INDEX.TABLE$(INDEX,3)="000"
300 NEXT INDEX
310 CLS
320 ' MAIN MENU
330 PRINT TAB(15);"PATIENT MENU"
340 PRINT TAB(5);"To access a record enter.........1"
350 PRINT TAB(5);"To add a record enter............2"
360 PRINT TAB(5);"To delete a record enter.........3"
370 PRINT TAB(5);"To end enter.....................4"
380 PRINT TAB(36);
390 INPUT RESPONSE
400 IF RESPONSE<1 OR RESPONSE>4 THEN BEEP:GOTO 310
410 IF RESPONSE=1 THEN GOSUB 1000
420 IF RESPONSE=2 THEN GOSUB 2000
430 IF RESPONSE=3 THEN GOSUB 3000
440 IF RESPONSE=4 THEN GOTO 460
450 GOTO 310
460 CLOSE #2
470 ' WRITE THE TABLE TO DISK
480 OPEN "SEQUFILE" FOR OUTPUT AS #1
490 FOR NO.OF.PATIENTS=1 TO N
500    WRITE #1, NO.OF.PATIENTS, INDEX.TABLE$(NO.OF.PATIENTS,2),
                 INDEX.TABLE$(NO.OF.PATIENTS,3)
510 NEXT NO.OF.PATIENTS
520 CLOSE #1
999 END
1000 ' ***** ACCESS PATIENT RECORD ****
1010 ' ACCESSING RECORD
1020 CLS
1030 INPUT "Enter the patient's name or room number";PATIENT$
1040 IF ASC(LEFT$(PATIENT$,1))<65 THEN GOTO 1150
1050 ' ACCESS BY NAME
1060 LET NO.OF.PATIENTS=1
1070 WHILE (NO.OF.PATIENTS<N AND INDEX.TABLE$(NO.OF.PATIENTS,2)
          <>PATIENT$)
1080    LET NO.OF.PATIENTS=NO.OF.PATIENTS+1
1090 WEND
```

Figure 11.13   Example Program for the IBM and TRS-80

```
1100 IF INDEX.TABLE$(NO.OF.PATIENTS,2)<>PATIENT$ THEN GOTO 1130
1110 GOTO 1220    'PRINT OUT THE RECORD
1120 PRINT:PRINT:PRINT
1130 INPUT "The patient you entered cannot be found.  If you wish to try again
            please enter a yes";ANSWER$
1140 IF ANSWER$="YES" THEN GOTO 1020 ELSE GOTO 1999
1150 ' ACCESS BY ROOM NUMBER
1160 CLS
1170 LET NO.OF.PATIENTS=1
1180 WHILE (NO.OF.PATIENTS<N AND INDEX.TABLE$(NO.OF.PATIENTS,3)
            <>PATIENT$)
1190    LET NO.OF.PATIENTS=NO.OF.PATIENTS+1
1200 WEND
1210 IF INDEX.TABLE$(NO.OF.PATIENTS,3)<>PATIENT$ THEN GOTO 1380
1220 ' PRINT OUT THE RECORD
1230 GET #2, NO.OF.PATIENTS
1240 CLS
1250 PRINT:PRINT:PRINT
1260 PRINT TAB(5);"PATIENT . . . . ";INDEX.TABLE$(NO.OF.PATIENTS,2)
1270 PRINT TAB(5);"ROOM NUMBER . . ";INDEX.TABLE$(NO.OF.PATIENTS,3)
1280 PRINT TAB(5);"ADDRESS . . . . ";ADDRESS$
1290 PRINT TAB(5);"CITY . . . . . ";CITY$
1300 PRINT TAB(5);"STATE . . . . . ";STATE$
1310 PRINT TAB(5);"ZIP CODE . . . ";ZIP.CODE$
1320 PRINT TAB(5);"NEXT OF KIN . . ";NEXT.OF.KIN$
1330 PRINT TAB(5);"ILLNESS . . . . ";ILLNESS$
1340 PRINT TAB(5);"CONDITION . . . ";CONDITION$
1350 PRINT:PRINT:PRINT
1360 INPUT "When you are ready to continue hit return",CONTINUE$
1370 GOTO 1999
1380 PRINT:PRINT:PRINT
1390 INPUT "The patient you entered cannot be found.  If you wish to try again
            please enter a yes";ANSWER$
1400 IF ANSWER$="YES" THEN GOTO 1020 ELSE GOTO 1999
1999 RETURN
2000 ' ***** ADD A PATIENT ************
2010 LET NO.OF.PATIENTS=1
2020 WHILE (NO.OF.PATIENTS<N AND INDEX.TABLE$(NO.OF.PATIENTS,3)<>"000")
2030    LET NO.OF.PATIENTS=NO.OF.PATIENTS+1
2040 WEND
2050 IF INDEX.TABLE$(NO.OF.PATIENTS,3)<>"000" THEN GOTO 2999
2060 CLS
2070 INPUT "ENTER THE PATIENT'S NAME";PATIENT.NAME$
2080 INPUT "ENTER THE ROOM NUMBER   ";ROOM.NUMBER$
2090 INPUT "ENTER THE ADDRESS       ";ADDRESS.ENTERED$
2100 INPUT "ENTER THE CITY          ";CITY.ENTERED$
2110 INPUT "ENTER THE STATE         ";STATE.ENTERED$
2120 INPUT "ENTER THE ZIP CODE      ";ZIP.CODE.ENTERED$
2130 INPUT "ENTER THE NEXT OF KIN   ";NEXT.OF.KIN.ENTERED$
2140 INPUT "ENTER ILLNESS           ";ILLNESS.ENTERED$
2150 INPUT "ENTER CONDITION         ";CONDITION.ENTERED$
2160 PRINT
2170 INPUT "Is the data correct?    ";ANSWER$
2180 IF ANSWER$="NO" THEN GOTO 2060
2190 LET INDEX.TABLE(NO.OF.PATIENTS,1)=NO.OF.PATIENTS
2200 LET INDEX.TABLE$(NO.OF.PATIENTS,2)=PATIENT.NAME$
2210 LET INDEX.TABLE$(NO.OF.PATIENTS,3)=ROOM.NUMBER$
2220 LSET ADDRESS$=ADDRESS.ENTERED$
2230 LSET CITY$=CITY.ENTERED$
2240 LSET STATE$=STATE.ENTERED$
2250 LSET ZIP.CODE$=ZIP.CODE.ENTERED$
2260 LSET NEXT.OF.KIN$=NEXT.OF.KIN.ENTERED$
2270 LSET ILLNESS$=ILLNESS.ENTERED$
2280 LSET CONDITION$=CONDITION.ENTERED$
2290 PUT #2, NO.OF.PATIENTS
2300 GOTO 2999
```

Figure 11.13   Example Program for the IBM and TRS-80 (Continued)

```
2310 PRINT "Sorry, there is no more room to add any patients"
2999 RETURN
3000 ' ***** DELETE A PATIENT *********
3010 CLS
3020 INPUT "Enter the name of the patient you wish to delete";PATIENT$
3030 LET NO.OF.PATIENTS=1
3040 WHILE (NO.OF.PATIENTS<N AND INDEX.TABLE$ (NO.OF.PATIENTS,2)<>PATIENT$)
3050    LET NO.OF.PATIENTS=NO.OF.PATIENTS+1
3060 WEND
3070 IF INDEX.TABLE$(NO.OF.PATIENTS,2)<>PATIENT$ THEN 3999
3080    LET INDEX.TABLE$(NO.OF.PATIENTS,2)="
3090    LET INDEX.TABLE$(NO.OF.PATIENTS,3)="000"
3100 GOTO 3999
3110 PRINT "Sorry, this patient does not appear on file"
3120 INPUT "If you wish to try again enter YES";ANSWER$
3130 IF ANSWER$="YES" THEN 3010
3999 RETURN
```

Figure 11.13   Example Program for the IBM and TRS-80 (Concluded)

REVIEW QUESTIONS

1. Explain what lines 1130 through 1230 do in the example program. (Obj. 5)
2. Explain what lines 1420 through 1480 do in the example program. (Obj. 6)
3. Explain how the accessing technique will work to access records by number and name in the example program. (Obj. 6)
4. Which file maintenance procedures were incorporated into the example program? Which procedure was not included? (Obj. 7)

VOCABULARY WORDS

The following words were introduced in this chapter:

indexed file   multiple indexing

KEYWORDS AND COMMANDS

No new keywords or commands were introduced in this chapter.

PROGRAMS TO WRITE

Complete the appropriate documentation for each of the programs before writing the code.

Program 1

Write a program using the indexed method of storage and retrieval to store five daily grades for up to 30 students with student name, number, and grade. The program should allow for interactive input of original data, ability to retrieve the record and add new grades to the individual records, and print a report of the grades.

Program 2

The local motel has 50 rooms available for rent. You are to write a program to set up an indexed registration system. The index may correspond to the room number, but the rooms are numbered beginning with 1000 (for example: 1001, 1002, 1003 . . . 1050). Through your menu-driven system you should be able to access the record based upon the name of the room registrant. Also, you should give them the option of listing all rooms that are occupied. This report should show the room number and the person's name. Use the following data when testing the program.

Room No.	Name of Guest
1012	Amelia Mendoza
1023	Frank Horgan
1037	Delores Kolb
1046	Chris Sonntag
1050	Joji Soga

Program 3

Because people tend to cancel reservations or change rooms, modify Program 2 to add the ability to retrieve records, make changes, delete information, or print more detail reports such as the person's name, address, city, state, and ZIP code. This information is used for public relations at a later date.

Program 4

Write a program to create a telephone directory. The program should store the name, address, city, state, ZIP code, and telephone number in an indexed file. Entries are to be retrieved by name. Therefore, the index should be sorted after it has been created to allow for rapid retrieval. The program should allow new entries to be made in the file, obsolete entries to be deleted, and existing entries to be examined and updated. Remember, the index will have to be resorted every time a new record is added.

Program 5

Develop an inventory control program to store the items usually found in a ski shop. Each of the inventory items has a five-digit number identifying the product as well as a 20 character or less description. You are to develop an indexed file system that will allow the retrieval of information on the basis of either the inventory number or description. The record stored on disk contains the inventory number, description, quantity on hand, unit price, and number of units back-ordered. The records should be retrievable at any time. New records will be added at any time. An inventory report will be requested periodically. Make sure that your system allows for these capabilities. Use the following data when testing your program.

Inventory Number	Description	Quantity	Price	Units Back-Ordered
27614	Cross-Country Skis	17	$79.99	18
53019	Poles	26	12.95	14
49233	Goggles	84	23.49	0
17240	Hats	77	15.00	24
82631	Ski Boots	5	35.99	36

Program 6

Modify Program 5 to include a binary search by product number. Add another 10 products to the file. Also, give the user an opportunity to print the report based upon the product groupings. For example, the user should be able to print a report of only the skis in inventory or only the ski boots in inventory.

CONTINUING PROJECTS

Before writing any progam of the continuing projects, be sure to complete all appropriate documentation.

Project 1

Write a program to print a payroll register. The program should be named (P1PAYREG) and accessed when the user selects the "print reports" option in the main menu. The payroll register should be constructed by matching the records in the master file, individual payroll detail file, and the weekly payroll transaction file. The tax tables must be loaded into tables prior to running the application to compute the payroll. Upon completion of the printing of the payroll register, the updated individual payroll detail file should be rewritten to the originally named data file. The payroll register should contain an appropriate title, column headings, output data, and summary totals. The output report should contain:

1. Social security number.
2. Name.
3. Hours worked.
4. Rate of pay.

5. Gross pay.
6. Federal tax.
7. State tax.
8. Net pay.

Project 2

The inventory maintenance system (P2MAINT) has been using a random file with a sequential search. Recognizing that an indexed accessing method would be more efficient, you are to rewrite the inventory maintenance system changing the access method from random with a sequential search to an indexed file processing system. After the system has been changed, you must test the complete system again to make sure that all elements are in working order.

## Chapter 12

Block Graphics

Objectives: 1. Define block graphics.

2. Describe the characteristics of a bar graph.

3. Describe the characteristics of a line graph.

4. Plan and code programs using block graphics.

The use of graphics (charts, drawings, pictures) can frequently make computer output easier to understand. In this chapter, we will look at one of the ways of producing graphic output.

Topic 12.1— PRINCIPLES OF USING BLOCK GRAPHICS

With many computers, the use of block graphics provides an easy way of producing some types of graphic output. In this section, block graphics will be defined. Then examples of their use in bar graphs and line graphs will be given.

DEFINITION OF BLOCK GRAPHICS

As background for learning the definition of block graphics, think about the way letters and numbers are placed on the screen. Each character is made of a matrix (row and column arrangement) of dots. With most computers, each character takes the same number of rows and columns. For example, each character might be eight dots wide and ten dots high. Study Figure 12.1, which shows examples of how the characters might be represented. Each character can be thought of as consuming one block on the screen. Remember that a character is printed by sending its ASCII code to the screen. Therefore, to print the A of Figure 12.2, the ASCII code of 65 is sent to the screen. To print the number 2, the ASCII code of 50 is sent.

Letter A   Number 2

Figure 12.1   Characters Are Made of Dots

Now that you are familiar with the terminology of a block of space on the screen, we are ready to define block graphics. Block graphics is a method of graphics in which characters representing shapes other than standard letters and numbers are printed on the screen. Depending on the computer being used, block graphics may be limited to simple shapes or they may allow the printing of rather complex shapes.

One of the most frequent uses of block graphics is to draw boxes or rectangles on the screen. To do this, characters representing different shapes are necessary. Shapes are needed for the corners of the box and for the horizontal and vertical lines. Refer to Figure 12.2 for the shapes required. While the shapes on a particular computer may vary, they will be somewhat similar to the illustration.

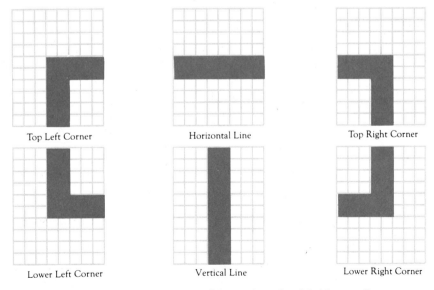

Top Left Corner   Horizontal Line   Top Right Corner

Lower Left Corner   Vertical Line   Lower Right Corner

Figure 12.2   Graphics Characters for Making a Box

By printing the contents of the various blocks, a box can be constructed. If desired, standard characters such as letters and numbers can be printed inside the box. Look at Figure 12.3 to see how the illustrated blocks can be combined to do this.

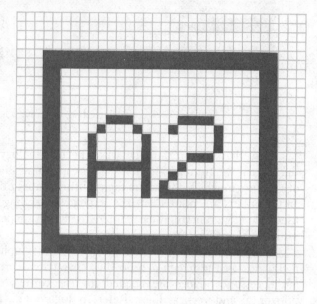

Figure 12.3   Blocks

BAR GRAPHS

A graph is a pictorial representation of data. A bar graph is a graph that uses bars to show different data. For example, a bar graph might be used to show a comparison of the sales at different store locations. Study the illustration of such a graph in Figure 12.4.

XR STORES CORPORATION
COMPARISON OF SALES, JULY 19--
(Stated in Ten Thousands)

```
0 - - - - - - - - 1 - - - - - - - - 2 - - - - - - - - 3 - - - - - - - - 4 - - - - - - - - 5
Store A  $$$$$$$$$$$$$$$$$$$$$$$$$$
Store B  $$$$$$$$$$$$$$$$$$$$$$$$$$$$$$$$$$$$$$$$$$$$$$$$$$$$
Store C  $$$$$$$$$$$$$$$$$$$$
Store D  $$$$$$$$$$$$$$$$$$$$$$$$$$$$$$$$$$$$$$$$$$$
```

Figure 12.4   Example of a Bar Graph

In Figure 12.4, note that each character in a bar represents $10,000 of sales. The amount to represent by each character in a bar is something that is decided by the programmer. Usually, a graph is easier to understand if the longest bar extends nearly all the way across the graph. The left end of each bar should almost always start at zero. Here is why this is important. By referring again to Figure 12.4 you can easily see that Store B sold about twice as much as Store C. Suppose, however, that we try to limit the width of the graph by not printing the entire width of the bars. Instead, we print only the parts of the bars that show change. By taking out the section of bars shown in Figure 12.5, we end up with the graph shown in Figure 12.6.

XR STORES CORPORATION
COMPARISON OF SALES, JULY 19--
(Stated in Ten Thousands)

```
          0---------1---------2---------3---------4---------5
Store A   $$$$$$$$$$$$$$$$$$$$$$$$$$$
Store B   $$$$$$$$$$$$$$$$$$$$$$$$$$$$$$$$$$$$$$$$$$$$$$$$$$
Store C   $$$$$$$$$$$$$$$$$$$$
Store D   $$$$$$$$$$$$$$$$$$$$$$$$$$$$$$$$$$$$$$$$$$$
```

Figure 12.5   This Bar Graph Shows the Common Sales Amounts for all Stores

XR STORES CORPORATION
COMPARISON OF SALES, JULY 19--
(Stated in Ten Thousands)

```
          -2---------3---------4---------5
Store A   $$$$$$
Store B   $$$$$$$$$$$$$$$$$$$$$$$$$$$$$$$
Store C
Store D   $$$$$$$$$$$$$$$$$$$
```

Figure 12.6   Incorrectly Constructed Bar Graph

After the "unnecessary" parts of the bars have been removed, the width of the graph is less, but look at what happened to the appearance. A quick look at the graph now seems to indicate that Store B sold many times more than Store C, which seems to have sold nothing. Obviously, this is misleading.

When constructing a bar graph with block graphics, any character desired can be used to construct the bars. Also, the bars may be vertical instead of horizontal. The previous graph done with vertical bars might look as shown in Figure 12.7.

XR STORES CORPORATION
COMPARISON OF SALES, JULY 19--

```
50000-
     -
     -                      $$$$
     -                      $$$$
     -                      $$$$
     -                      $$$$
40000-                      $$$$
     -                      $$$$
     -                      $$$$                      $$$$
     -                      $$$$                      $$$$
     -                      $$$$                      $$$$
30000-                      $$$$                      $$$$
     -                      $$$$                      $$$$
     -                      $$$$                      $$$$
     -          $$$$        $$$$                      $$$$
     -          $$$$        $$$$                      $$$$
20000-          $$$$        $$$$                      $$$$
     -          $$$$        $$$$        $$$$          $$$$
     -          $$$$        $$$$        $$$$          $$$$
     -          $$$$        $$$$        $$$$          $$$$
     -          $$$$        $$$$        $$$$          $$$$
10000-          $$$$        $$$$        $$$$          $$$$
     -          $$$$        $$$$        $$$$          $$$$
     -          $$$$        $$$$        $$$$          $$$$
     -          $$$$        $$$$        $$$$          $$$$
     -          $$$$        $$$$        $$$$          $$$$
    0-          $$$$        $$$$        $$$$          $$$$

              Store A      Store B      Store C       Store D
```

Figure 12.7   Example of Bar Graph with Vertical Bars

LINE GRAPHS

Line graphs use one or more lines to indicate changes over time. For example, changes in the price of gasoline might be shown by use of a line graph. Look at Figure 12.8 for an example of this.

PRICES OF REGULAR UNLEADED GASOLINE, 19--

	JAN	FEB	MAR	APR	MAY	JUN	JUL	AUG	SEP	OCT	NOV	DEC
1.46								□				
1.45							□		□			
1.44						□				□		
1.43												
1.42				□	□						□	□
1.41		□	□									
1.40	□											

Figure 12.8   Example of a Line Graph

Note on the line graph that each point is plotted at the intersection of a row and column. For example, the price of gasoline was $1.42 in May. Therefore, the point was marked on the $1.42 row and in the May column. Unlike the bar graph, the scale on the line graph need not start at zero. As long as the scale contains all the values to be graphed, it is sufficient. The example shows how a line graph looks when done with block graphics. Any character desired may be used to produce the graph. One character is placed at each point on the line of the graph; there is no way for the computer to connect the points together to actually form a line. It is perfectly acceptable, however, for you to connect the points with pen or pencil if you desire.

REVIEW QUESTIONS

1. What are block graphics? Why are they called block graphics? (Obj. 1)
2. How is a block graphic character represented by the computer? (Obj. 1)
3. How are shapes constructed using block graphics? (Obj. 4)
4. What are the characteristics of a bar graph? (Obj. 2)
5. What are the characteristics of a line graph? (Obj. 3)
6. For what kind of applications are bar graphs appropriately used? (Obj. 2)
7. For what kind of applications are line graphs appropriately used? (Obj. 3)

Topic 12.2— IMPLEMENTING BLOCK GRAPHICS USING BASIC

Most small computers have some degree of block graphic capability. Of the computers discussed in this text, block graphics are available on the Commodore, IBM, and TRS-80. Block graphics are not standard on the Apple, although software packages that produce block graphics can be purchased from various vendors.

No special keywords are necessary for producing block graphics under BASIC. The process involves two steps:

1. Determine where a graphic character should appear. This may be done by reading data from data lines or a data file, by input from the keyboard, or by computation from data.
2. Place the character in the determined position. The character can be placed by moving the cursor to the desired position and printing the character by using the CHR$ function. With some computers, it is easier to poke the graphic character's code into the memory position representing the desired screen location.

In the remainder of this chapter, we will show you examples of how to produce block graphics. First, we will draw a simple box. Then we will progress to bar graphs and line graphs.

DRAWING A BOX

It is so easy to draw a box that we will not complete formal documentation before showing how it is done. Rather, we will just explain how the box should look. At the top of the screen, you should draw a box using the first three lines. Within the box (on Line 2) you should place a title. The top of the screen should look like this:

```
┌──────────────────────────────────────┐
│              ALBUM SALES               │
└──────────────────────────────────────┘
```

The top horizontal line is in Row 1 of the screen; the bottom horizontal line is in Row 3 of the screen.

COMMODORE

On the Commodore, block graphics are probably done easiest by poking character codes into the desired memory locations. The top left corner of the screen is represented by memory location 1024. Since the row contains 40 characters, this means that the top right corner of the screen is represented by memory location 1063. Here are the memory locations of the first three rows:

Row 1: Locations 1024-1063
Row 2: Locations 1064-1103
Row 3: Locations 1104-1143

If we continued down the screen in this fashion, we would find that Row 24 (the last row) is represented by memory locations 1984-2023. The program to print the box follows. As you study it, pay particular attention to the REM statements to see how it works. Note that the character codes to be poked for each graphic character have been stored in variables for easy use.

```
10 REM EXC12E1
20 REM CLARK AND LABARRE--CHAPTER 12, EXAMPLE 1, COMMODORE
30 REM DRAWS BLOCK GRAPHIC BOX ON SCREEN
40 REM THE FOLLOWING LINES DEFINE GRAPHIC CHARACTERS TO USE
50 TL=85        :REM TOP LEFT CORNER
60 TR=73        :REM TOP RIGHT CORNER
70 BL=74        :REM BOTTOM LEFT CORNER
80 BR=75        :REM BOTTOM RIGHT CORNER
90 HL=67        :REM HORIZONTAL LINE
100 VL=66       :REM VERTICAL LINE
110 HT=102      :REM HALF-TONE (THIS WILL BE USED IN A LATER PROGRAM)
120 REM NOW DRAW THE BOX
130 PRINT "⌂"; :REM PRINT "SHIFT-CLR-HOME"
140 FOR J=1 TO 120       :REM PRINT AREA MUST BE FILLED WITH SPACES
150 PRINT " ";           :REM BEFORE CHARACTERS CAN BE POKED
160 NEXT J               :REM INTO THE SCREEN LOCATIONS
170 POKE 1024,TL         :REM PLACE THE CORNERS
180 POKE 1063,TR
190 POKE 1104,BL
200 POKE 1143,BR
210 FOR MEM=1025 TO 1062 :REM DRAW HORIZONTAL LINE ON ROW 1
220 POKE MEM,HL
230 NEXT MEM
240 POKE 1064,VL         :REM DRAW VERTICAL LINES
250 POKE 1103,VL
260 FOR MEM=1105 TO 1142 :REM DRAW HORIZONTAL LINE ON ROW 3
270 POKE MEM,HL
280 NEXT MEM
290 PRINT "⌂";           :REM PRINT "CLR-HOME" (SEND CURSOR HOME)
300 PRINT TAB(15);"⌂⌂ALBUM SALES";:REM CURSORDOWN/PRINT HEADINGS
310 GET Z$:IF Z$="" THEN 310 :REM HOLD SCREEN UNTIL USER IS READY
320 REM STOP EXECUTION ONLY WHEN KEY IS STRUCK
999 END
```

IBM

On the IBM, block graphics are done by locating the cursor at the desired position and printing the character. As you study the following example, pay particular attention to the REM statements to see how it works. Note that the CHR$ function has been used at the first of the program to place each character in a variable. This makes printing of the characters much easier.

```
10 ' EXC12E1
20 ' CLARK AND LABARRE, CHAPTER 12, EXAMPLE 1, IBM
30 ' DRAWS GRAPHIC BOX ON SCREEN
40 ' THE FOLLOWING LINES DEFINE GRAPHIC CHARACTERS TO USE
50 TL$=CHR$(201)  'TOP LEFT CORNER
60 TR$=CHR$(187)  'TOP RIGHT CORNER
70 BL$=CHR$(200)  'BOTTOM LEFT CORNER
80 BR$=CHR$(188)  'BOTTOM RIGHT CORNER
90 HL$=CHR$(205)  'HORIZONTAL LINE
100 VL$=CHR$(186) 'VERTICAL LINE
110 HT$=CHR$(178) 'HALF TONE (THIS WILL BE USED IN A LATER PROGRAM)
120 WIDTH 40      'SET SCREEN WIDTH TO 40
130 CLS
140 PRINT TL$;STRING$(38,HL$);TR$       'PRINT LINE 1
150 PRINT VL$;TAB(14)"ALBUM SALES";TAB(40);VL$  'PRINT LINE 2
160 PRINT BL$;STRING$(38,HL$);BR$       'PRINT LINE 3
999 END
```

TRS-80

On the TRS-80, block graphics are done by locating the cursor at the desired row and column position and printing the character. As you study the following example, pay particular attention to the REM statements to see how it works. Note that the CHR$ function has been used at the first of the program to place each character in a variable. This makes printing of the characters much easier.

```
10 ' EXC12E1
20 ' CLARK AND LABARRE--CHAPTER 12, EXAMPLE 1, TRS-80 MODEL III
30 ' DRAWS BLOCK GRAPHIC BOX ON SCREEN
40 ' THE FOLLOWING LINES DEFINE GRAPHIC CHARACTERS TO USE
50 TL$=CHR$(156)       'TOP LEFT CORNER
60 TR$=CHR$(172)       'TOP RIGHT CORNER
70 BL$=CHR$(141)       'BOTTOM LEFT CORNER
80 BR$=CHR$(142)       'BOTTOM RIGHT CORNER
90 HL$=CHR$(140)       'HORIZONTAL LINE
100 LVL$=CHR$(149)     'LEFT VERTICAL LINE
110 RVL$=CHR$(170)     'RIGHT VERTICAL LINE
120 HT$=CHR$(153)      'HALF-TONE (THIS WILL BE USED IN A LATER PROGRAM)
130 CLS
140 PRINT TL$;STRING$(38,HL$);TR$            'PRINT LINE 1
150 PRINT LVL$;TAB(14);"ALBUM SALES";TAB(39);RVL$ 'PRINT LINE 2
160 PRINT BL$;STRING$(38,HL$);BR$            'PRINT LINE 3
999 END
```

DRAWING A BAR GRAPH

The same principles used in drawing a box on the screen apply when doing more complex graphics such as a bar graph. You still determine a screen location and place a character there. Look at Figure 12.9 which shows the graph we will produce. Notice that the boxed heading from the previous example has become a part of the bar graph.

Once the heading has been placed on the graph, the next step is to place the scales. In this case, we must print the units up the side of the graph and print the album names across the bottom. In doing the scales, we will use constants and literals. For more advanced bar graphs, however, you could write a program that would look at the size of the data items and compute how the units scale should look.

After the scales have been printed, the bars will be drawn. For the example, we will get data from a DATA line, even though the data could have just as easily come from keyboard input or from a data file. The data will be given in millions—.8, 2.0, and 1.4. Since the scale is incremented in fifths while the data is incremented in tenths, a mathematical adjustment must be made in the length of the bars. A series of nested loops will be used to position the bars. As in the previous example, many REM statements are included in the code to help make the operation of the programs easier to understand. Refer to the documentation in Figure 12.10 as you study the following program for your computer.

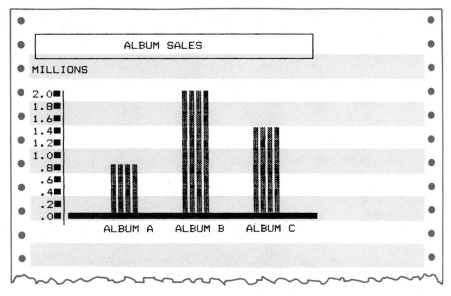

Figure 12.9   Bar Graph to be Produced

MODULE DOCUMENTATION	Program: EXC12E2	Module: MAIN Lines: 10-999

Module Description:

This program produces a bar graph on the screen.

Module Function (Program Design):

1. Set up variables containing the character codes to be used.
2. Clear the screen.
3. Use the block graphic codes to draw a box at the top of the screen and place the name of the graph in the box.
4. Print the vertical and horizontal scales on the graph.
5. Draw the bars on the graph.

Figure 12.10   Bar Graph Program Documentation

COMMODORE

The printing of the scales on the Commodore is straightforward. As was done previously, many values will be poked into memory to produce the graphics characters. Note that graphic characters have been chosen to print scale marks along with the numbers on the left. The Commodore uses different codes for pokes and for printing character strings. In other words, if you poke 91 into a memory position you will get one character; if you print CHR$(91) you will get a different character. Therefore, be sure you are looking at the correct code chart in the Commodore manual for the kind of operation you are doing. Here is the Commodore program.

```
10 REM EXC12E2
20 REM CLARK AND LABARRE--CHAPTER 12, EXAMPLE 2, COMMODORE
30 REM DRAWS BAR GRAPH ON SCREEN
40 REM THE FOLLOWING LINES DEFINE GRAPHIC CHARACTERS TO USE
50 TL=85          :REM TOP LEFT CORNER
60 TR=73          :REM TOP RIGHT CORNER
70 BL=74          :REM BOTTOM LEFT CORNER
80 BR=75          :REM BOTTOM RIGHT CORNER
90 HL=67          :REM HORIZONTAL LINE
100 VL=66:SM$=CHR$(164)+CHR$(165)  :REM VERTICAL LINE AND SCALE MARK
110 HT=102        :REM HALF-TONE
120 PRINT "J"; :REM PRINT "SHIFT-CLR-HOME"
130 FOR J=1 TO 120        :REM PRINT AREA MUST BE FILLED WITH SPACES
140 PRINT " ";            :REM BEFORE CHARACTERS CAN BE POKED
150 NEXT J                :REM INTO THE SCREEN LOCATIONS
160 POKE 1024,TL          :REM PLACE THE CORNERS
170 POKE 1063,TR
180 POKE 1104,BL
190 POKE 1143,BR
200 FOR MEM=1025 TO 1062  :REM DRAW HORIZONTAL LINE ON ROW 1
210 POKE MEM,HL
220 NEXT MEM
230 POKE 1064,VL          :REM DRAW VERTICAL LINES
240 POKE 1103,VL
250 FOR MEM=1105 TO 1142  :REM DRAW HORIZONTAL LINE ON ROW 3
260 POKE MEM,HL
270 NEXT MEM
280 PRINT "8";            :REM PRINT "CLR-HOME"
290 PRINT TAB(15);"  ALBUM SALES";:REM CURSORDOWN/PRINT HEADINGS
300 REM PRINT THE SCALE
310 PRINT:PRINT:PRINT "MILLIONS":PRINT
320 PRINT "2.0";SM$
330 PRINT "1.8";SM$
340 PRINT "1.4";SM$
350 PRINT "1.4";SM$
360 PRINT "1.2";SM$
370 PRINT "1.0";SM$
380 PRINT " .8";SM$
390 PRINT " .6";SM$
400 PRINT " .4";SM$
410 PRINT " .2";SM$
420 PRINT " .0";SM$;"_____"
430 PRINT TAB(11);"ALBUM A";SPC(3);"ALBUM B";SPC(3);"ALBUM C";
440 PRINT "8";            :REM PRINT "CLR-HOME"
450 PRINT "";             :REM CURSOR DOWN 6
460 FOR K=1 TO 10         :REM NESTED LOOP FILLS PRINT AREA WITH SPACES
470 PRINT "";             :REM CURSOR RIGHT 6 TO AVOID ERASING EXISTING SCREEN
480 FOR L=1 TO 34
```

Continued

```
490 PRINT " ";              :REM PRINT 34 SPACES ON EACH LINE
500 NEXT L
510 NEXT K
520 FOR COL=12 TO 32 STEP 10 :REM LOOP FOR THREE COLUMNS
530 READ MAGNITUDE
540 FOR R=1664 TO 1664-MAGNITUDE*5*40 STEP -40 :REM BAR SIZE LOOP
550 FOR BW=0 TO 3
560 POKE R+COL+BW,HT :REM POKE 4-WIDE BAR
570 NEXT BW
580 NEXT R
590 NEXT COL
600 GET Z$:IF Z$="" THEN 600:REM LOOP UNTIL USER STRIKES KEY
610 DATA .8,2,1.4
999 END
```

IBM

The printing of scales on the IBM is done by using normal PRINT statements. Note that graphic characters have been chosen to print scale marks along with the numbers on the left. The bars are printed by using the LOCATE statement to position the cursor. Remember that the rows on the IBM are numbered 1 through 25, while the columns are either 1 through 40 or 1 through 80, depending on the setting of the WIDTH statement. Once the cursor is in position, the characters are printed. Here is the IBM version of the program.

```
10 ' EXC12E2
20 ' CLARK AND LABARRE, CHAPTER 12, EXAMPLE 2, IBM
30 ' DRAWS BAR GRAPH ON SCREEN
40 ' THE FOLLOWING LINES DEFINE GRAPHIC CHARACTERS TO USE
50 TL$=CHR$(201)   'TOP LEFT CORNER
60 TR$=CHR$(187)   'TOP RIGHT CORNER
70 BL$=CHR$(200)   'BOTTOM LEFT CORNER
80 BR$=CHR$(188)   'BOTTOM RIGHT CORNER
90 HL$=CHR$(205)   'HORIZONTAL LINE
100 VL$=CHR$(186) 'VERTICAL LINE
110 SM$=CHR$(223)+VL$  'SCALE MARK
120 HT$=CHR$(178) 'HALF TONE
130 WIDTH 40       'SET SCREEN WIDTH TO 40
140 CLS
150 PRINT TL$;STRING$(38,HL$);TR$                'PRINT LINE 1
160 PRINT VL$;TAB(14)"ALBUM SALES";TAB(40);VL$   'PRINT LINE 2
170 PRINT BL$;STRING$(38,HL$);BR$                'PRINT LINE 3
180 ' PRINT THE SCALE
190 PRINT "MILLIONS":PRINT
200 PRINT "2.0";SM$
210 PRINT "1.8";SM$
220 PRINT "1.6";SM$
230 PRINT "1.4";SM$
240 PRINT "1.2";SM$
250 PRINT "1.0";SM$
260 PRINT " .8";SM$
270 PRINT " .6";SM$
280 PRINT " .4";SM$
290 PRINT " .2";SM$
300 PRINT " .0";STRING$(35,SM$)
310 PRINT TAB(11);"ALBUM A";TAB(21);"ALBUM B";TAB(31);"ALBUM C"
320 FOR COL=12 TO 32 STEP 10     'LOOP FOR 3 COLUMNS
330   READ MAGNITUDE            'READ NUMBER OF SALES
```

Continued

```
340      FOR ROW=15 TO (15-MAGNITUDE*5+1) STEP -1    'BAR SIZE LOOP
350         LOCATE ROW,COL                           'POSITION CURSOR
360         PRINT STRING$(4,HT$)                      'PRINT FOUR CHARACTERS
370      NEXT ROW
380 NEXT COL
390 Z$=INPUT$(1)   'LOOP UNTIL USER STRIKES KEY
400 DATA .8,2,1,4
999 END
```

TRS-80

The printing of scales on the TRS-80 is done by using normal PRINT statements. Note that graphic characters have been chosen to print scale marks along with the numbers on the left. The bars are printed by using the PRINT@ statement to position the cursor. If using the Model III, the top left position on the screen is position 0, with row 1 consuming positions 0-63. Row 2 uses positions 64-127, while row 3 uses positions 128-191. If using the Model 4, the cursor can be positioned by using row and column numbers rather than one position number. If using the Model 4 remember that the rows and columns start with number 0 rather than number 1. Once the cursor is in position, the characters are printed. Here is the TRS-80 Model III version of the program. If you are using the Model 4, you may refer to the IBM version of the program and substitute PRINT@ for each LOCATE in the program.

```
10  ' EXC12E2
20  ' CLARK AND LABARRE--CHAPTER 12, EXAMPLE 2, TRS-80 MODEL III
30  ' DRAWS BAR GRAPH ON SCREEN
40  ' THE FOLLOWING LINES DEFINE GRAPHIC CHARACTERS TO USE
50  TL$=CHR$(156)        'TOP LEFT CORNER
60  TR$=CHR$(172)        'TOP RIGHT CORNER
70  BL$=CHR$(141)        'BOTTOM LEFT CORNER
80  BR$=CHR$(142)        'BOTTOM RIGHT CORNER
90  HL$=CHR$(140)        'HORIZONTAL LINE
100 LVL$=CHR$(149)       'LEFT VERTICAL LINE
110 RVL$=CHR$(170)       'RIGHT VERTICAL LINE
120 SM$=CHR$(176)+LVL$   'SCALE MARK
130 HT$=CHR$(153)        'HALF-TONE
140 CLS
150 PRINT TL$;STRING$(38,HL$);TR$                'PRINT LINE 1
160 PRINT LVL$;TAB(14);"ALBUM SALES";TAB(39);RVL$ 'PRINT LINE 2
170 PRINT BL$;STRING$(38,HL$);BR$                'PRINT LINE 3
180 ' PRINT THE SCALE
190 PRINT "MILLIONS"
200 PRINT "2.0";SM$
210 PRINT "1.8";SM$
220 PRINT "1.6";SM$
230 PRINT "1.4";SM$
240 PRINT "1.2";SM$
250 PRINT "1.0";SM$
260 PRINT " .8";SM$
270 PRINT " .6";SM$
280 PRINT " .4";SM$
290 PRINT " .2";SM$
300 PRINT " .0";SM$;STRING$(35,SM$)
310 PRINT TAB(11);"ALBUM A";TAB(21);"ALBUM B";TAB(31);"ALBUM C";
320 FOR COL=12 TO 32 STEP 10    'LOOP FOR 3 COLUMNS
```

Continued

```
330    READ MAGNITUDE              'READ NUMBER OF SALES
340    FOR R=896 TO (896-((MAGNITUDE*4+1)*64)) STEP -64 'BAR SIZE LOOP
350       PRINT@R+COL,;              'POSITION CURSOR
360       PRINT STRING$(4,HT$);    'PRINT 4 CHARACTERS
370    NEXT R
380 NEXT COL
390 STZ$=INKEY$:IF Z$="" THEN 390  'LOOP UNTIL USER STRIKES KEY
400 DATA .8,2,1,4
999 END
```

DRAWING A LINE GRAPH

The drawing of a line graph is done in two stages. First, the heading and scales are printed in the same manner as used with a bar graph. Then the line is drawn. The line is drawn by plotting x and y coordinates. Each x value tells how far across the graph to go. Each y value tells how far up or down the graph to go. When using block graphics, each of the points is plotted by placing the cursor at the desired position and printing the character that has been chosen to represent the line.

As an example of a line graph, look back at Figure 12.8 showing the variation in the price of gasoline for the year. For another example, look at Figure 12.11 which shows the progress of a dieter over a period of 30 days.

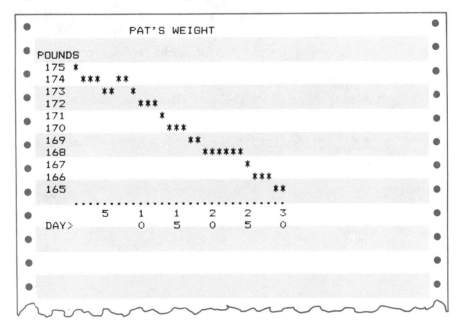

Figure 12.11   Sample Line Graph

This is the graph we will produce with an example program. Refer to the documentation in Figure 12.12 as you study the following program for your computer.

MODULE DOCUMENTATION	Program: EXC12E3	Module: <u>MAIN</u> Lines: <u>10-999</u>

Module Description:

This program produces a bar graph on the screen.

Module Function (Program Design):

1. Clear the screen.
2. Print the heading.
3. Print the vertical and horizontal scales on the graph.
4. Plot the line of the graph.

Figure 12.12   Steps in Producing a Line Graph

COMMODORE

In producing the bar graph in the previous section, we used POKEs on the Commodore. For this program, we will use cursor positioning and printing just to show how this method works. If you wish to use POKEs for drawing a line graph, you may. Here is the program.

```
10 REM EXC12E3
20 REM CLARK AND LABARRE--CHAPTER 12, EXAMPLE 3, COMMODORE
30 REM DRAWS LINE GRAPH
40 PRINT "⊐"   :REM PRINT "SHIFT-CLR-HOME"
50 PRINT
60 PRINT TAB(14);"PAT'S WEIGHT"
70 PRINT
80 PRINT "POUNDS"
90 REM PRINT SCALES
100 FOR WEIGHT=175 TO 165 STEP -1
110 PRINT WEIGHT
120 NEXT WEIGHT
130 PRINT "       ................................"
140 PRINT "          5    1    1    2    2    3"
150 PRINT " DAY>          0    5    0    5    0
160 REM PLOT WEIGHT
170 FOR DAY=1 TO 30
180 READ WEIGHT
190 PRINT "⬛"      :REM PRINT "CLR-HOME"
200 FOR R=1 TO 4+(175-WEIGHT)
210 PRINT "⬛";    :REM POSITION CURSOR TO ROW (CURSORDOWN)
220 NEXT R
230 PRINT TAB(DAY+4);CHR$(42);:REM PLOT POINT
240 NEXT DAY
250 GET Z$:IF Z$="" THEN 250:REM LOOP UNTIL USER STRIKES KEY
260 DATA 175,174,174,174,173,173,174,174,173,172
270 DATA 172,172,171,170,170,170,169,169,168,168
280 DATA 168,168,168,168,167,166,166,166,165,165
999 END
```

IBM

Here is the program for the IBM:

```
10 ' EXC12E3
20 ' CLARK AND LABARRE--CHAPTER 12, EXAMPLE 3, IBM
30 ' DRAWS LINE GRAPH
40 WIDTH 40
50 CLS
60 PRINT TAB(14);"PAT'S WEIGHT"
70 PRINT
80 PRINT "POUNDS"
90 ' PRINT SCALES
100 FOR WEIGHT=175 TO 165 STEP -1
110    PRINT WEIGHT
120 NEXT WEIGHT
130 PRINT TAB(6);STRING$(30,".")
140 PRINT "          5    1    1    2    2    3"
150 PRINT " DAY>          0    5    0    5    0"
160 ' PLOT WEIGHTS
170 FOR DAY=1 TO 30
180    READ WEIGHT
190    LOCATE 4+(175-WEIGHT),DAY+5
200    PRINT CHR$(42);
210 NEXT DAY
220 Z$=INPUT$(1)   'HOLD SCREEN UNTIL USER STRIKES KEY
230 DATA 175,174,174,174,173,173,174,174,173,172
240 DATA 172,172,171,170,170,170,169,169,168,168
250 DATA 168,168,168,168,167,166,166,166,165,165
999 END
```

TRS-80

Here is the TRS-80 Model III version of the program. If you are using the Model 4, refer to the IBM version of the program and substitute PRINT@ using a row and column number for each LOCATE in the program.

```
10 ' EXC12E3
20 ' CLARK AND LABARRE--CHAPTER 12, EXAMPLE 3, TRS-80 MODEL III
30 ' DRAWS LINE GRAPH
40 ' USING BLOCK GRAPHICS
50 CLS
60 PRINT TAB(14);"PAT'S WEIGHT"
70 PRINT "POUNDS"
80 ' PRINT SCALES
90 FOR WEIGHT=175 TO 165 STEP -1
100    PRINT WEIGHT
110 NEXT WEIGHT
120 PRINT TAB(5);STRING$(30,".")
130 PRINT "          5    1    1    2    2    3"
140 PRINT " DAY>          0    5    0    5    0";
150 ' PLOT WEIGHTS
160 FOR DAY=1 TO 30
170    READ WEIGHT
180    PRINT@64*(2+(175-WEIGHT))+DAY+4,;
190    PRINT CHR$(42),;
200 NEXT DAY
210 Z$=INKEY$:IF Z$="" THEN 210    'HOLD SCREEN UNTIL USER STRIKES KEY
220 DATA 175,174,174,174,173,173,174,174,173,172
230 DATA 172,172,171,170,170,170,169,169,168,168
240 DATA 168,168,168,168,167,166,166,166,165,165
999 END
```

REVIEW QUESTIONS

1. Describe the procedure for drawing a box with block graphics. (Obj. 4)
2. On the Commodore, how may the cursor be positioned for printing block graphics? (Obj. 4)
3. On the IBM, how may the cursor be positioned for printing block graphics? (Obj. 4)
4. On the TRS-80, how may the cursor be positioned for printing block graphics? (Obj. 4)

VOCABULARY WORDS

The following terms were introduced in this chapter:

graphics	graph	line graph
block graphics	bar graph	

KEYWORDS AND COMMANDS

No new keywords or commands were introduced in this chapter.

PROGRAMS TO WRITE

For each program, prepare the necessary documentation prior to writing the BASIC code.

Program 1

Write a program to produce a bar graph showing the number of engines available for four different automobiles. The bars should be vertical. Assume that a Gazelle has 3 available engines, a Martin has 5, a Sprite has 4, and a Portofino Roadster has 2.

Program 2

Write a program that draws a line graph showing the number of speeding tickets issued each day in a town. The graph should be for one month. The days of the month should be on the x axis; that is, the days go across. Here are the numbers of tickets issued:
3,2,1,3,2,2,2,1,1,2,2,3,3,4,5,4,4,4,3,3,2,3,0,0,0,1,2,1,1,0.

Program 3

Modify Program 1 so that the bars are horizontal.

Program 4

Modify Program 2 so that the days of the month are on the y axis.

Program 5

Many manufacturers of air conditioners have made their units more efficient. This increased efficiency is documented on the units by a higher number for the energy rating. Write a program that will produce a bar graph showing the increased efficiency of four brands of air conditioners. Use two bars for each brand; one for the efficiency rating last year and one for the efficiency rating this year. Here is the data:
Arctic,8.5,9.3,Coolair,7.6,8.7,Frosty,8.5,8.6,Windy,7.2,10.3.

Program 6

A company has two salespeople. Write a program to produce a line graph showing their performance for a year. Use different symbols to represent the line for each of the salespeople. In thousands, salesperson Robin had sales of 3,4,4,6,7,7,6,6,6,5,4, and 3. In thousands, salesperson Cleo had sales of 1,1,2,2,1,2,3,5,5,8,9, and 10.

CONTINUING PROJECTS

Before writing any program of the continuing projects, be sure to complete all appropriate documentation.

Project 1

Prepare a program module that will show the number of employees in each pay range. A pay range can be defined as a pay rate starting at an even dollar and continuing through 99 cents. For example, employees earning between $5.00 and $5.99 are in one range, while those earning between $6.00 and $6.99 are in another. Use a bar graph to make the presentation. Data should be read from the data files created by running other options of the project.

Project 2

Prepare a program module to show sales for each stock number as a multiple of the reorder point. One way of doing this might be to draw two bars, one representing the sales and the other the reorder point. The bars might be next to each other or one inside the other. The data for any stock number input by the user of the program should be read from the files and the graph created. In other words, the graph for one product at a time should appear on the screen, and the product that appears should appear at the command of the user.

## Chapter 13

Pixel Graphics

Objectives: 1. Define pixel graphics.

2. Describe how a bar graph is made using pixel graphics.

3. Describe how a line graph is made using pixel graphics.

4. Plan and code programs using pixel graphics.

In Chapter 12 you learned about a graphic method known as block graphics. In this chapter you will learn about a method known as pixel graphics.

Topic 13.1— PRINCIPLES OF USING PIXEL GRAPHICS

With many computers, the use of pixel graphics provides an easy way of producing some types of graphic output. In this section, pixel graphics will be defined. Then, examples of their use in bar graphs and line graphs will be given.

DEFINITION OF PIXEL GRAPHICS

Remember from Chapter 12 that each character is made of a matrix of dots. With most computers, all characters take the same number of rows and columns of dots. Each of these dots is known as a pixel, which is short for picture element. When using block graphics, the group of dots or pixels was handled as a character unit. When using pixel graphics, you can control each dot individually. To illustrate the difference, assume that each character in block graphics is eight dots wide and eight dots high. Therefore, the smallest unit that can be controlled on the screen by a program is 8 by 8, or 64 dots. In pixel graphics, on the other hand, each of the dots can be individually controlled. In this example, therefore, you might conclude that the use of pixel graphics gives you 64 times more control over the picture on the screen. While this conclusion would not be entirely correct, you do have the ability to show much more complex displays when using pixel graphics.

When using pixel graphics, think in terms of the entire screen rather than in terms of individual characters. The greater the number of pixels on the screen, the higher the resolution of the display. This simply means that the greater the number of dots, the greater the amount of detail that may be shown on the screen. For example, a screen of 640 x 200 pixels has higher resolution than one of 320 x 200 pixels.

When working with block graphics, you referred to row and column numbers to place the cursor before printing a character. When working with pixel graphics, you use x and y coordinates instead of rows and columns. The x coordinate tells how far across the screen to go, while the y coordinate gives the distance down the screen. If you are using a screen that is 320 x 200 in size, the maximum x coordinate is 319 and the maximum y coordinate is 199. Refer to Figure 13.1 for a diagram of the way the pixels are numbered. The diagram shows a 320 x 200 screen. For other screen sizes, the coordinate numbers would be different.

The pixel in this corner is 0,0. It is 0 pixels across and 0 pixels down.

Approximate center is 160,100. These numbers are half of the maximum coordinate values.

The pixel in this corner is 319,0. It is 319 pixels across and 0 pixels down.

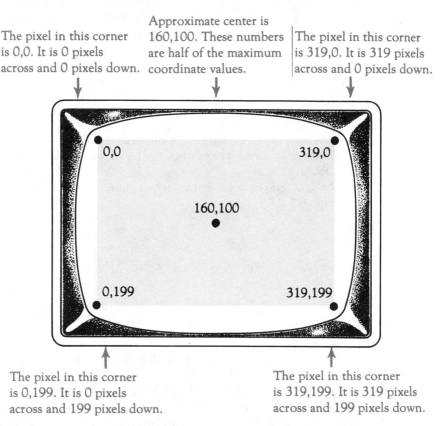

The pixel in this corner is 0,199. It is 0 pixels across and 199 pixels down.

The pixel in this corner is 319,199. It is 319 pixels across and 199 pixels down.

Figure 13.1   Coordinate Positions of 320 Pixels x 200 Pixels Screen

Any pixel on the screen can be individually turned on or off by referring to its coordinates. If you are using a computer with color capability, the color of each pixel can also be individually controlled.

When you were working with block graphics in Chapter 12, you used only keywords that you already knew. In using pixel graphics, however, there are many new keywords. Each of them is designed to perform a particular function in producing displays on the screen. For example, there are special keywords to draw lines from one point on the screen to another. There are also much greater differences from one computer to another when using pixel graphics.

USING PIXEL GRAPHICS TO DRAW GRAPHS

You learned in Chapter 12 that a bar graph is used to show comparisons of different data items; a line graph is used to show changes in the data item. Both these kinds of graphs can be made using pixel graphics instead of block graphics. There will not be a tremendous difference in the appearance of bar graphs, which are done by drawing horizontal and vertical lines to form bars. Line graphs, however, look much better and are much easier to read when done with pixel graphics. This is because the points on the graph may actually be connected by using the keywords to draw a line from one point to another.

REVIEW QUESTIONS

1. What are pixel graphics? Why are they called pixel graphics? (Obj. 1)
2. How is a pixel graphic character represented by the computer? (Obj. 1)
3. How are shapes constructed using pixel graphics? (Obj. 4)
4. Do bar graphs look better when done with block graphics or pixel graphics? (Obj. 2)
5. Do line graphs look better when done with block graphics or pixel graphics? (Obj. 3)

Topic 13.2— IMPLEMENTING PIXEL GRAPHICS USING BASIC

Many small computers have some degree of pixel graphic capability. Of the computers discussed in this text, pixel graphics are available on the Apple and IBM. Pixel graphics are not standard on the Commodore and TRS-80, although hardware and software packages that produce pixel graphics can be purchased from various vendors.

Doing pixel graphics requires special keywords. These words vary tremendously from one computer to the next. Using the special keywords required for producing pixel graphics under BASIC involves several steps.

1. Determine what kind of shape needs to be drawn and which keyword(s) can be used to draw it.
2. Determine where on the screen the shape should appear.
3. Use the chosen keyword to place the shape in the determined position.

In the remainder of this chapter, we will show you examples of how to produce pixel graphics. Versions of BASIC discussed in this chapter have rich vocabularies of pixel graphic keywords with which to work. Entire books can and have been written about using these graphics commands. Such detailed coverage of all the commands is beyond the scope of this chapter. However, the keywords introduced will serve to introduce you to the capabilities of the languages. It is suggested that you refer to the reference manual for your computer for a description of the other capabilities that are available for your use.

IBM

On the IBM, pixel graphics are available only if your machine is equipped with a color/graphics monitor adapter or if you are using a PCjr. If your machine uses a monochrome monitor adapter, none of the pixel graphic commands will work. When using graphics, you can still print text at any desired location on the screen by using the keyword LOCATE. In other words, you can print words in the middle of graphic shapes, label graphs, and so on.

First, let's look at some of the frequently used keywords for pixel graphics on the IBM. For each of these keywords, the general form and an example will be given. If possible, enter and try each of the examples.

SCREEN

As you learned earlier, the SCREEN statement is used on the IBM to indicate the mode in which the display should be operating. SCREEN 0 selects text mode, while one of the graphics modes given below must be used to do pixel graphics.

General Form: *line number* SCREEN *mode*

Example 1: 80 SCREEN 1

Example 1 places the computer in medium-resolution graphics mode (320 pixels across by 200 pixels down) with four colors.

Example 2: `80 SCREEN 2`

Example 2 places the computer in high-resolution graphics mode (640 pixels across by 200 pixels down); black and white are the only two colors available. If you are using a PCjr, there are additional modes; they are listed in the following examples.

Example 3: `80 SCREEN 3`

Example 3 places the computer in low-resolution graphics mode (160 x 200) with 16 colors.

Example 4: `80 SCREEN 4`

Example 4 places the computer in medium-resolution graphics mode (320 x 200) with four colors.

Example 5: `80 SCREEN 5`

Example 5 places the computer in medium-resolution graphics mode (320 x 200) with 16 colors (this requires 128K of memory).

Example 6: `80 SCREEN 6`

Example 6 places the computer in high-resolution graphics mode (640 x 200) with four colors (this requires 128K of memory).

All the examples that follow in this chapter assume that SCREEN 1 has been selected as the mode. In addition to changing modes, the SCREEN statement can do some other things, but they are of no use in pixel graphics.

PALETTE

On the IBM PC in graphics mode, you may select any of 16 colors for the background color. Each of these colors has a number and is listed in Table 5.1 in Chapter 5. Once the background color is selected, you work with a palette (group) of graphics colors. With modes 1 and 2, this group is chosen from one of two available palettes by using the COLOR statement. The two palettes contain the colors shown in Table 13.1.

Color Number	Palette 0	Palette 1
1	Green	Cyan
2	Red	Magenta
3	Brown	White

Table 13.1   Palette Colors on the IBM PC

If you are using a PCjr, you can change the colors in the palette you are using. This is done with the PALETTE statement as follows. Whichever palette is in use will be changed.

General Form: *line number* PALETTE *number on palette,color number*

Example: 80 PALETTE 2,14

The example assigns color number 14 (yellow) as the second color of the palette.

COLOR

The use of the COLOR statement varies slightly depending on the mode that has been selected with the SCREEN statement. In modes 1 and 2, the COLOR statement is used to set or change the background color and palettes. Once the palette is selected, individual graphics keywords determine which of the chosen palette's colors is actually used.

General Form: *line number* COLOR *background,palette*

Example: 90 COLOR 9,0

The example chooses a background color of 9, which is light blue, and selects palette 0, which consists of colors green, red, and brown. Therefore, any graphics displayed on the screen will be done in green, red, or brown on a light blue background. You are also allowed to do graphics in the color of the background, which means you can't see them unless you change the color after they are drawn. The COLOR statement can be used as many times as desired in a program. Its changes go into effect immediately. Suppose that you have drawn graphics on the screen using palette 0. If you use the COLOR statement again and change the palette to 1, the colors of the graphics already on the screen will change. As with many BASIC statements, unnecessary parts of the statement may be omitted. That is, if you want to change only the background color, you don't need to enter the comma and the palette number. If you want to change just the palette number and not the background, you may skip over the background color number; however, you will have to put in the comma as a "place holder". Any even number as the palette number will select palette 0. Any odd number will select palette 1.

When using any mode from 3 through 6, the general form of the COLOR statement is as follows:

> **General Form:** *line number COLOR foreground,background*
>
> **Example:**   `COLOR 2,1`

PSET

The most elementary pixel graphics statement is PSET, which stands for point set. It simply turns on any specified pixel on the screen. Its general form is as follows:

> **General Form:** *line number PSET(x,y),color number*
>
> **Example:**   `100 PSET(ACROSS,DOWN),2`

As a brief example showing the use of the PSET statement, look at a program that uses the random number generator to turn on pixels at random positions on the screen. We will also use random colors, and the program will continue until interrupted by CTRL-Break.

```
40 SCREEN 1
50 COLOR 9,0
60 WHILE Z$=""
70    X=RND*320
80    Y=RND*200
90    HUE=RND*3+1
100   PSET(X,Y),HUE
110 WEND
```

LINE

One of the most useful pixel graphics statements is LINE. In its simplest form, it draws a line from any point on the screen to any other point on the screen. It is also used for drawing boxes and filled-in boxes. Its general form is as follows:

> **General Form:** *line number LINE(from x,y)-(to x,y),color number*
>
> **Example:**   `100 LINE (0,0)-(319,199),2`

Output:

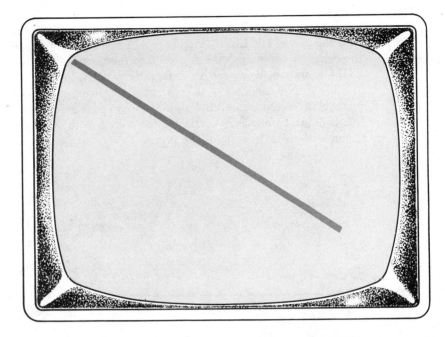

If a B (short for box) is placed at the end of the LINE statement, this causes the pairs of x and y coordinates to be considered as opposite corners of a box rather than as the beginning and ending points for a line.

Example:

```
LINE (20,10)-(60,80),3,B
```

Output:

If you want to fill in a box drawn with the line statement, you can add an F to the end of the LINE statement. The color is one of those contained in the currently chosen palette. If a color in the other palette is to be used, the COLOR statement is used to change the palette.

The LINE function is quite useful for drawing line graphs also. This is made easier because the function works when only a destination is given; the line is drawn from the last point on the screen to the new point. Here is an example showing how it can be done:

Example:

```
40  SCREEN 1
50  CLS
60  READ P
70  PSET(0,P),2                  ' SET BEGINNING POINT
80  FOR X=20 TO 319 STEP 20      ' VARIABLE X STEPS ACROSS THE SCREEN
90      READ P
100     LINE-(X,P)               ' DRAW LINE FROM LAST POINT TO NEW POINT
110 NEXT X
120 DATA 53,79,180,160,160,150,140,184,67,48,94,90,50,96,129,30
```

Output:

CIRCLE

Circles may be drawn by using the CIRCLE function. In its simplest form, it draws a circle of the desired size at any point on the screen. In a more advanced form, it can draw ellipses and partial circles. Its general form is as follows:

General Form: *line number* CIRCLE *(x,y of center),radius, color*
number

Example: `100 CIRCLE (160,85),50,2`

Output:

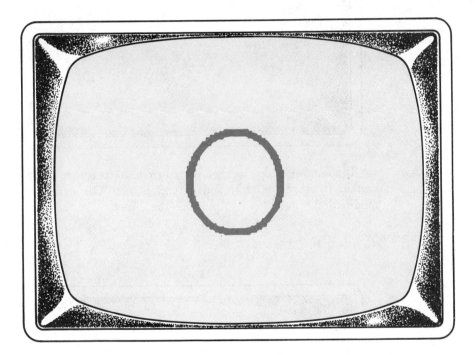

As with other pixel graphic functions, the color is chosen from the currently selected palette. If a color in the other palette is to be used, the COLOR statement is used to change the palette.

By adding start and end points to the CIRCLE function, a partial circle may be drawn. The start and end points are angles given in radians and may range from -2*PI to 2*PI. Remember that PI is 3.141593. Look at the following example.

Example:
```
100 PI=3.141593
110 CIRCLE(160,100),50,2,PI/2,PI
```

Output:

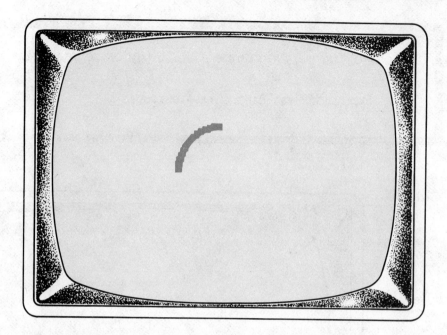

If you want to connect the partial circle to its center point, place a minus sign in front of the start and/or end points. The example above can be modified as shown here to produce the effect.

Example:

```
100 PI=3.141593
110 CIRCLE(160,100),50,2,-PI/2,-PI
```

Output:

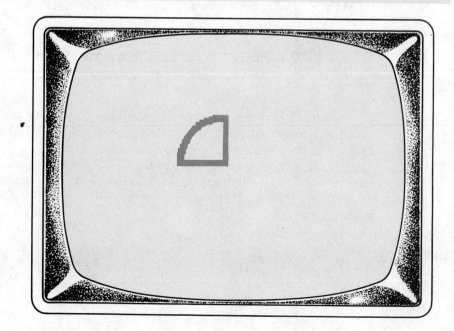

The final option to the CIRCLE function is to make the ellipse fatter or skinnier. This is done by adding an aspect ratio to the end of the statement. The aspect ratio is the ratio of the x-radius to the y-radius. Remember that there are more pixels across the screen than down. Therefore, if the same number of pixels were turned on going both across and down the screen, the circle would not be round. The aspect ratio provides a method of controlling this so the ellipse looks as desired. The aspect ratio may be either greater or less than one. If it is less than one, the radius specification of the ellipse is considered to apply to the x-radius. If the aspect ratio is greater than one, the radius specification of the ellipse applies to the y-radius. Look at the following program for an example.

Example: 100 CIRCLE(100,80),60,,,,2

Output:

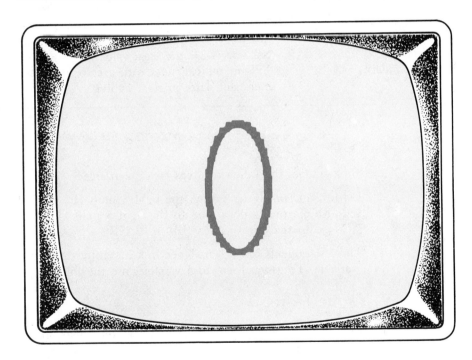

Note in this example that the color, start point, and end point were omitted. Therefore, they retained their old values.

DRAW

The DRAW statement is used to produce just about any desired shape. To use the statement, directions of movement are defined by using letters of the alphabet and giving distances. The letters of the alphabet for controlling direction of movement are shown in Table 13.2.

Command	Meaning
U*distance*	Move up
D*distance*	Move down
L*distance*	Move left
R*distance*	Move right
E*distance*	Move diagonally up and right
F*distance*	Move diagonally down and right
G*distance*	Move diagonally down and left
H*distance*	Move diagonally up and left
B*command from above*	Move, but don't draw while moving
N*command from above*	Return to original position after drawing
A*angle*	Set angle at 0-3, corresponding to 90, 180, 270, 360 degrees
TA*angle*	Set turn angle from -360 to +360 degrees (positive turns counterclockwise, negative turns clockwise)
C*color attribute number*	Set color (0-3 or 0-15 depending on screen mode)
S*scale factor*	Set size (1-255 are legal values)
P*paint,boundary*	Fills in the character with a color (see the paint command later in this chapter)

Table 13.2   Selected Commands for DRAW Statement

For example, the following steps create a triangle:

1. Move diagonally up and to the right 5 units (E5 in BASIC)
2. Move diagonally down and to the right 5 units (F5 in BASIC)
3. Move to the left 10 units (L10 in BASIC)

These statements can be combined in a literal for direct use or assigned to a variable. To assign them to a variable, use the following statement:

```
190 TRIANGLE$="E5F5L10"
```

To draw the triangle, use the DRAW statement in either of the following manners:

Example:

```
200 DRAW TRIANGLE$
```

Example:

```
200 DRAW "E5F5L10"
```

Output:

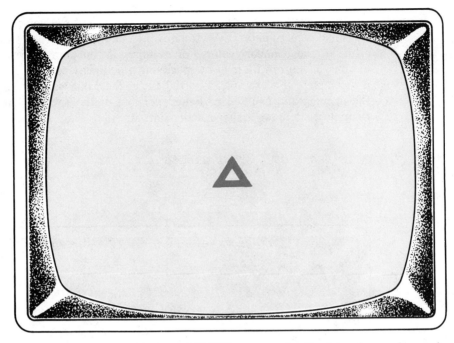

By using some additional DRAW commands, the triangle can be made to rotate and increase in size. This is done by using the commands called TA (turn angle) and S (scale) and placing them inside a loop. Here is how to do it.

```
190 TRIANGLE$="E1FIL2"    'Make the triangle very small

200 FOR A=1 TO 255 STEP 10

210    DRAW "TA=A;S=A;"+TRIANGLE$    'Turn angle and increase size

220 NEXT A
```

All values used with DRAW may be either entered as constants or placed in variables as was shown here with the turn angle and scale.

PAINT

The keyword PAINT is used to color in a graphic shape. Here is its general form:

General Form: *line number* PAINT(*begin x,y*),*color,boundary*

Example 1:   100 PAINT(160,85),2,3

In effect, you are setting down the paintbrush at the point designated by the x and y coordinates. Everything is then painted in until the brush reaches a line of the boundary color. For example, if you draw a circle using color number 2, you can fill it in by specifying a boundary color of 2. If any shape is incomplete (for example, a partial circle) the paint will "leak out" through the opening and paint in undesired portions of the screen. Here is a longer example that draws a shape and paints it.

Example 2:
```
100 DRAW "C3U40R50F20G20L50"
110 PAINT(170,70),1,3
```

Output:

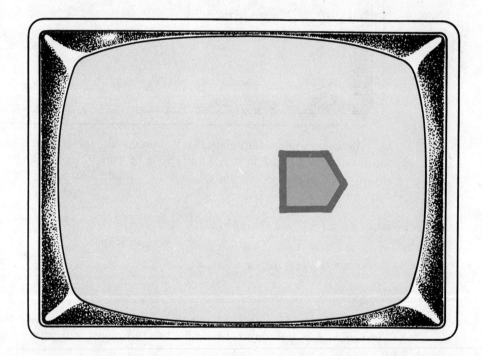

EXAMPLE PROGRAMS

This section shows two example programs that make use of many of the pixel graphics keywords and functions you have learned in this chapter. The first program, in Figure 13.2, draws a bar graph showing the unit prices of two different packages of the same product. The product name, package sizes, and package prices are entered by the user. The second program, in Figure 13.3, uses a line graph to plot the weight of a dieter over a one-month period. Follow each program's documentation as you study the program listings.

MODULE DOCUMENTATION	Program: EXC13E1	Module: MAIN Lines: 10-999

Module Description:

This program draws a bar graph showing unit prices of two different packages of the same product for the IBM.

Module Function (Program Design):

1. Read the input data.
2. Put the computer in graphics mode.
3. Draw a box around all of the screen except for the caption area at the bottom.
4. Compute the starting points and sizes for the bars.
5. Draw the bars.
6. Draw circles at the bottoms of the bars.
7. Print the unit-costs inside the circles.
8. Print the captions below the outer box.

```
10 ' EXC13E1
20 ' CLARK AND LABARRE--CHAPTER 13, EXAMPLE 1
30 ' DRAWS BAR GRAPH OF UNIT PRICES
40 ' GET DATA
50 KEY OFF
60 CLS
70 LINE INPUT "WHAT IS THE PRODUCT NAME?   ";NAM$
80 PRINT
90 INPUT "HOW MANY UNITS IN PACKAGE 1";U1
100 INPUT "WHAT IS THE PRICE OF PACKAGE 1";P1
110 PRINT
120 INPUT "HOW MANY UNITS IN PACKAGE 2";U2
130 INPUT "WHAT IS THE PRICE OF PACKAGE 2";P2
140 ' DRAW GRAPH
150 SCREEN 1
160 CLS
170 ' DRAW BOX AROUND MOST OF SCREEN
180 LINE(0,0)-(319,150),,B
190 ' COMPUTE STARTING POINTS AND SIZES
200 B1=P1/U1
210 B2=P2/U2
220 IF B1>B2 THEN MAX=B1 ELSE MAX=B2
230 MULTIPLIER=140/MAX
240 B1START=140-B1*MULTIPLIER
250 B2START=140-B2*MULTIPLIER
260 ' DRAW BARS
270 LINE(64,B1START)-(128,149),2,BF    'DRAW FIRST BAR
```

Figure 13.2   Documentation and Code for Example Program 1 (Continued)

```
280 LINE(192,B2START)-(256,149),2,BF   'DRAW SECOND BAR
290 ' DRAW CIRCLES AND PRINT UNIT COSTS
300 CIRCLE(96,125),25,1:PAINT(96,125),1
310 CIRCLE(224,125),25,1:PAINT(224,125),1
320 LOCATE 17,11
330 PRINT USING "#.##";B1
340 LOCATE 17,27
350 PRINT USING "#.##";B2
360 LOCATE 21,9
370 PRINT "PRODUCT 1"
380 LOCATE 21,25
390 PRINT "PRODUCT 2"
400 LOCATE 23,1
410 PRINT "COMPARATIVE UNIT COSTS FOR ";NAM$;
420 LINE INPUT Z$
999 END
```

Figure 13.2   Documentation and Code for Example Program 1 (Concluded)

MODULE DOCUMENTATION	Program: EXC13E2	Module: MAIN Lines: 10-999

Module Description:

This program uses a line graph to plot the weight of a dieter over a one-month period for the IBM.

Module Function (Program Design):

1. Put the computer in graphics mode.
2. Print the scales.
3. Read and plot the weight for the first day of the month.
4. Repeat for each remaining day of the month:
   a. Read the weight.
   b. Draw a line from the last weight to plot the point of the new weight.

```
10 ' EXC13E2
20 ' CLARK AND LABARRE--CHAPTER 13, EXAMPLE 2
30 ' DRAWS LINE GRAPH OF WEIGHT
40 SCREEN 1
50 CLS
60 PRINT TAB(12);"FREIDA'S WEIGHT"
70 PRINT
80 PRINT "LBS."
90 FOR WEIGHT=175 TO 165 STEP -1
100     PRINT MID$(STR$(WEIGHT),2)
110 NEXT WEIGHT
120 PRINT "      0...0....1....1....2....2....3"
130 PRINT "DAY->1   5    0    5    0    5    0"
140 ' PLOT WEIGHTS
150 READ WEIGHT
160 PSET (44,28+(175-WEIGHT)*8),4  'SET STARTING POINT; MULTIPLIER 8 AND STEP 8
170 FOR X=52 TO 276 STEP 8         'EQUATE GRAPH TO CHARACTER SCALES
180     READ WEIGHT
190  ' LINE-(X,28+(175-WEIGHT)*8),4   'CONNECT TO NEXT POINT
200 NEXT X
210 Z$=INPUT$(1)  'HOLD SCREEN UNTIL USER STRIKES KEY
230 DATA 175,174,174,174,173,173,174,174,173,172
240 DATA 172,172,171,170,170,170,169,169,168,168
250 DATA 168,168,168,168,167,166,166,166,165,165
999 END
```

Figure 13.3   Documentation and Code for Example Program 2

APPLE

On the Apple, pixel graphics are standard equipment. When using standard graphics, the screen may be totally devoted to graphics or may be divided into a graphics area at the top of the screen and a text area at the bottom of the screen. You cannot print text characters in the graphics portion and cannot print graphics in the text portion. Note, however, that these limitations can be overcome by using advanced procedures that are beyond the scope of this book or by using commercially available software.

Let's look now at some of the frequently used keywords for pixel graphics on the Apple. For each of these keywords, the general form and an example will be given. If possible, enter and try each of the examples.

GR, HGR, AND HGR2

The GR, HGR, and HGR2 statements are used to set the Apple to graphics mode. If you want low-resolution graphics, use GR. If you want high-resolution graphics, use HGR or HGR2.

General Form: *line number* GR *or* HGR *or* HGR2

Example 1:   80 GR

Example 1 places the computer in low-resolution graphics mode (40 pixels across by 40 pixels down) with sixteen colors. It also reserves four lines at the bottom of the screen for text.

Example 2:   `30 HGR`

Example 2 places the computer in high-resolution graphics mode (280 pixels across by 160 pixels down) with eight colors. It also reserves the bottom four lines of the screen for text.

Example 3:   `80 HGR2`

Example 3 places the computer in full-screen, high-resolution graphics mode (280 pixels across by 192 pixels down) with eight colors and reserves no space for text. One of the three graphics commands introduced above must be used before graphics can be done. All partial programs in this chapter that do not show the command assume that it has been used.

COLOR AND HCOLOR

The use of the COLOR or HCOLOR statement sets or changes the color used for pixel graphics. COLOR must be used when in low-resolution graphics mode (set with GR). HCOLOR must be used when in high-resolution grapics mode (set with HGR or HGR2).

General Form: *line number* COLOR *or* HCOLOR=*color number*

Example 1:   `90 COLOR=12`

Example 2:   `90 HCOLOR=1`

The examples choose a color of green, which is number 12 in low-resolution mode and number 1 in high-resolution mode. A color must be set before plotting any graphics. The color statements may then be used as many times as desired in a program. Their changes go into effect immediately. Tables 13.3 and 13.4 give the color numbers used.

Number	Color	Number	Color
0	black	8	brown
1	magenta	9	orange
2	dark blue	10	grey2
3	violet	11	pink
4	dark green	12	green
5	grey1	13	yellow
6	medium blue	14	aqua
7	light blue	15	white

Table 13.3   Apple Low-Resolution Graphics Colors

Number	Color
0	black1
1	green
2	violet
3	white1
4	black2
5	orange
6	blue
7	white2

Table 13.4   Apple High-Resolution Graphics Colors

PLOT

The most elementary pixel graphics statement is PLOT. It simply turns on any specified pixel on the screen. The general form is as follows, with PLOT being used only in low-resolution graphics.

General Form: *line number* PLOT *x,y*

Example: 100 PLOT ACROSS,DOWN

As a brief example showing the use of the PLOT statement, look at a program that uses the random number generator to turn on pixels at random positions on the screen. We will also use random colors, and the program will continue until interrupted by CTRL-C.

```
40 GR
50 X=RND(1)*40
60 Y=RND(1)*40
70 COLOR=RND(1)*16
80 PLOT X,Y
90 GOTO 50
```

HLIN

HLIN, used only with low-resolution graphics, draws a horizontal line. Here is its syntax:

General Form: *line number* HLIN *from, to* AT *vertical position*

Example: 100 HLIN 5,35 AT 12

The example says that a line is to be drawn across the screen beginning at pixel 5 and continuing through pixel 35. It is to be drawn in the twelfth row of pixels from the top of the screen.

VLIN

VLIN, used only with low-resolution graphics, draws a vertical line. Here is its syntax:

General Form: *line number* VLIN *from, to* AT *horizontal position*

Example: 100 VLIN 10,30 AT 15

The example says that a line is to be drawn up and down beginning at pixel 10 and continuing through pixel 30. It is to be drawn in the fifteenth column of pixels from the left of the screen.

HPLOT

One of the most useful pixel graphics statements for use with high-resolution graphics is HPLOT. In its simplest form, it lights up one designated pixel. In a more sophisticated form, it draws a line from any point on the screen to any other point on the screen. It may take any one of the following forms:

General Form: *line number* HPLOT *x,y*

Example 1: 100 HPLOT 30,40

This example will turn on the one pixel located 30 pixels across the screen and 40 pixels down the screen. The color last chosen with the HCOLOR statement will be used.

General Form: *line number* HPLOT *from x,y* TO *to x,y*

Example 2: 100 HPLOT 0,0 TO 279,159

This example draws a line from position 0,0 (the top left of the screen) to position 279,159 (the lower right corner of the screen).

General Form: *line number* HPLOT TO *x,y*

Example 3: 110 HPLOT TO 1,159

This example draws a line from the last point plotted to pixel 0,199 (the lower left corner of the screen. If Example 2 and Example 3 were used together, the output would be as follows:

Output:

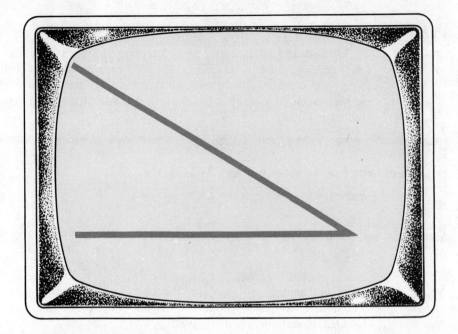

The HPLOT statement can be extended to draw more complex shapes such as rectangles. Study the following example:

Example: `100 HPLOT 0,0 TO 20,0 TO 20,100 TO 0,100 TO 0,0`

Output:

The HPLOT function is quite useful for drawing line graphs also. This is made easier because the function works when only a destination is given; the line is drawn from the last point on the screen to the new point. Here is an example showing how it can be done:

Example:

```
40 HGR
50 HCOLOR=2
60 HPLOT 0,0                 :REM SET BEGINNING POINT
70   FOR X=20 TO 279 STEP 20 :REM PLOT A POINT EVERY 20 PIXELS
80     READ P
90       HPLOT TO X,P         :REM DRAW LINE FROM LAST POINT TO NEW POINT
100 NEXT X
110 DATA 28,54,155,135,135,125,115,159,32,23,60,65,25,71
```

Output:

DRAW

The DRAW statement is used to produce just about any desired shape in high-resolution graphics. As an example of a shape that can be drawn, look at the following triangle:

The following steps created the triangle:

1. Repeat this process four times: Plot a point and move up; move right without plotting. This will take care of the left side.
2. Repeat this process four times: Plot a point and move right; move down without plotting. This will take care of the right side.
3. Repeat this process eight times: Plot a point and move left. This will take care of the base of the triangle.

The DRAW statement carries out instructions such as those above to make the desired shape on the screen. Before using the DRAW statement, however, the instructions for making the shape must have been defined previously and loaded into the computer's memory into what is known as a shape table. The shape table usually is created with one of several commercially available programs and stored on disk. If you want to create a shape table without using a shape table program, instructions are included in the Apple manuals. Creation of a shape table without using a program designed for the purpose is very tedious and time consuming, however.

Here is the general form of the DRAW command:

General Form: *line number* DRAW *shape number* AT *x,y*

Example: 100 DRAW 1 AT 140,95

The shape number specifies which of several shapes in the table to draw. If the portion of the statement telling where to begin drawing is left off, the shape will begin at the last point plotted by the previous HPLOT, DRAW, or XDRAW statement. XDRAW is a variation of DRAW. It works the same way except that each pixel is changed to the complementary color already existing at each point. That is, if a point was already white, it will be turned black; it if was already black, it will be turned white. Because of this quality, XDRAW is frequently used to erase a shape. For example, if a shape was drawn on the screen in white, XDRAW would change it back to black, effectively erasing it. The complementary color pairs are black and white, violet and green, and blue and orange.

Before using the DRAW statement, you should use other keywords to help tell the computer how to do the drawing. By using the keyword ROT (rotate), you can turn the shape from the way it was originally entered. By using the keyword SCALE, you can tell the computer to make the shape larger than it was originally stored in the shape table. Here is the way to use the keywords:

General Form: *line number* ROT = *rotation*

Example: 100 ROT=32

The number following ROT = should be in the range of 0 through 63. A zero draws the shape as it was created in the shape table. A one rotates the shape 1/64 of a circle, while a two rotates the shape 2/64 of a circle, etc. Thus, a number of 32, for example, will rotate the shape 180 degrees from the way it was drawn. A number of 64 starts the process over, since it is the same as zero.

General Form: *line number* SCALE = *multiplier*

Example: 100 SCALE=2

The number following SCALE = specifies how much larger than the original a shape is to be. A one means to draw the shape the same size as it was originally created in the shape table. A two means to draw it twice as big. The maximum multiplier is 255, meaning the shape is drawn 255 times as large as its original creation in the shape table.

Now, assume that the triangle described above has been stored in a shape table on disk by using commercial software. Here is how to use the DRAW command to make the shape appear on the screen.

```
40 PRINT CHR$(4);"BLOAD SHAPES"  :REM LOAD SHAPE TABLE INTO MEMORY
50 POKE 232,252:POKE 233,29      :REM TELL BASIC WHERE TO LOOK TO FIND TABLE
60 HGR                           :REM SWITCH ON HIGH RES GRAPHICS
70 HCOLOR=2                      :REM SET COLOR TO VIOLET
80 ROT=0                         :REM DRAW SHAPE TURNED AS CREATED
90 SCALE=2                       :REM DRAW SHAPE TWICE ITS ORIGINAL SIZE
100 DRAW 1 AT 140,80             :REM BEGIN SHAPE 140 PIXELS ACROSS AND 80 DOWN
```

All values used with DRAW may be either entered as constants or placed in variables. By putting statements inside a loop and using the loop variables to control the scale and amount of rotation, you can create interesting movement patterns with DRAW.

EXAMPLE PROGRAMS

The following programs make use of many of the pixel graphics keywords and functions you have learned in this section. The first program, shown in Figure 13.4, draws a bar graph showing the unit prices of two different packages of the same product. The product name, package sizes, and package prices are entered by the user. The second program, shown in Figure 13.5, draws a line graph of a dieter's weight loss. Follow the documentation as you study each program listing.

MODULE DOCUMENTATION	Program: EXC13E1	Module: MAIN Lines: 10-999

Module Description:

This program draws a bar graph showing unit prices of two different packages of the same product for the Apple.

Module Function (Program Design):

1. Read the input data.
2. Put the computer in graphics mode.
3. Draw a box around all of the screen except for the caption area at the bottom.
4. Compute the starting points and sizes for the bars.
5. Draw the bars.
6. Print the unit costs.
7. Print the captions.

```
10 REM EXC13E1
20 REM CLARK AND LABARRE--CHAPTER 13, EXAMPLE 1
30 REM DRAWS BAR GRAPH OF UNIT PRICES
40 REM GET DATA
50 HOME
60 INPUT "WHAT IS THE PRODUCT NAME?  ";NAM$
70 PRINT
80 INPUT "HOW MANY UNITS IN PACKAGE 1?  ";U1
90 INPUT "WHAT IS THE PRICE OF PACKAGE 1?  ";P1
100 PRINT
110 INPUT "HOW MANY UNITS IN PACKAGE 2?  ";U2
120 INPUT "WHAT IS THE PRICE OF PACKAGE 2?  ";P2
130 REM DRAW GRAPH
140 HGR
150 HCOLOR=2
160 REM DRAW BOX AROUND GRAPHICS PART OF SCREEN
170 HPLOT 0,0 TO 279,0 TO 279,159 TO 0,159 TO 0,0
180 REM COMPUTE STARTING POINTS AND SIZES
190 B1=P1/U1
200 B2=P2/U2
210 IF B1>B2 THEN MAX=B1
220 IF B1<=B2 THEN MAX=B2
```

Continued

```
230 MULTIPLIER=160/MAX
240 S1=160-B1*MULTIPLIER
250  IF S1=0 THEN S1=1
260 S2=160-B2*MULTIPLIER
270 IF S2=0 THEN S2=1
280 REM DRAW BARS
290 HPLOT 56,S1 TO 112,S1 TO 112,159 TO 56,159 TO 56,S1 :REM DRAW FIRST BAR
300 HPLOT 168,S2 TO 224,S2 TO 224,159 TO 168,159 TO 168,S2 :REM DRAW SECOND BAR
310 VTAB 21:HTAB 9
320 PRINT B1;
330 HTAB 25
340 PRINT B2
350 VTAB 22:HTAB 9
360 PRINT "PRODUCT 1";
370 HTAB 25
380 PRINT "PRODUCT 2"
390 VTAB 23:HTAB 5
400 PRINT "COMPARATIVE UNIT COSTS FOR ";NAM$
410 GET Z$
999 END
```

Figure 13.4   Documentation and Code for Example Program 1

MODULE DOCUMENTATION	Program: __EXC13E2__	Module: __MAIN_____ Lines: __10-999_____

Module Description:

This program uses a line graph to plot the weight of a dieter over a one month period for the Apple.

Module Function (Program Design):

1. Put the computer in graphics mode.
2. Print the bottom scale.
3. Read and plot the weight for the first day of the month.
4. Repeat for each remaining day of the month:
   a. Read the weight.
   b. Draw a line from the last weight to plot the point of the new weight.

```
10 REM EXC13E2
20 REM CLARK AND LABARRE--CHAPTER 13, EXAMPLE 2
30 REM DRAWS LINE GRAPH
40 HGR
50 PRINT "     0...0....1....1....2....2....3"
60 PRINT "DAY->1  5   0   5   0   5   0"
70 PRINT TAB(12);"FREIDA'S WEIGHT"
80 REM PLOT WEIGHTS
90 READ WEIGHT
100 HPLOT 36,(32+(175-WEIGHT)*8) :REM STARTING POINT (MULTIPLIER 8, STEP 32)
110 FOR X=42 TO 244 STEP 7        :REM EQUATE GRAPH TO CHARACTER SCALES
120    READ WEIGHT
130    HPLOT TO X,(32+175-WEIGHT)*8) :REM CONNECT TO NEXT POINT
140 NEXT X
150 GET Z$                        :REM HOLD SCREEN UNTIL USER STRIKES KEY
160 DATA 175,174,174,174,173,173,174,174,173,172
170 DATA 172,172,171,170,170,170,169,169,168,168
180 DATA 168,168,168,168,167,166,166,166,165,165
999 END
```

Figure 13.5   Documentation and Code for Example Program 2

REVIEW QUESTIONS

1. What is the general sequence of steps in a coded program using pixel graphics? (Obj. 4)
2. Describe each of the graphics modes available with the IBM PC and PCjr. (Obj. 4)
3. Describe each of the graphics modes available with the Apple. (Obj. 4)
4. For the computer you are using, which keyword is used to: (Obj. 4)
   a. Draw lines
   b. Draw circles
   c. Draw rectangles
   d. Draw just about any desired shape

VOCABULARY WORDS

The following term was introduced in this chapter:

pixel

KEYWORDS AND COMMANDS

The following keywords and commands were introduced in this chapter:

IBM:

SCREEN	CIRCLE	DRAW
PALETTE	PSET	PAINT
COLOR	LINE	

APPLE:

GR	HCOLOR	HPLOT
HGR	PLOT	DRAW
HGR2	HLIN	ROT
COLOR	VLIN	SCALE

PROGRAMS TO WRITE

Complete the appropriate documentation for each of the programs before writing the code.

Program 1

Write a program to draw two rectangles on the screen, one inside the other. Then connect the corners of the two rectangles so that it looks like you are peering into a box. The result should appear something like the following:

Program 2

Write a program that draws lines on the screen until it is interrupted. Each successively plotted point should be randomly chosen.

Program 3

A sporting goods store has its merchandise divided into several departments and would like a graph showing what proportion of its sales come from each department. There are three departments: Clothing, Shoes, and Equipment. The user should enter the sales figures for each department from the keyboard. The program should then draw a bar graph showing the sales for each department.

Program 4

Modify Program 3 so that it draws a different kind of graph. Instead of three bars, the program should produce one rectangle on the screen. The rectangle should be divided into three different sized areas representing the sales for each department.

Program 5

Write a program to produce a line graph of the sales of a store for the twelve months of a year. The sales figures should be on data lines. Here are the monthly figures for January through December, in thousands:
200,193,220,242,250,245,248,242,249,252,297,323.

Program 6

Modify Program 5 so that it shows sales of the store for two years. The figures from Program 5 are for the first year. The figures for the second year, which should be graphed in a different color, are as follows:
197,194,221,241,253,259,254,249,260,255,294,330.

CONTINUING PROJECTS

Before writing any program of the continuing projects, be sure to complete all appropriate documentation.

Project 1

Modify Project 1 from Chapter 12 so that it uses pixel graphics rather than block graphics.

Project 2

Modify Project 2 from Chapter 12 so that it uses pixel graphics rather than block graphics.

## Chapter 14

Advanced BASIC for System Development

Objectives: 1. Describe how programs may be written without line numbers.

2. Name the advantage of using decimal arithmetic.

3. Tell how independent modules are constructed and used.

4. Compare the definition and use of single-line and multiline functions.

5. List some of the ways in which additional input/output capability is being added.

6. Explain the function of advanced string handling facilities.

In the first thirteen chapters of this text, you have learned the versions of BASIC that come as "standard equipment" with the Apple II family, the Commodore 64, the IBM PC and PCjr, and the TRS-80 Models III and 4. This last chapter departs from that pattern; it does not explain a concept and then show its implementation with the four different versions of BASIC. Rather, it addresses advanced capabilities that are becoming available as more competent versions of BASIC are introduced. These abilities make programming easier and more efficient. The coding of these capabilities will vary from one advanced BASIC to another. Therefore, always refer to your reference manual for exact capabilities and syntax when using an advanced BASIC. Statements similar to those illustrated are becoming available in several versions of BASIC. The following paragraphs will introduce you to some of the better ways of writing programs with more-advanced versions of the BASIC language.

OMISSION OF LINE NUMBERS

All BASIC programs you have written to this point have used line numbers to indicate the order of steps to be performed. The line numbers were necessary in order to distinquish immediate execution statements from delayed execution (program) statements. Better versions of BASIC allow the line numbers to be omitted. This is possible under either of two circumstances. One, the version of BASIC may be compiled rather than interpreted. In this case, there is no immediate execution mode since all compiled languages function only in delayed execution mode. Second, the language may be set up as an incremental compiler. That is, small segments of code are compiled as entered, allowing them to be executed immediately thereafter by entering each name.

When line numbers are omitted, several problems must be resolved. The first is the order of execution. When using line numbers, the numbers determine the order. When the numbers are omitted, the physical sequence of the steps as entered determines the order. For example, when using line numbers you can enter:

```
400 PRINT A+B

200 A=5

300 B=10
```

The BASIC interpreter will place the lines in correct sequence, printing a result of 15 when the program is run. Entering the lines in the same order without numbers gives the following:

```
PRINT A+B

A=5

B=10
```

Running this version of the program will print a result of zero, since variables A and B have had no values assigned at the time that they are added and printed. Because of this difference, programs without line numbers must be entered with an editor that is capable of inserting new lines between existing ones whenever necessary.

A second difference that arises when line numbers are omitted is how to handle branches. With interpreted BASIC, for example, each GOSUB is followed by a line number telling the program where to branch. Without line numbers, this problem is addressed by using labels. Since a label generally consists of a word, it is easier to understand than the use of numbers. Compare the following two program segments, the first with line numbers and the second without line numbers. In the second example, note that the label is followed by a colon so BASIC can distinquish it from a variable name.

```
60 IF CATEGORY=1 THEN GOSUB 1000
1000 ' COMPUTE SALES TAX
1010 SALESTAX=MDSE*RATE
1020 RETURN

IF CATEGORY=1 THEN GOSUB COMPUTE.TAX

COMPUTE.TAX:
     SALESTAX=MDSE*RATE
     RETURN
```

Note how the use of a label rather than line numbers makes the program easier to read and adds to the internal documentation of the program.

DECIMAL ARITHMETIC

Most versions of BASIC store numeric values and do arithmetic in floating point format. For most purposes, this works fine. Occasionally, however, it results in undesired rounding problems. In financial computations, for example, a calculation might come out one cent wrong under some circumstances. When numbers are stored and arithmetic is done in a decimal format, such rounding problems don't exist. Computations using decimal arithmetic are set up by the programmer in the same way as those using floating point arithmetic. The difference is internal to the language; the most that would be required of the programmer might be specifying that certain variables are to be set up in decimal form.

INDEPENDENT MODULES

Think back for a moment to Chapter 8 dealing with searching a table to find desired data. In that chapter, we developed a search module that can be written into each program that needs to use it. In other words, if we have 15 programs that search tables for data, the module must be copied into each of the 15 programs. The use of a language allowing the use of independent modules eliminates this copying need. That is, the search module is entered one time. Then any program that needs it may call on it. Assume that we want to call the module by the name SEARCH. Here is how it can be structured to function as an independent module.

    1. Code the SEARCH program module. In coding the module, it must be given a name and a parameter list. In looking at the following

example, remember that the search routine needs to know the name of the table to search and the item for which to search; these items are the parameters. Here is how the module might look. The internal details are omitted to better show the structure; the actual program lines look the same as when the routine was first written in Chapter 8.

```
SUB SEARCH(LOOKIN,FIND,ROW)
ROW=0
      WHILE LOOKIN(ROW)<>FIND
            ROW=ROW+1
      WEND
END SUB
```

In this example, the keyword SUB indicates the begining of the subprogram. SEARCH is the name of the subprogram being written. The parameters function as follows: LOOKIN indicates the name of the table to be searched. FIND is the data to be located. When the data is located, its row number will be placed in the variable designated by ROW. The END SUB statement indicates the end of the subprogram.

2. Compile the SEARCH module and store it in a module library on the disk. The library may contain a number of different program modules, either related or unrelated to each other.
3. Call the SEARCH module from any program that may need to use it, without having to copy the module into the program. Assume that we have a program that needs to search a table called IDS to find a student whose number is stored in variable STUNUM. The row in which the name is found is to be placed in variable ROW. In the program, a CALL statement is used to bring the subprogram into use.

```
CALL SEARCH(IDS,STUNUM,ROW)
```

The keyword CALL is followed by the name of the subprogram to use. The variables to be used are included inside parentheses. Note that the actual variables used in calling the subprogram do not have to be the same ones used when coding the subprogram. This allows the subprogram to be used in many different programs regardless of the names of the variables the different programs are using.

MULTILINE FUNCTIONS

As preparation for understanding multiline functions, refresh your memory about single-line functions as you have used them. Suppose that we want to define a function to calculate the area of a rectangle. A program defining and using such a function might look as follows:

```
DEF FNAREAREC(L,W)=L*W
INPUT "WHAT IS THE LENGTH OF THE RECTANGLE";LENGTH
INPUT "WHAT IS THE WIDTH OF THE RECTANGLE ";WIDTH
PRINT "THE AREA OF THE RECTANGLE IS ";FNAREAREC(LENGTH,WIDTH)
```

The function in this example works nicely. However, suppose you need a function that will decide which of three entered numbers is the smallest. This cannot be done with just a simple equation on one line, so a multiline function may be used. Here is an example of how it might be done:

```
DEF FNMINIMUM(A,B,C)
    SMALLEST=A
    IF B<SMALLEST THEN SMALLEST=B
    IF C<SMALLEST THEN SMALLEST=C
    FNMINIMUM=SMALLEST
END DEF

INPUT"ENTER THREE NUMBERS";N1,N2,N3
PRINT "THE SMALLEST OF YOUR NUMBERS IS ";FNMINIMUM(N1,N2,N3)
```

Since the function being defined required more than one line, it was necessary to designate the ending point of the definition. This was done with the END DEF statement. Note also that it was necessary to use a let statement to assign the result of the function steps to the name of the function.

ADDITIONAL INPUT/OUTPUT CAPABILITY

Advanced versions of BASIC generally include additional input and output capability. Here are some of the possible additions.

Device-Independent Input and Output

In standard BASIC, the PRINT statement usually refers to the display, and the INPUT statement refers to the keyboard. Some standard BASICs also use these statements to refer to other devices. In device-independent input and output, a program can get input from any device or send output to any device without having to recode the program. In other words, on one program run, a program could get its input from the keyboard. While on another run, it could get its input from a file on disk. On one run, output could go to the display. While on another, it could be sent to the printer. As another example, the output produced by one program could be sent as input to another program.

Additional File Types

In this text you learned about index files and creating your own index. Some advanced BASICs have built-in capability to handle indexed files. In other words, they can set up the indexes without using any coding effort on the part of the programmer.

A Richer Collection of File Handling Keywords

With some advanced BASICs, the number of keywords dealing with file handling has been increased significantly. This helps the programmer do precisely what is needed by the program rather than having to contend with limitations of the file handling system.

ADVANCED STRING FUNCTIONS

String-handling capability is one of the strongest points of some standard versions of BASIC. This powerhouse feature is further enhanced by some newer versions. Here are some of the possible new keywords you may find.

LCASE$ and UCASE$

These two complementary keywords change uppercase letters to lower-case and vice versa. When a user may be entering input in either uppercase or lowercase, use of one of these functions can make checking for correct input much easier.

TRIM$, LTRIM$, and RTRIM$

These three functions remove leading and trailing blanks from data. TRIM$ removes leading and trailing blanks, while LTRIM$ and RTRIM$ only remove the blanks from one end of the data.

MATCH

MATCH is a powerful adaptation of the INSTR function with which you may already be familiar. Where INSTR has to look for particular characters, MATCH can look for patterns. For example, use of a number sign will tell MATCH to find any digit from 0-9.

REVIEW QUESTIONS

1. How can programs be written without line numbers? (Obj. 1)
2. Why is it preferable to use decimal arithmetic under some circumstances? (Obj. 2)
3. How can independent modules be constructed and used? (Obj. 3)
4. What are multiline functions? Under what circumstances are they preferable to single-line functions? (Obj. 4)
5. How is input/output capability being improved? (Obj. 5)
6. What are some of the increased string-handling capabilities of newer BASICs? (Obj. 6)

Glossary

ACTIVITY
The number of transactions processed within a file or the number of updates made to a file.   page 229

ALTERNATE ACTION
Often referred to as a case structure with several alternatives.   page 43

APPLICATION SYSTEM
A collection of several programs needed to carry out the requirements for one application.   page 54

ARITHMETIC OPERATORS
Mathematical symbols used in equations.   page 22

ARRAY
A table dimensioned to a certain size.   page 72

ASCENDING ORDER
Data arranged from smallest to largest.   page 185

AUDIT FILE
A chronological listing of all activities processed within a file.   page 233

AUDIT REPORT
A hard copy report of the activities processed within a file.   page 235

BAR GRAPH
A graph made of horizontal or vertical bars, usually showing comparisons between items.   page 302

BATCH PROCESSING
A file processing technique where all data is stored before any processing occurs.   page 73

BINARY SEARCH
An algorithm for searching an ordered table. The quantity of items under consideration is halved on each pass through the sort.   page 214

BLOCK GRAPHICS
A method of producing graphics by printing special chracters at designated locations on the screen.   page 301

BUFFER
A temporary memory location within main memory used to store data prior to writing to a file. It may also be used to temporarily store data retrieved from a file.   page 112

CASE
A program logic structure where several alternative actions are available.   page 43

CATENATE
To connect together two or more items of string data.   page 175

CATENATION
The connection of two or more data items to form a longer string.   page 77

CODING
Writing an algorithm in a computer language.   page 13

COMPILER
A program that translates a program written in a high-level language into machine language.   page 2

CONCATENATION
Connecting data items together. Also known as catenation.   page 77

CONDITIONAL BRANCH
A GOTO statement used with an IF ... THEN statement so that program control may or may not be transferred depending upon a condition.   page 42

CONSTANT
An actual number used for processing by the computer.   page 7

COUNTER
A variable used to store the number of occurrences or items processed or number of repetitions through a loop.   page 50

DATA BASE SYSTEM
A set of programs designed for storage, selection, and retrieval of data items.   page 212

DATA MODIFICATION
A technique of using either the left, middle, or right portion of the data stored in a variable.   page 74

DEBUG
The process of eliminating syntax errors within the program.   page 20

DELAYED REPLACEMENT
A sorting algorithm that finds the smallest item and places it first in the table, repeating the process on successive locations in the table until all items are in order.   page 186

DESCENDING ORDER
Data arranged from largest to smallest.   page 185

DETAIL FILE
A file used to store information related to the master file.   page 231

DIGIT EXTRACTION METHOD
A hashing scheme used to determine record numbers in a relative file   page 264
processing system.

DIMENSIONING
A procedure for setting the size of a table within the computer's memory.   page 82

DIRECT CURSOR POSITIONING
Using a BASIC statement to locate the cursor at any desired row and   page 142
column.

DIRECT ORGANIZATION
A file organization which enables the direct access of records without   page 259
processing any other records.

EXCEPTION REPORT
A report generated within a file processing system which would identify   page 235
situations that were not common to the processing of records.

FIELD
Separate data items in a record.   page 104

FILE
A collection of records.   page 104

FILE PROCESSING SYSTEM
An application program system which requires many programs to use the   page 229
same file or collection of files.

FILE SIZE
The volume of records stored in a file.   page 229

FILTER
A program module that screens certain characters of input and takes the   page 175
action desired by the programmer.

FLOATING DOLLAR SIGN
An editing feature where the dollar sign moves to the right as far as   page 30
necessary to be printed next to the most significant digit.

FOLDING
A hashing scheme used with relative file organization to permit direct   page 264
access to a record.

FUNCTION
A keyword used to perform a predetermined operation.   page 71

GRAPH
A pictorial representation of data.   page 302

GRAPHICS
Relating to a pictorial representation.   page 300

HARDCOPY
A paper copy of output from the computer.   page 36

HASHING SCHEME
A technique used to arrive at record numbers for records stored in a relative file. — page 259

HIERARCHY CHART
A diagram showing the relationship of the main module to the sub-modules in a program. — page 5

HIGH-LEVEL LANGUAGE
A computer language written in English-like instructions that must be translated into machine language prior to execution on the computer. — page 2

HIGHLIGHTED
Emphasized in some way, such as by inverse video or the use of a different color. — page 142

HIGH-RESOLUTION GRAPHICS MODE
A screen mode in which a large number of pixels is available for graphics. — page 146

HISTORY FILE
A file used to store all activities related to a specific record. — page 233

INDEXED FILE
A file accessed via an indexing routine. — page 281

INFINITE LOOP
A loop which creates a repetition of computer instructions without a logical exit. — page 18

INPUT DATA
Data input via a keyboard, DATA statement, or data file. — page 2

INTERNAL DOCUMENTATION
Remarks within the coded program designed to help the reader better understand the logic being performed. — page 15

INTERPRETER
A program that translates a program written in a high-level language into machine language. — page 2

INVERSE VIDEO
Reversed colors on the screen, such as black on white rather than the normal white on black. — page 142

ITERATION
A repetition of processing steps created by forming a loop. — page 43

KEYWORDS
English words in BASIC having a special meaning to the translator program. — page 3

LEADING ZERO
Zeros printed to the left of the most significant digit in a numeric value. — page 29

LINE GRAPH
A graph made of lines connecting points on the screen. — page 304

LINKED FILE
A file whose records are connected through the use of pointers.   page 259

LITERAL
A value enclosed in quotation marks.   page 7

LOOP
A series of statements repeated a number of times.   page 43

MACHINE LANGUAGE
A computer language generated as a result of translation of a high-level   page 2
language.

MASTER FILE
A file containing vital information which is mostly permanent.   page 230

MATRIX
A table of data elements. Often referred to as either a table or an array.   page 72

MEDIUM-RESOLUTION GRAPHICS MODE
A graphics mode in which a moderate number of pixels is available.   page 146

MODE
A method of operating, such as text or graphics.   page 144

MODULE
A series of logic steps to be performed as a segment of a program.   page 5

MODULE DOCUMENTATION SHEET
A form describing in detail the operation of a part or module of the   page 8
program.

MULTIPLE INDEX
An indexing system utilizing more than one index to permit access to   page 281
relative files.

NESTING
A loop totally contained within another loop. Often referred to as a   page 44
nested loop.

NULL
A nothing character designated by an ASCII code of zero.   page 82

NUMERIC FUNCTION
Used to perform an operation on numeric values.   page 71

NUMERIC VARIABLE
A variable containing a numeric value.   page 21

ONE-DIMENSIONAL TABLE
A table containing either rows or columns but not both.   page 71

OUTPUT
Processed information that may be displayed on a screen, printer, or may   page 2
be stored for future use.

PIXEL
A picture element, one dot on the screen.   page 318

POINTER
A field in a record that identifies the location of another record.   page 105

POINTER-BASED SORT
A sort algorithm that does not physically move the data being sorted.   page 197

PRIME AREA
The main area of a linked file where the first record with a record key is   page 259
stored.

PRIME NUMBER/REMAINDER DIVISION PROCEDURE
A hashing scheme used to determine record numbers for records stored in   page 262
a relative file.

PROGRAM
A series of high-level or machine language instructions designed to direct   page 2
the computer while processing data.

PROMPTS
A technique of printing instructions for the user of an interactive   page 73
program.

PSEUDOCODE
English-like statements that identify the steps to be completed in   page 8
performing logic.

RANDOM DATA FILES
Files permitting the user to read or write a record directly. Often referred   page 106
to as relative files.

RECORD
A collection of fields of data to be stored in a file.   page 104

RELATED FILE
A file containing information concerning either the master file or detail   page 231
file.

RELATIONAL OPERATOR
Symbols used in a condition which allows the computer to compare   page 45
variables or variables and constants.

RELATIVE RECORD NUMBER
A number used to identify a record location within a relative file.   page 259

REPETITION
A technique of processing the logic statements over and over several   page 43
times.

RESERVED WORD
A word with a specific meaning to the translator program; it may not be   page 21
used as a variable name.

REVERSE VIDEO
A reversal of the normal screen colors, such as black on white rather than   page 142
white on black.

SCROLLING
> The movement of data up and off the screen as new data is printed at the bottom of the screen.
> page 149

SELECTION
> A logic structure which requires the comparison of two variables to determine which branch is to be made.
> page 42

SEQUENCE
> A logic structure where the processing of instructions takes place one after another without interruption.
> page 41

SEQUENTIAL SEARCH
> A search algorithm that looks for an item in a table by starting at the beginning of the table and looking for each item in turn.
> page 213

SHELL-METZNER SORT
> A fast sorting algorithm named for its developers.
> page 189

SIZING
> A process of determining how many records will be stored within a file.
> page 259

SOURCE DOCUMENT
> A document that would be used to obtain input data.
> page 4

STATIC
> Descriptions of a file with a low volume of additions and deletions.
> page 230

STRING VARIABLE
> An alphanumeric variable containing either alphabetic or numeric information.
> page 21

STUBBING IN
> A technique of writing minimum code which will allow the user to test the branching instructions in the main module.
> page 20

SUBMODULE
> A subroutine containing logic that performs a specific function.
> page 5

SUBROUTINE
> A submodule containing logic designed to perform a specific function.
> page 5

SUBSCRIPT
> A numeric value which identifies the row or column of an element in a table.
> page 72

SYNONYM
> A duplicate record in a linked file.
> page 259

SYNTAX
> The structure of the language.
> page 15

SYNTAX ERRORS
> Mistakes in the structure of the language.
> page 34

TABLE
> A variable that may store more than one item of data at a time. Often referred to as an array.
> page 71

Quick Reference Guide to Commonly Used Keywords

Note: Keywords that vary on different computers and are unique to a particular computer are indicated in the computer column. Their usage can be checked on the referenced page. Computers will be indicated as (A)pple, (C)ommodore, (I)BM, and (T)RS-80. If the keyword is for the TRS-80 Model III only, it will be indicated as TIII. If the keyword is for the TRS-80 Model 4 only, it will be indicated as T4. It is assumed that all statements in the example column are preceded by line numbers. Each keyword is followed by a brief definition. Refer to the reference manual of your computer for keywords not included in this chart.

Keyword	Example	Page	Computer
ABS	ABS(x) Returns the absolute value of x.	81	A,C,I,T
ALL	CHAIN ALL An option that causes all variables in one program to be passed to another program.	55	I,T4
APPEND	Varies with computer. Allows data to be added to existing files.	116	A,C,I

ASC	PRINT ASC(Z$) Returns ASCII code of first character in string.	94	A,C,I,T
AUTO	AUTO 10,100 Generates a line number automatically after each time the ENTER/RETURN is pressed.	34	I,T
CHAIN	CHAIN 'PROG1' Used to transfer control to another program.	54	I,T
CHR$	Y$=CHR$(15) Returns the character equivalent of an ASCII number.	95	A,C,I,T
CIRCLE	CIRCLE(100,50),25 Draws a circle at x and y coordinates using the specified diameter.	326	I
CLEAR	CLEAR 2000 Varies with computer.	16	A,I,T
CLOSE	Varies with computer. Closes data files.	113	A,I,T
CLS	CLS Clears the screen.	17	I,T
COLOR	COLOR 2,1 (IBM) COLOR=3 (Apple) Used to set text and/or graphics color.	146, 323	A,I
COMMON	COMMON A$,B Used in conjunction with CHAIN to pass specific variables.	55	I,T
COS	A=COS(ANGLEX) Returns the cosine of angle x.	81	A,C,I,T
CTRL-0	PRINT 'CTRL-0' Turns off the reverse video.	159	C
CTRL-9	PRINT 'CTRL-9' Turns on the reverse video.	159	C

CVD	CVD(N$) Converts string variable types to numeric variable types.	128	I,T
CVI	CVI(N$) Converts string variables to integer variable types.	128	I,T
CVS	CVS(N$) Converts string variables to single precision variables.	128	I,T
DATA	DATA 10,TOM Holds data for access by a READ statement.	23	A,C,I,T
DEFDBL	DEFDBL B Declares a variable type as double precision.	79	I,T
DEF FN	DEF FNAREA=L*W*H Define and name a function.	80	A,C,I,T
DEFINT	DEFINT A Declares a variable type as integer.	79	I,T
DELETE	DELETE 40 Used to delete a line or a file.	35, 115	A,I,T
DIM	DIM A$(15) Dimensions a table.	82	A,C,I,T
DRAW	DRAW C$ (IBM) DRAW 2 AT 50,40 (Apple) Draws a predefined shape on the screen.	329	A,I
END	END Terminates processing.	19	A,C,I,T
EOF	IF EOF(1) THEN 2999 Used to check for the end of a sequential file.	113	I,T
EXP	X=EXP(Y) Calculates the exponential function of Y.	81	A,C,I,T
FLASH	FLASH Makes subsequently printed characters flash on and off.	155	A

FOR ... NEXT	FOR A = 1 TO 10 NEXT A Creates a FOR ... NEXT loop and establishes limits.	49	A,C,I,T
GET	Varies with computer.	89	A,C,I,T
GET #	GET #1,10 Reads the designated random record from the number file.	126	I,T
GOSUB	GOSUB 1000 Branches to a subroutine.	18	A,C,I,T
GOTO	GOTO 10 Branches unconditionally to a specific line number.	181, 118	A,C,I,T
GR	GR Switches to low-resolution graphics mode.	335	A
HCOLOR	HCOLOR = 4 Sets high-resolution graphics color.	336	A
HGR	HGR Switches to high-resolution graphics mode.	335	A
HGR2	HGR2 Switches to high-resolution graphics on Apple with no lines reserved for text.	335	A
HLIN	HLIN 5,20 AT 4 Draws a horizontal line in low- resolution graphics.	338	A
HPLOT	HPLOT x,y Turns on high-resolution pixels; also can draw lines.	339	A
HTAB	HTAB 15 Moves printing point to specified horizontal column.	154	A
IF ... THEN	IF A = B THEN 1000 A decision is made based upon a true/false condition.	45	A,C,I,T

IF ... THEN ... ELSE	IF A=B THEN 1000 ELSE 2000 A branch to one specific statement or another is completed based upon a true/false condition.	46	I,T
INKEY$	C$=INKEY$ Reads a character from the keyboard.	89	I,T
INPUT	INPUT 'ENTER YOUR NAME'; NAM$ Allows interactive data entry during execution.	87	A,C,I,T
INPUT$	C$=INPUT$(2) Reads a given number of characters from the keyboard.	90	I,T4
INPUT#	INPUT#1, A,B$ Reads items from disk files and assigns them to variables.	112	C,I,T
INSTR	A=INSTR(B$,' ') Searches for the first occurrence of a string and returns to the position at which it is found.	96	I,T
INT	PRINT INT(22.22) Returns the largest integer that is less than or equal to a given value.	81	A,C,I,T
INVERSE	INVERSE Switches to reverse video.	155	A
LEFT$	PRINT LEFT$(Z$,3) Returns the given number of left-most characters.	91	A,C,I,T
LEN	Varies with computer; used to return a number of characters in a string or to designate a number of characters in a record.	93	A,C,I,T
LET	LET A=20 Assigns the value of an expression to variables.	22	A,C,I,T

LINE	LINE(15,5)-(100,90) Draws a line between two specified points. Can also draw a box.	324	I
LINE INPUT	LINE INPUT NAM$ Allows input from keyboard to include blanks and punctuation.	88	I,T
LIST	LIST 10-100 Used to list some or all program statements.	34	A,C,I,T
LLIST	LLIST 10-1000 Used to list some or all program statements on paper.	36	I,T
LOAD	LOAD 'PROG1' (IBM, TRS- 80) LOAD PROG1 (Apple) LOAD 'PROG1',8 (Commodore) Loads a file from disk storage into memory.	35	A,C,I,T
LOCATE	LOCATE 12,15 Positions cursor to the indicated row and column.	145	I
LOF	X=LOF(1) Returns the length of a random file.	128	I,T
LOG	X=LOG(y) Returns the natural logarithm of value y.	81	A,C,I,T
LPRINT	LPRINT 'PRINT ON PAPER' Causes output to be printed on paper.	36	I,T
LSET	LSET RB$=X$ Places data in a random file buffer.	125	I,T
MID$	MID$(X$,2,4) Returns the requested part of a given string.	92	A,C,I,T
MKD$	LSET A$=MKD$(AMT) Makes a double precision number ready to write on disk.	127	I,T

MKI$	LSET A$ = MKI$(AMT) Makes an integer number ready to write on disk.	127	I,T
MKS$	LSET A$ = MKS$(AMT) Makes a single precision number ready to write to disk.	127	I,T
NAME	NAME 'A:DATAFILE:A$ 'A:FILE2' Renames a file to a new name.	236	I,T
NEW	NEW Deletes the current program in memory.	33	A,C,I,T
NORMAL	NORMAL Cancels INVERSE and FLASH.	155	A
ONERR or ON ERROR	ONERR GOTO 1000 Transfers control when error is detected.	117	A,I,T
ON ... GOSUB	ON NUMBER GOSUB 1000,2000,3000 Branches to one of several specified line numbers depending on the value of the variable.	48	A,C,I,T
ON ... GOTO	ON NUMBER GOTO 1000,2000,3000 Branches to one of several specified line numbers depending on the value of the variable.	48	A,C,I,T
ON KEY	ON KEY(N) GOSUB Sets up a line number for BASIC to branch to when a specific function key is struck.	49	I
OPEN	Varies with computer. Opens data files on disk.	111	A,C,I,T
OPTION BASE	OPTION BASE 1 Sets the minimum value for a table subscript at 1	82	I,T

PAINT	PAINT(50,20),2 Paints shapes in which x and y fall using the specified color.	331	I
PALETTE	PALETTE 2,3 Assigns a color to a position in the palette.	322	I
PEEK	PEEK(222) Returns the contents of specified memory location.	118	A,C,I,T
PLOT	PLOT 15,20 Turns on a pixel in low-resolution graphics.	337	A
POKE	POKE 1024,65 Places a character in memory. Effects vary tremendously depending on where the character is placed.	152	A,C,I,T
PRINT	PRINT 'THIS IS A LITERAL' Displays characters on the screen.	17	A,C,I,T
PRINT USING	PRINT USING '$#,###.##';12.33 Prints numbers using specified format.	28	I,T
PRINT@	PRINT@57,A$ Positions the cursor to the specified screen location.	151	T
PRINT#	PRINT #1,A,B$ Writes data sequentially to a file.	112	C,I,T
PR#0	PR#0 Designates the output that is to go to the screen.	36	A
PR#1	PR#1 Turns on the printer mode to receive output.	36	A
PSET	PSET(x,y),2 Turns on one pixel.	324	I

PUT#	PUT#1,10 Writes a record to the designated position of a random file.	125	I,T
READ	READ A,B$ Reads data from a DATA statement.	23, 117	A,C,I,T
REM	REM Allows explanatory remarks.	16	A,C,I,T
RESTORE	RESTORE Resets the pointer to the beginning of the DATA statements.	23	A,C,I,T
RETURN	RETURN Ends a subroutine and returns to the statement following GOSUB.	19	A,C,I,T
RIGHT$	PRINT RIGHT$(B$,3) Returns the right-most characters of a string.	91	A,C,I,T
ROT	ROT=12 Specifies the orientation of an object to be drawn with DRAW.	343	A
RND	Varies with computer. Returns a random number.	81	A,C,I,T
RSET	RSET A$=B$ Right justifies data set to the random buffer.	125	I,T
RUN	RUN Begins execution of a program.	34	A,C,I,T
SAVE	SAVE 'PROG1' (IBM and TRS-80) SAVE PROG1 (Apple) SAVE 'PROG1',8 (Commodore) Causes the program in memory to be stored on disk.	35	A,C,I,T

SCALE	SCALE=5 Specifies the size of an object to be drawn with DRAW.	343	A
SCREEN	SCREEN 1 Sets screen mode to text or graphics.	145, 321	I
SIN	PRINT SIN(X) Calculates the trigonometric sine function.	81	A,C,I,T
SPACE$	A$=SPACE$(5) Returns a string of the specified number of spaces.	97	I
SPC	PRINT SPC(15);'START' Prints the specified number of spaces.	28	A,C,I,T
SQR	PRINT SQR(X) Returns the square root of the argument.	81	A,C,I,T
STATUS	IF STATUS=64 THEN 110 Returns the status of the last input/output operation.	121	C
STEP	FOR X=1 TO 10 STEP 2 Specifies the increment in a FOR ... NEXT loop.	50	A,C,I,T
STR$	N$ STR$(20) Returns a string representation of a specified value.	95	A,C,I,T
STRING$	PRINT STRING$(80,'-') Produces the specified number of character symbols.	97	I,T
SWAP	SWAP A,B Exchanges the value of the two variables.	86	I,T4
TAB	PRINT TAB(15);'START' Tabs print position to a specified position.	26	A,C,I,T
TAN	PRINT TAN(X) Returns the trigonometric tangent of the argument.	81	A,C,I,T

WHILE ... WEND	WHILE N$<>'Y' WEND Sets up a loop which will continue while N$ is not equal to 'Y'.	53	I,T4
WIDTH	WIDTH 40 Sets the output line width.	144	I
WRITE#	WRITE #1,A,C,B$ Writes variables to a sequential file, using quotes and commas.	112	I,T4
VAL	PRINT VAL('-2') Returns the numerical value of a string.	96	A,C,I,T
VIEW	VIEW (0,0)-(100,50) Allows definition of windows on the screen.	148	I
VLIN	VLIN 2,9 AT 3 Draws a low-resolution vertical line.	338	A
VTAB	VTAB 8 Positions the cursor to the designated row of the screen.	154	A

ASCII Code

Inside the computer, each character is stored as a numeric code. The code is known as the American Standard Code for Information Interchange, or ASCII. There are 128 characters represented by the code, using code numbers of 0-127. Some computers use additional codes.

Codes 0-31 are known as control codes. Most of them do not have separate keys on the keyboard and do not appear on the screen when printed. If your computer has a control key (CTRL), the control codes can be produced by holding down that key while striking a regular character key. The characters represented by the codes may be printed by using the CHR$ function, such as PRINT CHR$(7). Codes used for the same purpose by most computers are described. Others are simply listed. Since the effects of control codes vary widely from one computer to another, check the reference manual for your computer.

ASCII CONTROL CHARACTERS

Code	Name	Control Key	Description
0		@	
1		A	
2		B	
3		C	
4		D	
5		E	
6		F	
7	BEL	G	Bell. On computers that can "beep," printing ASCII code 7 will produce the sound. For example, a BASIC statement of PRINT CHR$(7) may be used.
8	BS	H	Backspace. In addition to being produced by striking the H key while holding down the CTRL key, code 8 is produced by the backspace key.

Code	Name	Control Key	Description
9	HT	I	Horizontal tab. On computers with a TAB function, printing of this code moves the cursor to the next tab stop. Produced also by the TAB key, if present.
10	LF	J	Line feed. When printed, causes the cursor to move to the next line on the screen. It does not cause the cursor to return to the left side of the screen.
11		K	
12	FF	L	Form feed. With many printers, printing of this code causes the paper to move to the top of the next page.
13	CR	M	Return. Printing of the return code causes the cursor to move to the left side of the screen.
14		N	
15		O	
16		P	
17		Q	
18		R	
19		S	
20		T	
21		U	
22		V	
23		W	
24		X	
25		Y	
26		Z	
27	ESC	Varies	Escape. On computers with an escape key (ESC), this code is produced when that key is struck. The response of the computer to this key depends on the software being used.
28			
29			
30			
31			

ASCII CHARACTER CODES

The character codes are used for characters that appear on the screen when printed. Each code is produced by a key on the keyboard. Printing the CHR$ function of one of the codes is the same as printing the character inside quotation marks. For example, PRINT 'A' and PRINT CHR$(65) will both print the letter A on the screen. The codes for the letters and numerals are the same for all computers using the ASCII code. However, there is some variation from one machine to another on the codes for some of the symbols. For this reason, you should check the reference manual for your machine if using the codes for symbols. Here are the codes:

Code	Character	Code	Character	Code	Character
32	Space	64	@	96	`
33	!	65	A	97	a
34	'	66	B	98	b
35	#	67	C	99	c
36	$	68	D	100	d
37	%	69	E	101	e
38	&	70	F	102	f
39	'	71	G	103	g
40	(	72	H	104	h
41	)	73	I	105	i
42	*	74	J	106	j
43	+	75	K	107	k
44	,	76	L	108	l
45	- (hyphen)	77	M	109	m
46	.	78	N	110	n
47	/	79	O	111	o
48	0	80	P	112	p
49	1	81	Q	113	q
50	2	82	R	114	r
51	3	83	S	115	s
52	4	84	T	116	t
53	5	85	U	117	u
54	6	86	V	118	v
55	7	87	W	119	w
56	8	88	X	120	x
57	9	89	Y	121	y
58	:	90	Z	122	z
59	;	91	[	123	{
60	<	92	/	124	—
61	=	93	]	125	}
62	>	94		126	~
63	?	95	__ (underscore)	127	Delete

Flowcharting

Objectives:
1. Define flowcharting.
2. Explain the uses of various symbols in flowcharting.
3. Explain how to use flowcharting to document the control structures commonly used in programming.
4. List the advantages and disadvantages of using flowcharting.

WHAT IS FLOWCHARTING?

Some program designers find it convenient to use flowcharting to plan and document their programs. Flowcharting is a method of using pictorial representations to show the design of a program. Assume you wish to design a program to calculate sales tax on an item. The steps of the program design are listed below.

1. Assign the price of the item and the tax rate to variables.
2. Display the price.
3. Display the rate.
4. Calculate and display the sales tax.
5. End of problem.

To show the design of a program in flowchart form, each step of the program is placed inside a symbol that indicates what kind of action is taking place at each step. Arrows known as flowlines are used to connect the different steps. The steps generally go from top to bottom and left to right, though there can be exceptions.

At the simplest level, a rectangle can be used for all sequential steps. Since all steps of the program design we are currently working with are sequential, the rectangular symbol is all that will be required. Study Figure C-1 to see how the steps can be shown. Note that each step has simply been placed inside a rectangle.

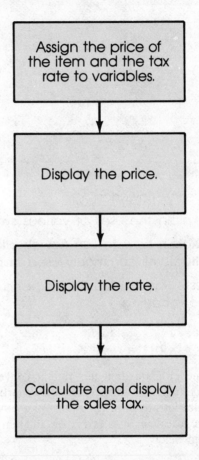

Figure C-1   Flowchart of a Sequential Program

SYMBOLS USED IN FLOWCHARTING

There are many symbols that can be used in flowcharting. However, the logic of just about any program can be shown by using only three symbols. Using a small number of symbols helps make the production of flowcharts much easier. Study Figure C-2, which shows the commonly used symbols and describes their use.

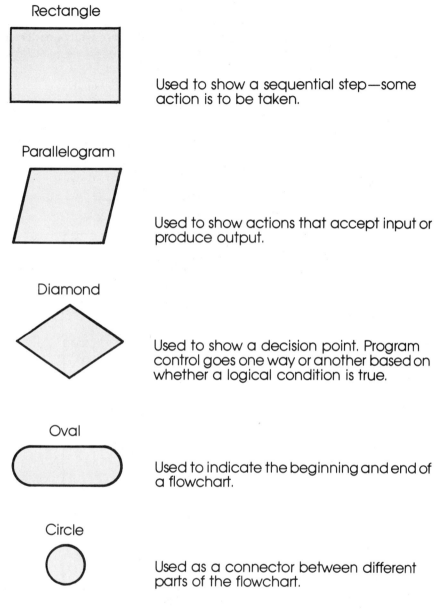

Rectangle

Used to show a sequential step—some action is to be taken.

Parallelogram

Used to show actions that accept input or produce output.

Diamond

Used to show a decision point. Program control goes one way or another based on whether a logical condition is true.

Oval

Used to indicate the beginning and end of a flowchart.

Circle

Used as a connector between different parts of the flowchart.

Figure C-2   Commonly Used Flowcharting Symbols

Use of the Rectangle for Steps in Processing

In the previous section, you became familiar with the rectangle that can be used to indicate all sequential steps in a program. When desired, the rectangle may be used to show input and output as well as computations. This is true in spite of the fact that a separate symbol has been designated for input and output operations.

Use of the Oval for Beginning and Ending the Flowchart

The oval may be used to indicate both the beginning and ending points of a flowchart. Look at Figure C-3 to see how the symbol has been added to the flowchart from Figure C-1.

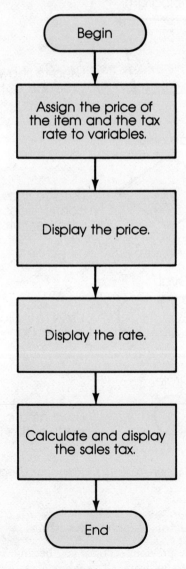

Figure C-3   Flowchart of a Sequential Program

Use of the Parallelogram for Input and Output

Now, look at how the flowchart from Figure C-3 can be changed to include the symbol used for output. This time, the steps that produce output will be in parallelograms. Look at the result in Figure C-4. Note that the original *calculate and display the sales tax* step from Figure C-3 has to be divided into two steps this time, since it does a computation as well as produces output.

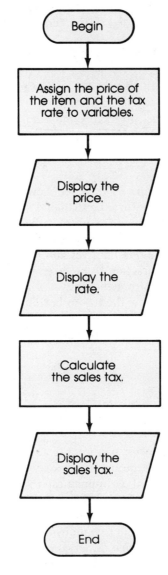

Figure C-4   Flowchart Showing Use of the Output Symbol

Use of the Diamond for Decisions

The diamond symbol is used whenever a decision must be made based on some logical condition. Assume you wish to design a program to calculate and print the gross pay for several employees. The steps of the program design are listed below:

1. Clear space for character storage (required for TRS-80 Model III).
2. Print the headings at the top of the report.
3. Read the employee's name, the hours worked, and the rate of pay.
4. Check to see if the terminator was read. If it was, go to the end statement.
5. Calculate the gross pay by multiplying the hours worked by the rate of pay.
6. Print the employee name, the hours worked, the rate of pay, and the gross pay.
7. Go back to step 3 and read the next record.
8. End.

Study Figure C-5 to see how the steps have been represented in a flowchart. Note that the diamond is used to represent step 4 of the program design. At this point, control either continues or is transferred to the end statement, depending on whether the terminator was read. The two possible answers to the question, yes and no, are written at points of the diamond to indicate the direction to be taken depending on the answer. The arrows then point the way from the answer. One thing that we have done to make the flow better follow the top to bottom guideline, is to place the end statement at the bottom of the flowchart. It could have been placed at the right of the decision symbol, though such a location would not be preferred.

Use of the Connector

The connector symbol, the circle, is used to connect different parts of a flowchart. This becomes necessary whenever the chart is too large for one page, or when it is impractical to draw a flow line in the required path. Connectors are labeled to show the connection; the label may be either alphabetic or numeric. Suppose we have a payroll program that calculates both hourly pay and commissions. The methods for doing these obviously vary and can become rather complex. Therefore, the flowchart for computing hourly pay might consume one page, while the flowchart for computing commissions might consume another page. A connection could be made to

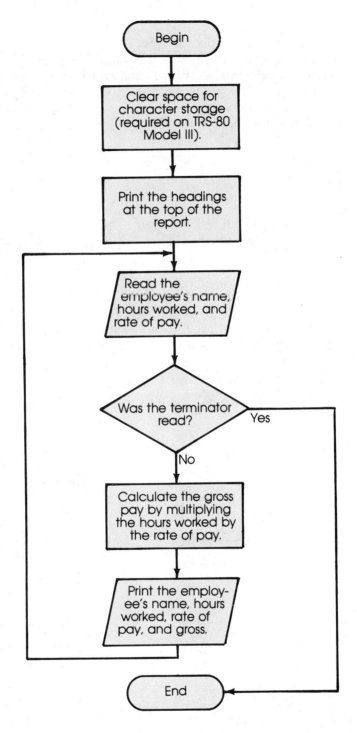

Figure C-5   Illustration of the Operation of a Decision Statement

either page based on the pay type. Figure C-6 shows the departure for the connections between the flowchart sections. This shows that if the pay type is hourly, control should go to the connector labeled as A, which will be on another page. If the pay type is commission, control will go to the connector labeled B, which will also be on another page. Note that the beginning of the flowchart is not shown.

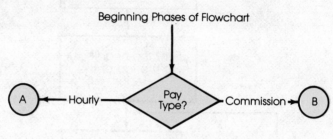

Figure C-6   Use of "Departure" Connectors

On the additional pages, each flowchart will begin with a circle containing the appropriate alphabet letter—either A or B. Figure C-7 shows how those flowcharts will look.

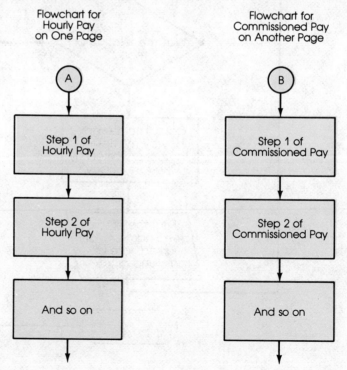

Figure C-7   Flowcharts Beginning With "Continuation" Connectors

USING FLOWCHARTS TO DOCUMENT PROGRAM DESIGN

There are four main design structures with which all programs may be written. Known as control structures, they are: (1) sequential steps, (2) alternate actions (IF . . . THEN . . . ELSE), (3) case (also known as selection), and (4) iteration. When drawing flowcharts, only these structures should be used. On the flowchart, each structure should be complete in itself, with one way to get in the structure and one way out of the structure. In other words, on a flowchart you should be able to identify everything as one of these four structures. If you encircled each structure, there should be only one flow line going into the box and one flowline coming from the box. This will help ensure the principles of structured programming are followed. The following sections illustrate how to flowchart each of the control structures.

Sequential Steps Structure

Sequential steps are shown in a flowchart as one symbol after another. The steps may indicate the beginning of a program, a computation or other action to take, an input step, an output step, or the end of a program. Figure C-8 indicates the general form of sequential steps in a flowchart.

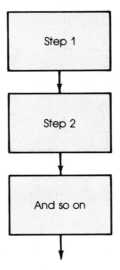

Figure C-8   Sequential Control Structure

Alternate Actions Structure

When alternate actions are to be taken based on a logical comparison, it is very easy to produce flowcharts that are difficult to follow. However, by using the pattern suggested here, flowcharts will be easier to construct and follow.

The most frequently occurring difficulty in flowcharting alternate actions is that of where to place the two different actions. That can be solved by, in effect, making two distinct flowcharts, one for each action. Then a decision is made as to which to follow, with the flowlines coming back together at the end of the actions. This maintains the idea of one way into and one way out of each control structure. Study Figure C-9 for an example of alternate actions to be taken. Note that the choices need not contain the same number of steps.

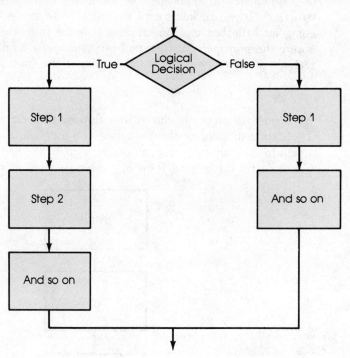

Figure C-9   General Form for Alternate Action Structure

In BASIC, an alternate action structure is most frequently implemented with an IF...THEN...ELSE statement. The logical condition is given after the word IF. The action to be taken if the logical condition is true is written after the word THEN; the action to be taken if the condition is false is written after the word ELSE. The actions can be contained in subroutines if they are several steps long.

Sometimes, an action is to be taken if a logical condition is true while no action of any kind is to be taken if the condition is false. When flowcharting such a structure, both possible outcomes are still shown. Figure C-10 shows how it is done. This type of structure is most frequently implemented in BASIC as an IF...THEN statement without the ELSE option.

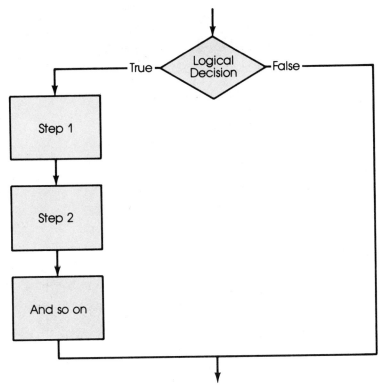

Figure C-10   General Form for Action/No Action Structure

Case Structure

The case structure, also known as selection, is used to cause a program to perform one action from a selection of possibilities. One of the most frequent applications is in the use of menus, where the user chooses which of several actions the program should take. Other applications might involve selecting from among multiple types of pay methods to process, or taking different actions depending on how far past due an account receivable is.

While the case structure may be drawn in several ways in a flowchart, one of the better ones involves the use of connectors. Each connector indicates a separate flowchart documenting the steps to be performed in that case. Study Figure C-11 for an example of the case structure for a menu. The beginning and end of the case structure are easy to see. Note that only one of the cases is true when the program is executed. Therefore, only one of the flowcharts referenced by the connectors will come into play. In case the selected choice is invalid, no action will be taken. While most versions of BASIC do not have a real case structure statement, the ON . . . GOSUB statement can handle most cases.

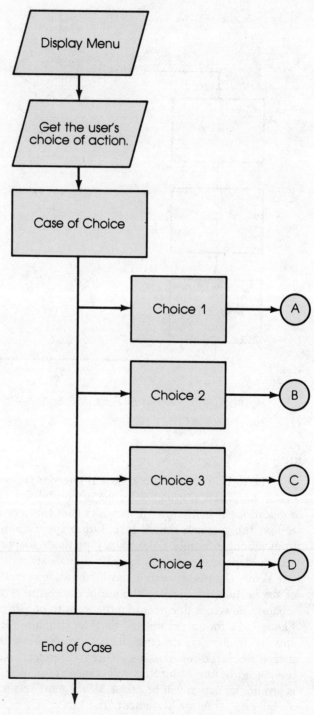

Figure C-11   Flowchart of Case Structure

Iteration Structure

Iterations, commonly known as loops, may be of two types as far as structure is concerned. Both types repeat until some terminating condition becomes true. The difference is that one type tests for the terminating condition before taking action, while the other tests for the terminating condition after taking action. In making flowchart segments for these two kinds of loops, we still follow the guideline of one way in and one way out. Examine the following two figures to learn how to make these structures. Figure C-12 shows the "test first" loop, while Figure C-13 shows the "test last" loop.

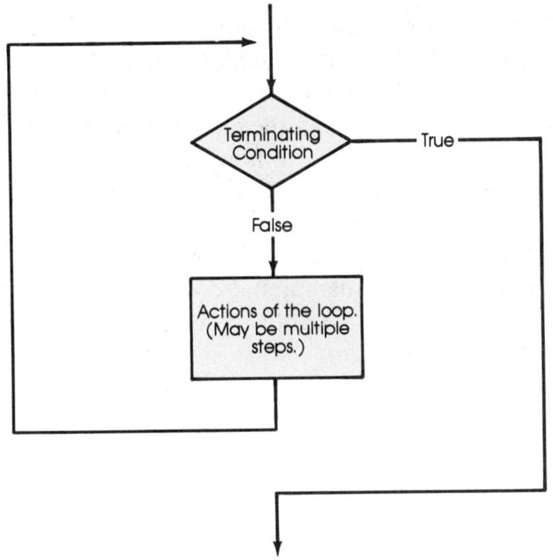

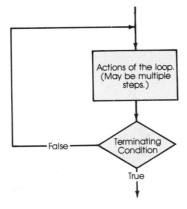

Figure C-12   "Test First" Loop

Figure C-13   "Test Last" Loop

ADVANTAGES AND DISADVANTAGES OF FLOWCHARTING

Whether to use flowcharting has been a topic of much discussion. There are some factors in favor of flowcharting. Flowcharting may make the design of a program easier for someone other than the designer to understand. Also, it may point out some logic problems before coding of a program begins.

On the negative side of flowcharting, there are also some factors. First, the preparation of flowcharts is very tedious and time consuming. Most programmers will not make flowcharts unless directed to do so by their superiors. At that, they may be made only after a program is completed, contributing nothing to the planning process. The biggest disadvantage, however, has to do with program maintenance. Remember that one of the most important purposes of program documentation is to enable someone else to make corrections or modifications in the program. Remember also that the programmers spend much of their time making program modifications. Assuming that a flowchart has been made originally, it is next to impossible to keep it up to date as changes are made in a program. Therefore, it becomes useless. It is much better to make the code of the program as self-documenting as possible. When the code is self-documenting, there is no doubt that the program and documentation match. In other words, the ideal is for a person to be able to determine how a program works by reading the program itself.

Index